Confluence of Thought

Confluence of Thought

Mahatma Gandhi and
Martin Luther King Jr.

BIDYUT CHAKRABARTY

Oxford University Press is a department of the University of Oxford.
It furthers the University's objective of excellence in research, scholarship,
and education by publishing worldwide.

Oxford   New York
Auckland   Cape Town   Dar es Salaam   Hong Kong   Karachi
Kuala Lumpur   Madrid   Melbourne   Mexico City   Nairobi
New Delhi   Shanghai   Taipei   Toronto

With offices in
Argentina   Austria   Brazil   Chile   Czech Republic   France   Greece
Guatemala   Hungary   Italy   Japan   Poland   Portugal   Singapore
South Korea   Switzerland   Thailand   Turkey   Ukraine   Vietnam

Oxford is a registered trademark of Oxford University Press
in the UK and certain other countries.

Published in the United States of America by
Oxford University Press
198 Madison Avenue, New York, NY 10016

© Oxford University Press 2013

Library of Congress Cataloging-in-Publication Data
Chakrabarty, Bidyut, 1958- author.
Confluence of thought : Mahatma Gandhi and Martin Luther King, Jr. / Bidyut Chakrabarty.
pages cm
Includes bibliographical references and index.
ISBN 978-0-19-995123-9 (pbk.)—ISBN 978-0-19-995121-5 (cloth)
1. Nonviolence. 2. Gandhi, Mahatma, 1869-1948—Influence. 3. Gandhi, Mahatma,
1869-1948—Political and social views.   4. King, Martin Luther, Jr., 1929-1968—
Influence.   5. King, Martin Luther, Jr., 1929-1968—Political and social views.   I. Title.
HM1281.C46 2013
303.6'1—dc23
2012050207

9 8 7 6 5 4 3 2 1
Printed in the United States of America
on acid-free paper

Dedicated to those fighting for human dignity

CONTENTS

FOREWORD

Bidyut Chakrabarty has written one of those unusual books that actually delivers more to readers than is suggested by the title. His book succeeds not only as a concise and cogent comparative discussion of the ideas of Mahatma Gandhi and Martin Luther King Jr., but also as an insightful examination of the broader historical and intellectual context from which both leaders emerged. Informed by Dr. Chakrabarty's familiarity with the extensive literature regarding Gandhi and King, *Confluence of Thought* sheds light on the political, cultural, religious, and intellectual milieus that shaped the worldviews of the twentieth century's preeminent advocates of nonviolent resistance. This book provides an engaging, thought-provoking, and well-researched examination of the lives and times of two of the most influential figures of the twentieth century.

Since becoming the editor of King's papers a quarter century ago, I have come to realize that King cannot be understood apart from his intellectual encounter with Gandhian nonviolence. Although the Hindu beliefs that Gandhi absorbed during his formative years were quite different from the Christian teachings that King absorbed as the son of a Baptist minister, both were receptive to unconventional religious and philosophical ideas. Both were drawn to existing traditions of nonviolent activism and human rights, and both were skilled at adapting the ideas of other activist intellectuals. Both were eclectic rather than original thinkers, although their eclecticism eventually led each of them to develop a distinctive body of ideas. Early in their lives, both Gandhi and King were influenced by the nineteenth-century American nonconformist Henry David Thoreau, who provided them with a convincing rationale for civil disobedience.

It is hardly surprising that Gandhi would exert considerable influence over King's intellectual development. Despite their very different upbringings, they had many qualities in common. Both men benefited from exceptional educational opportunities that made them familiar with the ideas of European-American intellectual elites, but they also acquired unshakeable commitments to egalitarianism and social justice. Even as King completed his graduate studies in modern Euro-American theology, he discovered that Gandhi's "emphasis on love and nonviolence" provided "the method for social reform" he was seeking. By the time he rose to national and international prominence as a spokesperson for the Montgomery bus boycott movement of the mid-1950s, King had become an articulate proponent of Gandhian thought. His "pilgrimage to the Land of Gandhi" in 1959 deepened his understanding of and firm commitment to Gandhian precepts. Afterward, he inherited Gandhi's legacy and played a crucial role in disseminating Gandhian ideas throughout the world.

My growing understanding of the ties between the two leaders prompted me to teach a course on Gandhi and King at Stanford University and then, along with my Stanford colleague Linda Hess, teach a three-week seminar on "Gandhi and His Legacy." This seminar brought fifteen of my Stanford students to India late in the summer of 2008. Although I prepared for the course and the seminar by reading Gandhi's major writings and several biographies of him, I nonetheless found that my conversations with Gandhi's contemporary followers and critics reshaped my understanding of him. The experience made me aware of the ways in which he, like King, was part of a sustained mass movement that was beyond the control of any one leader. I came to see that both leaders faced considerable challenges in their effort to guide unruly freedom movements. Both encountered strong challenges from other leaders who advocated alternative tactics and strategies. Both were assassinated and left behind contested legacies.

In February 2009, I traveled to India as part of an official American delegation to commemorate the fiftieth anniversary of King's 1959 trip to India, which he described as a "pilgrimage." The delegation included the Atlanta congressman John Lewis, the former chair of the Student Nonviolent Coordinating Committee (SNCC), a group that had utilized Gandhian strategies in the sit-ins and freedom rides of the early 1960s. We were joined by King's eldest son, Martin Luther King III, and by other former civil rights activists who had been closely associated with King, such as the former US ambassador to the United Nations, Andrew Young, and former US senator Harris Wofford, who had spent time in India during the 1930s and 1940s and whose writings on Gandhian nonviolence had influenced King's views. This tour increased my awareness of the many links not only between Gandhi and King but also between the Gandhi-inspired Indian independence movement and the modern African American freedom struggle. Perhaps the most important contribution of Dr. Chakrabarty's study is that it makes clear that Gandhian ideas were evident in the African American struggle years before King adopted Gandhian ideas. *Confluence of Thought* demonstrates that King's Gandhian convictions were at least as much the result of his contact with American Gandhians as with Gandhi's writings and his Indian followers.

Most of all, I appreciate that Dr. Chakrabarty has placed the two leaders and the mass movements they inspired in a comparative framework. He has avoided the tendency of some scholars to advocate—wittingly or unwittingly—Great Man theories that depict Gandhi and King as leaders who single-handedly changed the course of history. He recognizes that their greatness resulted in large part because of their involvement in great movements. They rose to prominence within these movements, he suggests, because of their ability to synthesize the ideas of other activists and intellectuals. Both men were able to articulate these adopted ideas with extraordinary clarity and passion to a global audience.

By placing Gandhi and King in a proper historical context, Chakrabarty draws needed attention to many leaders who played important roles in the freedom struggles in India and the United States. Gandhi and King can best be understood in relation to other leaders who influenced them or in some cases criticized them, thereby forcing them to clarify and strengthen their arguments. Chakrabarty thus demonstrates the historical significance of figures such as M. N. Roy, Rabindranath Tagore, and B. R. Ambedkar in India and W. E. B. DuBois, Howard Thurman, and Bayard Rustin in the United States. By drawing attention to less widely known intellectuals and political activists, Chakrabarty offers a useful corrective to the narrowly focused biographies and studies of Gandhi and King. He shows that neither Gandhi nor King can be fully understood apart from the movements that enabled them to transform themselves from talented professionals into historically significant political leaders.

Chakrabarty's notion of Gandhi and King as products of their eras by no means diminishes their historical significance. Instead, his study enables us to see these leaders as crucial participants in history's greatest freedom struggle: that is, the succession of mass movements against European and American domination that have affected the lives of a majority of humanity. During the past three centuries, the toiling masses of the world have struggled, individually and collectively, to liberate themselves from entrenched systems of oppression. Even as European empires expanded their global control, chattel slaves, servants, serfs, peons, and other landless laborers and peasants found ways to resist or escape from systems of racial and class dominance.

To a large extent, the freedom struggles of the modern era have been sparked by individualized resistance or grassroots movements. Even as European nations have imposed their political and economic dominance over Africa and Asia, they encountered persistent resistance. Slave and peasant revolts produced few victories and could not reverse the overall trend toward European domination of the world, but the international campaign to abolish slavery ultimately succeeded and left behind an enduring legacy of tactics and strategies of resistance. Moreover, some nonwhite leaders adapted for their own purposes the egalitarian sentiments associated with Christianity, the European Enlightenment, the American Revolution, and the French Revolution, transforming rationales for racial domination into rationales for racial equality.

Gandhi and King lived during an era when a sustained global movement to transform peasants into citizens reached its climax. By revealing the historical context that made possible their rise to international prominence, Dr. Chakrabarty helps us understand the thread of commonality that ties together the historical experience of today's peasants and descendants of peasants who are still seeking to overcome the enduring consequences of past oppression. In learning about Gandhi and King, we also enhance our understanding of a shared story of the ongoing global quest for freedom and justice.

Clayborne Carson,
Professor of History & Director,
Martin Luther King Jr. Research and Education Institute, Stanford University

PREFACE

The book examines the ideas, projects, and sensibilities of two great apostles of peace and nonviolence: Mohandas Karamchand Gandhi, popularly known as the Mahatma, and Martin Luther King Jr. This is not a clear-cut intellectual history, but an intellectual effort at conceptualizing "the confluence of their thought" with reference to its historical roots.

To maintain historical accuracy, I have used the term "Negro," which was a generally accepted term to identify African Americans, at least in the first half of the twentieth century. Martin Luther King Jr. and his colleagues, who had challenged racial segregation in the context of the civil rights campaign and even earlier, did not find the expression "Negro" objectionable. To them, "nigger," which was the distorted version of the term "Negro," was far more pejorative and was thus unacceptable. Throughout the book, I have used Negro, black, and African American interchangeably, but when I have quoted from the original text, I have reproduced verbatim the expression of the author.

I was drawn to the topic of racial segregation after having read two famous novels: Harriet Beecher Stowe's *Uncle Tom's Cabin* (1852) and Harper Lee's *To Kill a Mockingbird* (1960). While the first novel is perhaps the most revealing account of the brutality of slavery in the United States, the latter stands out by bringing out the true nature of racial segregation, even after the 1863 Emancipation Declaration that outlawed slavery. *To Kill a Mockingbird* is also a sharp comment on the racial tilt of the US judiciary and a testimony to how white liberals, of which Atticus Finch was a true representative, fought racial discrimination tooth and nail, within the liberal-democratic framework of politics. There were also three films that inspired me to understand the era of the civil rights campaign with reference to the African American endeavor to fight racial discrimination. The first film that set the ball rolling was *Mississippi Burning*, a 1988 American crime drama based on an FBI investigation into the real-life murder of three civil rights workers in Mississippi in 1964. The second film that acted as a catalyst was *Separate but Equal,* a 1991 American movie narrating the story of the 1954 landmark Supreme Court judgment in *Brown vs. Board of Education,* banning the separate but equal system of racial segregation in public schools. Finally, set in the Jim Crow South, *The Help* (2011), based on the 2009 bestseller by Kathryn Stockett, is another film that sought to capture bitter race relations between the whites and blacks in Jackson, Mississippi. It depicted the day-to-day life experiences of the black maids and their white employers.

Besides its intellectual appeal, *Confluence of Thought* will be remembered by my family for a different reason: our school-going daughter, Urna Chakrabarty, has, through her persuasive editorial suggestions, improved the text. I salute her effort and wish her grand success in her mission to become a creative writer.

The book has been a long time in gestation in the sense that I have been nurturing this project since I began working on Gandhi in 2006. I completed the manuscript in the early part of 2012, in the serene atmosphere of the Shenandoah Valley in Virginia. In the articulation of the arguments, I was benefited by the comments of the reviewers and also by the comments of my colleagues at James Madison University, Virginia who, with their well-thought-out inputs, enabled me to improve the text in a substantial way. I am also thankful to those who made useful comments on the project when it was presented at seminars and workshops in various university campuses in North America and Europe. By his encouraging e-mails from Stanford, Dr. Clayborne Carson instilled in me the confidence of working on a project that requires interdisciplinary training in the true sense of the term. He was a great source of inspiration, and by sharing his expertise on the sociopolitical ideas of Martin Luther King Jr., he contributed immensely to the shaping of my approach to the complex issues of the civil rights movements in the United States. Dr. Peter Stearns, the Provost of George Mason University, supported the project since it was conceptualized. I am grateful to him. Dr. Bob Kolodinsky of the Business School of James Madison University helped improve the text by providing useful intellectual inputs. Besides his intellectual support, he made our stay away from home joyous by his regular visits with his lovely daughter Katie.

I am thankful to my doctoral students and now colleagues, Dr. Prakash Chand of the University of Delhi and Mr. Arindam Roy of Burdwan University, for their support during the preparation of this book. Without the support of Ms. Angela Chnapko of Oxford University Press, New York, the project would not have been available for public consumption. I am thankful to her. Last, and not the least, I express my gratitude to my family, who sustained my zeal for intellectual creativity despite all odds.

ABBREVIATIONS

ACMHR Alabama Christian Movement for Human Rights
AICC   All-India Congress Committee
CORE   Congress of Racial Equality
FOR   Fellowship of Reconciliation
MIA   Montgomery Improvement Association
MOWM   March on Washington Movement
NAACP   National Association for the Advancement of Colored People
NUL   National Urban League
SCLC   Southern Christian Leadership Conference
SNCC   Student Nonviolent Coordination Committee
UNIA   Universal Negro Improvement Association

Confluence of Thought

Introduction

Nonviolence is not merely a mental construct; it is a powerful ideology inspiring people to fight against injustice despite adverse consequences. By drawing on complementary intellectual and ideological sources, Mohandas Karamchand Gandhi and Martin Luther King Jr. fulfilled a historical mission in specific historical contexts. It is true that their roles in mobilizing specific groups of victims of circumstances were critical; nonetheless, their success can also be attributed to the assistance of those who fought along with them against any form of injustice. Their creative intervention in politics in British India and racially segregated America, respectively, was theoretically refreshing and practically useful in grasping the change that they sought.

Despite being raised in a relatively well-off family in the Dixie state[1] of Alabama, King was also subject to racial segregation in a country that drew its inspiration from the Jeffersonian idea that "all men are created equal." Segregation had, in his view, been not only "the Negroes' burden [but also] America's shame,"[2] since it was contrary to the core values of American democracy. The civil rights campaign was thus geared to the attainment of the founding fathers' secular goal. From such a perspective, there was nothing abnormal in King's conceptualization of antiracist theoretical discourse, since it was based on the fundamental values upon which America, as a nation, was built. Even in regard to the political method of nonviolence, he drew on Christian ethics. Ideologically, he seemed to have been governed by the liberal democratic ethos and the Christian ethical code of conduct for individuals. Gandhi was certainly a significant influence much later, building on the Sermon on the Mount philosophy. It is therefore fair to argue that King was instinctively drawn to nonviolence. This concept was obviously linked with what he learned from his "family of pastors" and also from his interaction with colleagues and teachers, first at Crozer and later during his graduate studies at Boston University. His attraction to Gandhian sociopolitical ideas supporting nonviolence appears to have been prompted by the success that Gandhi had, first in South Africa and then in India, in partly removing the sources of visible political oppression. One can also argue that Gandhian ideas struck an emotional chord with those fighting against racial segregation in America, presumably because of their cultural roots in Christianity and also the success of the black church in the Deep South in instilling faith in nonviolence.

Nonviolence remained an inspiring ideal for both King and Gandhi, though the nature of the context in which they evolved nonviolent mass resistance was slightly different: while Gandhi led a majority against a minority British ruling authority, King spearheaded a campaign of a historically underprivileged minority against a majority. Gandhi thus had an obvious advantage in that a struggle against colonial power was likely to create constituencies of support rather automatically. King faced a more difficult situation because blacks were in a country which purportedly was theirs and yet they were subject to torture and humiliation and considered inferior. Nonetheless, both of these great men of peace had identical aims in their long struggle to remove oppression against humanity.

The aim of this book is to understand the complex evolution of the sociopolitical ideas of Gandhi and King and also their confluence in the specific contexts of India and America, respectively. Two important areas will be addressed in this introduction: the Jim Crow laws and the African American dialogue with Gandhi. American racism was rooted in what was euphemistically described as "the Jim Crow laws," an articulation of racial discrimination in legal terms. Part of American history is confined to movements challenging the Jim Crow discriminatory practices, which were also legally codified. Gandhi had experienced his share of racial abuse in South Africa, but not to the extent King suffered as an African American born and raised in a Dixie state where the Jim Crow laws were legally binding. Hence, here in the introduction, I shall focus on the Jim Crow laws and their sociohistorical roots to comprehend their complex nature. Equally important to consider is the African American dialogue with Gandhi, which was articulated in two ways: (1) through personal interactions between African Americans and the Mahatma in India and (2) through an intellectual pilgrimage to the Gandhian texts and a conceptualization of the unique Gandhian methods and ideology. As will be shown later in this chapter, the encounter between black activists and Gandhi had a long history. Black activists visited Gandhi primarily to understand the exact nature of Gandhian nonviolent protest in socioeconomically diverse India—presumably to comprehend its applicability among the socioculturally stratified American blacks. What is most striking here is the fact that the dialogue between Gandhi and his visitors appeared to have reconfirmed their faith in a nonviolence that had its roots in Christianity. In other words, Gandhi was certainly a significant influence in the civil rights campaign, which seemed to have drawn on an ideological application of nonviolence not only in regard to shaping interpersonal relationships, but also in regard to interracial and international interactions.

|

Jim Crow was about racial segregation in the American South. It occurred through an elaborate process that physically separated the races based on social custom and stringent legal stipulations. The term "Jim Crow" was derived from a nineteenth-century minstrel show in which Thomas Dartmouth "Daddy" Rice, a white entertainer, performed in blackface a song-dance sequence, *Jump Jim Crow*, which portrayed the Negro in a very comical and funny fashion. Rice was reported to have based his caricature on a performance by an elderly slave, owned by a Mr. Crow in Louisville in 1828.[3] The minstrel show ceased to be mere entertainment once it set in motion a process of racial segregation, particularly in the South, on the basis of well-defined social codes and equally strict laws. Given the peculiar power relationships in the Dixie states and the well-entrenched and historical racial prejudices, Jim Crow flourished, subjecting the disinherited Negroes to innumerable constraints and also inhuman torture. Even before Jim Crow became a reality, the blacks, especially in the Deep South, were subject to various kinds of racial constraints. For instance, there was the infamous "grandfather clause," which meant that a person was not eligible to vote unless his grandfather had been a voter. Given the legal validity of slavery before the 1863 Emancipation Proclamation, this piece of legislation effectively disenfranchised almost the entire black population. Another effective racist device was the retrospective imposition of a high poll tax: in order to vote, a black had to pay the poll tax, which made the exercise of voting rights an expensive proposition. The trick was thus "almost as effective as the grandfather clause because very few black people could afford to pay that much to vote."[4]

Segregation gradually encompassed every element of Southern culture: the racial difference was not a mere description, but a source of power for the dominant whites over the peripheral blacks in America. It was therefore obvious that the difference was politically contrived to justify the hegemony of one racial group over another; Jim Crow was accordingly translated in laws and in the social code of conduct for the underprivileged blacks who had come to the United States as slaves. In this sense, Jim Crow was the perpetuation of slavery in a different garb; it was sustained by creating complementary codes of conduct for the blacks, backed by equally strong legislation. Jim Crow was so all-pervasive that the Negroes could hardly escape racial discrimination so long as the system prevailed. As John W. Cell explains,

> When they rode public transportation, they sat in the black section in the rear. If they wanted to drink, eat, or to go to the toilet, they might be lucky enough to find facilities reserved for them; otherwise, they had to do without. Parks, beaches, golf courses, tennis courts, and swimming pools excluded them; again comparatively rarely they might find separate but undoubtedly inferior facilities. If they ran afoul of the law, they were sworn on separate-but-equal Bibles and, if convinced by usually all-white juries, were sentenced by white judges to segregated jails. When they died, they were embalmed in black funeral parlors...and buried in black cemeteries.[5]

The arrangement was so deeply entrenched that Jim Crow restrictions affected every bit of Negro life from birth to death. Also striking were the elaborate legal stipulations to maintain such a racially biased system of segregation. In his influential assessment of Jim Crow, C. Vann Woodward provided a candid account of how the system became an integral part of the white mind-set, which preceded the actual legislations endorsing racial discrimination. Reminding Negroes constantly of their inferior social position, the segregation statutes or Jim Crow laws, argued Woodward,

> constituted the most elaborate and formal expression of sovereign white opinion upon the subject. In bulk and detail as well as in effectiveness of enforcement the segregation codes were comparable with the black codes of the old regime, though the laxity that mitigated the harshness of the black codes was replaced by a rigidity that was more typical of the segregation code. That code lent the sanction of law to a racial ostracism that extended to churches and schools, to housing, to jobs, to eating and drinking. Whether by law or by custom, that ostracism extended to virtually all forms of public transportation, to sports and recreations, to hospitals, orphanages, prisons, asylums and ultimately to funeral homes, morgues and cemeteries,[6]

This detailed description of how Jim Crow laws were articulated shows how pervasive the impact was of such an arrangement on Negroes' social lives. It is also true that legally endorsed discriminations became formidable presumably because of favorable white mind-sets that appeared to have become normal, if not natural, in those circumstances due to obvious socioeconomic and political advantages. Segregation laws were also designed "to encourage lower class whites to retain a sense of superiority over blacks, making it far less likely that they would sustain inter-racial political alliances aimed at toppling the white elite."[7] The Jim Crow system thus became a time-tested mechanism to avoid class hostility. In the light of the increasing importance of Jim Crow and racial segregation in American social life, the 1863 Emancipation Proclamation seemed to have lost its validity. Segregation thus became integral to a white thought process that could not be so easily transformed. In this sense, de facto segregation preceded de jure segregation: laws were likely to be strong and stringent once they were complemented by a conducive mind-set that evolved over a period of sustained appreciation of certain values and mores. The relationship between these two types of segregations was thus dialectically textured: they drew on each other. Such a complementarity explains the continuity of Jim Crow even after the landmark 1954 *Brown v. Board of Education* judgment reversing the 1896 Plessy "separate-but-equal" Supreme Court decision that legally endorsed "segregation in the field of public education." As a result, various devices, including separate housing and social services, poll taxes, and educational qualifications for voting rights, were fused into the legal system across the South. The segregation of races was thus "a political stratagem employed by the emerging Bourbon interests in the South to keep the Southern masses divided and Southern labour the cheapest in the land."[8]

How was Jim Crow articulated? As contemporary accounts show, racial segregation was maintained and politically defended by the whites for obvious partisan interests. The Southern states were the worst hit, and the Negroes remained victims of circumstances despite occasional protests. What was strange was the tacit approval of discriminatory practices by states other those in the South. For example, Ray Sprigle, a New York–based black youth, expressed his helplessness at having to ride a Jim Crow coach from Union Station, Washington, DC, to Alabama when he said, "I quit being white, free and an American citizen [once] I climbed aboard that [Alabama-bound] Jim Crow coach in the station. From then on, until I came out of the South four weeks later, I was black, and in bondage—not quite slavery, but not quite freedom, either. My rights of citizenship were a mere description without substance."[9] Not only is Sprigle's account revealing, it is also indicative of how stringent the Jim Crow laws were in the Dixie states. It was hard for him to believe that he still lived in an America that always valued human dignity more than anything else. What upset him most was the deliberate distortion of those major political institutions that the founding fathers had built to strengthen the democratic fabric of the country, especially the rule of law. Referring to what he experienced in the state of Alabama, he elaborated by saying that

[f]rankly and openly, the courts and the law in the South let the Negroes know that their sworn testimony in courts is not to be given the same weight as that of a white man. Automobile insurance companies, when they do sell insurance to a Negro automobile owner, never go to court when he is in a collision with a white driver. They just pay. So, too when a Negro without insurance collides with a car owned by a white man. There rarely is any question as to who was at fault. The Negro is told how much he is going to pay, [and] pays it.[10]

The situation was more or less identical everywhere. Negroes had to be at the receiving end regardless of whether that was fair or not in the light of the fundamental canons of American democracy. In his reminiscences, Sprigle further provided innumerable instances to graphically illustrate how well entrenched the Jim Crow mentality was in the Dixie states:

> If a white man attacks [a Negro], he'd better not resist. If he does he's due for lynching. That is why Negroes, if they do resist a white man, generally try to kill him. If you are going to be killed, better give the white folks something to kill you for, the black man figures.
>
> . . .
>
> If [a Negro] goes to a white doctor or dentist, he'll probably get service. But he will wait until all the white patients have been cared for. If it's time for the physician to quit when the Negro patient reaches his desk, he's told to try it again some other time.
>
> . . . .
>
> [A Negro] can't enter a white library. But if there's a colored branch library in his town he can go there and any book he wants is obtained from the white library.
>
> . . .
>
> In nearly every Southern town, you'll find not one but two honor rolls, one for white and one for black, sometimes side by side, oftener the Negro honor roll hidden in the dingy Negro section [because] no Negro is allowed to contaminate the white race by getting his name on the same honor roll with a white man even if he did die a hero in the service of his country."[11]

As is evident, racial segregation was easily maintained because of the color prejudices of the dominant whites who, for obvious benefits, upheld the separation as appropriate for social tranquility. One of the common expressions of abuse was the word *nigger*, which "has been a familiar part of the vocabularies of whites high and low."[12] In fact, so well-entrenched were racist prejudices among the white supremacists that they were terribly annoyed when Booker T. Washington dined at the White House. A senator from South Carolina, Benjamin Tillman, reportedly declared that "the action of President Roosevelt in entertaining that nigger will necessitate our killing a thousand niggers in the South before they will learn their place again."[13] Besides evoking such a strong reaction, which was also translated into action on various occasions, Negroes were always subject to racial hatred; they "forever [are] fighting," argued Martin Luther King Jr. "a degenerating sense of nobodiness,"[14] an obvious outcome of racial segregation which was highly immoral because "it treats men as means rather than ends, and thereby reduces them to things rather than persons."[15] Malcolm X remembered that during his childhood, after his family fell apart following the murder of his father, the whites who served as his local guardians always referred to blacks as "niggers." And then there was his encounter with a white teacher, Mr. Ostrowski, who was very upset when Malcolm expressed his desire to become a lawyer because "a lawyer—that's no realistic goal for a nigger"; instead, he was advised to pursue a career in carpentry because he was good with his hands.[16]

At its core a system of exclusion and discrimination, Jim Crow was the outcome of sustained processes of socialization spanning one's entire childhood and
its aftermath. Separate rules of racial etiquette evolved for black and white children, respectively. Jim Crow was both codified in statutes and lived out, every
minute of every day in the South. Black children were taught to be subservient
to their white counterparts because it was perhaps the best strategy for survival,
though it came at the cost of self-dignity. The Jim Crow etiquette thus demanded
that the black children "suppress (although not entirely forget) their individual
and contrary impulses in a process that inevitably shaped the children themselves."[17] White children imbibed the spirit of segregation by demanding "defer-
ence and using racial key words to distance and subordinate blacks."[18] Senior
members of the family and community were critical in such a process. The goal
was to instill a sense of superiority in white children's minds so that the idea of
segregation between blacks and whites did not appear to be odd, but natural.
The superior race had a moral responsibility toward those identified as inferior.
So, in this sense, the Negroes needed to be subservient for their own benefit. The
physical slavery led to "the paralysis of mental slavery,"[19] and the Negroes started
believing that "perhaps they were less than human."[20] So racial peace was maintained by evolving an appropriate sociopsychological design in which Negroes
were forced "patiently to accept injustice, insult and exploitation."[21] This was how
racial segregation was justified and gained legitimacy in circumstances in which
the authority of the supremacists was hardly effectively challenged.

Jim Crow was a threat to American constitutionalism. Yet it continued with
a lot of vigor presumably because of a supportive supremacist mindset that also
gained enormously with adequate backing from the local political authorities.
As a result, the values of the Constitution remained unrealized. In view of the
recurring incidents of lynching, murder, and various other forms of lawless-
ness, "our nation has [thus] become," lamented a group of black ministers of
Washington, "the laughing stock of civilized peoples throughout the world, and
unless something is done to make human life more valuable and law more uni-
versally respected, we feel that our beloved country is doomed to destruction
at no distant date."[22] This was a challenge to the Jim Crow laws and also a well-
argued defense of the institutional sanctity of the Constitution (which was appropriated by the majority at the expense of a minority). What was striking in this
appeal was the overwhelming faith of these black ministers in liberal democratic
institutions, including the court of law. In fact, they appeared to have endorsed
the general feelings of the civil rights activists who, besides adopting various
nonviolent means, always defended their ideological stance with reference to the
Constitution and other fundamental doctrines of equally important constitutional significance. This was invariably the underlying spirit in which civil rights
campaigns were organized and molded. It was therefore not surprising when
King felt that "if the Constitution were today applied equally and impartially
to all of America's citizens, in every section of the country, in every court and
code of law, there would be no need for any group of citizens to seek extra-legal
redress."[23] In other words, the claim that the United States was a paragon of civil

liberty and democratic fortitude was "absolutely futile so long as it maintained its embarrassing attachment to outdated racial attitudes."[24] Jim Crow was finally rescinded following a mass-based civil rights movement, backed by the liberal US Supreme Court and a shifting domestic and international milieu.

Jim Crow died with the official acceptance of the 1964 Civil Rights Act and the 1965 Voting Rights Act by the US Congress. Legally it was banned. But in its place has emerged "a new leviathan of racial inequality" that lacks "the brutal simplicity of the old Jim Crow system, with its omnipresent 'white' and 'colored' signs [and] yet it is in many respects potentially far more brutalizing, because it presents itself to the world as a correctional system that is theoretically fair and essentially colorblind."[25] A new Jim Crow is being implemented by the mass incarceration of blacks and also the termination of voting rights to ex-felons. It is not surprising that the proportion of black men going to prison is staggeringly high in comparison with their white counterparts. As one study has shown, in 2008, one in nine blacks between the ages of twenty and thirty-four years and one in fifteen blacks above eighteen years of age were incarcerated, compared to one in 106 whites.[26] The reasons are plenty. In general, crimes flourish in poverty and ignorance. Blacks may have the political right to vote but continue to suffer in abject poverty and ignorance due to lack of literacy. The high proportion of black prisoners in US jails corroborates the widespread belief that this situation is "compatible with the American creed [suggesting] that their imprisonment can be interpreted as their own fault."[27] There is a powerful sociopsychological argument here: if the crime and consequent prison sentences are shown to be a natural outcome of their culture and fragile family life, then society is "absolved of responsibility to do anything about their conditions."[28] Hence King always felt that mere political rights might not be meaningful unless they are accompanied by adequate economic guarantee for a respectable existence.

By setting "economic equality" for Americans irrespective of color as a goal for the 1963 March on Washington, King sought to build a multiracial coalition for economic justice. The march was, it has been argued, directed "to shake the foundation of the power structure and force the government to respond to the needs of the ignored underclass."[29] Earlier movements were directed at race-specific grievances, but the March on Washington set in motion the argument that racial justice required overhauling of social institutions and a dramatic restructuring of the economy. As King argued in his 1968 address to the Southern Christian Leadership Conference (SCLC) workers, "[T]he changes [that are visible now] are basically in the social and political areas: the problem we now face—providing jobs, better housing and better education for the poor throughout the country—will require money for their solutions, a fact that makes those solutions all the more difficult."[30] Most of the gains—desegregation in public schools, guaranteeing voting rights or the appointment of few black officials in positions of power—cost nothing. Now "white America must recognize that justice for the black people cannot be achieved without radical changes in the structure of our society. The comfortable, the privileged cannot continue to tremble at the prospect of change in the status quo."[31]

With the removal of the Jim Crow laws of segregation, those committed to racial hierarchy evolved newer mechanisms to legitimize racism. Barred by law from invoking race explicitly, the supremacists still utilized the bogey of law and order to effectively continue with the old system of racial segregation. The high proportion of blacks in jail is attributed to the fact that their presence in society is not conducive to law and order; even without following the due process of law, they are kept in prison. It was therefore not surprising that the civil rights movement was designated as a threat to law and order and that those who participated were dubbed as criminals. The jails, particularly those in the Southern states, suddenly became overburdened with these civil rights activists. After so much struggle, the Jim Crow restrictions were withdrawn only to resurface later in a different form. Defining racial segregation as integral to structural racism, William Manning Marable argued that the Jim Crow discriminatory practices are largely rooted in the white mentality, backed by an appropriate legal system.[32] On top of it remains the general colorblindness to racial differences due to historical reasons. Blacks lag behind because they continue to be deprived of the opportunities that are readily available to their white counterparts. The well-entrenched colorblindness, it has been argued, "prevents us from seeing racial and structural divisions that persist in society—the segregated, unequal schools; the segregated jobless ghettos; and the segregated public discourse—a public conversation that excludes the current pariah caste."[33] It was King who thus felt that despite having voting rights for the Blacks, colorblindness and indifference to racial groups were serious impediments to racial equality. Racism survived, according to King, because of the intellectual and spiritual blindness of those whites who decided to remain ignorant of its actual socioeconomic and political roots. He further elaborated by saying that

> the tragic blindness is also found in racial segregation, the not-too-distant cousin of slavery. Some of the most vigorous defenders of segregation are sincere in their beliefs and earnest in their motives. Although some men are segregationists merely for reasons for political expediency and political gain, not all of the resistance to integration is the rearguard of professional bigots. Some people feel that their attempt to preserve segregation is best for themselves, their children and their nation. Many are good church people, anchored in the religious faith of their mothers and fathers....What a tragedy! Millions of Negroes have been crucified by conscientious blindness....Jesus was right about those men who crucified him. They knew not what they did. They were inflicted by terrible blindness.[34]

The Jim Crow system of racial segregation that made its first appearance in the mid-nineteenth century continued to remain effective as long as, wrote Malcolm X, "white men dominate politics, control the nation's wealth and write rules by which everyone else is forced to live."[35] Undoubtedly, the civil rights campaign led to the legal banning of this brutalized system of discrimination on the basis of skin color. Legally endorsed racial segregation was discontinued with the approval of the Civil Rights Act of 1964 and Voting Rights Act of 1965. But despite the removal of the horizontal modes of separation and subordination and the simultaneous insistence of equal opportunity—colorblindness—in procedures for public employment or any other role in the public sphere, the situation did not improve to the extent expected. This was because "the increasing isolation of blacks in core cities and suburban ghettos concentrated those blacks who could not escape where they were least likely to reach entry level jobs, interracial schools, and effective political power."[36] In stressing processes rather than the outcome, the steps toward equal opportunity became vacuous, given the long history of black deprivation of basic human requirements. It was not the clear-cut explicit "blacks not allowed racism...but a series of small encumbrances, sudden obstacles, hard stares, or refusals to notice or acknowledge [one's] presence [that] added up to the message: blacks not welcome."[37] By accepting a case-by-case prove-discriminatory-intent approach to remedying inequality, "equal opportunity [thus] militated against systematic changes."[38] Negroes had the legal right to eat in any restaurant and sleep in white motels, but they did not have the economic means to fulfill these desires. Poverty was and is "a concomitant of segregation."[39] "It is murder," exhorted King, "to deprive a man of a job or income,"[40] and he thus saw the slums as "the handiwork of a vicious system"[41] that remained even after the elimination of segregation. By attacking poverty, King called into question "fundamental patterns of American life"[42] in which "the conditions of black Americans without education and economic opportunity remained, as King once described, "a lonely island of poverty in an ocean of material wealth and affluence."[43] The elimination of segregation was not adequate, it was thus argued, as long as the continuity of those "policies that deprive workers of a living wage, undermine educational opportunity, and seek to balance budgets by cutting assistance to the poor, to the sick, and the vulnerable do not reflect the values of the America [that he] loved."[44] Thus, without a substantial and radical overhaul of the prevalent power relationships, racism was able to survive and also thrive.

II

Gandhi never set foot in the United States, yet he became known to the Americans through his interactions with the leading intellectuals and activists of the period.[45] For most Americans, Gandhi was an exotic figure, and his ideas seemed weird in the American context. There were some who found in Gandhi's ideas a possible threat to the racial hierarchy, given his success in mobilizing the underprivileged, first in South Africa and later in India. A third group, mainly pacifists, valued Gandhi's political ideology and its articulation in the context of his struggle against British colonialism. For them, the Gandhian nonviolent civil resistance was a source of learning and inspiration because Gandhi provided a powerful voice to the oppressed. Therefore it was not surprising that Gandhian ideas were in circulation long before African Americans undertook trips to India.

African Americans were drawn to the idea of nonviolent civil resistance, which Gandhi had successfully applied in South Africa to challenge racism and other forms of injustice. What appeared to have impressed the pacifists in America was Gandhi's zeal for nonviolence despite adverse circumstances. There are, however, indications that given the long Quaker traditions in the United States, it was easier for nonviolence to strike roots. The fact that most of those who championed nonviolence were Christians was thus not a strange coincidence. Given their ideological affinity, Christians came together rather easily when the Fellowship of Reconciliation (FOR) was founded in 1965 by sixty-eight pacifists, including A. J. Muste, Jane Adams, and Bishop Paul Jones to pursue interfaith peace and justice in the United States. Christianity thus became an instrument of change for the oppressed regardless of color. The duty of all Christians was therefore "to follow God's moral order and to enact it in fellowship [which also meant that] each must be willing to sacrifice for others [because] each can fulfill his or her own potential only by serving others."[46] The involvement of FOR radically altered the prevalent perception of Christian nonviolence, which was no longer merely "a counsel of perfection" directed to individuals who wanted to live a heavenly life on earth, but was seen as "a method, indeed the best method, for improving life on earth for everyone."[47]

Gandhi became a source of inspiration to the African Americans who found in his nonviolent satyagraha [civil disobedience] a meaningful instrument for salvation. Nonviolence was not an alien idea, presumably because of its roots in Christian ethics. Hence it was easier for Marcus Garvey, the founder of the Universal Negro Improvement Association (UNIA) in his native Jamaica in 1914, when he came to the United States to champion the cause of the racially segregated blacks. Garvey opened an American chapter of UNIA in Harlem in 1916, and it immediately became "the largest and most dramatic black mass movement ever to exist in America."[48] Not only did he introduce Gandhi to the American blacks, he also popularized his nonviolent method as perhaps the most effective in adverse circumstances of torture and brutality. To him, Gandhi was both a source of inspiration and a personification of meaningful challenge to atrocities and injustice against humanity. This was evident in his 1922 speech when he declared that "Leadership means sacrifice; leadership means martyrdom. Hundreds of thousands of men as leaders have died in the past for the freedom of their country—the emancipation of their respective peoples—and we will expect nothing else from Gandhi but that self-sacrifice and martyrdom that will ultimately free his country and his countrymen."[49] Despite being highly popular, the UNIA and Garvey were vehemently opposed by the National Association for the Advancement of Colored People (NAACP), especially by its leaders, including A. Philip Randolph and W. E. B. DuBois. Nonetheless, there was no doubt that it was Garvey who not only introduced Gandhi to the African Americans, but that he, by highlighting his role as a successful campaigner of nonviolence, also provided them with a mechanism to challenge the state for its discriminatory policies toward America's one-tenth black population. In that sense, the dialogue that Garvey began with Gandhi seems to have ushered in a new era of political struggle involving the disinherited blacks against society-driven and politically backed color prejudices. That the campaign that he started thrived even after he was deported was a testimony to how strong it became even when Garvey was not on the scene.

Though he was dismissive of Garvey's contribution, W.E.B. DuBois, like Garvey, felt that African Americans fighting for justice needed a black Gandhi. In his personal magazine, *The Crisis*, DuBois regularly wrote about Gandhi and the movement that he had led in South Africa and later in India. The first serious effort that DuBois made to assess Gandhi was an article in *The Crisis* entitled "Gandhi and India" in which he characterized Gandhi as "a man who professes to love his enemies and who refuses to take advantage of or embarrass [the] government in crisis."[50] In his 1928 novel *Dark Princess*, DuBois, while critiquing Garvey-driven black militancy, prepared the ground for Gandhian nonviolent resistance, which was, according to him, a time-tested device for ameliorating the conditions of the downtrodden and underprivileged sections of society.[51] In response to a request from DuBois, Gandhi also wrote "a little love message" for African Americans in *The Crisis* that was quoted extensively by the activists during the campaign: as Gandhi stated, "[L]et not the 12 million Negroes be ashamed of the fact that they are the grand children of slaves. There is no dishonor in being slaves. There is dishonor in being slave-owners."[52] This brief message immediately connected Gandhi with the disenfranchised blacks who appeared to have found in the Mahatma an ideological instrument to effectively articulate their voice of protest. Comparing Gandhi with Buddha, Muhammad, and Jesus, DuBois was also appreciative of his simple lifestyle, which easily linked him with the disinherited masses. In his column in the *New York Amsterdam News*, while explaining the rising importance of Gandhi in India, DuBois thus pointed out that

> Gandhi has few of the characteristics that [black people] have been taught to associate with greatness. He is not a great orator but speaks slowly and in a low voice. He is not an impressive figure of a man but small and thin, weighing only about 100 pounds. He describes himself [as] ugly and he dresses cheaply and quietly, after the manner of Indian peasants. He is an ascetic, eating little, playing little and believing in peace and sacrifice, fasting and thought.[53]

The purpose here was to draw people's attention to the simple life that Gandhi maintained to associate with the poorest of the poor. Not only did he integrate easily with the masses, he also taught them how to challenge ruthless authority nonviolently. In his perception, political action had to always be backed by spiritualism and asceticism. For the African Americans, this did not appear to have made sense unless understood with reference to the Sermon on the Mount, which Gandhi translated in his nonviolent civil resistance in India. Many African Americans had an instant liking for Gandhi because "he is the living embodiment of the command: He that denieth not himself cannot be

My disciple."[54] Gandhi was thus not merely a political leader but also a spiritual leader who epitomized Christian ethics in its totality. It was not surprising that African Americans looked for a Gandhi in their fight against racist oppression. The *Chicago Defender* eloquently put this forth in its editorial "Will a Gandhi Arise?" by saying,

What we need in America is a Gandhi who will fight the cause of the oppressed. One who, like Gandhi, can divorce himself from the greed for gold, one who can appreciate the misery of the oppressed and respond in spirit to their needs and requirements.

We have fought a continuous battle largely under the baneful influence of artificial leadership. Men who have spoken for us have chosen their words with their personal gain.

The name Gandhi is synonymous with the good intent of all who are struggling for a peaceful adjustment of spiritual differences. The observation can be safely made that the most essential thing needed by the world today is a better understanding of one's self. It is through this personal knowledge of ourselves that we are able to sense the value of our fellow men.[55]

Besides highlighting the relevance of Gandhi in the struggle against racial seg-regation, this editorial, in one of the well-publicized news magazines, seems to be a watershed in black thinking in at least two fundamental ways: first, Gandhi was no longer a mere idea of nonviolent resistance; he became a source of inspi-ration for the underprivileged in adverse circumstances. It was the Indian politi-cospiritual leader who, while leading the unarmed and yet ideologically inspired Indians against the well-equipped British colonialists, set a powerful example of how to nonviolently oppose adversaries in unfavorable circumstances. Gandhi gave nonviolence a meaningful substance and utilized it most effectively in his confrontation with the British Empire. So, Gandhi, through his sociopolitical activities during his fight for justice, initiated a new wave of thinking among the blacks, which was backed up by their commitment to Christian ethics. Second, what impressed the black leadership was Gandhi's selfless attachment to India's political cause, an attachment that was sadly missing in the case of black leader-ship. Owing to their greed for gold, the black leaders, apprehended the *Chicago Defender*, were simply not equipped to genuinely address the sources of racial segregation. Here Gandhi provided a fresh air of sacrifice and selfless abdication of worldly comfort for a bigger cause that was worth emulating; otherwise, the campaign against racism was sure to collapse long before the attainment of the goal for which it was undertaken.

The dialogue with Gandhi continued, and it was Reinhold Niebuhr who car-ried it forward. Despite being critical of Gandhian nonviolence, Niebuhr did not rule out the redemptive power of nonviolence. He stated that

[t]here is no problem of political life to which religious imagination can make a larger contribution that this problem of developing non-violent

resistance. The discovery of elements of human frailty in the foe and, con-
comitantly, the appreciation of all human life as possessing transcendent
worth, creates attitudes which transcend social conflict and thus miti-
gates its cruelties. It binds human beings together by reminding them of
the common roots and similar character of their vices and virtues.... These
attitudes...require a sublime madness which disregards immediate appear-
ances and emphasizes profound and ultimate unities."[56]

But while appreciating Gandhi's strategy of nonviolence as a means for political mobilization, Niebuhr did not endorse the claim that nonviolence was absolutely free from violence. In his conceptualization, nonviolence was also coercive
because "destruction is not the intended but the inevitable consequences of
non-violent coercion."[57] The consequences of nonviolent resistance were always
negative since boycott, an important ingredient in Gandhi's repertoire, "may
rob a whole community of its livelihood, and if maintained long enough, it will
certainly destroy life."[58] Nonviolence thus resulted in social consequences not
entirely dissimilar from those of violence.

Nonetheless, Gandhi was perhaps a unique individual in history who evolved
a pragmatic strategy by drawing upon basic human instincts supporting nonviolence. To Gandhi, nonviolence required voluntary submission to the penalty
for noncooperation with evil. In so doing, the Mahatma built tremendous good
will for his endeavor and automatically drew people toward him. Thus, nonviolent resistance created a solid political platform that gradually gained credibility
largely due to Gandhi's unflinching commitment to nonviolence as a means of
underplaying the importance of ends in his political strategies. As a true liberal,
he committed himself to nonviolent resistance, in which there always remained
scope for dialogue. He was too realistic to undermine the importance of the liberal techniques of conflict resolution. In Gandhian political strategy, truth force
or soul force created, for instance, a conducive environment for dialogue and
discussion by "an appeal to the reason and goodwill of an opponent in a social
struggle."[59]

While making a comparative assessment of the ideas of Niebuhr and Gandhi,
King also endorsed the same point by saying that "pacifism is not unrealistic
submission to evil power, as Niebuhr contends [but] a courageous confrontation of evil by the power of love, in the faith that it is better to be recipient of
violence than the inflicter of it, since the latter only multiplies the existence of
violence and bitterness in the universe, while the former may develop a sense of
shame in the opponent and thereby bring about a transformation and change
of heart."[60] Similarly, self-suffering that "appeals not to the intellect, [but] it
pierces the heart"[61] was a powerful idea in political mobilization under adverse
circumstances since it involved the willingness to sacrifice notwithstanding the
consequences. Gandhi thus "harmonizes the insights of a saint with the necessi-
ties of statecraft [which was] indeed a very difficult achievement."[62] On the basis
of his own comprehension of Gandhi's sociopolitical ideas, Niebuhr redefined
the nature of the Gandhian strategy of nonviolence, which drew its sustenance

not only from the moral convictions of its participants, but also from a realistic assessment of the circumstances rendering nonviolence "a plausible practical orientation in politics."[63] Niebuhr's critique of the Gandhian strategy of non-violence thus brought out the exact nature of politics that Mahatma refined in the context of India's freedom struggle. He was, after all, a pragmatist who had articulated a powerful voice of opposition by drawing on the religious and ethical resources of what he defined as "satyagrahi soldiers."[64]

Similar to Niebuhr, Richard Gregg contributed significantly to popularizing Gandhian ideas of nonviolence among Americans. A Harvard-trained corporate lawyer, Gregg went to India in 1925 and stayed about four years, part of it at Gandhi's Sabarmati ashram, to learn about the country that gifted the strategy of nonviolence to the world. Gregg felt that in Gandhi nonviolence had become more than an inner conviction; it was an articulation of specific programs, based on a moral dialogue with the public and seeking to elicit support and sympathy from the perpetrators of violence and their sympathizers. According to him, nonviolence "sought to combine moral and spiritual principles with the strategic dramatization of those principles."[65]

Gregg systematically articulated his ideas in *The Power of Non-Violence*, published in 1934. He defined nonviolent resistance as "a means of communicating feelings and ideas."[66] According to him,

The object of non-violent resistance is partly analogous to the object of war—namely, to demoralize the opponent, to break his will, to destroy his confidence, enthusiasm and hope. In another respect it is dissimilar for non-violent resistance…does not break the opponent's will but alters it; does not destroy his confidence and enthusiasm and hope but transfers them to a finer purpose.…[N]on-violent resistance [thus] demoralizes the opponent only to re-establish in him a new morale that is finer because it is based on sounder values."[67]

He believed that Gandhian satyagraha "involved many of the same virtues as military training, yet was part of the much more humane and psychologically healthy means of solving conflicts."[68] Hence it was a sort of moral jiu-jitsu, according to Gregg. While elaborating his point he thus argued that

"[t]he nonviolence and good will of the victim act like the lack of physical opposition by the user of physical jiu-jitsu, to cause the attacker to lose his moral balance. He suddenly and unexpectedly loses the moral support which the usual violent resistance of most victims would render him. He plunges forward…into a new world of values. He feels insecure because of the novelty of the situation and his ignorance of how to handle it. He loses his poise and self-confidence. The victim not only lets the attackers come, but…pulls him forward by kindness, generosity and voluntary suffering.…The user of non-violent resistance, knowing what he is doing and having a more creative purpose and perhaps a clearer sense of ultimate

values than the other, retains his moral balance. He uses the leverage of a
superior wisdom to subdue the rough direct force or physical strength of
his opponent."[69]

The aim of nonviolence was not to inflict defeat on the opponent, but to convert
the opponent and to change his sense of values so that "he will join wholeheart-
edly with the resister in seeking a settlement truly amicable and truly satisfy-
ing to both sides...under which both parties can have complete self-respect
and mutual respect."[70] In a typical Gandhian way, Gregg also highlighted the
importance of "self-suffering" and "humility" in realizing the goal that a nonviolent resister sought to accomplish. To him, nonviolence was a persuasion-
driven mechanism, and "if the changes are to be made by persuasion instead
of by violent coercion," Gregg believed, "the persuader must take as much as
possible of the suffering involved."[71] The other human criterion that needed to be
juxtaposed with suffering to successfully pursue nonviolent civil resistance was
"humility," which was "confused, in the west, with weakness, cowardice and lack
of self-respect."[72] This was a clear distortion, as Gregg strongly argued, because
humility was not "mere lowliness, but a consciousness that distinctions of size,
rank and other temporal and spiritual qualities are relatively unimportant, irrelevant and often misleading because of their transcendence by things of the spirit'
[which thus makes] humility a sort of equalitarianism."[73]

Not only did Gregg inspire many African American political activists in
their struggle against racial segregation, he also put forward a model of nonviolent resistance to those involved in the 1955 Montgomery bus strike. Bayard
Rustin, one of King's most trusted lieutenants, translated Gregg's suggestion
into specific steps in the context of the transport strike by insisting on being
absolutely nonviolent despite the provocations by the local police. The movement was so peaceful and nonviolent that local authority was at a loss when
confronting the resisters. Besides providing a strategy, Gregg was also a strong
intellectual influence on King, who was deeply influenced by Gregg's book, *The
Power of Non-Violence*, which provided the idea of nonviolence with "a more
realistic and depthful interpretation."[74] He was also persuaded to believe that
"under the influence of Gregg's ideas, the Montgomery bus boycott gradually
became a Gandhian project."[75] This was also evident in King's autobiographical
essay entitled "Pilgrimage to Non-Violence,"[76] which drew on Gregg's conceptualization of nonviolence. Like Gregg, King sought to combine the aggressive qualities of nonviolent resisters with human sentiments of love, hate, and
shame. During the bus strike, Gregg, persuaded by the aim of the movement,
came forward to help organize people against injustice. The Montgomery
incident gave him an opportunity to effectively implement Gandhi's ideas by
involving people in activities for the community including "clean-up, paint-up,
tidy-up, creation of sanitation and good physical order." Such a program, felt
Gregg, "would add to people's self-respect, increase their solidarity, use their
emotions and energy on permanent constructive self-help as well as the efforts
of protest."[77]

Unlike other pacifists and Quakers, Richard Gregg stood out because of his effort at articulating Gandhian ideas of nonviolence in the form of a meaningful strategy for the disinherited sections of the people. He successfully blended Christian ethics with the basic human concern for care, compassion, and sympathy. This was a Gandhian effort and at the same time went beyond it because Gregg's formulation of moral jiu-jitsu had visible elements of coercion that Gandhi strategically underplayed. Militant nonviolence was thus an authentic description of an ideology that did not entirely abdicate violence. It thus became, in Gregg's conceptualization "a practical instrument with a clear political form that could help usher in the Kingdom of God on earth."[78]

In popularizing Gandhi and his distinctive ideas among the African Americans, the role of Krishnalal Sridharani was no less insignificant. A student of Columbia University, Sridharani published his doctoral dissertation, titled *War without Violence: A Study of Gandhi's Method and Its Accomplishments*, in 1939. Drawing on Gregg's "realism," Sridharani reiterated some of Gregg's familiar arguments by saying that "the absence…of any sort of physical resistance deprives the attacker of an immediate incentive, much needed if he is to continue his act of violence. He [thus] loses his momentum, and feels himself ridiculous and baffled."[79] It was moral jiu-jitsu that he upheld. A veteran of the 1930 Dandi March, Sridharani aimed at building a nonviolent world, and his book helped him reach a wide range of American people. Although he was not very sure at the outset whether nonviolence was appropriate for the West, he later revised his opinion by saying that

[m]y contact with the Western world has led me to think that, contrary to popular belief, satyagraha, once consciously and deliberately adopted, has more fertile fields in which to grow and flourish in the West than in the Orient. Like war, satyagraha demands public spirit, self-sacrifice, organization, endurance and discipline or its successful operation, and I have found these qualities displayed in Western communities more than in my own. Perhaps the best craftsmen in the art of violence may still be the most effective wielders of non-violent direct action.[80]

Sridharani was not wrong, because his book was readily accepted by the pacifists. Seeing it as a guide book, James Farmer asked his Congress for Racial Equality (CORE) members to read *War without Violence* during the Chicago campaign. *Fellowship*, the intellectual organ of the Fellowship for Reconciliation (FOR), also published an abridged version of the book for its members. What was unique about this text was that it reiterated the basic Gandhian formulations on satyagraha in simple language so that it was intelligible to a wider section. It was also a powerful exposition of the Sermon on the Mount teachings, written in a typical Gandhian language. This attracted African Americans presumably because Gandhi built his idea on love and righteousness, which were integral to Christian ethics. The text was thus not only intellectually refreshing, it also provided readers with an idea about how to organize a nonviolent campaign for radical social change. Nonviolence did not mean "acquiescence, as most people at that time, when they heard of nonviolence, assumed that it was.... [I]n this book, Sridharani had outlined Gandhi's steps of investigation, negotiation, publicity and then demonstration. And we adopted those steps as our method of action."[81]

Gandhi was thus a transnational influence, as Sridharani's *War without Violence* demonstrates. The argument that Sridharani advanced was similar to the one that Richard Gregg pursued in his formulation of moral jiujitsu. Nonetheless, the book became "a guide and also a rule book" to African American activists presumably because it was recognized by the CORE and FOR leadership. What attracted attention was the idea that nonviolence was not merely a spiritual idea, but one with clear practical application in circumstances where violence seemed to have been a preferred device. In Sridharani's conceptualization, Gandhi's rearticulation of nonviolence was effective because he approximated the sense in which the Sermon on the Mount was verbalized. This linkage was significant for African Americans.

What Gregg and Sridharani had learned from Gandhi through personal interaction was articulated clearly in their written works. Gandhi became a household name, at least for those African Americans who took part in movements opposed to racial segregation. By the 1930s, there was growing interest in Gandhian ideas, which, though approximated to Christian ethics, were differently textured (presumably because of India's unique socioeconomic context). People felt the need for a black American Gandhi because "if non-cooperation brings the British to their knees in India, there is no reason why it should not bring the white man to his knees in the South."[82] In order to understand Gandhi better and to get a sense of what he stood for, a delegation comprising Edward G. Carroll, Phenola Carroll, Howard Thurman, and Sue Bailey Thurman traveled to India in 1935. This delegation was on "a pilgrimage to friendship" mission in response to an invitation by the Student Christian Movement of India, Burma, and Ceylon (now Sri Lanka). The historic meeting between Gandhi and the delegation took place in Bardoli, Gujarat, in February 1936. The discussion revolved around various issues: two important issues pertaining to the nature of the Gandhian movement in India and its articulation elsewhere seemed to have attracted maximum attention. While responding to the first issue relating to the nature of the nonviolent campaign in India, Gandhi explained its weaknesses in terms of the failure of the participants to internalize the spirit of nonviolence. He provided a detailed answer by saying that

[t]he effectiveness of a creative ethical ideal such as non-violence, ahimsa or no killing depends upon the degree to which the masses of the people are able to embrace such a notion and have it become a working part of their total experience. It cannot be the unique property or experience of the leaders; it has to be rooted in the mass assent and creative push. The result is that we first began our movement, it failed and it will continue to fail until it is embraced by the masses of the people.... They could not sustain this ethical

ideal long enough for it to be effective because they did not have enough vitality. [The masses lack vitality] because they are hungry [due to non-availability of food] and are also unable to stand on their own [since] there are hardly avenues for fruitful employment in India [given] the presence of a colonial power.... The *second* reason for the lack of vitality was the loss of self-respect [not]...because of the presence of conqueror in our midst, but because of the presence of untouchability in Hinduism.[83]

Howard Thurman was struck with Gandhi's formulation that nonviolence, to succeed, needed to be embraced by the victims at large; otherwise, it was not going to yield results, as demonstrated by movements that Gandhi had launched. Nonviolence was thus required to be inculcated among the masses as part of their being. It was not an easy task since people remained hungry and lacked self-respect. What was striking to Thurman was the relationship that morality and ethics had with physical vitality. He thus realized that the key to a success-ful political mobilization of the African Americans against racial injustice was not the biblical text, nor the instinctive moral values, but a meaningful solution to the socioeconomic problems confronting them. This was a typical Gandhian approach to human problems, which were to be tackled not only from a spiritual point of view, but also through adequate sources for gratification of human needs.

The second important point that figured in the discussion between Gandhi and the African American delegates was about his visit to the United States. The Mahatma had declined to visit since it would serve no practical purpose. He explained his inability by stating that

[t]he only condition under which I come would be that I would be able to make some helpful contributions toward the solution of the racial trouble in your country. I don't feel that I would have the right to try to do that unless or until I won our struggle in India. And, out of that discovery and disclo-sure, I may be able to have some suggestion about the problems involving race relations in your country and the rest of the world'.[84]

Gandhi's reluctance to visit the United States rekindled Thurman's belief that being independent politically was necessary to effectively challenge racial injus-tice. During the conversation, Thurman conveyed that Gandhian nonviolence was already part and parcel of the Negro psyche due to their strong ground-ing in the Sermon on the Mount. It would therefore not be difficult for African Americans to imbibe the spirit of nonviolence and to articulate a strong voice of protest drawing on Christian ethics. To this, Gandhi prophetically pronounced that "if it comes true, it may be through the Negroes that the unadulterated mes-sage of nonviolence will be delivered to all men everywhere."[85]

The 1936 Bardoli encounter between Gandhi and the African American del-egates was an important event in the black struggle against racial segregation in two significant ways: first, it was a meeting of hearts, because both Gandhi and Thurman came together on the basis of their appreciation for identical human concerns. However, their appreciation sprang from different sources: in the case of Gandhi, it was the colonial context of India that was critical, while for Thurman, it was the racially segregated nature of America that remained significant in shaping the views of the victims of racism. Second, the discussion was political. Nonviolence was a spiritual tool, and it was Gandhi who transformed nonviolence into a technique for bonding regardless of class, clan, and color. Thurman was thus persuaded to believe that Christianity-driven nonviolence was an adequate source of strength for the blacks presumably because it would come naturally to them given their unquestionable allegiance to Christianity. Gandhi's endorsement of nonviolence (corresponding with the spirit in which the Sermon on the Mount was conceptualized) provided a meaningful and effective alternative to African Americans in their struggle for political rights in racially divided America.

The relationship between Thurman, his colleagues, and Gandhi was further strengthened by another trip made by Benjamin E. Mays and Channing H. Tobias, who traveled to India to participate in the 1936 World Congress of the YMCA. Mays, then dean of Howard University's School of Religion, was already known for his forthright views on black issues and Christianity, especially for his candid comments on religion, politics, and education. A national secretary of the YMCA, Tobias was drawn to Gandhian nonviolence during his youth and was very excited when Mays agreed to take him to meet Gandhi in person. After their meeting with Gandhi at Wardha Ashram, both Mays and Tobias were convinced that nonviolence was perhaps the best device in the black struggle against racism. As Gandhi had shown, nonviolence was "invisible" and perfected through sustained practices, and thus "cannot be preached." Once it became active, nonviolence "travels with extraordinary velocity [effecting] miracle." Besides highlighting the strength of nonviolence, Gandhi also persuaded them to believe that nonviolence, if it was practised by the masses, could be an effective means of challenging socioeconomic atrocities. For Mays, this was a significant message, and he carried it from Wardha for the African Americans.[86]

Mays's meeting with Gandhi reconfirmed his belief in nonviolence as perhaps the best option under the circumstances. Like Thurman, he also believed that nonviolence was not an alien concept to the black Christians. The four cardinal values of Gandhian nonviolence remained integrally linked with Christianity. However, despite having a similar conceptual base, the African Americans hardly matched the Indians in terms of social progress, given their failure to rise as a collectivity against oppression. Hence Mays argued that

[t]he Negro people have much to learn from the Indians. The Indians have learned what we have not learned. They have learned how to sacrifice for a principle. They have learned how to sacrifice position, prestige, economic security and even life itself for what they consider a righteous and respectable cause. Thousands of them in recent times have gone to jail for their cause. Thousands of them died for their cause.[87]

What was striking to Mays was Gandhi's ability (a) to instill a sense of self-respect among the victims of colonialism in India and (b) to raise nonviolence as an invincible mechanism for radical socioeconomic and political changes. It was possible for Gandhi to attain the goal primarily because his unflinching commitment was steadfast, regardless of the consequences. There is no doubt that Gandhi had given "the Indian masses a new conception of courage…to face death, to die [or] to go to jail for the cause without fear and without resorting to violence."[88] This was not a mean achievement in a diverse country like India, which was clearly divided in sociocultural parameters. Nonetheless, the Mahatma, through his sustained work among the Indians had made "the Indian masses proud of their cultural roots, has instilled in them a feeling that 'it's great to be an Indian.'"[89]

Gandhi thus remained a constant source of inspiration to the African Americans, illustrating the importance of self-sacrifice in fulfilling specific sociopolitical aims. Those who came in contact with Gandhi were also persuaded that nonviolence was the only option for the disinherited African Americans in their ideological fight against racial segregation. The tradition continued. In 1947, Mordecai Johnson, the president of Howard College, led another delegation to India to meet Gandhi. King was reportedly drawn to Gandhian teachings only after he heard Johnson speak about them, having learned about them during his trip to India. Johnson's speech was "so profound and electrifying," recalled King later in his life, "that [he] left the meeting and bought a half a dozen books on Gandhi's life and works."[90] This encounter with Johnson enabled King to realize how love could be an effective force in the realm of social reform. He was now convinced that "the ethics of Jesus," based on "the love your enemies philosophy" was not merely a guiding principle for individual conduct, but was also a powerful ideological instrument to achieve larger social goals. It was Gandhi who, argued King, "was probably the first person in history to lift the love ethic of Jesus above mere interaction between individuals to a powerful effective social force on a larger scale."[91] The Johnson lecture in Philadelphia's Fellowship House in the spring of 1950 was a watershed event in King's life: not only did he understand the power of nonviolence, he also appeared to have found a powerful political philosophy to defend his ideological allegiance to the African American cause—in contrast with other prevalent philosophical discourses. He categorically stated that

[i]t was in the Gandhian emphasis on love and nonviolence that I discovered the method for social reform that I had been seeking for so many months. The intellectual and moral satisfaction that I failed to gain from the utilitarianism of Bentham and Mill, the revolutionary methods of Marx and Lenin, the social contract theory of Hobbes, the back to nature optimism of Rousseau, the superman philosophy of Nietzsche, I found in nonviolent resistance philosophy of Gandhi.[92]

What was striking to King was also the fact that Gandhian philosophy was not merely an explanatory model, it was also a praxis theory in the sense that it provided the struggling masses with a clearly designed ideological instrument to fight for justice. India's attainment of political freedom in 1947 through nonviolent civil resistance was illustrative of the effectiveness of Gandhian means. King was thus convinced that "this was the only morally and practically sound method open to oppressed people in their struggle for freedom."[93]

The story of the African American encounter with Gandhi will never be complete without reference to the activities of A. Philip Randolph, James Farmer, and Bayard Rustin because it was they who successfully translated Gandhian ethics of nonviolence into the context of the black struggle for racial desegregation. They were baptized by another Gandhi admirer, A. J. Muste (1885–1967), who, after having met Gandhi in 1931, was convinced that nonviolence was the only way out in circumstances of well-entrenched social, economic, and political oppression. As one of the founding members of the FOR, Muste mentored black activists, including Rustin and Farmer, who became most critical in challenging discriminatory socioeconomic practices. In a typical Gandhian way, he firmly believed that "pacifism must be an inner experience, an inner attitude, a way of life, not merely a tool or device which [an] individual uses in certain circumstances."[94] Hence, to him, nonviolence or pacifism was not a value that could be imposed from outside; it was something that needed to be consciously inculcated in individuals because

[i]f you want a revolution, you must be revolutionized. A world of peace will not be achieved by men who in their own souls are torn with strife and eagerness to assert themselves....He who would save me and heal strife must unite himself both reconciliation and new order.[95]

While Muste philosophized Gandhian ideas for the African American resisters, Randolph and his younger colleagues, Rustin and Farmer, built movements opposing racial segregation by drawing on the Gandhian model of nonviolent civil resistance. As will be shown later in the book, it was Randolph who found in Gandhi's 1930 Dandi March a useful technique for political mobilization—a technique that was translated in the 1941 March on Washington. Although the march was withdrawn after racial discrimination in the military was revoked, it was one of the first instances of nonviolent civil resistance in America to be conceptualized in Gandhian terms. This was evident in Randolph's statement before the Senate Committee on the eve of the march:

We would participate in no overt acts against our government....Ours would be one of non-resistance,...non-cooperation [and] non-participation in the military forces of the country [for which] we would be willing to absorb the violence, absorb terrorism, to face the music and to take whatever comes, and we, as a matter of fact, consider that we are more loyal to our country than the people who perpetuate segregation and discrimination on Negroes because of color or race.[96]

Seeking to articulate a powerful voice, Randolph, like Gandhi, sought to instill a sense of self-respect among the Negroes. He strongly felt, as his colleague in the FOR, Benjamin E. Mays, underlined in the past, the success of the black movement for justice was impossible without self-reliance among the victims of racism. "Negroes have no moral right," stressed Randolph, "to delegate their responsibility to any other organizations in America; they must themselves carry out this mandate of history."[97] What thus separates Randolph from other African American radical thinkers who articulated racism in clear theoretical terms was his insistence on "a mass organization with an action programme, aggressive, bold and challenging spirit" to pursue the struggle against the racial discrimination that was contrary to the fundamental canons of American constitutionalism.[98]

This spirit reverberated among the members of CORE, an organization that was founded in 1942 with the objective of establishing racial equality in America. One of CORE's founding members was James Farmer, who, after having been baptized in Gandhian nonviolence by Howard Thurman at Howard University, played a critical role, along with Randolph, Rustin, and other black activists, in the struggle against racial injustice. Like Randolph, he strongly felt the need for an organization backed by "genuine commitments" of those who regardless of race held Gandhian nonviolence in its totality. According to Farmer, Gandhi provided a political philosophy that, along with the laying of the intellectual foundation for nonviolent struggle, also articulated a nonviolent course of action that was both practical and rooted in human experiences. It was reflected in his reminiscences when he stated that

[s]egregation will go on as long as we permit it. Words are not enough; there must be action. We must withhold our support and participation from the institution of segregation in every area of American life—not an individual witness to purity of conscience, as Thoreau used it, but a coordinated movement of mass non-cooperation as with Gandhi. And civil disobedience when laws are involved. And jail where necessary. More than elegant cadre of generals we now have, we also must have an army of ground troops. Like Gandhi's army, it must be nonviolent. Guns would be suicidal for us.[99]

Persuaded by the Gandhian techniques of human salvation, Farmer went to the extent of declaring that "Gandhi has the key for [him] to unlock the door to the American dream…of Hebraic-Christian ethos of universal brotherhood."[100] The idea resurfaced with much vigor in another committed black activist, Bayard Rustin, a contemporary of Muste and Randolph, who, after a detailed study of Gandhian texts, came out clearly in favor of Gandhian civil resistance by saying that "no situation in America has created so much interest among Negroes as the Gandhian proposals for India's freedom."[101] Besides underlining the importance of a self-reliant organization to support the movement, Rustin had a concern similar to that of his colleague Randolph, of building a multiracial political platform with the involvement of white liberals. Here he was drawn to Gandhi because of his success in building a multiclass and multicaste political platform for India's freedom from the British rule. According to Rustin, Gandhi taught that

in a situation where the objectives of a social movement are accepted as valid by the majority, protest movement becomes an effective tactic to the degree that it elicits brutality and oppression from the power structure....[Therefore] it was not the civil rights movement's program which aroused the conscience of the nation, but the sight of small children entering a Little Rock High School accompanied by a federal troop escort that could not protect them from the jeering cadences of an ugly and irrational mob."[102]

He was convinced—and Gandhi had proved—that the aim of the civil rights movement could be achieved only through self-suffering. "Negroes gained moral authority," felt Rustin, "not because Americans opposed segregation, but because black people were suffering, because churches were bombed and children fire-hosed."[103] Success was possible only if the participant "uses, in his struggle, non-violent direct action—a technique with the ends he desires;...but as Gandhi has said, 'freedom does not drop from the sky,' one has to struggle and be willing to die for it."[104] He was also aware that one or a couple of successful political movements against racism were not adequate to conclusively abolish discriminatory practices supporting segregation. The abolition of segregation in public transport following the 1955 Montgomery bus strike was no doubt a significant achievement, but

it would have no permanent meaning in the racial struggle unless it led to the achievement of a dozens of similar victories in South. In practical terms, this meant that the movement needed a sustaining mechanism that could translate what we had learned during the bus boycott into a broad strategy for protest in the South.[105]

This was a realistic assessment of the circumstances leading to a successful organization of movements against racial injustice. As a strategy, nonviolence worked well presumably because it instantly caught the imagination of the African Americans who appeared to have found in this an expedient means for gratifying their socioeconomic and political goals.

The above brief discussion of the meetings between the African American civil rights activists and Gandhi is a clear testimony of the growing importance of the latter in shaping the movement against racial segregation. Although King stole the limelight with his reputation as a powerful critic of racism, the contribution of those African American intellectuals and political activists who also fought relentlessly against racial prejudices cannot be ignored. The civil rights movement in the United States was thus a combination of efforts that were directed towards King's goal. His equally adept colleagues helped him to sustain the momentum of various movements, beginning with the 1955 Montgomery bus strike and culminating in the 1965 removal of racial segregation and promulgation of the Civil Rights Act. The movements in which King reigned as the supreme leader were Gandhian at least in form because he deployed nearly "the entire Gandhian arsenal"[106]—from picketing, boycotts, and strikes to marches, flooding the jails, bearing witness, and the skillful mobilization of the media. The result was obvious: the civil rights campaign, which was generally confined to the Dixie states, gradually became a national phenomenon challenging the very intellectual foundation of racial discrimination. By meaningfully blending the Christian ethos with the Gandhian message for nonviolence, King did more than just to inculcate a new tradition; he provided "a bridge between Gandhi-inspired activists and church-centered followers of Jesus [which]...set in motion energy which helped to transform the nation."[107] In this entire process, the contribution of those leading African American civil rights activists was also equally significant: their close study of the Gandhian nonviolent civil resistance in India enabled them to conceptualize satyagraha (civil disobedience) in America through the fight against injustice and the articulation of a common cause for humanity. With their firm belief in the Gandhian mode of protest in circumstances other than India, these politically conscious African American protestors "also helped to change societies" that were socioculturally different from that of India by nurturing basic human values of love, compassion, and empathy for others.[108] Nonviolence thrilled the participants with substantial achievement and opposition was silenced by "the spectacle of sacrificial display."[109] A unique political model of protest, the Gandhian nonviolent civil resistance thus gradually became universal in both substance and spirit.

III

This study is about the sociopolitical ideas of Mahatma Gandhi and Martin Luther King Jr., also known as "Negro Gandhi."[110] My primary aim is to focus on the confluence of thought between these two great apostles of nonviolence. The book has four substantial chapters besides the introduction and conclusion. Chapter 1 seeks to identify the intellectual roots of Gandhi's and King's sociopolitical ideas. Both of them seem to have represented a well-entrenched tradition to which their predecessors contributed rather significantly. Divided into two complementary parts, this chapter focuses on those texts that acted critically in shaping what finally became the distinctive ideas of Gandhi and King. What separated them from their predecessors was their effort to articulate their ideas through the action victims of oppression must take against their perpetrators. This is how they stand out among those who, like them, comprehended the reality in its most complex manifestation, but seldom provided a course of action to radically alter the existing power relationships. Chapter 2 focuses on the liberal critique that Gandhi and King articulated while challenging the prevalent power relationships in India and America. It is not a strange coincidence that both Gandhi and King defended their opposition to the existing system of governance with reference to the fundamental values of the Enlightenment. In the case of Gandhi, colonialism in India was a threat to British liberalism because it took away the fundamental values that constituted the core claims of the latter. King followed the same argument while challenging racial segregation, which was contrary to the principles that informed the Declaration of Independence, the American Constitution, and the 1863 Emancipation Declaration. So, racism in America was not derivative of the Enlightenment tradition, but an outcome of a deliberate distortion made by the pseudo liberals. Chapters 3 and 4 focus on how Gandhi and King sought to change the system of governance in colonial India and racist America that sustained its hegemony by willful negligence of basic human concerns. While chapter 3 focuses on those movements that Gandhi led to accomplish his ideological goal, chapter 4 identifies the unique nature of King's political ideology by providing a concise analysis of the movements in which King had a critical role. Given the organic connection that Gandhi and King had evolved by their active participation with these specific movements in India and America, respectively, a careful study of these movements will also help us understand their contextual nature in conjunction with what acted as inspirational ideologies. There are a whole range of ideas that Gandhi and King upheld to articulate their distinctive approaches to human existence. What is striking is that, while the political career of each was cut short abruptly because of assassination, both of them were engaged in creating circumstances free from hunger, poverty, and oppression. Although they failed to fulfill their own ideological missions because of their sudden deaths, they nonetheless set in motion a transformative movement involving the disengaged and disinherited sections of the people.

The book is an attempt to understand the complex evolution of Gandhi's and King's sociopolitical ideas with reference to their immediate contexts and ultimate ideological sources of inspiration. Gandhi was a child of his age and set in motion a political agenda for change. The Mahatma was able to fulfill his goal because of a unique interplay of factors that allowed his ideas to be meaningfully articulated in the form of nonviolent civil resistance and brought disparate people together under a common political platform with an identical ideological aim of freedom from British rule. Like Gandhi, King never supported racial segregation because it was inhuman, unfair, and contrary to what constitutes the core values of American constitutionalism. Besides the Evangelical roots he derived from being raised in a family of Baptist pastors, the Montgomery hero drew on the ideas of political predecessors who were equally charged against racial discrimination. What explains King's success in leading a campaign toward its set goal was his ability to transform a mere Christian belief of human compassion and empathy into a formidable source of organization for the disinherited African Americans. The distinctive nature of the civil rights campaign stems from the fact that, despite its distinctive

Christian roots, it was informed, if not inspired by, the Gandhian approach to politics. It was King who, by grafting Gandhi onto American Christianity, not only redefined the nature of the civil rights campaign in the United States by identifying its "secular" roots, but also created circumstances for the multicultural political platform to strike roots.

CHAPTER 1

The Intellectual Roots of
Confluence of Thought

Ideas do not emerge in a vacuum. The context seems to play a significant, if not determining, role in the dialogue that unfolds in pursuance of an ideology. What emerges as a text in a particular context is dialectically structured in the sense of an interrelationship between text and context. The crucial interdependence between text and context is what lays the foundation stone for this study of the confluence of thought between the two great minds of the twentieth century, Mohandas Karamchand Gandhi and Martin Luther King Jr. By their distinctive approach to contemporary sociopolitical and economic issues, they sought to build a unique theoretical model of liberal democracy that is both different from and identical to its classical form: identical because while pursuing their ideological goals they drew on fundamental values of liberalism that had failed in the specific contexts of India and America; different because their modes of argumentation and theoretical discourse diverged from the core values of liberalism. Both these apostles of peace, nonviolence, and human fraternity challenged successfully the existing system of exploitation and racial segregation not because it was inhuman, but because it was contrary to the fundamental tenets of any human religion and also the foundational values of the Enlightenment. Hence their campaign against the system was just and legitimate.

Gandhi's political ideas were rooted in the larger socioeconomic and political processes of the nineteenth and twentieth centuries. The sociohistorical and cultural perspective of British India, for obvious reasons, constantly referenced the Mahatma. Gandhi conceptualized a model that, for a variety of reasons, gained currency both as a nationalist strategy for political mobilization and as a blue-print for India's future. What was unique about Gandhi was his ability to guide the nation toward a goal that followed a model based on different kinds of poli-tics. The same argument is followed while relocating King's sociopolitical ideas in the context of racial segregation in America. This was a liberal America in which the illiberal Jim Crow laws seemed to take organic roots for various com-plex socioeconomic reasons. Racial segregation became integral to American society, especially in the Southern states: whites endorsed it because it gave them privileges they did not want to abdicate; blacks accepted it (though reluctantly) as perhaps the best option to avoid humiliation, torture, and even lynching. Protest movements were crushed immediately and ruthlessly to prevent the par-ticipants from organizing again. Nonetheless, the black voice of protest that fol-lowed the adoption of the 1863 Emancipation Proclamation continued to gain momentum over the course of several revolutionary verdicts, including the 1954 *Brown v. Board of Education* judgment of the US Supreme Court.

One thus cannot meaningfully comprehend the rise and acceptance of Gandhi and King as leaders of protest movements in the last century without reference to the context. This was a context of innovative thinking, based on concern for underprivileged and disinherited human beings. Besides the leading figures of these protest movements, Gandhi and King, there emerged a galaxy of creative thinkers who were not only associated with the campaign for justice but were also critical in conceptualizing the political challenge within a liberal demo-cratic framework. Neither Gandhi nor King ever was illiberal in their action; in fact, their rigid stance was, on occasions, a source of irritation and pain to their colleagues. The primary focus of this chapter is to understand the evolution of Gandhi and King as political activists with clear ideological visions in sup-port of their respective sociopolitical and economic goals. Not only will there be attempts to locate the sources of their ideas in the prevalent religious, political, and other texts of contemporary relevance, there will also be an emphasis on assessing the role of equally important individual thinkers who, while critiquing the ideas of Gandhi and King, also provided an alternative politico-theoretical discourse.

THE SOCIO-ECONOMIC AND POLITICAL CONTEXTS OF MAHATMA GANDHI AND MARTIN LUTHER KING JR.

Both Gandhi and King were the products of socioeconomic and political con-texts of racism, human exploitation, and severe injustice. While Gandhi con-fronted an unjust political rule in both racist South Africa and colonized India, King faced an equally ruthless political authority and well-entrenched racism in America. The prevalence of Jim Crow laws justifying segregation between blacks and whites in the South remained an immediate reference point for King, who easily mobilized opinion when he raised his voice against such an inhuman sys-tem. The Jim Crow laws, with historical roots in contemporary socioeconomic circumstances, led to and also consolidated racist bias against blacks. In fact, King's father, "Daddy" King, a sharecropper's son, graphically explained the inevitability of the situation, given the obvious advantages that the whites accrued by forcing the blacks to provide "free labor." He thus stated,

> [t]he Blacks had no right...that the White man was bound to respect....He wasn't nothing but a nigger, a workforce....[White] men owned the land, he owned the mules, he owned everything. You paid for half of the guano that was used to make the cotton grow, and half of some of the seed....And then you work just for half, and whatever grew on the farm, they'd rob you out of it. Then you weren't supposed to question them. You just worked and let them take from you.[1]

Gandhi viewed colonialism and imperialism as predatory tendencies wielded by morally corrupt and economically insatiated countries. Hence, to solve Industrial Revolution problems of availability of raw materials and large consumer markets, these countries started colonizing various parts of the world. Lack of moral and humanist considerations on the part of the colonializing powers added vigor and speed to a project that infringed on the rights and domains of other people.

Gandhi saw the rise of European imperialism as a natural expression of the inherent impulse of aggressiveness and exploitation underlying the heart of modern civilization.[2] To Gandhi, the very structure of modern civilization revolved round the idea of exploiting one's fellow human beings. The dynamics of the market economy were such that commercial transactions could not be hampered by moral or ethical considerations. Such considerations would compromise or threaten the commercial viability of an enterprise. Moreover, modern economic activities must be conducted in a highly rational manner in which emotions, sentiments, passions, human values, and noncommercial considerations are kept aside. Only then will economic ventures be viable, and exploitation of one person by other is considered perfectly justified.

Colonialism and imperialism seek to cut native people from their roots and mold them in the typical colonial value system so that they start emulating the colonial ways of life. Such a process gradually robs native people of their indigenous ideals and values and converts them into blind followers of the artificially planted habits, institutions, values, and ideals of the colonial country. To Gandhi, colonialism was an ideology that dispossessed native people not only of their material belongings but also of their moral and spiritual self. Hence, as Gandhi saw it, colonialism contributed to the moral corruption and spiritual degeneration of native people and societies with a view toward furthering its own sinful interests. At the same time, he pointed out that the goal of any national movement should not be confined to waging a relentless negative battle against colonial forces. Rather, it should bring about a positive reorientation in the outlook of people through constructive program and moral and spiritual regeneration.

An analysis of Gandhi's views on colonialism and imperialism reveals two interrelated aspects of his critique. First, Gandhi conceptualized the ideology of colonialism and imperialism as offshoots of the modern Western civilization that itself could not withstand his critical scrutiny. Gandhi was quite convinced that the material basis of modern Western civilization would never yield space to a moralist and ethical philosophy of life capable of deterring Western countries from the path of colonialism and imperialism. Moreover, he noted that the unbridled quest for money and other material possessions motivated these countries to forgo all norms of civilized and humanist conduct even in relation to their own people. Hence, Gandhi was not surprised when the colonial masters let loose a reign of terror on the hapless colonies in response to even the slightest murmur against British rule in India. Second, in Gandhi's perspective of life, moral and ethical considerations carried more weight than the material and physical considerations that motivated ideologies such as colonialism and imperialism. Hence, what pained Gandhi more was the unavoidable impact that colonialism and imperialism had on the moral and ethical standing of the people in society. To Gandhi, long years of colonial rule were likely to lead to moral and spiritual decadence in the post-independence times. Hence, Gandhi saw colonialism and imperialism as the bane of not just the people of the colonies, but also of humanity.

INTELLECTUAL PILGRIMAGE TO NONVIOLENCE: GANDHI

For Gandhi, thought had no meaning unless it was lived out. A new idea provoked interest in him only if it was worthwhile. Once a book gripped his imagination, he always meditated over its message and put the message into action to uncover its truth. His reading interest was varied, though he preferred to read religious and moral literature. He not only read Plato's *Apology* and William Salter's *Ethical Religion* (1889), but also translated and summarized them in his mother tongue, Gujarati. Four of the several great books that influenced Gandhi when he was in South Africa were Henry David Thoreau's essay on *Civil Disobedience* (1849), which was, according to him, "a masterly treatise"; Leo Tolstoy's *The Kingdom of God Is Within You* (1893), which not only "overwhelmed" him but also "left an abiding impression on him" and in which he claimed to have first discovered the doctrine of nonviolence and love;[3] Edward Carpenter's *Civilization: Its Cause, Cure and Other Essays* (1889), the spirit of which reverberated in Gandhi's critique in *Hind Swaraj* (1909) of mechanized Western civilization; and John Ruskin's *Unto This Last* (1862), which "brought about instantaneous and practical transformation in [his] life" and a determination "to change [his] life in accordance with the ideals of the book."[4]

Gandhi's devotion to nonviolence was based on internalizing the ideas of these authors, as well as the long nonviolent traditions of the major religions of India, including Hinduism. Besides acknowledging his mother, who instilled in him "saintliness,"[5] Gandhi confessed that "[t]hree moderns have left a deep impress on my life and captivated me: Raychandbhai by his living contact; Tolstoy by his book, *The Kingdom of God Is within You*; and Ruskin by his *Unto This Last*.[6] Gandhi was drawn to Raychandbhai, whom he met in Bombay before his departure for England, because of "his deep intellect,...moral earnestness, and...a conviction that he would never willingly lead [Gandhi] astray...[and] put him in the right spiritual path."[7] He was clearly inspired by Leo Tolstoy's *The Kingdom of God Is Within You* in two significant ways. First, Gandhi was drawn to the Sermon on the Mount, which figured prominently in *The Kingdom of God Is within You*. From this work, he learned about the five cardinal values of human existence reflecting qualities like compassion, humility, self-criticism, forgiveness, and renunciation of material gain—which, in other words, is articulated in what is known as "the turn of the other cheek" philosophy. The second important idea that Gandhi drew from Tolstoy was love. In his letter to Gandhi, Tolstoy elaborated that love was the only means to rescue humanity from all ills, and the only method of saving the people from enslavement. In very ancient times, he further argued, love was proclaimed with "special strength and clearness among your people to be the religious basis of human life." Love, and forcible resistance to evil-doers, involved such "a mutual contradiction as to destroy utterly the whole sense and meaning of the conception of love."[8] This was evident in Gandhi when he articulated "the Christian message of 'resist not evil'—not a passive principle but the positive power of soul force, the infinite possibilities of universal love."[9] Like Tolstoy, the Mahatma strongly felt that the sole meaning of life was to serve humanity by contributing to the establishment of the kingdom of God, or "the reign of inward perfection, truth and love."[10]

The other thinker who had a strong bearing on Gandhi's thought was John Ruskin, especially his text *Unto This Last and Other Essays*. According to Gandhi, "[T]he book was impossible to lay aside once I had begun. I determined to change my life in accordance with the ideas of the book."[11] Ruskin helped him discover "some of his deepest conviction[s] of life [that] made [him] transform his life."[12] Two significant ideas of Ruskin that seemed to have critically influenced Gandhi were (a) dignity of labor and (b) concerns for the poor. Drawing on this, Gandhi thus argued that "the good of the individual is contained in the good of all," and, echoing Thomas Aquinas, that God was the owner of the universe and human beings were mere "trustees"—God alone has the absolute dominion over material nature." According to Gandhi, Ruskin redefined wealth not in terms of "the quantity of cash," but in terms of the "happiness" that it brought to human life in "a righteous" manner.

The third major figure who significantly influenced Gandhi was Henry David Thoreau, especially his famous text—*Civil Disobedience and other Essays* (1849). Gandhi was persuaded to believe in civil disobedience, which meant "disobedience to the state" within the accepted social forms. Similar to Thoreau, he also felt that "there will never be a really free and enlightened State until the State comes to recognize the individual as a higher and independent power, from which all its own power and authority are derived, and treats him accordingly."[13]

Edward Carpenter, the famous English socialist poet, also had a significant influence on Gandhi. Being critical of modern Western civilization, Carpenter proposed, in his *Civilization: Its Cause, Cure and Other Essays*, that civilization was "a form of disease that human societies pass through." Drawing on the analogy of a "diseased human body," Carpenter further clarified the point by saying that

just as…in [the] human body, when the inner and positive force of Health has departed from it, that it falls a prey to parasites which overspread and devour it; so when the central inspiration departs out of social life does it writhe with mere maggots of individual greed, and at length fall under the domination of the most monstrous egoist who had been bred from corruption.[14]

Gandhi elaborated this point in a more poignant way in his *Hind Swaraj*[15] by comparing modern civilization with a crippling "snake coil" that harmed human civilization in more than one way. Similar to Thoreau, who justified civil disobedience against a brutal state, Carpenter defended protest as inevitable because "the protest is not merely or chiefly against specific forms of injustice; it is rather to all intent and purposes, a protest against our present social system itself as intrinsically undemocratic, and as necessarily contributing to poverty and dependence on the one hand and excessive wealth and injustice on the other."[16] In a similar fashion, Gandhi justified protest against colonialism as perhaps the only way to save humanity. Despite being a loyal subject of the British Empire, he challenged its authority since it deviated from the well-established norms of governance and basic democratic values and principles.

Gandhi instinctively learned about nonviolence presumably because of his grounding in India's socioeconomic circumstances. As he narrated in his *Autobiography* (1925), his faith in nonviolence was rooted in his instinctive appreciation of religion-driven critique of violence. Despite being born in a typical Hindu family, he was also drawn to other religious traditions. Because his father was keen to learn about other religious texts from Islam, Jainism, and Christianity, he always encouraged discussions at home. Gandhi was privileged to have had access to these discussions, which inculcated in him "toleration for all faiths."[17] Although he appreciated the Sermon on the Mount,[18] he disliked Christianity presumably because of the alleged role of the Christian missionaries in "forcible conversion [and] also pouring abuse on Hindus and their gods."[19] His dislike of Christianity was due not only to the aggressive evangelical style of Christian missionaries, but also to the abuse the new converts usually heaped on "the religion of their ancestors, customs and their country."[20] Despite hailing Jesus Christ as "a living inspiration and a spiritual power,"[21] he was not comfortable with Christianity because "it compelled one to eat beef, drink liquor and change one's own clothes."[22] It is thus fair to argue that although Gandhi was highly impressed by the values that the biblical texts upheld,[23] he was equally appalled by the discrepancy between its humanitarian creed and the discrimination it perpetuated in the then-racist South Africa and colonial India.

In conceptualizing his argument for nonviolence, Gandhi was thus indebted to several intellectual sources, including major religions. His ideas were thus an outcome of his constant engagement with those texts that clearly charted a nonviolent course of action. He may have been attracted to this strategy because of the context in which nonviolence was preferable to other contending ideological alternatives. The best exposition of what led Gandhi to prefer nonviolence was made by Gandhi himself when he stated that

[i]t was the New Testament which really awakened me to the rightness and value of Passive Resistance. When I read in the Sermon on the Mount such passages as 'resist not him that is evil, but whosoever smiteth thee on thy right cheek turn to him the others also, and Love your enemies and pray for them that persecute you, that ye may be sons of your Father which is in heaven, I was simply overjoyed, and found my opinion confirmed where I least expected it. *The Bhagavad Gita* deepened the impression, and Tolstoy's *The Kingdom of God Is Within You* gave it a permanent form.[24]

CRITIQUE OF GANDHI: M. N. ROY, RABINDRANATH TAGORE, AND B. R. AMBEDKAR

This section draws on the critiques of M. N. Roy, Rabindranath Tagore, and B. R. Ambedkar for the reason that they not only provide refreshing theoretical interventions, they also helped Gandhi reformulate some of his early ideas. While Roy provided a Marxist critique of Gandhi, Ambedkar evaluated Gandhi on the basis of his conceptualization of distributive justice, privileging "the untouchables" or *dalits* over others. Tagore's critique of Gandhi is perhaps the most creative response, being both indigenous and Western-influenced. These varied critiques dialectically influenced Gandhi and transformed his ideas on occasion. So the blueprint of future India that the Mahatma sought to articulate reflected various but authentic influences. Here lies the significance of the dialogue that Gandhi had with his colleagues on issues of socioeconomic and political importance. Although Roy, Tagore, and Ambedkar articulated their ideological critiques of Gandhi in different voices, their critiques were largely theoretical, as none of them were involved in the Indian nationalist movement as organically as Gandhi was.

Notwithstanding the significant contribution of M. A. Jinnah in articulating a sovereign state for the Muslims, this section does not deal with his critique of Gandhi for two reasons: (1) the critical literature on this theme is abundant, and hence the discussion will merely be repetitive; and (2) since both Jinnah and Gandhi were primarily political activists, it would be improper to deal with the dialogue without contextualizing the issues that figured in their discussion. Just like Gandhi, Jinnah too carved out an independent place in the Indian freedom struggle that culminated in the bifurcation of British India following his two-nation theory.

M. N. ROY AND GANDHI

M. N. Roy (1887–1954) provided a well-argued Marxist critique of Gandhi's social and political ideas. Gandhism was, according to him, the most important of all the ideologies of class collaborations within the Indian nationalist movement. Roy predicted that the Indian nationalist movement, actuated by the spirit of nonviolence, was bound to fail, and that it would "fall victim to its own contradictions."[25] The inability of the Mahatma to comprehend the changing nature of social and political forces opposed to the prevalent nationalist movement remained at the root of its failure. Sharing Gandhi's criticism of capitalist civilization, Roy was however critical of the alternative that Gandhi provided simply because it was neither "realistic" nor "practicable." He further argued that "one need not be a sentimental humanitarian, nor a religious fanatic in order to denounce the present order of society in the countries where capitalism rules." Capitalism was unavoidable and "will not collapse because sentimental humanitarians find it full of cruelty and injustice, [but because] of its own contradictions."[26] Illustrative of "the satanic Western civilization," British rule in India provided the most obvious missing link in India's growth as a national economy. Gandhi's role was significant in conceptualizing the adverse economic impact that capitalism, feverishly introduced in the form of large industries at the cost of handicrafts and other indigenous efforts, would have on India. Not only did he decry the devastating nature of Western capitalism, he also radically altered the nature of the anti-British political campaign of the erstwhile moderate and extremist varieties. The former was extremely cautious not to disturb British rule by being submissive to its authority; the latter failed to arouse the masses because of [a] their caste and religious prejudices and [b] their uncritical acceptance of violence while pursuing the nationalist goal.[27]

So Gandhi was a clear departure from the past. Despite the inherent weaknesses and limited goal of satyagraha, it had "penetrated the villages, it had rudely shaken the resignation of the masses of India people." Roy characterized this mass movement as "a huge popular upheaval," caused essentially by "economic exploitation not alone by imperial capital, but by native agencies as well." Roy therefore concluded that "the imminent popular upheaval," inspired by Gandhi and organized on the principles he devised, was "a social outburst, the rise of a socially revolutionary force uncompromising, unrelenting, implacable, which would mark the commencement of the inevitable class war."[28] As evident, Roy was critical of the ideology of nonviolence and satyagraha for being politically restrictive; and yet, he found in Gandhi the most effective political leadership that extended the constituencies of nationalist politics by involving the peripheral sections of society.

For Roy, nonviolence was a cloak "to serve the interests of those who have built castles of social privilege and economic exploitation. If the end of nationalism is to glorify the privileged few, then non-violence is certainly useful; but to nationalism of a broader kind, which is the expression of the desire of the entire Indian people, it is a positive hindrance."[29] At the same time, the cult of nonviolence was a convenient tool for both the Gandhi-led nationalist political forces and those supporting imperialism. Roy predicted that both these forces "will bury their hatchet [in due course] in order to carry on the crusade against those forces of revolution which menace the security of vested interests."[30] It was clear to Roy that nonviolence was tuned to protect the vested interests and that noncooperation was the best strategy to contain the revolutionary fervor of the masses. In other words, this strategy was ideologically governed and dictated in order to "thwart the development of dynamic revolutionary forces which threaten to push Indian nationalism dangerously farther than the so-called politically-minded middle class desired it to go."[31] By drawing attention to the sudden withdrawal of the Noncooperation Movement, Roy sought to prove the point. According to him, Gandhi called off the movement because he apprehended a revolutionary outburst challenging the ideological basis of the Noncooperation Movement: "[W]ith one single breath, the Mahatma thus blows up the beautiful castle built so laboriously during all these years of storm and stress."[32] Not only did Gandhi stall a revolutionary upsurge, he also became an instrument at the hands of the colonial power to contain movements threatening its very foundation. As Roy put it, Gandhi was immediately released as soon as the movement was withdrawn simply because the government understood that "he will be a very valuable asset in the coming game of change of heart."[33] Furthermore, in releasing Gandhi, the government was not generous but calculative because "none will appreciate this act of generosity more than the Mahatmaji who will pay it back [in some form or another] when required."[34]

Roy criticized Gandhi's *swaraj* as doomed to fail because "the time is gone when the people could be inspired by a vague promise of Swaraj." He was convinced that this Congress-led movement was bound to fail since it aimed at protecting exploitation and ignored "the political rights of the workers and peasants." As a Marxist, he also felt the need to join hands with "the proletariats" elsewhere, as, otherwise, these movements remain just ripples. He therefore suggested that "the revolutionary nationalists should, therefore, not only join hands with the Indian workers and peasants, but should establish close relations with the advanced proletariat of the world."[35] By attributing the abject poverty in India to the British policy of "forcibly making India an agricultural adjunct to industrial Britain," Roy was, for obvious reasons, critical of India's dominion status within the empire. Hence he argued that "neither Self-government realized progressively by Non Cooperation will change the economic condition of the toiling [masses]...Therefore, the interests of the majority demand *complete separation from all imperial connection and the establishment of a Republican State* based on the democratic principles of *Universal Suffrage*" (emphasis in the original).[36]

Roy's analysis of Gandhi's constructive programs clearly suggests that they were basically verbal, couched in sentiments, rather than effective programs involving the masses. In view of the serious weaknesses, these programs failed to achieve the goal that the Mahatma so assiduously set for the masses. According to Roy, these programs "should be such as to appeal to the immediate interests of the masses of the people." For him, the nonpayment of taxes that already had galvanized the peasants in Uttar Pradesh, Bengal, and Punjab into action should have been pursued with zeal. Advising the Congress to adopt the agenda of the masses, Roy recommended that "the preparatory work consists of demonstrating practically and not by sentimental humanitarian cant, that the Congress is the leader of the worker and peasant population. [Only then] Civil Disobedience can be inaugurated with all the possibilities of a revolutionary development."[37] As demonstrated, Roy carved a space for himself by providing a critique of Gandhi's social and economic ideas. Despite his admiration for Gandhi's infusing India's struggle for independence with new zeal, Roy was perhaps one of those few who was never swayed by the charisma of the Mahatma when it involved social, economic, and political issues affecting the masses. Hence, his critique remains a significant intervention underlining both the weaknesses and the natural strengths of the ideology that the Mahatma sought to articulate as an activist-theoretician.

What is clear in M. N. Roy's thought is an attempt to conceptualize his response to the Indian nationalist movement by drawing upon Marxism and his specific experiences in this context. Gandhi was a constant referent for obvious reason. In fact, political radicalism acquired a completely different connotation with the growing participation of the so-called "peripheral" sections of society. As will be shown in Chapter 3, it was during the Noncooperation Movement that the constituencies of the Indian National Congress went beyond the cities and educated the middle class. Roy seemed to have captured this moment of colonialism in India and provided a theoretical framework that largely drew on Marxism. In other words, by seeking to capture the "neglected voice" of the people, Roy performed a historical task, along with those radicals striving to involve the subalterns in the nationalist movement. Whether his radicalism was politically viable in that particular context is debatable, though there is no doubt that his ideas were ideologically refreshing simply because they took into account the growing revolutionary ferment among the masses. Like his radical counterparts in the nationalist movement, Roy put forward a well-argued theoretical model that explained the predicament of the Gandhi-led nationalist leadership in its failure to comprehend the mass fervor confronting both the colonial power and also the indigenous vested interests. Yet Roy's analysis of Gandhi from a strictly Marxist point of view, though creative, failed to understand "the cultural power of Gandhi," and its ability to fashion weapons of political struggle out of unorthodox material. This led him to misconstrue what, in retrospect, was the strength of Gandhi's politics as "an impotent mysticism."[38]

RABINDRANATH TAGORE AND GANDHI

Rabindranath Tagore's critique of Gandhi was based on a certain reading of Indian civilization and actual political processes that unfolded in the context of the struggle against imperialism. But while Gandhi hardly responded to Roy, he remained in a constant dialogue with Tagore. Not only did they interact regularly on various philosophical issues pertaining to India as a civilization—either through personal correspondence or through the media—they also exchanged views on the mundane political agenda of the Indian National Congress. As a poet who was not directly involved in the nationalist agitation, Tagore sought to articulate the concerns of the Indian public consciousness.

Tagore was perhaps the first to emphatically argue that identity in the sub-continent was not unidimensional. Challenging the concept of "nation," which, he believed, undermined the multilayered Indian identity, Tagore reminds us of the combined role of the "little" and "great" traditions in shaping what he loosely defined as the Indian nation.[39] India's diversity, Tagore felt, was her "nature [and] you can never coerce nature into your narrow limits of convenience without pay-ing one day very dearly for it."[40] Not only "have religious beliefs cut up society into warring sections...social antagonisms [between the Hindus and Muslims] have set up impassable barriers every mile—barriers which are guarded night and day by forces wearing the badge of religion."[41] For Tagore, the gulf between the communities was largely due to "the cultural forces" released by British colonialism that "fractured the personality of every sensitive exposed Indian and set up the West as a crucial vector within the Indian self."[42] As India's social system got distorted, "[l]ife departed," argued Tagore, "from her social system and in its place she is worshipping with all ceremony the magnificent cage of countless compartments that she has manufactured."[43] Interrogating the "totalizing" dimension of the nationalist project—where a single entity, called "nation," always prevails over other forms of identity—Tagore sought to provide an alternative to an "essential-istic" invocation of identity in the shape of a nation. According to him, in articu-lating the civilizational identity of India, the importance of underlying cognitive and ethical claims, which are invariably lodged in and emanate from contradic-tory social locations, could never be undermined. So the European modular form of nation was conceptually futile and politically inapplicable presumably because India's civilizational identity was not singular but multiple and thus difficult to capture on a single axis.

Gandhi held identical views. Like Tagore, he rarely used the term "nation" in the sense Jinnah referred to it. Yet Gandhi failed to halt the historical processes whereby the Indian Muslims became a nation and bargained successfully for a separate Muslim state. Jinnah's role was equally significant. In the penulti-mate year of the transfer of power, the Jinnah-led Muslim League secured parity with the Congress, and in the 1946 Shimla conference, the Muslim League and the Congress had an equal number of representatives to pursue their respective points of view[44] What came in the form of the 1940 Lahore Resolution became feasible. And Jinnah's appeal to "unsettle the settled notions...of Muslims being a minority [that] had been around for so long"[45] was finally translated into reality. So, not only did the *Quaid-i-Azam* (great leader) succeed in dramatically alter-ing the role of the Muslims in the overall constitutional settlement on the eve of the Great Divide, he also transformed the Muslim community into a nation[46] by ascertaining "territorial sovereignty to a heterogeneous community turned homogeneous nation."[47] The Muslim community for Jinnah was, therefore, not "an abstract historical-political entity...but a separate nation with distinct interests [which] could not be treated only as a minority."[48]

Gandhi's opposition to the concept of nation was based on two specific arguments: first, he put forward a contextual argument by saying that the logic of creating a religion-based nation-state was faulty because religion could neither be "a stabilizing nor a unifying factor in humanity," but "divisive." So, by seeking to gloss over the obvious diversities among the Indian Muslims for a sovereign state, Jinnah ignored the long-drawn historical processes in their community formations. For Gandhi, nation was hardly a criterion for conceptualizing the complex and deeply heterogeneous communities in the subcontinent regardless of religion. Couched in a humanitarian fashion, the second argument dwells on the devastating consequences of conceptualizing Hindus and Muslims as separate nations. Holding politics responsible for the Hindu-Muslim schism, Gandhi pledged to "rescue people from this quagmire and make them work on solid ground where people are people. [Therefore his] appeal [was] not to the Muslims as Muslims nor to the Hindus as Hindus, but to ordinary human beings who [had] to keep their villages clean, build schools for their children and take many other steps so that they [could] make life better."[49] To Gandhi, nation as a categorizing device was perhaps the narrowest in its manifestation, as it ignored the inherent diversities of the communities. Conceptually nonviable and practically inappropriate, the application of nation as a category weakened the anti-British struggle, he argued, because of the clash of interests between the Hindus and Muslims once they were characterized as separate nations.

The honeymoon was shortlived because soon Gandhi and Tagore came out sharply against each other once the 1919–21 Noncooperation Movement was inaugurated. Gandhi's idea of burning foreign clothes, for instance, evoked much unease in Tagore, who wondered if Gandhi was not encouraging the flames of narrow nationalism and xenophobia. As he argued,

[T]he clothes to be burnt are not mine, but belong to those who most sorely need them. If those who are going naked should have given us the mandate to burn, it would, at least, have been a case of self-immolation and the crime of incendiarism would not lie at our door. But how can we expiate the sin of the forcible destruction of clothes which might have gone to women whose nakedness is actually keeping them prisoners unable to stir out of the privacy of their homes?[50]

Similarly, during the noncooperation movement, withdrawal from the schools and colleges never appeared to be a wise call. Tagore refused to endorse the campaign because "the great injury and injustice which had been done to those boys who were tempted away from their career before any real provision was made, could never be made good to them."[51] He was not persuaded to believe that Western education "injured" young minds and should be altogether rejected. According to Tagore, the root of the misconception lay elsewhere. As he pointed out, "[w]hat has caused the mischief is the fact that for a long time we [have] been out of touch with our own culture and therefore the Western culture has not found its perspective in our life; very often [it has] found a wrong perspective, giving our mental eye a squint."[52] Tagore adopted a nuanced argument vis-à-vis the Noncooperation Movement, which was a relatively successful political campaign involving a wider section of the population across the length and breadth of India.

Tagore's critique of the Noncooperation Movement drew on the "constructive work" that he experimented with during the 1905–08 Swadeshi Movement in Bengal. He was opposed to coercion because his experience of the Swadeshi Movement had shown its adverse consequences. When the movement was at its zenith, Tagore denounced its reliance on coercion and the alienating impact it had on the masses it claimed to enthuse and activate. His critique of the Noncooperation Movement followed the same logic. He regarded the pervasive use of social boycott and other forms of coercion "as evidence of the Swadeshi activist's failure to persuade people to their cause."[53] He thus argued that "we have not been patient enough to work our way gradually towards winning popular consent."[54] That was at the root of the nationalist failure to unite all Indians in "a grand patriotic mobilization." The debate between Gandhi and Tagore brought out their contrasting perspectives on this subject. While Gandhi was confident that the noncooperation agenda was most appropriate sociopolitically, Tagore expressed fear that the "narrow political aim" of the movement was likely to jeopardize its wider goal and objectives. The debate remained inconclusive, but raised certain major questions about Gandhi's influential social and political ideas.[55]

Just like the debate over the strategy of noncooperation, the exchange of views between Gandhi and the poet on *charkha* and *khaddar*[56] laid bare their different perspectives. Tagore was not persuaded, let alone impressed, by the campaign for charkha. As he admitted,

> [T]he depths of my mind have not been moved by the charkha agitation...for its inherent weaknesses [and he therefore apprehended] that all intense pressure of persuasion brought upon the crowd psychology is unhealthy for it [because] it will create blind faith on a very large scale in the charkha...which is liable to succumb to the lure of short cuts when pointed out by a personality about whose moral earnestness they can have no doubt."[57]

Tagore was not convinced because unless the cultivators accepted charkha as complementary to their well-being, it would be difficult to draw them to the campaign that Gandhi had launched for self-reliance through khaddar and charkha. He thus offered two reasons in support of his argument against khaddar and charkha: first, the cultivator acquired a special skill with his hands, and special bent of mind by dint of consistent application to his particular work. Hence, "to ask the cultivator to spin is to derail his mind; he may drag on with it for a while, but at the cost of disproportionate effort and therefore waste of energy."[58]

Second, if charkha was imposed on disinclined cultivators it would lose its significance and effectiveness. In other words, the acceptance of charkha was not spontaneous, and hence the consequence could be devastating. As Tagore most eloquently said,

> [I]t would be wrong to make the cultivator either happier or richer by thrusting aside, all of a sudden, the habits of body and mind which have grown upon him through his life....To tell the cultivator to turn the charkha instead of trying to get him to employ his whole energy in his own line of work is only a sign of weakness [*sic*]. We cast the blame for being lazy on the cultivator, but the advice we give him amounts rather to a confession of the laziness of our mind.[59]

According to Tagore, spinning was not creative, for "by turning its wheel man merely becomes an appendage of the charkha; that is to say, he but does himself what a machine might have done; he converts his living energy into a dead turning movement. [In the process] he becomes a machine, isolated, companionless."[60] Instead, Tagore suggested concrete steps that were organically linked with human life. For instance, as he perceived, the village that sustained itself economically and supported each of its inhabitants could lay the foundation of swaraj in the true sense of the term. As he most unambiguously put it, "[T]he village of which people come together to earn for themselves their food, their health, their education, to gain themselves the joy of so doing, shall have lighted a lamp on the way to swaraj."[61]

Gandhi responded to the poet's critique in his rejoinders in the magazine *Young India*. Instead of countering Tagore's arguments, the Mahatma, in a very cryptic way, defended charkha as indispensable for India's economic well-being. In response to the charge that he insisted on spinning to the exclusion of all other activities, Gandhi argued that he never wanted "the Poet to forsake his muse, the farmer his plough, the lawyer his brief and the doctor his lancet. [Instead], he asked the 'famishing' to spin for a living and the half-starved farmer to spin during his leisure hours to supplement his slender resources."[62] He was not opposed to a machine per se; his concern was that machine civilization would make human labor redundant, a consequence most devastating where human labor was in abundance. As Gandhi argued,

> [M]achine must not be allowed to displace the necessary human labour. An improved plough is a good thing. But if by some chance one man could plough up by some mechanical invention of his the whole of the land of India and control all the agricultural produce and the millions had no other occupation, they would starve, and being idle, they would become dunces, as many have already become....[i]t is therefore criminal to displace hand labour by the introduction of power-driven spindles unless one is at the same time ready to give millions of farmers some other occupation in their homes.[63]

The charkha was a symbol of involvement with the day-to-day life of the poor and thus a powerful device to conceptualize that reality. Gandhi suggested to the poet that "if [he] spun half an hour daily his poetry would gain in richness [for] it would then represent the poor man's wants and woes in a more forcible manner than now."[64] Gandhi also replied to the charge that the charkha was calculated to bring about a deathlike sameness in the nation. To him, the charkha was "intended to realize the essential and living oneness of interest among India's myriads."[65] The charkha was not simply an economic activity. Instead, it brought people together by involving them in an activity that was (a) a source of supplementary income and (b) a device to link them automatically with the rest of India politically.[66] Spinning, for Gandhi, was therefore a symbolic form of identification with the masses; Tagore, however, was suspicious of any such appeal that tended to gloss over the inherent diversity among the Indian people.

Apart from these major issues, an interesting debate took place following Gandhi's characterization of the Bihar earthquake in February 1934 as "divine chastisement" for the great sin committed against those known as harijans.[67] Tagore took serious note of this by saying that "it has caused me painful surprise to find Mahatma Gandhi accusing those who blindly follow their own social custom of untouchability of having brought down gods' vengeance upon certain parts of Bihar."[68] Since it was said by the most revered political leader of the country, the statement, he felt, was most devastating for its obvious impact on interpersonal relationship between harijans and others. So, it should not go "unchallenged."[69] Tagore prefaced his critique of this superstitious view of Gandhi by saying that "it is all the more unfortunate, because this kind of unscientific view of things is too readily accepted by a large section of our countrymen." Underlining that "physical catastrophes [like earthquakes, etc.] have their inevitable and exclusive origin in [a] certain combination of physical facts," he further argued that

> if we associate ethical principles with cosmic phenomena, we shall have to admit that human nature is morally superior to Providence that preaches its lessons in good behaviour in orgies of the worst behaviour possible....What is truly tragic about it is the fact that the kind of argument that Mahatmaji uses by exploiting an even of cosmic disturbance far better suits the psychology of his opponents...[He thus felt] profoundly hurt when any words from [Gandhi's] mouth may emphasize the elements of unreason...which is a fundamental source of all the blind powers that drive us against freedom and self-respect.[70]

Gandhi retorted against Tagore's views equally strongly. Reiterating his views on the Bihar earthquake, the Mahatma argued,

> [T]o me, the earthquake was no caprice of God nor a result of a meeting of mere blind forces....Visitations like droughts, flood, earthquakes and the like, though they seem to have only physical origins, are, for me, somehow

connected with man's morals. Therefore, I instinctively felt that the earthquake was visitation for the sin of untouchability. [He firmly believed]
that our sins have more force to ruin the structure than any mere physical
phenomenon.[71]

On this occasion, both of them held diametrically opposite views. A scientific
Tagore upheld reason, while a moralist Gandhi privileged faith over reason. The
point here is not to ascertain the validity of their respective arguments objectively, but to ascertain their appropriateness in the context of India's struggle
for swaraj. Tagore's was a reasoned argument with a limited application, while
Gandhi's had a wider application, given his influence over the masses. It was,
as it were, a Gandhian preemptive measure, based on his wider acceptability
as a political leader. What informed Gandhi's view was perhaps his confidence
in dissuading people from practicing untouchability and warning them of
god's impending wrath. For Gandhi, linking the Bihar calamity with the sin of
untouchability, though unscientific logically, was a significant step in his battle
against untouchability. In other words, the statement on the Bihar earthquake
had different connotations, which one may not comprehend without gauging the
Mahatma's popularity among the masses. So, given the typical Gandhian meth-
odology of mass mobilization for freedom, it was just another method to launch
an effective and meaningful campaign against untouchability.

As is evident, the differences between Tagore and Gandhi regarding specific
political strategies for mass mobilization were fundamental. Unlike Gandhi,
Tagore never appreciated the noncooperation strategy, for instance, because of
its in-built weaknesses. Similarly, in the case of charkha and khaddar, the poet
was critical of the Mahatma since they neither provided an appropriate alternative to the masses nor adequately addressed the problem of poverty. It was
largely "a hollow political slogan," as Tagore believed, and would cause obvious
adverse political and economic consequences for the masses if forced on them.
Despite the validity of Tagore's wider argument, there is no doubt that charkha
and khaddar instrumentalized the Gandhi-led mass movement; they, in other
words, became symbols of mass involvement in the anti-imperial struggle. But
while the two men differed in regard to politico-economic strategies, they held
uniform views on nationalism. Given the disparate nature of the Indian masses,
"nation," to both of them, never appeared to be a viable organizing principle.
Tagore was perhaps the first to confront the devastating consequences of the
principle of nationalism in the context of the Swadeshi Movement of 1903–08
in Bengal, when the schism between the Hindus and Muslims was articulated in
a nationalist language. The growing strength of the Muslims, defined later as a
separate nation by Jinnah, the architect of Pakistan, caused a permanent fissure
between these two major religious communities. This schism ultimately led to
the 1947 partition of the subcontinent. Articulating their views in a nonnational-
ist language, Gandhi and Tagore, perhaps the finest products of the Indo-British
cultural encounter, provided the most creative and also challenging response to
the nationalist "oneness" of the Western world.

B. R. AMBEDKAR AND GANDHI

Critical of the nationalist movement that upheld caste and untouchability at the behest of Gandhi, Bhimrao Ramji Ambedkar (1891–1956) sought to articulate an alternative political ideology by challenging the very foundation of the "Hinduised" nationalist movement. According to him, Gandhism was "a paradox" because he "stands for freedom from foreign domination [and] at the same time it seeks to maintain intact a social structure which permits the domination of one class by another on a hereditary basis which means a perpetual domination of one class by another."[72] Ambedkar saw Gandhi's loyalty to Hinduism as supporting "untouchability" as it is integrally linked with and justified by Hinduism. This assumption, however, was the opposite of what the Mahatma sincerely believed. According to him, "[U]ntouchability is not a sanction of religion; it is a device of Satan….There is neither nobility nor bravery in treating the great and uncomplaining scavengers of the nation as worse than dogs to be despised and spat upon."[73]

Ambedkar criticized Gandhi further for having eulogized the Indian villages as illustrative of a unique unit of social, economic, and political equilibrium. Instead, Ambedkar argued, Indian villages

> represent a kind of colonialism of the Hindus designed to exploit the Untouchables. The Untouchables have no rights. They are there only to wait, serve and submit. They are there to do or to die. They have no rights because they are outside the village republic and because they are outside the so-called republic, they are outside the Hindu fold. This is a vicious circle. But this is a fact which cannot be gainsaid.[74]

For Gandhi, the village was the basis for building a republican society[75]; for Ambedkar, the structure of village settlements reflected basic tenets of Hinduism that never recognized *dalits* as equal. In other words, villages contributed to and simultaneously sustained the divisive nature of the Hindu society, where the untouchables always remained "outside the fold." As Ambedkar most eloquently put it,

> [T]he Hindu society insists on segregation of the untouchables. The Hindu will not live in the quarters of the untouchables and will not allow the untouchables to live inside the Hindu quarters….It is not a case of social separation, a mere stoppage of social intercourse for a temporary period. It is a case of territorial segregation and of a cordon sanitaire [*sic*] putting the impure people inside the barbed wire into a sort of a cage. Every Hindu village has a ghetto. The Hindus live in the village and the untouchables live in the ghetto.[76]

The conflict between Gandhi and Ambedkar on the issue of separate electorates for untouchables and the depressed classes reflected two contrasting perspectives that fundamentally altered the nature of political participation by the scheduled castes and tribes in British India and during its aftermath. Once the Congress conceded a separate electorate for the Muslims through the 1935 Government of India Act, Ambedkar argued that the dalits should be allowed to constitute a separate electorate and elect their own representatives to the central and provincial legislatures. He further defended the claim by saying that since voting was severely restricted by property and educational qualifications, the geographically disparate depressed classes were unlikely to have any influence in the decision-making process. So, the solution lay in establishing a separate electorate for them. Ambedkar held the view that untouchables were absolutely separate from Hinduism and hence he tried "to find a solution to their problem through political separatism."[77] In order to substantiate, he further argued that the Hindus "had much to lose by the abolition of untouchability, though they had nothing to fear from political reservation leading to this abolition."[78] The matter was "economic" rather than "religious." In an unambiguous way, Ambedkar brought out the economic dimension of untouchability by stating that

the system of untouchability is a gold mine to the Hindus. In it the 240 millions of Hindus have 60 million of Untouchables to serve as their retinue to enable the Hindus to maintain pomp and ceremony and to cultivate a feeling of pride and dignity befitting a master class, which cannot be fostered and sustained unless there is beneath it a servile class to look down upon. In it the 240 millions of Hindus have 60 millions of Untouchables to be used as forced labourers…in it the 240 millions of Hindus have 60 millions of Untouchables to do the dirty work of scavengers and sweepers which the Hindu is debarred by his religion to do and which must be done by non-Hindus who could be no other than Untouchables. In it the 240 millions of Hindus have 60 millions of Untouchables who can be kept to lower jobs.…In it the 240 millions of Hindus have the 60 millions of Untouchables who can be used as shock-absorbers in slumps and deadweights in booms, for in slumps, it is the Untouchables who is fired first and the Hindu is fired last and in booms the Hindu is employed first and the Untouchables is employed last. [So, untouchability is not a religious] but an economic system which is worse than slavery.[79]

Gandhi's protest against the extension of the separate electorate to the dalits was double-edged: on the one hand, he sincerely believed that the separate electorate would split from Hindu society and absolve the latter of its moral responsibility to fight against the practice of untouchability. On the other hand, argues Bhikhu Parekh, there were clear political calculations that governed Gandhi's protest, for "the separate electorate would have reduced the numerical strength of the Hindu majority, encouraged minority alliance against it, and fragmented the country yet further."[80] So, the Gandhian intervention was the result of skillful political strategy as well as of his passionate concern for Indian unity. Ambedkar was equally assertive and insisted on a separate electorate as the best device to protect the social, economic, and political interests of the dalits. As he stated, "I trust [that] the Mahatma would not drive me to the necessity of making a choice between his life and the rights of my people. For I can never consent to deliver my people bound hand and foot to the caste Hindus for generations to come."[81] No solution was visible. For Gandhi, a separate electorate for the untouchables would divide Hindu society further, perpetuating the dalits being inferior. Ambedkar denounced this as a strategic argument for using the untouchables as "weightage for the Hindus against the Muslims."[82]

When the British government endorsed the separate electorate in the Communal Award of August 1932, Ambedkar had an edge over his rival. The only course of action open to Gandhi was to embark on a fast. He went on a fast rather than approve the demand of the separate electorate for the depressed classes. Gandhi, who was in Yervada prison in Poona, began the fast on September 20, 1932, and ended it on September 24 only when Ambedkar agreed to accept the reservation of seats for dalits within the caste-Hindu constituencies.[83] An agreement between Gandhi and Ambedkar, known as the Poona Pact, was signed in 1933, and the depressed classes were given a substantial number of reserved seats, but remained within the Hindu electorate.

The Poona Pact represented a victory for the Mahatma in two ways: it established that untouchability was (a) "a social" and not "a political problem" and (b) that it was a problem of Hindu religion and not of the Hindu economy. Nonetheless, what was unique about the pact was that it, for the first time, placed the backward classes (later classified as the "scheduled castes" in the 1935 Government of India Act) on the center stage of Indian politics and endowed them with a separate identity. From now on, the scheduled castes would invariably figure in any discussion on national identity. Although the scheduled castes found a powerful leader in Ambedkar, they continued to remain a politically significant "minority" with narrow social, economic, and political goals. As a dissenter bent on dismantling an oppressive caste system, Ambedkar therefore "fulfilled the historical role of dissent not only to question the hateful religious dogma but also unbuckle the consolidating ambitions of the secular state within which former religious orthodoxies are subsumed."[84]

Ambedkar's diatribe against Gandhi and Hindu society can be found in his lecture entitled "Ranade, Gandhi and Jinnah."[85] The lecture has two clearly defined parts: the first part is Ambedkar's critique of Hinduism, based largely on an analysis of Hinduism by M. G. Ranade, the liberal Indian politician;[86] the second part dwells on his criticism of the roles of Gandhi and Jinnah as political leaders of "the respective groups of Hindus and Muslims" in India. While appreciating Ranade for his assessment of Hinduism, Ambedkar stated that Ranade was the first Indian politician who argued that "there were no rights in the Hindu society,... there were privileges and disabilities, privileges for a few and disabilities for a vast majority." Linking this argument with his criticism of Gandhi, Ambedkar felt that there was no alternative for the Mahatma but to support Hinduism and the caste system simply because "Mr Gandhi wants the untouchables to remain as Hindus... [n]ot as partners but as poor relations of

Hindus."[87] Characterizing Gandhi as "a Tory by birth as well as faith"[88] because of his rigid views on social and religious issues, he accused the Mahatma of "demoralizing" his followers and also "politics." He alleged that like Jinnah, Gandhi had made "half of his followers fools and the other half hypocrites." He attributed the rise of Gandhi to

> the aid of big business and money magnates. As a result, Indian poli-
> tics, at any rate the Hindu part of it, instead of being spiritualized has
> become grossly commercialized, so much so that it become a byword of
> corruption....Politics has become a kind of sewage system intolerably
> unsavoury and insanity. To become a politician is like going to work in
> the drain.[89]

Ambedkar's sharp critique not only problematized the twin concepts of justice and freedom by taking into account the dalit point of view, it also posed
new social, economic, and political issues involving the peripheral sections of
Indian society. Ambedkar's intervention illuminated a serious gap in the nationalist sociopolitical thought. Gandhi, despite being universal in his approach,
had failed to incorporate the specific dalit issues while organizing the campaign
for freedom. That Gandhi represented all regardless of class, caste, and creed
was based on assumptions inflating his claim to amicably settle the conflicting sociopolitical and economic interests of the diverse Indian population. Not
until the 1932 Poona Pact, did Gandhi effectively negotiate with the dalits as
an emerging and socially formidable constituency of India's nationalist politics. Congress leadership formally accorded a legitimate space to the dalits
only after this pact. The role of the British government was not insignificant
either. By accepting Ambedkar as the representative of the dalits in the 1932
Round Table Conference, the ruling authority deflated Gandhi's claim to epitomize India as a whole. Gandhi was pushed to the periphery, and Ambedkar was
brought in presumably because of his success in articulating the issues concerning dalits, which, though important, were never adequately addressed either by
the nationalist political leadership or by the colonial government. So, justice
and freedom acquired new connotations in the changed milieu when dalits had
already emerged as a politically significant constituency under the stewardship
of B. R. Ambedkar. By providing a new conception of emancipatory politics,
Ambedkar went beyond a comprehensive "delegitimation" of slavery, which
was but another name for untouchability. It entailed, as shown, a wide-ranging
program of equality and equity measures seeking to fulfil a variety of material and nonmaterial needs of those identified as untouchables. It is this total
program of societal transformation that constituted his conception of swaraj,
which was not just freedom from colonialism; it was a just freedom.[90] Swaraj,
thus defined, was not merely political and economic freedom from colonialism,
as conceptualized by Gandhi, but a significant sociopolitical package striving to
ameliorate the conditions of those "outside the fold." It would not be wrong to
argue, therefore, that the Gandhi-Ambedkar debate is theoretically innovative

and politically crucial in grasping the most volatile phase of Indian nationalism when the Mahatma no longer remained the undisputed leader of the freedom struggle.

INTELLECTUAL ROOTS OF KING'S SOCIOPOLITICAL IDEAS

Like Gandhi, King was also influenced by various thinkers who helped him not only to articulate but also to defend his position while leading the civil rights campaign in the United States. The emotional basis of King's thought was rooted in the black man's struggle for equality and social justice. Before being trained as a pastor, he read the biblical tracts at an early age. He was fortunate to have had his father's guidance. Martin Luther King Sr., also known as Daddy King, was a role model for young King, who admired his father for being "a genuine Christian...a man of real integrity, deeply committed to moral and ethical principles."[91] As pastor of Ebenezer Church, King Sr. was known for his "frankness" and never hesitated "to tell the truth and speak his mind, however cutting it may [have been]"[92] in a dominant culture of segregation that stereotyped blacks as childish and sycophantic clowns. He was involved in Negro voter registration drives, participated in the National Association for the Advancement of Colored People (NAACP), and was also a member of the board of Morehouse College. On the whole, he was an active participant in the movement against the Jim Crow laws of racial segregation, which, King Sr. always felt, were contrary to Christian ethics. King had learned a lot about Christianity at the dinner-table discussion in which both his parents took part: one of the major ideas that remained integral to King's philosophy and which he had imbibed out of such dinner-table talks was one of racial harmony. Hatred toward white men was, according to King Sr., contrary to Christian ethics. This became one of the fundamental pillars of his sociopolitical ideas. This was further strengthened by his close interaction with Benjamin E. Mays, the president of Morehouse College, who influenced a generation of black students. It was easy for King to appreciate Mays's views, as his father had already instilled in him Christian ethics and the idea that "without God, nonviolence lack[ed] sustenance and potency."[93] The idea of an omnipresent God was always present in King's regular sermons. While conceptualizing God, he appeared to have been influenced by Mays's argument that "the Negro's idea of God grew out [the] social situation in which he finds himself."[94] It is therefore obvious that the social experiences of slavery, legalized segregation, and discrimination produced a unique conceptualization of God, and King and his colleagues drew on the language of Christian ethics in challenging the Jim Crow laws. The black church culture that King personally experienced in the intimacy of his family and in the church where his father and grandfather were ministers, along with the instruction from Benjamin E. Mays, were "the institutional carriers of a uniquely-defined image of God [which] always remained an instantaneous point of reference for King while making a political point regarding the issue of race and racial segregation."[95] The starting point of King's philosophy as well as his final vision were thus basically religious, dependent on his faith in God and in the power of love to transform the hearts and minds of men. These two great forces were seen as responsible for holding together the universe, and as being continually manifest throughout the unity of creation. King's entire philosophy is derived from this perception of spiritual unity. Man, rooted in God, depended on his relationship to God for his growth and self-expression. That he was persuaded to appreciate the human face of Christianity was evident in his 1955 doctoral dissertation, in which he compared the views of Tillich and Wieman on Christianity by reiterating his faith in "the idea of a personal God" and "Christ's Sermon on the Mount."[96] Like Gandhi, he was also impressed by Thoreau's theoretical justification for civil disobedience against "unjust laws that a majority inflicts on a minority that is not binding on itself."[97] He further argued that "segregation is an existential expression of man's tragic separation, an expression of his awful estrangement, his terrible sinfulness," created and maintained through the racist ideology that blacks were naturally incapable without support of the whites. So challenging the segregation ordinances was justified because "they are morally wrong."[98] Two important ideas of Thoreau seem critical in King's approach to resistance: first, following Thoreau, King endorsed "the right to refuse allegiance and to resist the government when its tyranny or its inefficiency are great and unendurable."[99] If the state failed to ensure the gratification of individual well-being, its members had a natural right to challenge unjust laws; as Thoreau argued, "I do not lend myself to the wrong which I condemn."[100] The second significant influence in King's thought was Thoreau's very definitive concept of liberalism, in which the individual remained the pivot. As Thoreau argued, "[T]here will never be a really free and enlightened State, until the State comes to recognize the individual as a higher and independent power from which all its own power and authority are derived."[101] Based on such an assumption, the rebel, who had opposed the 1846–48 Mexican War, found the right to vote "most precious." It was, to him, "not a strip of paper merely, but [one's] own influence."[102] King also had similar concerns: central to his politics was the individual, and the right to vote was a powerful weapon in liberal dispensation, and hence he paid considerable attention to the drive for the registration of the disenfranchised Negroes. It was therefore not surprising that one of the main agenda items of the 1963 Birmingham campaign and later the 1965 Selma agitation was the removal of constraints that Negroes were subject to while registering as voters.

SOURCES OF INSPIRATION

King's doctoral dissertation gave him the opportunity to join together the two indispensable elements of Christianity: faith and works. In doing this, he brought to the fore his own Christian beliefs grounded in the African American religious traditions, where God is perceived as a loving, caring, personal force capable of interceding in history. In 1960, those beliefs would enable him to write,

> "[I]n recent months, I have also become more and more convinced of the reality of a personal God....I am convinced that the universe is under the control of a loving purpose and that in the struggle for righteousness man has cosmic companionship. Behind the harsh appearance of the world, there is a benign power." And he optimistically concluded, "[I]n a dark, confused world the spirit of God may yet reign supreme."[103]

This principle was grounded in the New Testament and in particular in Jesus of Nazareth's Sermon on the Mount: "Love your enemies, bless those who curse you, do good to those who hate you, and pray for those who spitefully use you and persecute you; [never] to resist an evil person, [b]ut who ever slaps you on your right cheek, turn the other cheek." This sermon lay at the heart of the nonviolent pacifist message preached by both Gandhi and King. The nonviolent core of Jesus's sermon was elegantly summarized for both Gandhi and King in the Second Commandment: "You shall love your neighbor as yourself; there is no other commandment greater than this." Being committed to the Sermon, King, as an activist Baptist pastor, sought to institutionalize the support of the blacks around the symbols of Christianity. It is therefore not surprising that the cross remained a very powerful device for political mobilization in the struggle for civil rights. According to him, the cross was not merely a religious symbol, but a symbol of freedom. "The Cross we bear," argued King, "precedes the crown we wear. To be a Christian, one must take up," he further stated, "his Cross, with all of its difficulties and agonizing and tension-packed content and carry it until that very Cross leaves its marks upon us and redeem us to that more excellent way which comes through suffering."[104] This was a source of inspiration and sustenance to the Southern Christian Leadership Conference (SLCC), which upheld Christianity presumably for its capacity to bring people together, regardless of socioeconomic differences. King's training as a pastor made him easily acceptable to the community despite strong criticisms from other civil rights organizations. It was a strategy that King refined not only by reconceptualizing the basic Christian ethos, but also by drawing on the available texts supporting his argument. A large contingency of theologians were critical in King's thought process, both during its formation and aftermath. Of all the thinkers, the three who were significantly influential in "rescuing Christianity from distortions" were Walter Rauschenbush, Howard Thurman, and Reinhold Niebuhr: besides Rauschenbush, all of them had had direct interaction with Gandhi in India and sought to imbibe the Gandhian spirit of nonviolence while reinterpreting Christianity in the changed milieu. Christianity was, they felt, "appropriated" by vested interests and had thus become a doctrine without substance. Pointing out such deliberate distortions of the fundamental values of Christianity enabled King to mobilize the victims of racially segregated Christianity against its white adherents. These theologians, who did not find racial segregation congruent with Christianity, thus found the task of rallying black Christians relatively easy.

One of the leading thinkers seeking to redefine the goal of Christianity was Walter Rauschenbusch (1861–1918). He was born in upstate New York to a German preacher who taught at the Rochester Theological Seminary. His fundamental aim was to spread the idea of the Kingdom of God, not through fiery or aggressive preaching, but by leading a Christlike life. For him, the Kingdom of God was an ideal that everybody should aspire to establish well-being for all. This was not "a utopia" because it meant "justice, freedom and fraternity." He also insisted that the "old ideal need[ed] to be defined in modern terms, in the terms of modern democracy, of the power machine, of international peace and of evolutionary science." Seeking to meaningfully blend the old with the new, he wanted "to embrace the new ideal with the old religious faith and ardor, so that we can pray over it."[105] On the basis of his general understanding of Christianity, he offered four supporting arguments in his defense: first, he sincerely believed that "Jesus was always on the side of the common people long before democracy was on the ascendant. He loved them, felt their worth, trusted their latent capacities, and promised them the Kingdom of God."[106] In Rauschenbusch's perception, Jesus laid the foundation of modern democracy by being sensitive to the needs of the underprivileged. He saw Christianity, even when impure and under the control of the upper classes, as "the historical basis for the aspirations of the common people." Second, in order to translate the core goal of Christianity, he devised three social principles: (a) life and personality remained sacred, (b) the growth of humanity depended on collective cooperation, and (c) the strong must stand with the weak and defend their cause. Based on the Sermon on the Mount, these principles were articulated as efforts at identifying specific human activities to establish the Kingdom of God on earth. The third social principle related to the creation and consolidation of a collective moral ideal for the individual and race. "Every man," Rauschenbush emphasized,

> must have a conscious determination to help in his own place to work a righteous social order for and with God. The race must increasingly turn its own evolution into a conscious process. It owes that duty to itself and to God who seeks a habitation in it. It must seek to realize its divine destiny.... This is the conscious evolutionary programme of Jesus [combining] religion, social science and ethical action in a perfect synthesis.[107]

The final argument that Rauschenbush provided deals with the actual difficulty in implementing the ethical principles laid down in the Sermon on the Mount. Practical to the core, he was also aware that genuine and sincere efforts to establish the Kingdom of God were likely to be countered by "the recalcitrant and stubborn instincts of human nature and the conservative forces of society." This had been historically true because Jesus had to encounter "the wealthy men who controlled the economic outfit,...the official groups who held...political power and the lawyers, theologian, priests and zealots who dominated the religious life of a very religious people: together they constituted an oligarchy that controlled human life."[108] While explaining the continuity of the oligarchy, Rauschenbush put forward a fundamental theory of class contradiction that remained at the root of the exploitation of human beings by human beings. Class rivalry was natural to human society given the antagonistic relationship between the two fundamental classes: the one "is born to toil, and gets its class characteristic by toil. The other,…characterized by the pleasure and arts of leisure, is physically developed by leisure, and proud and jealous of its leisure."[109]

Adopting a very unusual radical tone, this upstate New York priest made a profound statement by submitting that the wealthy class, conscious and protective of its class privileges, flourished "on the labor of many" and that in order to sustain its hegemony, it controlled "political power, military outfit, the power of making, interpreting and executing the laws and the forces forming public opinion."[110] There was no option for the poor when the rich ceased to be Christian in their attitudes toward them; the "life of the rich is thus wedged farther and farther from the poor, [as evident] in the differences in housing, eating, dressing and speaking."[111] The outcome was devastating, because "if we allow deep and permanent inequality to grow up in our country, it is as sure as gravitation that not only the old democracy and frankness of manners will go, but even the theory of human equality, which has been part of our spiritual atmosphere through Christianity, will be denied."[112] How to arrest such degradation? Despite being a committed evangelical Christian, Rauschenbush did not agree with the suggestion that the role of the ministers remained critical in spreading the message of "true" Christianity. In his words,

[T]he new evangel of the Kingdom of God will have to be carried into the commons consciousness of Christiandom by the personal faith and testimony of the ordinary Christian man. It is less connected with the ministrations of the Church and therefore will be less the business of the professional ministry than the old evangel of the saved soul. It is a call to Christianize the everyday life, and the everyday man will have to pass on the call and make plain its meaning.[113]

Rauschenbush articulated a "Christian liberalism" that left "an indelible imprint on [King's] thinking."[114] His persuasive logic in favor of the Kingdom of God inspired King to develop his notion of "the beloved community." Nonetheless, he was not persuaded to appreciate Rauschenbush's "unwarranted optimism concerning human nature" presumably because of the whites' endorsement of racism, which, according to Rauschebush, not only sustained but also consolidated an artificial boundary between racially segregated African Americans and their white counterparts. Furthermore, Rauschenbusch's argument linking "the kingdom of God with a particular social and economic system" did not auger well because the formulation, as King saw, was "highly restrictive." Notwithstanding these shortcomings, King underlined that Rauschenbush gave to American Protestantism "a sense of social responsibility that it should never lose." The gospel at its best deals, he further argued, "with the whole man, not only his soul, but his body, not only his spiritual well-being but his material being."[115] Rauschenbush's impact on King was so fundamental that King underlined the human face of Christianity by stating that

[a]ny religion that professes to be concerned about the souls of men and is not concerned about the slums that damn them, the economic conditions that strangle them and the social conditions that cripple them is a spiritually moribund religion awaiting burial.[116]

In King's own words, Rauschenbusch's ideas gave him "a theological basis for the social concerns which had already grown up in [him] as a result of [his] early experiences." Despite having disagreed with him on some points of interpretation, he found that Rauschenbush had done "a great service for the Christian church by insisting that the gospel deals with the whole man, not only his soul, his body; not only his spiritual well-being but his material well-being."[117] King thus concluded that religion that did not take care of the material well-being of the believers was futile in so far as human beings were concerned. Rauschenbush gave King specific direction when he was groping in the dark and put him in a better position to articulate his notion of a Christianity that contributes to human well-being irrespective of clan and color.

King held these views until he encountered the writings of Reinhold Niebuhr. Unable to appreciate Rauschenbusch's optimism, Niebuhr believed that the former's uncritical acceptance of love to bring about the Kingdom of God was entirely misplaced because "man's selfishness was the major barrier to justice in society and men in privileged groups were the most persistent in obstructing any efforts to improve society." Hence he concluded that "disproportion of power in society is the real root of social injustice...and relations between groups [are] predominantly political rather than ethical."[118] The arguments of Niebuhr and his friend Kenneth Smith at Crozer "moved King away from his earlier blind attachment to the optimism that pervaded not only Rauschenbusch's social gospel, but indeed all of evangelical liberalism."[119] After having read Niebuhr, King seemed to have reassessed his concept of the "natural goodness of man and natural power of human reason." Niebuhr made him "a realist" by presenting to him "the complexity of human motives and the reality of sin on every level of man's existence."[120] Such a realization was very helpful for understanding the roots of racial segregation, which were based on "the sinful nature" of human beings. As long as human beings remained "self-centered," the Kingdom of God, warned King, could hardly be realized. Niebuhr appeared to have influenced King in another very critical way: King's unquestionable faith in American liberalism was tempered significantly by this New York Baptist preacher. Despite having appreciated the role of schools established by the white philanthropists in spreading education among the black children and youth, Niebuhr was also aware that such an effort was likely to gain "little" because "it is made within a given system of injustice" [in which]...the Negro schools, conducted under the auspices of white philanthropy encourage individual Negroes to higher forms of self-realization, but they do not make a frontal attack upon the social injustices from which the Negro suffers.[121] This was a point that reverberated in King's famous "Letter from Birmingham Jail" of 1963 in which he, as discussed later in this chapter, was critical of the role of the white moderate Christians who, despite being "good" to the blacks, were reluctant to join the campaign against racial segregation because it was contrary to both Christianity and American constitutionalism. Hence he was categorical while assessing the role of the white moderates by saying that

> the Negro's greatest stumbling in the stride toward freedom is not the White Citizen's councilor or the Ku Klux Klanner, but the white moderate who is more devoted to 'the order' than to justice; who prefers negative peace which is the absence of tension to a positive peace which is the presence of justice.... The white moderates [fail] to understand that law and order exist for the purpose of establishing justice, and that when they fail to do this they become dangerously structured dams that block the flow of social progress."[122]

What King achieved by reinterpreting the social gospel in the light of the Rauschenbush-Niebuhr debate was a rearticulation of the core values of Christianity—love, empathy, and forgiveness—that had been distorted by those with political and economic power. In this sense, both Rauschenbusch and Niebuhr fulfilled a historical role by providing King with persuasive arguments to relocate the social roles of Christianity as not merely a doctrine of righteous principles, but also as a well-defined design to accomplish obvious human goals—goals that were integral to human fulfillment and gratification.

Like Walter Rauschenbush, Howard Thurman (1899–1981) reinforced King's perception of Christianity as a liberating ideology. The distinction that Thurman made between "Christianity" and "religion of Jesus" enabled King to reinterpret Christianity as a set of rejuvenating socioeconomic ideals. According to Thurman, Jesus was a true genius "who was conditioned and organized himself that he became a perfect instrument for the embodiment of a set of ideals—ideals of such dramatic potency that were capable [of] changing the calendar, rechanneling the thought of the world, and placing a new sense of the rhythm of life in a weary, nerve-snapped civilization."[123]

In 1936, Thurman led "a Negro Delegation of Friendship" to South Asia, including India, where he met Gandhi. His conversation with Gandhi, Thurman felt, broadened his theological and international vision. In his seminal 1949 book, *Jesus and the Disinherited*, he provided an interpretation of the New Testament gospels that enabled the civil rights activists to understand Christianity in a new fashion. Thurman presented the idea that the basic goal of Jesus was to help the disinherited of the world so that they would be empowered to challenge oppression irrespective of consequences. The task was not easy given the well-entrenched vested interests. According to him, there was "a striking similarity between the social position of Jesus in Palestine and that of the vast majority of American Negroes. It is the similarity of a social climate at the point of a denial of full citizenship which creates the problem for survival for the Negroes."[124] By echoing the voice of Rauschenbush, he argued that love, rooted in "the deep river of faith," would help the oppressed to overcome persecution. Thurman metaphorically compared human life to a river that "may twist and turn, fall back on itself and start again, stumble over an infinite series of hindering rocks, but at last the river must answer the call to the sea."[125] In a similar way, despite uncertainty because of contingent difficulties, human beings were sure to achieve the Kingdom of God on earth because of the unflinching faith in "those values which led Jesus to sacrifice his life for his children." In his perception, Jesus, who was born in a poor Jewish family, always fought for justice despite having had to pay a heavy price. He stood for self-pride and assertion of the colonized under the tyranny of Rome that had to be fought by the human spirit for freedom. Christianity was thus forged "as a technique of survival of the oppressed....Wherever his [Jesus] spirit appears, the oppressed gather fresh courage, for he has announced the good news that fear, hypocrisy and hatred, the three hounds of hell that track the trail of the disinherited, need have no dominion over them."[126] Thurman articulated his views in this widely read book (which King was reported to have always carried with him) for "the disinherited," with the assumption that Jesus was a member of the oppressed and that his message was a survival strategy for them. It is a concise statement of the meaning of Jesus's message for those who live with their backs against the wall. According to him, "fear, deception and hatred," which he described as "the hounds of the hell" could easily be defeated through the power of love. Besides attempting to reinvent social gospel and the role of Jesus for the disinherited, Thurman paid a great deal of attention in recovering the slaves' lost history. He thus concentrated on slave songs, which, besides being great works of art, also powerfully and subtlely articulated a powerful message against the Jim Crow laws of segregation. Appreciative of the social roles of these songs, he stated that

> the genius of the slave songs is their unyielding affirmation of life defying the judgment of the denigrating environment which spawned them. The indigenous insights inherent in the Negro spirituals bear significantly on the timeless search for the meaning of life and death in human experience. I sought to establish a beachhead of thought about the slave's religious creativity...with the hope that ideas generated would open the eyes of the blind and deliver those in another kind of bondage into a new freedom. Thus, however briefly, they and the slave would stand side by side together as children of life.[127]

Despite being grounded in the liberal philosophical tradition, King also drew on the philosophy of Georg Hegel, who articulated the role of the dialectical trio as critical to human progress. Drawing on Hegel, King constantly sought the middle/higher ground of synthesis with a clear direction for further argument.

The conflict and crisis became an opportunity for growth rather than something to be avoided. In his *The Strength to Love* (1963), King states that "life at best is a creative synthesis of opposites in fruitful harmony. The philosopher Hegel said that truth is found neither in thesis nor the anti-thesis, but in an emergent synthesis which reconciles the two."[128] He went on to say that Jesus recognized the need to blend opposites. In sending his disciples out into the hostile world of politics, Jesus gave them a formula of action: "Be you therefore wise as a serpent and harmless as doves."[129] In such a conceptualization, King seemed to have attempted a creative blending of Rauschenbusch's stress on "love" and the Hegelian stress on "realism": the balanced Christian, argued King, "must be both loving and realistic....As an individual in complex social relations he must realistically meet mind with mind and power with power....Whereas love seeks out the need of others, justice...is a check upon ambitious individuals seeking to overcome their own insecurity at the expense of other."[130] Justifying the use of coercion to avoid injustice, King appeared to be drawn more to Niebuhr and less to Rauschenbusch because of the complexity of the social situations that needed to be tackled with élan and determination. He seemed to have endorsed the utility of coercive forces as a purely temporary measure while arguing, in a typical Niebuhrian way, that "since man is so sinful, there must be some coercion to keep one man from injuring others," though the wielder of authority "must not seek revenge."[131]

In articulating his voice of protest, King was indebted to W. E. B. DuBois, another famous African American author. DuBois coined a phrase, "the color line," to conceptualize the racial segregation that existed in the United States after the abolition of slavery. In his *Souls of Black Folk* (1903), DuBois most graphically developed the theme of the color line as a segregating device in a supposedly free America. For him, the color line was integral to grasping racism within the context of the color prejudices of the whites against the blacks because it reinforced that "the Negroes are a segregated servile caste with restricted rights and privileges; before the courts, both in law and custom, they stand on a different and peculiar basis [and] taxation without representation is the rule of their political life."[132] The color line was, DuBois further argued, organic to American social life because "at the back of the problem of race and color lies...the fact that so many civilized persons are willing to live in comfort even if the price of this is poverty, ignorance and disease of the majority of their fellowmen [and] to maintain this privilege men have waged war...and the excuse for this war continues largely to be color and race."[133] Persuaded by DuBois, King also firmly believed that the color line was a structural evil of racism because the concept indicated a collection of habits—no matter how intentional or unintentional they might be—that perpetuated an imbalance of power between black and white collective realities. Racism was justified logically because it came out of a thought process. Without blaming any particular white person or without denying that there were powerful black influences on American life, the logic of nonviolence nevertheless asserted that a structure of racism applied to collective relationships among groups. Furthermore, racism was a moral problem, because it perpetuated systemic injustice against the African Americans on the basis of the infamous Jim Crow laws.

As is evident, King was heavily influenced by the major African American thinkers who laid the foundation for his campaign against segregation. While conceptualizing nonviolence, King was also drawn to the ideas of Reinhold Niebuhr, who felt that man had ceased to become moral because of the rise and consolidation of an immoral society. In his *Moral Man and Immoral Society* (1932), Niebuhr justified nonviolence as perhaps the most effective means to resolve social disputes. He argued,

> [T]he advantage of non-violence as a method of expressing goodwill lies in the fact that it protects the agent against the resentments which violent conflict always creates in both parties to a conflict, and that it proves this freedom of resentment and ill will to the contending party in the dispute by enduring more suffering than it causes....one of the most important results of a spiritual discipline against resentment in a social dispute is that it leads to an effort to discriminate between the evils of a social system and situation and individuals who are involved in it. Mr. Gandhi never tires of making a distinction between individual Englishmen and the system of imperialism which they maintain.[134]

For religious spiritualism to succeed one needs, as Niebuhr further stated,

> [a] sublime madness [which] is not conceivable in the West, disregards immediate appearances and emphasizes profound and ultimate unities. It is therefore no accident that the spirit of non-violence has been introduced into contemporary politics by a religious leader of the Orient. Because occidental man lacks the spirit of non-violence he is incapable of engaging in non-violent social conflict. Western man's spiritual bankruptcy is the result of being deprived of religion. Lacking meaningful religious life, the white man has become a beast of prey.[135]

Like Gandhi, Niebuhr was very critical of machine-centric Western civilization, which had robbed human beings of human values. He also felt that the outcome of machine-induced development harmed the natural growth of a lively human civilization, which always remained the exalted aim of Christianity. Worried by the growing influence of the mechanical civilization of the contemporary era, he argued that "the religious heritage of the disinherited white man has been dissipated by the mechanical character of civilization and by the sentimentality and moral confusions introduced by the comfortable and privileged classes into the Christian religion."[136] While Niebuhr provided a macro perspective to King by drawing his attention to the wider socioeconomic context of racism, Walter Rauschenbush provided a micro perspective by emphasizing the importance of the contextual influences in interpreting Christianity and its value system.

While these thinkers provided King with theoretical insights to understand nonviolence as an extension of Christian ethics, it was Gandhi who made him realize its instrumental value in sociopolitical movements against injustice. After hearing Mordecai Johnson, the Howard University president who also had met Gandhi in India, King became extremely eager to explore Gandhian ideas further. As he stated, Gandhi's message was so profound and electrifying that he felt compelled to immediately procure texts on Gandhi and by Gandhi to know more about the ideology of nonviolence. He was now persuaded to believe in the power of love, which was the driving force behind the nonviolent struggle that Gandhi had waged against the British Empire in India. Discussing Gandhi's idea about the efficacy of love as an instrument for change, King mentioned that

> prior to reading Gandhi, I had almost concluded that the ethics of Jesus were only effective in individual relationships. The Turn of other cheek philosophy and love your enemies philosophy were, I felt, when individuals were in conflict with other individuals; when groups and nations were in conflict a more realistic approach seemed necessary. But after reading Gandhi, I saw how utterly I was mistaken.[137]

In making nonviolence the main element of the struggle against racial injustice, King was also indebted to Bayard Rustin, who finally persuaded him to consider the idea. In his regular meetings with King, besides talking about the strategies of their struggle, Rustin always discussed the Gandhian approach to nonviolence. King was "eagerly learning all that he [could] about nonviolence" though he was, as Rustin admitted, reluctant to use Gandhi's expression of "satyagraha" because it was likely to be misunderstood by Americans, presumably because of the non-American etymological roots of the word. Hence, he preferred to use the term "passive resistance" while explaining his protest methods. By following Niebuhr, he also felt that coercion was necessary to resist evil and combat oppression. In response to Rustin's question as to whether a "gun was compatible with a nonviolent movement," King was reported to have answered affirmatively by saying that "those holding even a gun tended to harm no one unless violently attacked." Only after he was told by Rustin that "the presence of guns were contrary to the philosophy that he was articulating," did King appear to have accepted nonviolence as a strategy.[138] This was perhaps the beginning of a new phase in King's political career, in which he began to distance himself from what he had learned from Reinhold Niebuhr. He saw two serious limitations to Niebuhr's critique of pacifism: first, Niebuhr's interpretation of pacifism was highly "negative" in the sense that it meant "a sort of passive non-resistance to evil[,] expressing naïve trust in the power of love." Gandhi had taught him, that "true pacifism is not non-resistance to evil, but nonviolent resistance to evil." Gandhi resisted evil with "as much vigour and power as the violent resister, but he resisted with love, instead of, hate."[139] True nonviolent struggle was thus not "unrealistic submission to evil power," as Niebuhr made us believe; it was rather, argued King,

> a courageous confrontation of evil by the power of love, in the faith that it is better to be recipient of love that the inflicter [sic] of it, since the latter only multiplies the existence of violence and bitterness in the universe, while the former may develop a sense of shame in the opponent, and thereby bring about a transformation and change of heart.[140]

Second, there was an obvious contradiction between Niebuhr's support (though qualified) of coercion and Christian ethics. According to King, the fundamental idea that came out of the Sermon on the Mount was about unconditional love even for the perpetrators of violence or injustice. Under no circumstances could this be compromised. By recollecting his father's instruction, King thus argued that not only should he not hate a white man, but it was also his "duty as a Christian to love him."[141]

It is true that King was indebted to the rich African American tradition while conceptualizing nonviolence as a political strategy; it is also true that Gandhi provided him with ways to articulate nonviolence as a method of action in the face of adverse consequences. Nonviolence was thus not merely an ideal, but an actual method of struggle in which the participants came together because of compassion, empathy, and concern for one another. According to King, the 1955 Montgomery bus strike was the first opportunity to challenge the perpetrators of racial oppression with nonviolence. Once he was convicted, he expressed confidence in nonviolence as an effective ideological tool for mobilizing the unarmed and disinherited blacks. He appeared happy and welcomed the sentence by metaphorically saying that he was sentenced because of his

> crime of joining my people in a non-violent protest against injustice. It was the crime of seeking to instill within my people a sense of dignity and self-respect. It was the crime of desiring for my people the unalienable rights of life, liberty and the pursuit of happiness. It was above all the crime of seeking to convince my people that non-cooperation with evil is just as much a moral duty as is cooperation with good.[142]

The Montgomery bus strike was a watershed moment in King's rise as a civil rights activist because it "did more to clarify [his] thinking on the question of non-violence than all of the books that [he] had read....Living through the actual experience of the protest, non-violence became more than a method...[it] became," as King confirmed, "a commitment to a way of life [and] many issues that [he] failed to understand intellectually concerning non-violence [became] crystal clear in the sphere of practical action."[143]

King reiterated this sentiment in his famous 1963 "Letter from Birmingham Jail" where he further said that "I have said to my people—Get rid of your discontent. Rather, I have tried to say that this normal and healthy discontent can be channeled into the creative outlet of non-violent direct action."[144] In Gandhi's idea of nonviolence, King had found perhaps the most effective instrument of fulfilling his Christian philosophy of live-and-let-live. King thus said in his Noble Peace Prize address in Norway in December 1964 that

> non-violence is the answer to the crucial political and moral question of our time—the need for man to overcome oppression and violence without resorting to violence and oppression....Negroes of United States, following the people of India, have demonstrated that non-violence is not servile passivity, but a powerful moral force which makes for social transformation.[145]

The first occasion when he put his nonviolent method to test was the 1955 Montgomery bus strike. While explaining nonviolence as a mechanism of mass protest, he thus stated,

> non-violence means a willingness to suffer and sacrifice. It may mean going to jail. If such is the case the resistor must be willing to fill the jail houses of the South. It may even mean physical death. But if physical death is the price that a man must pay to free his children and his white brethren from a permanent death of the spirit, then nothing more could be more redemptive.[146]

Similar to Gandhi, King also believed that the key to success in nonviolent protest movements regardless of the context was "willingness to suffer," which was sure to change the heart of the perpetrators of violence. To fulfill the goal of nonviolent protest, one needed to be strong, as Gandhi emphatically declared when he wrote that

> non-violence does not mean meek submission to the will of the evil-doer, but it means the pitting of one's whole soul against the will of the tyrant....And so I am pleading for Indians to practise non-violence because she is weak. I want her to practise non-violence being conscious of her strength and power.[147]

Pursuing a similar conviction, King, following the 1955 Montgomery bus boycott, declared,

> [W]e will match your capacity [that of whites] to inflict suffering with our capacity to endure suffering. We will meet your physical force with soul force. Do to us what you will and we will still love you. Bomb our homes and threaten our children; send your hooded perpetrators of violence into our communities and drag us out on some wayside road, beating us and leaving us half dead, and we will still love you. But we will soon wear you down by our capacity to suffer....You feel defeated and secretly ashamed. You know that this man is as good a man as you are; that from some mysterious source he has found the courage and the conviction to meet physical force with soul force.[148]

He echoed Gandhi when he explained what he meant by nonviolent struggle, which was not the weapon of the weak, but of the strong. According to King, nonviolent resistance "is not a method for cowards; it does resist. The non-violent resister is not physically aggressive towards the opponent. But his mind and emotions are always active, constantly seeking to persuade the opponent that he is mistaken."[149]

So, for King, nonviolence was a strategy that appeared to be most effective in the context of the Negro struggle against racial oppression. Gandhi provided him with a model of political struggle that was tested most successfully in South Africa and later in India. He thus confessed that after having read Gandhian texts, he came to realize the effectiveness of nonviolence as an ideological tool. But his acceptance of nonviolence as a method was made possible because of his religious background as a true Christian. Hence he argued that

the whole spirit of non-violence came to [him] from Jesus of Nazareth. Its central idea was that you counteract an unjust system through direct action and love your opponents at the same time: [through] sit-ins and boycott, . . . you hope to be able to bring an end to your opponent's self-defeating massacre and that he will change his attitude.[150]

While explaining the role of love in nonviolent resistance, he always referred to the Christian texts. In his perception, "love is the greatest force in the [entire] world... [and] it was Jesus [who] realized it in real life. This is our legacy [and]...we may go on with love in our hearts that will change us and change the lives of those who surround us;...God's kingdom will be a reality."[151] What remained a constant reference in King's sociopolitical ideas was the hegemonic influence of "the moral and ethical ideas of Christianity." Even while acknowledging the contribution of Gandhi to the Negroes' struggle against injustice, King hardly wavered from his commitment to Christianity because "religion has been real to [him] and closely knitted to life [and] the two cannot be separated."[152] What he gathered from the fundamental principles of Christianity became real in Gandhi's nonviolent resistance against injustice and oppression. Hence King found that while Christ "furnished the spirit and motivation,...Gandhi furnished the method."[153] This was a unique blending which was most effective in the nonviolent struggles of Negroes in America against racial segregation. In the context of the 1955 Montgomery bus strike, he came to realize that "a synthesis of Gandhi's method of non-violence and the Christian ethic of love [was] the best weapon available to the Negroes for [their] struggle for freedom and human dignity." It was Gandhi who made him understand that "it is possible to resist evil and yet not resort to violence."[154] Noncooperation with evil was as much a moral obligation as was cooperation with good. Gandhi was credited with the idea that violence, despite being effective temporarily, "creates newer problems and thus cannot contribute to permanent peace." The Gandhian method was a method of the strong because it had taught us how "to resist evil...without resorting to external violence or violence of the spirit." Only after having internalized the spirit of Gandhism, King was confident that nonviolence was an adequate weapon to challenge and also remove racial segregation in America. As he argued, "[B]efore I read Gandhi, I felt that the Christian ethics of love was meaningful only in regard to individual relationships." He was clueless as to how it worked in social conflict. With his introduction to the Gandhian ideas, he thus realized that it was Gandhi who "raised the ethic of love, as revealed in Jesus, to a social strategy for social transformation [which] was far effective than violence."[155] King also felt that unless the Gandhian principle of nonviolence was adequately appreciated, "we may end up by destroying ourselves through the misuse of our instruments." The choice was no longer, he further warned, "between violence and non-violence [but]...between non-violence and non-existence."[156]

King's zeal to eradicate the sources of injustice was thus strengthened by his introduction to the life and teachings of Gandhi. The more he read Gandhi's writings, the less he doubted the validity of the philosophy based on love. He stated that "[a]s I delved deeper into the philosophy of Gandhi my skepticism concerning the power of love gradually diminished, and I came to see for the first time that the Christian doctrine of love operating through Gandhian method of non-violence was one of the most potent weapons available to oppressed people in their struggle for freedom."[157] He now appeared to have discovered a specific, and also powerful, way to fight against segregation laws because Gandhi, according to him,

was probably the first person in history to lift the love of ethic of Jesus above mere interaction between individuals to a powerful and effective social force on a large scale. Love for Gandhi was a potent instrument for social and collective transformation. It was in this Gandhian emphasis on love and non-violence that I discovered the method for social reform that I had been seeking for so many months.

The intellectual and moral satisfaction that I failed to gain from the utilitarianism of Bentham and Mill, the revolutionary methods of Marx and Lenin, the social contract theory of Hobbes, the back to nature optimism of Rousseau and the superman philosophy of Nietzsche, I found in the non-violent resistance philosophy of Gandhi. I came to feel that this was the only morally and practically sound method open to oppressed people in their struggle for freedom.[158]

Gandhi made King realize the importance of nonviolence in his struggle against injustice. According to King, the Gandhian method of nonviolence was nothing but a revelation of Christian ethic. Reflecting on the success of the 1955 Montgomery bus boycott, King thus announced that "from the beginning, a basic philosophy guided the movement. It was the Sermon on the Mount. As the day unfolded however, the inspiration of Mahatma Gandhi began to exert influence." No longer skeptical about the power of love, King further argued, "Gandhi was probably the first person in history to lift the love ethic of Jesus above mere interaction between individuals to a powerful and effective social force on a large scale."[159] He strongly felt that "the Christian doctrine of love" operated most meaningfully through the Gandhian method of nonviolence that perhaps caught him by surprise as he himself exclaimed that "it is ironic, yet inescapably true that the greatest Christian of the modern world was a man who never embraced Christianity."[160]

King's philosophy is the outcome of a complex blending of both religious and existential sources: from the New Testament came the initial inspiration; Thoreau and Gandhi strengthened his faith in the theory of nonviolent social change. While Christ's Sermon on the Mount, with its emphasis on compassion, humility, self-criticism, forgiveness, and the renunciation of material gain drew King to nonviolence, Thoreau's commitment to civil disobedience taught him the rightfulness of protest against an unlawful state, and Gandhi confirmed the effectiveness of mass nonviolent resistance to the state. So, the teachings of Jesus, Thoreau, and Gandhi laid the foundation for King's political ideology. This was a synthesis, manifested in a simple philosophy of love. It was not merely a theory; it was an alternative to conflict and disharmony that remained usually associated with social progress in the modern era. Drawn on the teachings of intellectual giants of the past, King thus argued that

> non-violence is a powerful and just weapon. It is a weapon unique in history which cuts without wounds and ennobles the man who wields it. It is a sword that heals. Both a practical and a moral answer to Negro's cry for justice; nonviolent direct action proved that it could win victories without losing wars.[161]

The driving force for nonviolent struggle was unconditional love. While seeking to clarify the nature of love that King had in mind, he compared the three Greek words for love that figured in the New Testament: *eros, philia, and agape*. Eros refers to romantic or aesthetic love; philia is reciprocal love, the kind of love that may exist between close friends; agape is a dispassionate, redemptive love that embraces all men. Agape is an overflowing love that seeks nothing in return; it is "the love of God operating in the human spirit."[162] At this level of love, man can love his enemies while yet hating their actions. It is a love in which the individual seeks not his own good, but the good of his neighbor. Agape was free, a gift, or in theological parlance, a grace: it was not "willed or self-adopted attitude, it happened to a person or something that broke into one's life and consciousness from outside."[163] Nondiscriminating, seeking the best in every man, agape springs from the need of every person to belong to the best of the human family. The idea of agape, rooted in Christian ethic, was "unmotivated" and "overflowing" because it was

> love of God operating in human heart. The greatness of it is that you love every man, not for your sake, but for his sake. And you love every man because God loves him. And so it becomes all inclusive....You hate the deed that he does if he's your enemy and he's evil, but you love the person who does the evil deed.[164]

In his *Stride toward Freedom* (1958), King further elaborated,

> Love in this connection means understanding redemptive good will....When we speak of loving those who oppose us...we speak of a love which is expressed in the Greek word *agape*. *Agape* means understanding, redeeming good will for all men. It is an overflowing love which is purely spontaneous, unmotivated, groundless and creative. It is not set in motion by any quality or function of its object. It is the love of God operating in human heart.[165]

So love in the sense of agape remained most critical in the King-led nonviolent resistance. As an evangelical Christian, King justified nonviolent resistance to "unjust laws of segregation" because these laws were contrary to God's will. He thus argued that

> your highest loyalty is to God, and not to the mores or folkways, the state or the nation or any man-made institution. If any earthly institution or custom conflicts with God's will, it is your Christian duty to oppose it. You must never allow the transitory, evanescent demands of man-made institutions to take precedence over the eternal demands of the almighty God.[166]

King's uncritical faith in Christianity and the ideas he drew from the major biblical texts suggests that he epitomized evangelical liberalism. His stress on the humanity of Jesus and his emphasis on love, the dynamic nature of history, and God's action remained the key themes of the evangelical liberalism that King embraced quite early in his intellectual pilgrimage.[167] Central to King's ideology was Christianity, the teachings of Jesus, and the notion that "at the heart of the universe is the reality of God and the brotherhood of man, to which all Christians owe their allegiance."[168] Racial segregation was, felt King, "a blatant denial of this universal brotherhood [and was] thus a tragic evil that is utterly un-Christian."[169] He drew on Christianity probably because it enabled him to build and consolidate support among the blacks who were Christians as well, and it also helped him to expand his constituency to the white moderates, who were likely to be persuaded that segregation was contrary to Christianity. While pursuing his political goal, he thus insisted on clinging to its core values with his pledge to "let us be Christian in all of our actions."[170] It was thus not conceptually odd to find that King specifically referred to the identity of Rosa Parks as a devout Christian or the people of Montgomery as committed members of the Southern Black Baptist Church.

CONCLUDING OBSERVATIONS

What was common between Gandhi and King was their determination to challenge the existing power relationships within the liberal democratic framework;

their ideas challenged because they contradicted the fundamental values of liberalism. They confronted two different socioeconomic circumstances, but ones that inflicted more or less similar institutional constraints over human endeavors for change. As Gandhi drew upon India's rich religious and intellectual texts to defend his point of view, King drew his intellectual genealogy from rich African American intellectual traditions of nonviolence and peace, including the creative intervention of W. E. B. DuBois. Keeping these interventions in mind, my purpose is to focus on those ideas of King that had clear roots in Gandhi's sociopolitical philosophy. A. Philip Randolph, A. J. Muste, and Bayard Rustin remained critical influences on King's approach to civil rights issues; but Reinhold Niebuhr, Howard Thurman, Walter Rauschenbush, and, of course, W. E. B. DuBois were equally important in influencing King's sociopolitical ideas, which clearly resonated with Gandhi's conceptual framework. This is, to me, a confluence of thought that was made possible because of the well-informed African American intellectuals and also because of the white Americans who held views similar to that of Gandhi. It is true that these ideas were rooted in an uncritical faith in Christianity; but it was Gandhi who provided them with a strategy (through the idea of nonviolence) that drew on a fundamental Christian assumption based on "the Sermon on the Mount." Just as Gandhi, who despite being appreciative of Christianity, was very critical of the role of Christian missionaries in India,[171] King sought to rescue Christianity from the white Americans who, as he believed, distorted religion to fulfill partisan goals. He saw the role of the church as no less significant because "while flowing through the stream of history [the Church] has picked-up the evils of little tributaries, and the evils of these tributaries have been so powerful that they have been able to overwhelm the main stream."[172] In assessing the role of the church in such a critical fashion, King was undoubtedly influenced by other prominent intellectuals, like Niebuhr, Rauschenbusch, and Thurman, who did not appear to have been happy with the way some of the white churches endorsed racial segregation. Their principal argument challenging racism stemmed from the fact that color-driven separation was a blatant denial of Christian ethics. King, in his own assessment of the role of the specific churches, echoed this sentiment. I am thus inclined to argue that it may not have been possible for Gandhi or King to comprehend some of the critical issues without the creative intervention of their colleagues or co-workers. Both Gandhi and King were favorably disposed toward nonviolence as a strategy to combat a well-entrenched political authority (which was both brutal and prejudiced); they received an endorsement of their ideas from their colleagues who were enlightened and also intellectually committed to the cause.

NATURE OF PROTESTS

Gandhi fought racism in South Africa and colonial exploitation in India; King successfully accomplished his goal of racial desegregation, at least legally, in

America. Both of them pursued their political aims through nonviolent means against institutionalized forms of injustice and atrocities. It was simply odd to them that despite being part and parcel of the countries to which they belonged, they were discriminated against because of racial differences. Gandhi challenged the British authority on its clear deviation from the well-established canons of Enlightenment philosophy and he thus never found the campaign against the system of governance in South Africa or India undemocratic or inappropriate. His fight was for equal rights regardless of color, creed, or socioeconomic difference. King started from the same ideological basis in developing his own political vision: a fundamental element in King's dream was the Jeffersonian conviction that "all men, created alike in the name of God, are inseparably bound together." According to him, this was the substance of the Christian gospel and American constitutionalism, which was clearly articulated in the preamble to the constitution of the SCLC, an organization that he had established and led. The preamble stated,

> [O]ur nation came into existence as a protest against tyranny and oppression. It was created upon the fundamental assumption that all men are created equal and endowed with inalienable rights. The Government exists to protect the life and liberty of all without regard to race, color or religion.[173]

Gandhi might have drawn his inspiration from major religious texts, but he did not use religious language consciously to gain political mileage. In other words, he evolved an ideology that was rooted in religion and yet was not religious in the sense that King conceptualized his responses to injustice against the blacks. The reason is perhaps located in "the forms and language of the Christian biblical tradition of the Black southern Church heritage from which he came."[174] Given the success of the 1955 Montgomery bus strike, the 1963 March on Washington, and later the 1965 Selma-Montgomery March, it can be argued easily that the support that King obtained from the black Southern church was most critical in organizing an effective campaign. Not only did the church lay the foundation of the campaign, it also consolidated it by making the ideal of brotherhood a reality and exposing the irrationality of the fears and suspicions that were rooted in racial hatred. Given their easy acceptance among the believers, the churches remained the most effective institutions capable of showing that "the Negroes are not innately inferior in academic, health and moral standards, and that they not inherently criminal [because]...poverty and ignorance breed crime whatever the racial groups may be, and that it is a tortuous logic to use the tragic results of segregation as an argument for its continuation."[175]

Gandhi was perhaps the first among the nationalists to have realized the political inadequacies of the urban-centric national movement in a diverse society like India. Indian nationalism, starting from a very narrow constituency became mass-based and geographically widespread. Similarly, King had the distinction of raising the level of protests for civil rights to one that had previously been inconceivable, despite the efforts of his predecessors. Earlier movements for racial equality had fizzled out presumably because they lacked a unified black leadership and were carried out in a political environment in which racial segregation was more enthusiastically accepted than in King's era. The 1954 reversal of the 1896 separate-but-equal doctrine ushered in a new era of hope. Following the *Brown* case, blacks were encouraged to believe in the effective roles that the institutions of liberal democracy could play in radically altering the prevalent system of racial segregation. And, also, by being sensitive to the genuine black demands, the Kennedy-led government facilitated the process of racial desegregation that culminated in the passage of the 1964 Civil Rights Act and the 1965 Voting Rights Act.

RELIGION AND NONVIOLENCE

Both Gandhi and King had strong religious convictions, but the influence of religion in the strategies of the two thinkers was often distinctive. Gandhi, aware of the religious pluralism in India and also the subterranean animosity between Hindus and Muslims, generally employed secular arguments to advance his political goal. King did not have to deal with such a constraint and his appeals to religious texts were thus straightforward and persistent.

In articulating his goal of eradicating racial segregation and framing pacifism as a form of bravery, not only did King draw on a rich African American intellectual tradition, he also internalized the deep, motivating force of Christian ethics of love. Gandhi's nonviolence provided him with an instrument for mobilization that was readily accepted by African Americans because it was already deeply entrenched in their religious traditions. So for King, religion was a cementing factor, and he was not hesitant in utilizing religious bonding among the blacks for a political cause because he believed that "religion is not a private matter [though] it is intensely personal;...It is completely social as we human beings are."[176] King's uncritical view of religion as a liberating force was the result of his belief in the importance of the church in spreading the true message of Christianity over thousands of years. He thus admired the church as "a great institution which has gathered together the various insights of spiritual giants through the ages and welded them into a body of belief and conviction which has passed from one generation to another with cumulative conviction."[177] It is therefore not odd that King argued very persuasively that the Christian doctrine of love, operating through the Gandhian method of nonviolence, was one of the most potent weapons available to disinherited blacks in their struggle for justice. So, King was a Gandhian to the extent that he accepted and refined the technique of nonviolence, which had American roots as well.

By being moralists to the core, both Gandhi and King drew on God and sought to perfect humans through action aimed at improving human social conditions. For instance, Gandhi understood "unmerited suffering in terms of the law of karma, with its goal of salvation through an accumulation of mer-its. Implicit in King's version is a related Christian idea of brotherly love [based on] the belief that such love means taking upon oneself a burden of unmer-ited responsibility."[178] So, unconditional love, in the sense of agape, remained the guiding criterion: white Americans who believed in black inferiority were not evil but "misguided."[179] King described the Montgomery officials seeking to retain segregation as misguided because "when they seek to preserve segregation, they seek to preserve only what their folkways have taught them right."[180] Even when he was kicked and tortured by the Montgomery police during the 1955 Montgomery campaign, King was reported to have expressed "compassion" for the perpetrators of violence because they were "victims of their environment."[181] In order to meaningfully articulate his notion of universal brotherhood, King never endorsed sanctions against the individuals who happened to be misguided and misled and were thus taught "wrong" despite their role in their misdeeds.[182] His efforts were thus directed against the forces of evil rather than against those responsible for evil deeds.[183] The thing to do was "to get rid of the system and thereby create a moral balance within society."[184] Following his success in the Montgomery bus strike, King suggested that

[w]e must act in such a way as to make possible a coming together of white people and colored people on the basis of real harmony of interests and understanding. We seek an integration based on mutual respect.... We must now move from protest to reconciliation.[185]

Gandhi had a similar perception: he was opposed to English rule in India because it was unfair and based on misconceptions about human beings; his campaign was thus directed against the unjust system and not against individual Englishmen. "I have no hate in me for a single Englishman," argued Gandhi.[186] "My enmity is not," he further stated, "against the Englishmen, it is against their rule." It was a historical duty that he was born to perform in a most nonviolent way; hence, "if a hair of an Englishman was touched, he [would] feel the same grief as he [would] over such a mishap to [his] brother."[187]

In regard to nonviolence, Gandhi and King did not seem to adopt the same techniques. Two important techniques in King's protest movements were sits-in and boycotts, which the Montgomery bus strike of 1955 successfully employed. The 1965 Washington March corresponded with the Gandhi's Dandi March of 1930. There were various other steps, including voluntary resignation from gov-ernment jobs, renunciation of property, fasting, usurping of government func-tions, the formation of institutions performing governmental functions, and nonpayment of government tax (which Gandhi used to embarrass the British). King never showed any inclination toward these typical Gandhian steps. These differences can be attributed to the fact that while Gandhi sought complete polit-ical independence from the British rule, King sought to establish racial equality. Furthermore, it was possible for Gandhi to execute his plan of action because he led a campaign of the majority against a minority, while King led a black minority (who constituted barely one-tenth of the American population) against the white majority. Nonetheless, by adopting nonviolent civil resistance in a situation of well-entrenched racial prejudices, King crafted an alternative ideological discourse that, despite being rooted in the Sermon on the Mount, was articulated in clear Gandhian terms.

Mahatma Gandhi and Martin Luther King Jr.: Defying Liberals, but Deifying Liberalism

My primary aim in this book is to bring together various social, political, and intellectual influences to narrate a complex story woven around the two great apostles of nonviolence—Mahatma Gandhi and Martin Luther King Jr.—in two different socioeconomic and political contexts. Despite being located in two clearly different contexts, both Gandhi and King seemed to have appreciated the path of nonviolence presumably because of shared philosophical and religious dispensations. King's political language was clearly religious because of his role as a pastor in black Christian churches in the Southern states of the United States. Gandhi's political idioms may have had religious roots, but they were always articulated in secular terms, presumably because of the multi-class/religious nationalist platform that he assiduously nurtured. This is my fundamental point: King succeeded in mobilizing people for civil rights through his religious appeal, whereas Gandhi attained the nationalist goal of political mobilization by avoiding religious language. Religion may have played a role in constructing a discourse, but its articulation was far from being religious. This is how Gandhi distanced himself from M. A. Jinnah, who drew on religious differences between Hindus and Muslims to fuel his demand for the separate state of Pakistan and whose language of mobilization was unambiguously religious.

There is undoubtedly a confluence of thought between Gandhi and King because both of them found in nonviolence an effective instrument for mass mobilization for specific political goals. How do we conceptualize the growing acceptance of nonviolence in two different cultural milieus? Rather than being attached to a particular set of normative or institutional assumptions, this work is based on a search for meaning through engagement with thinkers who are not exactly Western in their perception. Gandhi introduced ideas and techniques that, despite their roots in the Enlightenment, were articulated differently in the context of the nationalist agitation against colonialism. King justified non-violence by reference to Christian ethics. This tactic appears to have persuaded people readily because of the importance of religion in their daily life. A careful study of the confluence of thought is a significant step toward a new genre of philosophy in which there is a critical engagement with various theoretical tra-ditions. So there are definite elements of cosmopolitan political thought in this book, in which, while describing the confluence of thought between Gandhi and King, "liberalism and other Westcentric modes of thought take their place in a series of plural and coeval engagements of thinkers and texts from all traditions."[1]

POLITICS OF DIFFERENCE

The argument in favor of the confluence of thought is made within the theoretical format of "the politics of difference," which draws sustenance from well-nurtured and also age-old "prejudices" based on a constructed notion of superiority-inferiority syndrome. Prejudice is usually accompanied by the pronouncement and also defense of "difference," as a marker of natural, obvious talents, and hierarchy as articulated in the difference between man and woman, black and white, Hindus and Muslims, modern and primitive, civilized and barbarians, Christians and Jews, and so on. The construction and proclamation of difference form "the core of the majority of judgments on the question of enfranchisement and disenfranchisement, the privilege of unmarked citizenship on the one hand, and the handicap and marginality, on the other."[2] The dominant political dis-course always justifies the denial of basic human dignity to a group of people as proper and appropriate and endorses the continued economic and cultural supremacy of the traditional dominant classes. It also offers perpetual support to the means of violence (psychological, physical, legal, and illegal) to sustain an inegalitarian system. It is not easy to overturn "the long habits of stigmatiza-tion, degradation and denial in the minds of the oppressors, nor the fear that accompanies them in the minds of oppressed."[3] The prevalence of what DuBois described as "the color line" is thus obvious, and what Gunnar Myrdal charac-terized as "the American dilemma" does not appear to be entirely concocted, but an outcome of socioeconomic and political processes that shaped racism and rearticulated the African American question in the United States. Even while articulating one's own self, white prejudice against blacks continues to remain prominent, as Walter White, an important leader of the National Association for the Advancement of Colored People (NAACP), most forcefully argued by saying that "I was a Negro, a human being with an invisible pigmentation which marked me as a person to be hunted, hanged, discriminated against, kept in poverty, and ignorance, in order that those whose skin was white would readily have at hand a proof of their superiority. No matter how low a white man fell, he could always hold fast to the smug conviction that he was superior to two-thirds of the world's population."[4] Such a conceptualization of a clearly primordial nature is at odds with the liberal philosophy that questions discrimination of any type. In other words, it is obvious that sustained racist prejudices against one-tenth of the American population, institutionalized through the Jim Crow laws, strike at the very foundation of American democracy and the modernity that it has brought about. A country that inculcates and also accepts constitutionally the spirit of bourgeois liberalism and upholds the importance of individual liberty and dignity, protected by an impartial judiciary regardless of race, creed, and clan, can never tolerate "prejudice," except at a heavy social cost. However, discriminatory practices are allowed to remain. This is a contradiction that poses important challenges to the power and authority of whites over blacks once the latter begin asserting their rights as citizens with equal political and cultural rights, greater social justice, and human worth. The civil rights movement and other movements of the 1950s and 1960s in the United States clearly overturned the racial equation between African Americans and whites by establishing firmly the conditions for the former's basic liberal rights. This happened despite the organized opposition by the perpetrators of racism based on an uncritical acceptance of the politics of prejudice that justified discrimination because of "sociocultural differences" among human beings.

There is one fundamental point that needs to be highlighted to reiterate the argument that the politics of positional differences clearly focuses on the issues of inclusion and exclusion. Given the roots of prejudice in the processes of inclusion and exclusion, it is obvious that its structural characteristics are context-specific. A product of structural inequality, racism is thus an articulation of prejudice-driven difference to engineer an artificial boundary among human beings. Racism based on differences (skin color, hair type, facial features) "constructs [a] hierarchy of standard or ideal type against which others appear inferior, stigmatized, deviant or abject."[5] By segregating those considered differently textured, racism produces and reproduces the "segregation of members of these racialized groups [and] renders deviant the comportments and habits of these segregated persons in relation to the dominant norms of respectability."[6] The stigma associated with the African American in the United States is rooted in the institution of slavery. While slavery was abolished more than a century and a half ago, "the racialized positions in the social division of labour remain."[7] Hence, "the least desirable work with the lowest pay, least autonomy and lowest status is the hard physical work, the dirty work and the servant work."[8] What is critical here is the assumption that structural inequality gets articulated in various well-designed forms and that whenever a challenge is mounted, the social equilibrium must be maintained for the well-being of everybody living in the affected social space. Being white is always a predetermined superior social status, just like being black means being inferior and suited to a particular kind of treatment, however objectionable that could be from the liberal point of view. Thus it was not inconceivable for Viola Andrews, a black woman of Georgia, to suggest that "the white man could not [lose]; the colored man could not win; the whites looked down upon everyone else, not only Niggers, as they called them, but all races, Orientals, Asians."[9] Racism is thus a double-edged sword: on the one hand, it creates and also re-creates a system of domination on the basis of prejudice-driven differences; it also contributes to reasons for its sustenance, on the other, by making segregation seem good for the racialized community. Hence, the argument that race-based discrimination can be dismantled by "race-blind principles" of equality and other liberal benefits does not appear to be viable at all. Instead, racism, given its organic roots in a particular mindset and social processes, needs to be addressed as an important foundation of structural inequality that cannot be meaningfully combated unless the processes and institutions providing a supporting cushion to the discriminatory practices are made completely defunct.[10] It is true that the civil rights movement, which was based on antiracist sentiments, has achieved a lot in initiating several new steps toward racial equality; but it may not be enough to eradicate the roots of racism, which has, presumably, become integrally linked with structural inequality. Mere change of government policy is certainly indicative of a change in the social fabric, a noticeable change under specific circumstances, though it may not be adequate to radically alter the institutionalized humiliation created by historically nurtured prejudice against the racialized minority. This is perhaps the fundamental lacuna in the liberal logic of universal equality. Liberal impartiality is thus vacuous in its claim of universality simply because it denies difference. There is no way these two can be reconciled because this is "an impersonal point of view on a situation, detached from any particular interests at stake."[11] Whether it is a challenge against racism in the United States or against any kind of sociopolitical and economic discrimination elsewhere, the politics of difference clearly articulates a specific point of view. The King-led civil rights movement was undoubtedly a serious step toward establishing racial equality in the United States, but it was not adequate to get rid of the roots of structural inequality.

Gandhi, who spearheaded the campaign against racism in South Africa and colonial exploitation in India, strengthened his claims on the basis of the prejudice-driven differences between the political authority and the governed. What was most critical to both Gandhi and King was to build their opposition to illiberal politics by reference to the differences between the dominating and dominated races. Gandhi transformed the nature of politics from an elite-based constitutional campaign to one of mass participation in which the visible (or other) differences from the colonial Other constituted an important source for political mobilization. The entire Gandhian assault—whether in South Africa or India—seems to have drawn its sustenance and gradually consolidated its grip on the masses from the sense of cultural differences between the ruled and ruling race that Gandhi had built during his campaign. The Mahatma employed various "rhetorical strategies...to open up this space of difference [and also to] articulate a political discourse which sought to reconcile differences within Indian society in order to project a unified difference against colonial power."[12]

By highlighting the differences, the nationalist project was directed at creating a hegemonic domain of nationalism where colonialism was never allowed to intervene. The contradiction between the colonizers and colonized clearly separated their respective domains. On this basis, the anticolonial nationalist struggle created its own domain of sovereignty confronting the imperial power. This is usually explained in a theoretical format by dividing this domain between "material" and "spiritual" or "inner" and "outer." The material domain constituted the economy, science, technology, and statecraft with which the West proved its superiority and the East had "succumbed." There was, however, an inner domain drawn on the unique spiritual and cultural resources of the East. Although the West was politically dominant, its role was marginal in the inner domain presumably because of its failure to comprehend the complexity of the spiritual and cultural world of the East. This had a significant consequence. Reacting against the growing influence of the West in the public sphere, the nationalist project increasingly sought strength by looking to the inner domain. By drawing upon the spiritual and cultural strength of the imagined nation, those seeking to identify its "distinctiveness" vis-à-vis the West initiated a major process that came to a head when Gandhi held the colonial power responsible for undermining India's age-old "civilization," thereby organizing a mass protest. Similarly, Bal Gangadhar Tilak's critique of the 1891 Age of Consent Bill[13] is part of a wider nationalist agenda seeking to protect the distinct Hindu identity, of which caste remained a nonnegotiable dimension. In Tilak's perception, the bill needed to be resisted because it struck at the foundation of caste, and the Sudharaks undermined "the power of caste panchayats" by allowing the colonial ruler to intervene in an exclusive domain of Hindu society.[14]

Just as Gandhi drew on the principle of difference and simultaneously created and sustained an independent domain of nationalist politics, King built and consolidated the antisegregation campaign on the same logic. Until then, segregation was justified because "the inferior social, economic and political position was good for the Negroes [who] were incapable of advancing beyond a fixed position and would therefore be happier if encouraged not to attempt the impossible."[15] In reality, it was culturally justified hatred that wrongly created and consolidated a difference that was unlikely to be bridged due to the well-entrenched prejudices of the whites against their black counterparts. One of the obvious outcomes of such a biased mindset was that the Negroes were always abused as "niggers, black apes and black cows."[16] While sharpening his argument against segregation based on racist prejudices, King described black resentments as "most natural" given the historical wrongs against the racialized minority. Seeking to illustrate the plight of the tormented blacks, King thus argued that

> when you take a cross-country drive and find it necessary to sleep night after night in the uncomfortable corners of your automobile because no motel will accept you; when you are humiliated day in and day out by nagging signs reading "white" and "colored"; when your first name becomes "nigger" and your middle name becomes "boy" (however old you are) and

your last name becomes "John," and when your wife and mother are never given the respected title "Mrs."; when you are harried by day and haunted by night by the fact that you are Negro, living constantly at tiptoe stance never quite knowing what to expect next, and plagued with inner fears and outer resentments; when you are forever fighting a degenerating sense of nobodiness.[17]

The agonized blacks thus continued to suffer due to specific socioeconomic circumstances in which a challenge to the status quo was always considered unwelcome and countered as ruthlessly as possible. So the principle of difference worked at two levels: at one level, it created and consolidated a black unity because difference-driven division was artificially created to endure and also defend racial inequality and discrimination; at another level, the deliberate efforts at maintaining racial segregation by laws and other coercive state apparatuses helped build and also prolong an unjust system of governance. As in the case of Gandhi, it was possible for King to spearhead and sustain a meaningful campaign by drawing on the unbridgeable differences between the whites and the racialized black minority. Difference, instead of being a source of confrontation, remained an important resource for civilizational growth.

To both Gandhi and King, liberalism, to be universal, needed to be alert to differences; otherwise, diversity, which remained an important source of human progress and change, could not be adequately appreciated. What is theoretically most inept, as the argument goes, is the effort at essentializing liberal values and its accompanying ethos regardless of socioeconomic and political contexts. In other words, the idea of "sameness" shall remain a refreshing idea as long as it gives room for contextual flexibility. Here comes the importance of the challenges that Gandhi and King spearheaded against a liberalism that projected universality as a means to fulfill partisan sociopolitical and economic designs. Besides taking into account Gandhi's and King's individual contributions, the argument defending the confluence of thought between Gandhi and King is uniquely textured by a challenge to efforts aimed at reducing "ethnopolitical subjectivity to a unity distracting from the situational specificities."

THE PROBLEMATIQUE

In the twentieth century, two main apostles of nonviolence were Mohandas Karamchand Gandhi and Martin Luther King Jr. Gandhi led a nonviolent civil resistance to win freedom from British colonialism, while King mobilized the American blacks against the law of segregation, popularly known as the Jim Crow laws.[18] A person of impeccable integrity and high moral values, Gandhi succeeded in his mission by drawing on nonviolence, which was instinctively upheld by the people at large. Success did not come so quickly, though the circumstances were generally favorable, given the general instinctive tilt of the Indians toward nonviolence. It will not therefore be wrong to argue that the support base that Gandhi drew upon in his campaign against colonialism was largely natural in view of the roots of nonviolence in the Indian psyche. This is one side of the story. The other part of the story concerns the issues that drew people to nonviolent struggle despite adverse consequences. Gandhi fought against racism and injustice during his almost sixty-year political career, first in South Africa (1893–1914) and later in India (1914–1948).[19] By challenging the exploitation of human beings by human beings, he articulated a powerful voice, hitherto undermined, if not gagged, for those extremely aggrieved—but not strong enough to air their grievances. There are three interrelated, but chronologically different, phases in Gandhi's active political life: the first phase is rather an innocent phase since he, at that point, had hardly evinced any inkling of what he would later articulate; just like his contemporary colleagues, Gandhi was keen to study hard for a better job. After successfully passing the school-leaving certificate (which was then called matriculation in India), Gandhi was persuaded to study law in England to firmly establish his claim for the post of Diwan (the highest administrative post in Porbandar in Gujarat), which his father had held. Gandhi's mother did not appear to have endorsed the idea because she was not sure whether it was "possible for [him] to stay in England without prejudice to [his] own religion,…culture and family tradition."[20] When Gandhi failed to persuade his mother, he requested Becharji Swami, a Jain monk who was a family adviser, to help him out. As Gandhi narrated in his autobiography, the Swami came to his aid. He was allowed to go to England on accepting three conditions of staying away from "wine, women and meat."[21] This readily convinced Gandhi's mother. The second phase, that of the loyalist Gandhi, emerged in the context of South Africa, where he went as a lawyer to fight a legal battle. Gandhi was appointed by a South Africa–based Indian firm, Dada Abdullah, to fight a legal battle against Taib Haji Khanmamad over a long-standing dispute for financial compensation. This is where he evolved his technique of nonviolent civil resistance to challenge the "unjust" policies of the government. For Gandhi, the South African experience was "a rich and formative one, moulding him into a very special kind of public figure, far greater in range and experience than most [of the contemporary] Indian politicians."[22] Nonetheless, he articulated his voice of protest as a loyalist because, as Gandhi believed, it was incumbent on the citizens of the empire to be "loyal" to the authority. This loyalty was, for him, "more in the nature of obligation." He thus "vied with Englishmen in loyalty to the throne; [not only did he] learn the tune of the national anthem [he also joined] in the singing whenever it was sung." So committed was Gandhi to the empire that "whenever there was an occasion for the expression of loyalty without fuss or ostentation, [he] readily took part in it."[23] He defended his loyalty, despite having encountered the well-entrenched racist bias of the government, by arguing that "the color prejudice" that he was subjected to in South Africa was "quite contrary to British traditions" and was thus ephemeral in existence. The final phase in Gandhi's political career saw the consolidation of a rebel Gandhi, and began once he got involved in struggles against the colonial authority in India. Not only did he challenge British rule in India, he mobilized people to overthrow a prevalent colonial authority that had lost its "moral claim over the Indians." What is striking in this phase is Gandhi's uncritical acceptance of liberal techniques of political opposition against the British Empire. He was convinced that British rule in India was a clear distortion of Enlightenment philosophy. Evolved over centuries of struggle against vested interests and appreciative of social virtues, benevolence, compassion, and tolerance, the Enlightenment inculcated and also helped consolidate those basic values that were not only enlightening, but also critical to human existence. Gandhi believed that British liberalism, as a product of the Enlightenment tradition, had laid the foundation of representative democracy, ensuring the political equality of citizens and also protecting certain inalienable human rights, irrespective of race or ethnicity. Based on three pillars of the liberal creed—rationality, individual liberty, and human dignity—British liberalism contributed to a certain variety of moral universalism. Consistent with its normative commitments to the citizens of the British Empire, liberalism did not endorse discrimination, since it was contrary to the Enlightenment tradition, both in spirit and substance. This ideology of sameness seemed to have crystallized from values that were integral to the conceptualization of the Enlightenment philosophy. There was a clear "disconnect" between British liberalism and the unjust and exploitative colonial practices in India given the Queen's 1858 Proclamation, which guaranteed equal rights to the Indians and their European counterparts. Reflective of liberal faith in its undiluted form, the proclamation states that

we hold ourselves bound to the natives of our Indian territories by the same obligations of duty which bind us to all our other subjects, and those obligations, by the blessings of the Almighty God, we shall faithfully and conscientiously fulfill.... We declare it to be our royal will and pleasure that none be in anywhere favoured, none molested or disquieted, by reason of their religious faith or observances, but that all shall alike enjoy the equal and impartial protection of the law.... [And] it is our further will that, so far as may be, our subjects, of whatever race or creed, be freely and impartially be admitted to offices in our service, the duties of which they may be qualified, by their education, ability, integrity, duty to discharge.[24]

The organic roots of sameness in British liberalism informed the empire, and one of its fundamental tenets was "fair play and impartiality of justice." Gandhi sharpened his attack on the political authority in South Africa precisely because Indians, despite being citizens of the British Empire, were denied fair play and impartiality of justice. In other words, Gandhi articulated and also defended his argument challenging the unjust policies on the basis of "difference" and "universalism" of British liberalism.

Was Gandhi's commitment to liberalism unique? The answer is an unequivocal "no." Gandhi was the product of a milieu that appeared to have uncritically upheld British liberal values. The opposition to colonialism was institutionalized in a typical liberal way with the establishment of the Indian National Congress, in 1885, by a retired British civil servant, A. O. Hume. Based on liberal values, the Congress articulated the nationalist language in a rather moderate fashion that, while questioning the prevalent British administration, remained committed to the empire. The most clearly articulated expression of such a commitment was the inaugural speech of Dadabhai Naoroji, the second president of the Congress. Being appreciative of the liberal ethos, Naoroji had no hesitation in saying that

> [i]t is our good fortune that we are under a rule which makes it possible for us to meet in this manner. It is under the civilizing rule of the Queen and the people of England that we meet here together, hindered by none and are freely allowed to speak our minds without the least fear and without the lest hesitation. Such a thing is possible under British rule and British rule only.[25]

This perception was shared not only by the early generation of the nationalist leadership but also by their later counterparts. For instance, G. K. Gokhale, Gandhi's political mentor and a leading nationalist voice in India in the twentieth century, had no qualms in appreciating British liberalism. He said, "I want my people [to] feel that the whole of [their] aspiration can, in essence and its reality, be realized within this Empire....Despite occasional lapses—and some of them most lamentable lapses—despite prolonged reactions, inevitable in human affairs, [no one can deny] the genius of the British people, as revealed in history, [in articulating] political freedom [and] constitutional liberty" as meaningful goals.[26] It is evident that the nationalist ideology from the very outset was heavily grounded in the dominant British liberal discourse that flourished in India in the wake of British rule. Like his mentor Gokhale, Gandhi articulated his voice of protest in a typical liberal way that was readily accepted by his nationalist colleagues and co-workers, presumably because of the sociopolitical ambience that favored British liberalism. His challenge to British colonialism was hardly "illiberal," but was based on the fundamental tenets of the Enlightenment, which, by seeking to establish the basic principle of universal human dignity, hardly favored discrimination due to creed, color, or race. The hinge of this loyalty to the British Empire was, argued Judith Brown, "a deep-rooted belief that its fundamental values were those of the British constitution...[which] included love of justice, fair dealing, equality and liberty."[27] As early as 1906, Gandhi thus stated that "we have no hesitation in saying that one of the greatest secrets of the success of the Empire is its ability to deal with even-handed justice. [The British administration] serves as a beacon-light to tell the Indians...that they need not be without hope so long as the fierce sun of justice beats on the Empire."[28] His optimism led him to support the British in the Boer War because "it is a golden opportunity to prove how committed Indians are to the Empire."[29] Besides proving his loyalty, such a commitment was expected of the citizens of the empire since Gandhi believed that "so long as the subjects owe allegiance to a state, it is their clear duty to accommodate themselves and to accord their support to the act of the state."[30]

Being a supporter of universalist liberal values, Gandhi could never reconcile to the racist prejudices of the South African rulers, which, he was persuaded to believe, were locally engineered distortions of noble constitutional principles. It was thus legitimate for the Indians in South Africa to claim their rights because, as Gandhi argued, "our existence [here] is only in our capacity as British subjects [and] we have been proud of our British citizenship."[31] What was unique in Gandhi's challenge to racism in South Africa and later to British colonialism in India was that he drew on liberalism to build his argument challenging British rule and also to mobilize people politically against its continuity. In other words, liberalism remained a significant driving force behind Gandhi's conceptualization of British colonialism as "a deviant form of governance," and also behind his organization of movements against a political authority that had lost its legitimacy given its failure to appreciate the basic British liberal ethos. There is therefore no doubt that "Gandhi's core values and assumptions were built on a number of unexpressed presuppositions that are deeply rooted in the entire British liberal tradition."[32] In this sense, it is also fair to argue that Gandhi shared "a common intellectual heritage"[33] with the leading exponents of liberalism. This provided him with a perspective to understand racism in South Africa and British colonialism in India, and also to combat an illiberal rule in India. There is no doubt that Gandhi responded to these distortions in governance on the basis of his actual experience of living and campaigning within an empire. His sociopolitical ideas evolved out of specific contexts of South Africa and later India that "made him forge his distinctive political attitudes"[34] by drawing on the fundamental canons of British liberalism.

GANDHI'S "LIBERAL" DILEMMA

Gandhi succeeded in meaningfully mobilizing aggrieved people around those issues that weakened the socioeconomic claims of the prevalent political authorities in South Africa and India. The rising popularity of Gandhi and his nonviolent strategy for mass-awakening was not, at all, coincidental, but an outcome of a process with organic roots in the contemporary socioeconomic and political milieu. It is, however, a strange coincidence that Gandhi fought only for the Indians in South Africa and he did not take up the exploitation of the blacks there.[35] It was not his racial prejudice, but political realism, that seems to have "guided Gandhi in limiting his agenda to the eradication of the disabilities of his countrymen in South Africa."[36] To fulfill his mission in the context of the unrelenting hostility of the Europeans and colonial government, he had to evolve an appropriate strategy with a well-defined agenda—an agenda for protecting the rights of the colored people that incorporated the well-defined liberal techniques of prayer, petition, and protest. That he was a loyal British subject was also evident in the way that he searched for a solution to the issues of racism and injustice within the legal parameters of British colonialism. The Gandhian parameters, however, gradually changed as he arrived on the Indian scene in 1914.

Gandhi's attitude toward the racist South African government was governed by his sincere commitment to British liberalism. He found racism and discrimination of any kind incongruent with the fundamental liberal tenets. It is surprising to note that although Gandhi realized both the black and brown races were suffering due to racist prejudices, he, more or less, had the same racist bias toward the local blacks as his European counterparts. In 1896, two years after his arrival in South Africa, Gandhi campaigned for separate entrances for Indians and local blacks at the Durban post offices (they shared a common entrance). In his petition to the government, Gandhi defended segregation because the Indians "felt the indignity too much and many respectable Indians were insulted and called all sorts of names by the clerks at the counter."[37] The petition was granted, and a separate entrance was built for the Indians. Gandhi had achieved the goal, but at the cost of alienating the blacks, who began questioning his commitment to fight against racism. This divide was deepened by various steps that he took to champion the cause of the Indians at the cost of their black counterparts, whom he referred to as *Kaffirs*, a pejorative South African term for blacks. He used this term despite being aware of its negative connotation. On one occasion he argued emphatically that Europeans diluted Indian racial superiority by lumping them with the Kaffirs. He stated that "[o]urs is one continual struggle against a degradation sought to be inflicted upon us by the Europeans, who desire to degrade us to the level of the raw kaffir whose occupation is hunting, and whose sole ambition is to collect a certain number of cattle to buy a wife with, and, then pass his life in indolence and nakedness."[38] He further expressed his annoyance by firmly arguing that "the British rulers take us to be so lowly and ignorant that they assume that, like the Kaffirs who can be pleased with toys and pins, we can also be fobbed off with trinkets."[39] Since Kaffirs "are, as a rule, uncivilized,"[40] Gandhi insisted in his petition to the Town Council of Durban that "the Town Council must withdraw the Kaffirs from the location [because] this mixing of the Kaffirs with the Indians...is very unfair to the Indian population."[41] Similarly, he characterized a Durban court verdict as "most satisfactory"[42] when it debarred the Kaffirs from travelling in the same tram compartment with the Indians. What is surprising is the fact that Gandhi seemed to have nurtured his apparent racist prejudices as late as 1909, when he succeeded in building a strong opposition to the unjust rule in South Africa based on the core liberal principle of "sameness." He was anguished when he found that some Indian prisoners were "happy to sleep in the same room as Kaffirs. This is a matter of shame to us [because] we cannot ignore the fact that there is no common ground between them and us in the daily affairs of life."[43] There is no doubt that Gandhi, like his liberal European counterparts, appreciated segregation on the basis of a cultural logic that stated that "if there is anything which the Indian cherishes more than any other, it is the purity of type."[44] This purity was likely to be diluted if segregation was not maintained. His commitment to fight such "a social imbalance" was total, and hence he urged his colleagues and followers to continue fighting "so long as cultured Indian passive resisters and conscientious objectors are treated as though they were aboriginal native fellows of the worst type."[45] He was thus opposed to the policy that dictated equal treatment of Indians and Kaffirs, since Indian civilization was far more superior to the Kaffir civilization.[46] While he might not have taken the blacks as partners in his political campaign for Indian equality, he was the first one to provide medical help to the Zulus during their 1906 rebellion. The British medical officers refused to treat the Zulus when they were wounded. With the help of the Indian Ambulance Corps (which Gandhi was instrumental in creating, along with his colleagues), and despite threats from the Europeans, he did not hesitate to serve the wounded, presumably because the call to serve humanity knew no bounds.[47] He, however, justified his involvement in this medical mission for the Zulus with a paternalistic suggestion that they needed his support. By 1922, when he was articulating his views on satyagraha in South Africa, he revised his opinion on the Zulus by saying that "they are not the barbarians we imagined them to be."[48] He characterized his earlier assessment as reflective of "a clear prejudice" saying that "[i]t is only vanity which makes us look upon the Negroes as savages."[49] He was also of the belief that since civilization is gradually making headway among the Negroes,[50] the situation was likely to change, and given their acceptance of "the importance of education and pious values of Christianity,"[51] the Zulus would soon be on par with other civilized communities.

It appears that Gandhi's views on liberalism and constitutionalism were linked with his conceptualization of morality, which remained critical in his sociopolitical thought.[52] Given Gandhi's upbringing in the liberal political order, as prevailed in Britain in the main, he naturally had firsthand experience of the theory as well as practice of the ideology of liberalism and constitutionalism. However, Gandhi's religious and moralistic beliefs, as evident in most of his formulations, could not be reconciled with the predominantly legalistic overtones in the main body of liberal philosophy.[53] Gandhi's liberalism was a unique interpretation of liberalism that drew its sustenance from well-defined moral parameters. In the context of the nonviolent civil resistance in South Africa, which gave him the first opportunity to fine-tune his strategy, Gandhi always couched his argument within a moral mold. Gandhi justified his morality in the name of God, given the well-entrenched religiosity of his colleagues and supporters. He thus explained that "to pledge ourselves or to take an oath in the name of God or with him as witness is not something to be trifled with. If having taken such an oath we violate our pledge we are guilty before God....A man, who deliberately and intelligently takes a pledge and then breaks it, forfeits his manhood."[54] In order to strengthen his argument further, he argued that "just as a copper coin treated with mercury not only becomes valueless when detected but also makes its owner liable to punishment, in the same way a man who lightly pledges his word and then breaks it becomes a man of straw and fits himself for punishment here as well as hereafter."[55] Hence, the main thrust of Gandhi's views on liberalism and constitutionalism has been nothing more than a critique of the theory for not being adequately moral; Gandhi thus sought to refurbish its fundamental foundations with moral justification. But such an assertion may appear superficial if one looks at the basic dichotomy between Gandhi's understanding of liberalism and that of the theory's other proponents. Historically, the rise and growth of liberal political philosophy in Europe was preceded by the dismantling of the decaying feudal economic order and its gradual replacement by an incipient capitalism. It was realized at that time that capitalism would not likely be a viable economic replacement for feudalism unless it was backed by something other than intellectual explanations of its numerous operational principles. Thus, it was in this background that liberalism emerged as a solid philosophy to ideologically explain and justify the fundamental tenets of the capitalist system. It soon became obvious that liberalism was being used by the capitalist class to protect its class interests rather than as a means for bringing about a moral regeneration among the masses. As a result, the basic concepts of liberalism provided a legalistic, contractual, competitive, bargaining code for serving class interests. Even the sense of accommodation in the doctrines of liberalism was prevalent only to the extent needed to keep the socioeconomic and political order intact without putting it at risk of greater and sudden upheavals. Such one-sided and seemingly self-driven postulates of liberalism were unconvincing to Gandhi, who was a moralist to the hilt and who emphasized a theory's ethical foundations over and above its legalistic or mechanical components. Hence, what Gandhi did was to provide some sort of improvisation in the theory of liberalism in view of its moralist imperatives. But it must be pointed out that Gandhi's brush with liberalism did not end just there. He also tried to detect the problem of overabstraction in many key components of the theory of liberalism, including in the notion of justice. He found that the whole idea of justice was philosophized in such a way that it could not be operationalized on the ground, and that the presence or absence of just order in society could only be assessed with reference to its existence either in the court of law or in the structuring of institutions of governance in a country. Gandhi criticized such an abstract notion of justice and called for its deep rooting in larger values of human fellowship and solidarity. Gandhi, thus, tried to enrich the ideology of liberalism and constitutionalism by imbuing it with ethical and moral perspectives.

Two fundamental points come out of the above discussion: first, Gandhi's critique of racism in South Africa and British colonialism in India was based on his appreciation of Enlightenment philosophy. He was simply not agreeable to a regime that, despite being based on liberalism, had a discriminatory nature. This was a contradiction that, Gandhi felt, needed to be meaningfully addressed to avoid further distortions in governance in South Africa and India. At another level of his critique, Gandhi sharpened his counterattack on the regime for its failure to uphold the basic values of liberalism while governing the citizens of the empire. His insistence on Indians being treated equally as citizens of the empire followed from the liberal tenets of his European counterparts. What was unique in Gandhi's approach to racism and colonialism was his emphatic faith in liberalism, which was, he strongly felt, an empowering ideology because of its egalitarian nature and its desire to create "sameness" in humanity. The second point relates to the contradiction that Gandhi himself became aware of while treating his fellow blacks in South Africa. He seemed to have had the same prejudices that the white liberals had toward the colonized brown people: they were excluded because they were different. What remained at the foundation of such a conceptualization was "paternalism," based on an apparent superiority of what was construed by the colonizers as British "civilization." And colonialism was always benign to the colonized because of the obvious benefits that accompanied "a munificent rule," drawing on the distinct social virtues of benevolence, compassion, and tolerance. This is how colonialism survived and also thrived, because in order to remain the only possible option for the colonized, colonialism undertook simultaneously two complementary sets of activities of "civilizing others" and also keeping them in perpetual "otherness."[56] Gandhi thus confronted "the system of difference and exclusion while at the same time maintaining his overall trust in the universalist ideals of liberal theory,"[57] that was seriously compromised in his attitude toward the Zulus or Kaffirs, as he preferred to characterize the local blacks in South Africa. He thus appeared to have been caught in a dilemma that clearly reflected the predicament of the liberals who, despite being appreciative of the Lockean sameness, were not inclined to support, without qualification, the idea of political equality of citizens and the protection of certain inalienable human rights regardless of race or ethnicity. Notwithstanding Gandhi's revolutionary sociopolitical views, he hardly could escape from the well-entrenched Victorian cultural prejudices, based on paternalism and also the arrogance of power, which always created "an inferior other" to justify the obvious distortions in an otherwise enlightening liberal ideology. The unequal treatment that was meted out to Gandhi was simply unacceptable to him because it stood in contradiction with the basic principles of liberalism—though it hardly deterred him from being "abusive" to the fellow blacks in South Africa. What it suggests is that Gandhi was a revolutionary at one level and a status-quoist at another level. His condemnation of the blacks as Kaffirs may not constitute sufficient proof to demonstrate his complicity in racism; it is nonetheless a clear indicator "of the psychological violence inherent in his construction of the African other [which] casts some doubt on his professed ability to resolve the dilemma of reconciling ethical and political power."[58] This was perhaps a dilemma of the age when liberal principles were selectively, if not conveniently, endorsed for a specific sociopolitical goal. The Mahatma, despite having spearheaded perhaps the most effective no-violent nationalist campaign against racial discrimination in South Africa and colonial exploitation in India, was hardly free from such a predicament. It is thus safe to argue that Gandhi failed to rise above the well-entrenched cultural prejudices in rearticulating liberal ideas.

MARTIN LUTHER KING JR. AND THE AMERICAN ENLIGHTENMENT

For Martin Luther King Jr., the scene was not substantially different except that he fought against racism and injustice in an independent United States within a much shorter adult life than Gandhi. As a trained pastor in a black Southern church, King was introduced to nonviolence at a very young age presumably because of his exposure to the biblical emphasis on nonviolence, particularly from his father, who was also a preacher. As King admitted in his autobiography, he "did not have much choice, but to become religious because [he] grew up in the church. [His] father is a preacher, [his] grandfather was a preacher, [his] great-grand father was a preacher, [his] only brother is a preacher, [his] daddy's brother is a preacher."[59] There is no doubt that King was introduced to nonviolence purely as a Christian. The Sermon on the Mount remained, to him, the most critical resource for justifying nonviolence as a meaningful device and also as a technique for mobilizing the affected against the organized adversaries.

The constituency that nurtured King in his campaign for nonviolence consisted mainly of blacks. He was motivated by "his strong social consciousness, together with his normal youthful rebellion against tradition,...especially the emotionalism of the church he knew [because] he believed in a relevant social gospel which few ministers preashed at that time."[60] He fought against racism and injustice, as practised by the Southern states. It was thus a specific context that led the young pastor to raise his voice against discrimination of a worse variety, and he drew blacks around him to nonviolently challenge the perpetrators of injustice. Like the racist South African context, which Gandhi had confronted the prevalence of legal segregation between the blacks and whites in the Southern states created circumstances in which his campaign against racism and injustice easily gained acceptance. So it is fair to argue that the contexts that led to the rise of Gandhi and King appear to be identical. Furthermore, both of them were drawn to the nonviolent religious traditions of the people they mobilized for political struggle. Gandhi was aware of the religious pluralism in India and the possibility for deep cleavages between Hindus and Muslims in India, and accordingly frequently employed secular arguments to advance his position. King did not have to deal with the same political realities, and his appeals to religious texts were straightforward and persistent. It is true that for Gandhi, nonviolence was a "given" since it remained integrally linked with India's major religious traditions. The same cannot be said for the American blacks who, despite being Christians, had suffered through the history of the brutal articulation of racism in America. Hence King addressed his relatively difficult task most intelligently by linking Christianity with nonviolence, especially by reiterating the five cardinal principles of the Sermon on the Mount. He thus underlined qualities like compassion, humility, self-criticism, forgiveness, and renunciation of material gain. King therefore instrumentalized the "turn the other cheek" philosophy, which was not, at all, an abstract call for political mobilization. It was an inspiring idea to the African Americans, given their emotional attachment to "a prophetic tradition that runs through David and Isaiah in the Old Testament through Augustine and Martin Luther to Reinhold Niebuhr in the twentieth century."[61]

King's attachment to liberalism is undoubtedly the continuation of a legacy of the past. The tradition appeared to have begun with Booker T. Washington, a born slave who became free following the Civil War. His autobiography—*Up from Slavery* (1901)[62]—remains, today, perhaps the most authentic account of how the victims of slavery became drawn to the liberal ethos in their struggle against racial prejudices. As one committed to humanism, Washington forcefully proclaimed that "[t]he great human love that in the end recognizes and rewards merit is everlasting and universal, [which] remains the most inspiring idea in the struggle that is constantly going on in the hearts of both the Southern white people and their former slaves to free themselves from racial prejudice."[63] Although he was aware of the devastating role played by the Ku Klux Klan in sustaining (and also consolidating) racial prejudices, he was confident that such prejudice was a temporary phase in American social life.[64] He also challenged the conventional view that the "Negro was so constituted that he could not learn from books, and [therefore] efforts and money would be thrown away in trying to teach him to master the studies of the ordinary school curriculum."[65] This was a revolutionary claim at that time, though he was later criticized for his apparently "lenient" view toward those perpetrating racial segregation. Perhaps the most trenchant and yet constructive critique of Washington was provided by W. E. B. DuBois, one of the most creative African American authors and an important influence on King in his struggle against racism. Washington represented, argued DuBois, "in Negro thought the old attitude of adjustment and submission; but adjustment at such a peculiar time as to make his program unique."[66] Submission was a context-driven strategy, and the aim was to build self-respect among the Negroes, who still carried the slave mindset. Instead of making high demands for Negroes to be recognized as men and as American citizens, which was likely to provoke a backlash from the whites, Washington preferred to concentrate on "industrial education, the accumulation of wealth and the conciliation of South."[67] Insisting that "the manly self-respect is worth more than lands and houses," he was thus favorably inclined toward giving up, at least for the present, the demands for "political power, civil rights and higher education for Negro youth."[68] Whether this was an appropriate strategy or a meek surrender to white supremacy is debatable, though his comments remain an immediate reference point for the struggle against racism. DuBois provided a powerful critique of Washington's assessment of the Negro issue, which is also known as "the Atlanta Compromise."[69] DuBois suggested that Washington's compromise with the main black demands helped the racist whites to fulfill their partisan goals. As a result of his soft-paddling with the critical issues, "there have occurred," mentioned DuBois, "the disenfranchisement of the Negroes, the legal creation of a distinct status of civil inferiority for them and the steady withdrawal of aid from institutions for their higher training."[70] The argument that Washington provided had thus obvious weaknesses, argued DuBois, because "nine millions of men can[not] make effective progress in economic lines if they are deprived of political rights, made a servile caste, and allowed only the most meagre chance for developing their exceptional men."[71] According to him, Washington suffered from "the triple paradox," which is articulated as follows:

1. His striving to make Negro artisans business men and property owners is utterly impossible under modern competitive methods for working

men and property-owners to defend their rights and exist with the right of suffrage.

2. His insistence on thrift and self-respect along with "a silent submission to civic inferiority...is bound to sap the manhood of any race in the long run."

3. His advocacy for common school and industrial training and de-recognizing the importance of institutions of higher learning for the Negroes was unrealistic unless a pool of teachers appreciating the cause was created, which remained a distant goal in adverse socioeconomic circumstances.[72]

On the basis of his well-argued critique of Washington's position, DuBois thus concluded by saying that "the Washington doctrine has tended to make the whites, North and South, shift the burden of the Negro problems to the Negro shoulders and stand aside as critical and rather pessimistic spectators [when] in fact the burden belongs to the nation and the hands of none of us are clean if we bend not our energies to righting these great wrongs."[73] This was a typical liberal argument, based on a contextual reading of the Negro question that was both historical and contemporary. For DuBois, a meaningful resolution to the conundrum facing American society would be possible once the fundamental liberal values, espoused by the founding fathers, were adequately appreciated. By drawing on the Jeffersonian values of constitutional equality, he thus emphatically argued that "by every civilized and peaceful method we must strive for the rights which the world accords to me, clinging unwaveringly to those great words which the sons of the Fathers would fain forget: we hold these truths to be self-evident: that all men are created equal; that they are endowed by their Creator with certain inalienable rights; that among these are life, liberty and the pursuit of happiness."[74] In view of such a proclamation, how can one justify, asked DuBois, "the Jim Crow laws of segregation," which, with a complementary American mindset, had created perhaps the most disgraceful system of racial discrimination. Instead, the Jeffersonian ideals had been distorted to create circumstances in which "Negroes spend their lives looking for insult or for hiding places from them—shrinking (instinctively and despite desperate bolstering of courage) from blow that are not always, but ever; not each day, but each week, each month, each year."[75] What is critical to note here is that the rationalization of the inhuman treatment to which the blacks were subjected did not appear to be justified in the light of the core values of American constitutionalism that the founding fathers so assiduously nurtured and defended.

DuBois's critique of racism is conceptually challenging and intellectually stimulating because it was based on a specific reading of liberal values that, he believed, if meaningfully applied to the American context, would have resolved most of the issues driven by racial prejudices. Racism, a product of "the structural deformities of the American state-society interactions," defied the core beliefs of American constitutionalism.[76] While racism remained a sociological fact of life in America, it should not have been an impediment toward racial integration because the African American, argued DuBois,

> ever feels his twoness—an American, a Negro…in one dark body, whose dogged strength alone keeps it from being torn as under. The history of the American Negro is the history of this strife—this longing to attain self-conscious manhood, to merge his double self into a better and truer self. [In the process], the American Negro simply wishes to make it possible for a man to be both a Negro and an American.[77]

In his 1910 essay entitled "White Co-Workers," he defended his position by unambiguously stating that

> "the Negroes of the United States of America wish to be Americans, but refuse to belong to the subject caste. They demand American citizenship with every right that inheres, but what they ask for themselves they grant just as freely to others. They believe in Negro blood and Negro genius; they seek, in voluntary unions, to develop a new Negro ethos—a music, a literature, a school of art and thought; but they will do this as freemen in a free democracy, joining wholeheartedly with their fellows of all colors whenever that freedom is menaced. Not narrow, excluding, other-hating particularism, but broad, sympathetic, all-embracing nationalism is our aim and spirit."[78]

Two issues are critical here: first, DuBois's argument is a theoretical defense of "sameness," the core conceptual liberal category. A survey of the efforts directed at racial equality in the United States shows that the claim to sameness, to equal rights and opportunities, and an end to discriminatory practices, prejudicial and judicial, remained the hallmark of the African American struggle for justice. Liberalism was thus a powerful tool to attain "a double victory"—victory for democracy and freedom and also victory against the perpetrators of racism and racial exploitation. The second issue relates to the distinct racial character of the Negroes, who made significant contributions to global history and culture to create an inclusive and "all-embracing" nationalism. Racism was thus to be effectively challenged as an impediment to the creation of amity and goodwill among the Negroes and their white counterparts; otherwise, the fundamental goals to which the founding fathers aspired remained distant.

This is one side of the story, showing the critical importance of liberal values in articulating a socioeconomic and political argument for avoidance of racial hatred and hostility. The other equally important part of the story is linked to the main pillars of what William Manning Marable characterized as a "structural racism" that draws its sustenance from "prejudice, power and privilege."[79] The prejudice was the outcome of an unquestioned belief in the natural superiority of white people over nonwhites. A belief in white racial superiority automatically degraded the blacks. According to DuBois, in the minds of white people, "darker people are dark in mind as well as in body; of dark, uncertain,

and imperfect descent; of frailer, cheaper stuff;...they have no feelings, aspirations and lovers....They are not simply dark men; they are not men in the
sense that Europeans are men."[80] By following a prejudiced argument, the
whites had, argued DuBois, exposed the artificiality of their commitment to
the fundamental liberal values on which the edifice of American constitutionalism was erected. The democratic process of government was thus crippled
"not simply through the disenfranchisement of Negros but through a process
[whereby]...power was left in the hands and under the control of the succes-
sors to the planter dynasty in the South."[81] A challenge to the liberal values, as
this argument was a testimony, was a serious threat to the creation of a milieu
in which both the white and black races intermingled in mutual appreciation
for the foundational principles of inclusive democratic framework of governance in the United States. DuBois was also aware that black commitment
to liberal values might not be an adequate shield against building up hatred
against the whites since "the worse fruit of prejudice is retaliatory prejudice
[and] the black folk have gradually adopted the reciprocal habit of hating white
skins, of being suspicious of every white action, and particularly of talking and
acting as though even those white people who are not prejudiced, or who earnestly desire not to be, belonged to the unfortunate majority."[82]

What was the way out? DuBois's solution stemmed from his uncritical faith
in the basic liberal values that remained integrally linked with the American
Declaration of Independence of 1789. In his 1897 address to the American Negro
Academy,[83] he thus proclaimed,

1. We believe that the Negro people, as a race, have a contribution to make
   to the civilization and humanity which no other race can make.
2. We believe it the duty of the Americans of Negro descent, as a body, to
   maintain their race identity until this mission of the Negro people is
   accomplished and the ideal of human brotherhood has become a practical possibility.
3. As a means to this end we advocate, not such social equality between
   these races as would disregard human likes and dislikes, but such a
   social equilibrium as would, throughout all the complicated relations of
   life, give due and just considerations to culture, ability and moral worth
   whether they be found under white or black skins.
4. We believe that the first and greatest step toward the settlement of the
   present friction between races—commonly called the Negro problem—lies in the correction immorality, crime and laziness among the
   Negroes themselves, which still remains as a heritage from slavery. We
   believe that only earnest and long continued efforts on own part can
   cure these social evils.
5. We believe that the second great step toward a better adjustment of
   the relations between the races, should be a more impartial selection
   of ability in the economic and intellectual world, and a greater respect
   for personal liberty and worth, regardless of race. We believe that only

earnest efforts on the part of the white people of this country will bring much needed reform in these matters.

6. On the basis of the foregoing declaration, and firmly believing in our high destiny, we, as American Negroes, are resolved to strive in every honourable way for the realization of the best and highest aims, for the development of strong manhood and womanhood, and for the rearing of a race ideal in America and Africa, to the glory of God and the uplifting of the Negro people.

In DuBois's conceptualization, color and race remained the twin powerful forces shaping the contemporary world. He consistently argued against color prejudices, which, he felt, were responsible for social, economic, and political turmoil in humanity. According to him,

The world problem of the 20th century is the problem of the color line [defining] the relation of the advanced races of men who happened to be white to the great majority of the undeveloped or half-developed nations of mankind who happen to be yellow, brown or black...; the question as to how far differences of race—which show themselves chiefly in the color of the skin and the texture of the hair—will hereafter be made the basis of denying to over half the world the right of sharing to their utmost ability the opportunities and privileges of modern civilization."[84]

DuBois further argued that this relationship is essentially one of domination, exploitation, and "narrow opportunity" for the people of color. Although he grew up in the majority white town of Great Barrington, Massachusetts, and received his elementary and high school education in the North, he was quite conversant with the racist discrimination that the blacks in the South encountered. He confronted racist prejudices at Fisk University in Tennessee. He found such prejudice difficult to swallow since he was "an American" too. He described his first memory of being different as "a certain suddenness that I was different from others...and shut from their world by a vast veil" [which, in his perception] contributed to a double consciousness among the whites and blacks in America." He further argued that veil became a mechanism of

always looking at one's self through the eyes of others, of measuring one's soul by the tape of a world that looks on in amused contempt and pity. One ever feels his two-ness- an American, a Negro; two souls, two thoughts, two un-reconciled strivings; two warring ideals in one dark body, whose dogged strength alone keeps it from being torn asunder.[85]

The veil was an impediment to the growth of America as "an inclusive society" because "double consciousness" along with the disenfranchisement and perpetuated ignorance about the African American community had caused "a sad havoc with the courage and faith and deeds of a significant section of the nation."[86] The most devastating effect of the veil was that "it not only divides the individual self, it also fissures the community, nation and society as a whole."[87] In order to bring about an inclusive America, DuBois challenged the paternalistic ideology of the whites while simultaneously psychologically empowering the victimized African American. The veil continued to remain because of the social milieu in which it was produced and reproduced.[88] What sustained the color line was therefore the socially justified veil, an idea that seemed to have been organically linked with the American mind-set. In his 1900 Address to the Nations of the World on behalf of the first pan-African Congress, DuBois elaborated his stance by stating that "the problem of the twentieth century is the problem of the color line, the question of how far differences of race—which show themselves chiefly in the color of skin and the texture of the hair—will hereafter be made the basis of denying to over half the world the right of sharing to their utmost ability the opportunities and privileges of modern civilization."[89] The color line is a unifying category in DuBois's thinking that never lost its salience. In his conceptualization of race, "color became synonymous with inferiority."[90] It became a designation of devaluation, degradation, and domination. Race stripped of all its pseudoscientific claims is essentially a sociobiological category used to assign human worth and social status using whites as the paradigm. In such a construction, the closer one is to the paradigm, the higher one's human worth and social status. And likewise, the farther a person or people is away from that paradigm, the lower their human worth and social status.[91] So fundamental was the concept of the color line in his overall philosophical position on racism that DuBois reiterated an identical argument as late as 1953 in his preface to the new edition of *The Souls of Black Folk* by stating that

> I still think today as yesterday that the color line is a great problem of this century. But today I see more clearly than yesterday that back of the problem of race and color, lies a greater problem which both obscures and implements it: and that is the fact that so many civilized persons are willing to live in comfort even if the price of this is poverty, ignorance and disease of the majority of their fellowmen; that to maintain this privilege men have waged war until today war tends to become universal and continuous, and the excuse for this war continues largely to be color and race.[92]

DuBois's analysis of racism and race relations seems to have significantly shaped King's conceptualization of civil rights issues. King identified three important issues in his appreciation of DuBois's contribution to reconceptualizing the Negro issue within the liberal political ideas of America's sociopolitical history. First, as King argued, by recognizing that the key to racist oppression was "the myth of Black inferiority," he exposed a carefully nurtured social lie that depicted "the black people as inferior, born deficient and deservedly doomed to servitude to the grave." This lie was sustained by "the brutality and criminality of conduct toward the Negro" and was defended by a twisted logic justifying "if the black man was inferior he was not oppressed [and] his place in society was appropriate to his meager talent and intellect." Second, King felt that history needed to attend to DuBois "[because] of his relentless fight to expose the myth-makers of Negro history." Not only was he "a tireless explorer and a gifted discoverer of social truths [he was also] one of the few scholars of America's recent history who took on alone…the propagandists who [deliberately] twisted historical facts to fulfill their partisan aim at the cost of the black people [who remained] as integrally connected with America as their white counterparts."[93] King zeroed in on the three main objectives of DuBois's campaign, namely, the right to vote, civic equality, and the education of the youth according to ability. If these three objectives were attained within the African American community, "the patriarchal color line that both economically and socially hindered [the growth of] the nation, particularly the South, would ultimately give way to progress, and eventually reform."[94] In a 1933 address, DuBois became far more militant in addressing the problem of the color line that appeared to have been accepted as "normal" even by the victims of racism. "American Negroes will be," warned DuBois,

> beaten into submission and degradation if they merely wait unorganized to find someplace voluntarily given them in the new reconstruction of the economic world. They must themselves force their race into the new economic setup…or else drift into greater poverty, greater crime, greater helplessness.[95]

Third, DuBois continued to be critically important to the history of America as a whole. He was its conscience keeper, due to his unflinching commitment to the fundamental constitutional values of American democracy, cherishing liberty, equality, and fraternity. He not only reminded "the white Americans of the importance of these great values in building our great nation," but also, by challenging their myopic vision about nationhood, he played a historical role in fulfilling an ideological mission of the founding fathers. When the white Americans, argued King, "corrupted Negro history, they distorted American history because Negroes are too big a part of the building of this nation to be written-off. White America," he further affirmed, "drenched with lies about Negroes, has lived too long in the fog of ignorance [and DuBois] gave them a gift of truth for which they should be eternally indebted to him."[96] Finally, King was indebted to DuBois because DuBois's effort to build a campaign on the local issues of class, education, and other discriminatory practices helped King to evolve a bottom-up approach to the problem of the color line. In contrast to the white-sponsored paternalistic top-down approach, deeply rooted in racial prejudice, King's approach was effective in mobilizing people against the prejudiced system of governance that sustained the color line to justify discriminatory racist practices. Furthermore, King's success in persuading a large section of the white moderates seems to have followed DuBois's strategy of not antagonizing or ostracizing one group over others. The color line was a distinct reality; nonetheless, DuBois did not pursue the argument to its logical end presumably to avoid unnecessary bitterness between the African Americans and whites. While DuBois was careful to not blame the federal government for the failures of Reconstruction, Du Bois also realized that "if anything were going to solve the problems of the African American community, the community, itself, would have to be stabilized first."[97] For the radical partners of King, such a strategy was tantamount to surrendering to the privileged whites and was thus likely to delay fulfillment of the sociopolitical goals for which African Americans were fighting. The most powerful voice was, of course, that of Malcolm X, who, while indicting King for being content with immediate gains, was never convinced of the positive (and also meaningful) roles that the white moderates were expected to play in movements challenging their sociopolitical and economic supremacy in America. Nonetheless, Du Bois remained a significant point of reference for King and his colleagues, who felt that their task was made easier with the support of the white moderates in the South. There is no doubt that the civil rights campaign became stronger with the involvement of "the exceptional white southerners who out of a moral commitment actively aided the movement [and] found themselves compelled to break with the segregationists in order to restore social peace, a good business climate, or the good name of their city in the national headlines."[98] Despite being accused of violating the Southern way of life and betraying their race, these middle-road Southerners, by their demographic strength and social standing, "undermined the credibility of the attackers."[99] Their role in the civil rights movement was undisputed, though their motives for supporting the campaign were "a mixture of altruism, pragmatism, paternalism, guilt and numerous other idiosyncratic sentiments."[100] Whatever the reasons the middle-road Southerners supported the King-led movement, the fact remains that their endorsement for demands of racial equality weakened the arguments that Malcolm X made to undermine the civil rights campaign. In fact, Malcolm X reportedly accepted the DuBois strategy of welcoming the white moderates as an effective strategy in those circumstances where the victims of oppression were demographically less preponderant than the perpetrators and also socio-economically disadvantaged.[101] He thus admitted that the application of such a strategy was thus most appropriate given the circumstances in which King organized the movement. On the whole, the civil rights movement not only created a joint platform involving even the white Southerners, but also gave the blacks confidence in their ability to successfully challenge and overcome white power structures.

AN AMERICAN DILEMMA AND ITS IMPACT

Perhaps one of the best-argued expositions of the liberal dilemma over the Negro question is Gunnar Myrdal's 1944 classic study of the contemporary socioeconomic and political circumstances responsible for racial segregation, *An American Dilemma: The Negro Problem and Modern Democracy*. Similar to DuBois, Myrdal attributed deliberate white misconceptions about blacks being socially, economically, and politically backward to the belief in the generic inferiority of the blacks. He was perplexed at the gap between democratic ideals and racial practices in America because Americans, more than any other people, were "practical idealists who wanted to be rational and just."[102] He charged Americans with deliberately distorting the principles that they held so dearly "to cover up their moral inconsistencies concerning the blacks."[103]

Gunnar Myrdal characterized the American dilemma in terms of the coexistence of American liberal ideals and the miserable situation of blacks. He saw a serious dilemma in the way "the American creed" stood in contradiction with the sociopolitical treatment of the American Negroes. As Junfu Zhang puts it, "[O]n the one hand, enshrined in the American creed is the belief that people are created equal and have human rights; on the other hand, blacks, as one tenth of the population, were treated as an inferior race and were denied numerous civil and political rights." Myrdal thus frankly concluded that "the Negro problem" is a "white man's problem," which means that the whites as a collective were responsible for the disadvantageous situation in which blacks were trapped.[104]

At the center of Myrdal's work in *An American Dilemma* was his postulate that political and social interaction in the United States is shaped by an "American Creed" that is traceable to "the Enlightenment, English law, the American Revolution (and its shining symbol, the Declaration of Independence) and Christianity."[105] This creed emphasizes the ideals of liberty, equality, justice, and fair treatment of all people. Myrdal claimed that the "American Creed" keeps the diverse melting pot of the United States together. It is the common belief in this creed that enables all people—white, Negroes, rich, poor, male, female, and foreign immigrants alike—to have a common cause and to coexist as one nation.[106] Myrdal's concept was laudable, though the reality was that the Negroes were hardly treated at par with their white counterparts. Hence Myrdal argued that individual white Americans faced a dilemma between the ideals of "the American Creed"—values of democracy and equal opportunity—and the realities of the Jim Crow laws. "The American Negroes," further argued Myrdal, "know that they are a subordinated group experiencing more than anybody else in the nation, the consequences of the fact that the Creed is not lived up to in America."[107] Myrdal failed to fathom that this subordination was evident in every walk of life because the principle that "Negroes are entitled to justice equally with all other people" had constitutional sanction and was held supreme in regard to law-making.[108] Negroes appeared to have been betrayed because they were denied what was their entitlement by virtue of being in a country that aspired to be a liberal state with no discrimination against its people. As a result, the Negroes, on their side, were

> hurt in their trust that the law is impartial, that the court and the police are their protection, and, indeed, that they belong to an orderly society which has set up this machinery for common security and welfare. They will [thus] not feel confidence in, and loyalty toward, a legal order which is entirely out

of their control and which they sense to be inequitable and merely part of the system of oppression.[109]

The Negroes suffered on counts of being both "racially inferior" and poor. In his study, Myrdal also found out that there were deficiencies in the working of "the machinery of the law" despite the fact that the ruling authority accepted the universality of the American Creed. Those who were responsible for administering justice were "not free from prejudices against people of lower economic and cultural levels" and, for historical reasons, the American blacks constituted a majority in this category. The discrimination against them was more pronounced even in the nature of punishment. As Myrdal mentioned, "[I]n matters involving offenses by Negroes against whites, Negroes will often find the presumptions of the courts against them, and there is a tendency to sentence them to a higher penalty than if they had committed the same offense against Negroes....A more serious matter is the treatment of the Negroes by the police;...Negroes are more likely than whites to be arrested under any suspicious circumstances."[110] Myrdal's assessment of the Negro situation in the United States seemed to have shaped a powerful critique of the "racist" prejudices of the white Americans toward their Negro counterparts. Violating the American Creed, the system of governance that evolved in the United States was a serious challenge to its philosophical foundations. King may not have thoroughly studied Myrdal's voluminous work, but it is evident from his critique of the racist rule in America that King had internalized the spirit of the argument. As a realistic thinker, King was aware that there was no quick solution to overcoming the system of psychological domination that had resulted from centuries of oppression and discrimination. It needed to be addressed within the liberal framework of American governance. What Myrdal saw as the American dilemma, King viewed as "the theistic dilemma." As a Christian, he believed in what is usually described as "eschatological hope," though he, as a pragmatic thinker, rejected the idea an "erroneous." He developed his argument in his essay "The Christian Pertinence for Eschatological Hope" while searching for "the spiritual meaning of four Christian concepts: the second coming of Christ, the Day of Judgment, immorality, and the Kingdom of God. He asserted that in 'a Copernican universe,' a literal interpretation of these concepts is quite absurd. And, he further added that 'we must realize that these beliefs were formulated by an unscientific people who knew nothing about a Copernican universe or any of the laws of modern science'; only the superficial optimist who refuses to face the realities of life fails to see this patent fact."[111]

Several black intellectuals, including W. E. B. DuBois, E. Franklin Frazier, Richard Wright, and Adam Clayton Powell Jr., considered Myrdal's contribution as a positive contribution to their cause. Persuaded by Myrdal's argument, King too endorsed that the ill-treatment meted out to the Negroes challenged the American creed of liberty, equality, and fraternity. His essay "The Problem of Evil," which he wrote at Crozer, explored a parallel theme of "theistic dilemma" by drawing on Myrdal's book. King found that there was a "power that is behind all things good; but on every hand the facts of life seem to contradict such a faith." As a Christian, his dilemma was centered on the contradiction between the principles of the Gospel and their implementation.

Myrdal and King shared a fundamental belief about the race issue beyond the idea that "it was a mere moral question." To address the disequilibrium in race relations, King, like Myrdal, also felt the need for a specific kind of social engineering through the creation of new institutional devices.[112] It was not an automatic process but one that required support from whites and black alike. Besides inculcating appropriate moral values, Myrdal also emphasized the need for leadership, education, and also necessary government decisions. Similar to Myrdal, King had great faith in the American judiciary, which, as Myrdal argued, "may not change the heart, but can restrain the heartless."[113] King was confident that laws were thus capable of significantly changing the habits and attitudes of the affected whites. Having endorsed the basic goodness and rationality of mankind, both King and Myrdal sought to conceptualize the racial imbroglio within the liberal framework. In other words, King shared Myrdal's optimism in seeking to institutionalize a system of governance that appreciated the blacks as integral to America. However, Myrdal's idea of a "gradual mental revolution, accompanied by adequate institutional changes" alienated radical blacks. The Swedish social scientist "envisioned a peaceful, orderly and limited revolution in racial arrangements [and] the battle would not [therefore] be one of raw power, group against group, culture against culture, but a struggle within the white conscience."[114] King appeared to have been persuaded by the spirit in which Myrdal made this argument. Hence the movement that he launched was confined to demands for legal equality and equal opportunity, later realized institutionally in the 1954 *Brown* decision and the 1964 Civil Rights Act.

REINHOLD NIEBUHR AND KING

Besides DuBois and Gunnar Myrdal, the other thinker who appeared to have had a significant influence on King's conceptualization of liberalism happens to be Reinhold Niebuhr. The neo-orthodox theologian, as King described Niebuhr, provided critical inputs to him in rejecting orthodox pessimism and liberal optimism about human nature. A liberal to the core, Niebuhr, who accepted readily "the modern Christian man as a guilty sinner," pursued a political argument in his *Moral Man and Immoral Society* to objectively comprehend the prevalent socioeconomic and political circumstances. Five major arguments that he provided to defend his position are as follows:

1. "Dominant groups indulge in hypocrisies beside the claim of their special intellectual fitness for the powers which they exercise and the privileges which they enjoy. Frequently they justify their advantages by the claim of moral rather than intellectual superiority. Thus the rising middle classes of the eighteenth and nineteenth centuries regarded

their superior advantages over the world of labor as the just rewards of a diligent and religious life."[115]

2. "Sometimes a dominant group feels itself strong enough to deny the fitness of a subject group to share its privileges without offering any evidence of a lack of qualification. The fact is asserted dogmatically without effort to prove it.... It has always been the habit of the privileged groups to deny the oppressed classes every opportunity for the cultivation of innate capacities and then to accuse them of lacking what they have been denied the right to acquire. The struggle for universal education in the nineteenth century prompted the same kind of arguments from the privileged in every country."[116]

3. "The rise of modern democracy, beginning with the eighteenth century, is sometimes supposed to have substituted the consent of the governed for the power of the royal families and aristocratic classes as the cohesive force of national society. This judgment is partly true but not nearly as true as the uncritical devotees of democracy assume [because]...the creeds and institutions of democracy have never become fully divorced from the special interests of the commercial classes who conceived and developed them. It was in their interests to destroy political restraint upon economic activity, and they therefore weakened the authority of the state and made it more pliant to their needs."[117]

4. "Society is perennially harassed not only by the fact that the coercive factors in social life (which the limitations of human intelligence and imagination make inevitable) create injustice in the processes of establishing peace; but also by the tendency of the same factors, which make for an uneasy peace within a social group, to aggravate inter-group conflict."[118]

5. "Southern whites in America usually justify their opposition to equal suffrage for the Negro on the ground of illiteracy. Yet, no Southern State gives equal facility for Negro and white education; and the educated, self-reliant Negro is hated more than the docile, uneducated one."[119]

These five points inform the Niebuhrian conceptualization of liberalism that was critical to King's understanding of liberal values and its deliberate distortion by the privileged for selfish desires. Niebuhr's major contribution to human history was, according to King, "a persistent reminder of the reality of sin on every level of human existence."[120] It was Niebuhr who, he admitted, "helped him recognize the complexity of man's social involvement and the glaring reality of collective evil."[121] Given their fundamental commitment to Christian ethics, they were keenly aware of "the complexities of human motive and of the relation between morality and power."[122] The other significant dimension in their approach to liberalism relates to the importance of love and justice as critical to politics and governance. In their thought, the relationship between ethics, power, and politics was always intertwined with their ideas on interlinkages between love and justice. This remained the fundamental point of reference for both King and Niebuhr despite having different (and also obvious) cultural perspectives in their approach to Christianity. Nonetheless, it is fair to assume that King, while taking a position vis-à-vis the American Enlightenment and liberalism, was clearly indebted to Niebuhr. His merit stemmed from the fact that not only did he, argued King, see "the problem of our age in its proper relations and dimensions [with intelligible solutions he also set] forth with rigour and profundity in analysis and criticism the fundamental weaknesses and inevitable sterility of the humanistic emphasis."[123] Justice was, as King felt, "a restraint on the sinful man to overcome his own insecurity at the expense of others; [it therefore] limits freedom to prevent its infringement upon the rights and privileges of others." Neither liberals nor orthodox Christians understood the complex relationship between love and justice or the complexities of Christian ethics. While orthodox Christianity, sensing the inevitability of sin in human conduct, remained pessimistic about the availability of pure love, liberalism was, by itself, not a panacea unless backed by a complementary mind-set. This was inconceivable due to the well-entrenched prejudices against the Negroes, who were not "even recognized as human beings." Paternalistic in their attitude toward the blacks, white Americans defended their stance by saying that Negroes "are subjugated by a superior people with an advanced way of life [and] the master race will be able to civilize them to a limited degree if only [they] will be true to [their] inferior nature and stay in [their] place."[124] Many whites thus accepted, argued an analyst, "the caste system with a sense of moral righteousness and ethical duty—as though it were the translation of the Kingdom of God."[125] Having agreed with Niebuhr's assertion that the privileged always resist change because "they are the beneficiaries of social injustice," King thus contended that "enlightened on the law of love, but insensitive to the inevitability of sin in history, liberalism vainly seeks to overcome justice through purely moral and rational suasions. Perfect justice," he further elaborates, "will not come by a simple statement of the moral superiority of brotherhood in the world, for men are controlled by power, not mind alone,…but by realistic means which must be employed to coerce society into the approximation of that ideal."[126] We required a coercive authority, drawing on Christian ethics to establish justice and love. Here King appreciated Niebuhr for being pragmatic because Christian ethics was, according to the latter, "an impossible possibility" given the difficulty in its articulation in reality. It remained "a distant goal" because human beings privilege "egoism and vested interests" while conducting themselves as part of a collectivity.

Like Niebuhr, King emphasized the importance of "government" as perhaps the only effective coercive instrument for establishing justice, given the fact that "men are controlled by power, not mind alone." As a liberal, committed to the rule of law-based governance, King, just like Niebuhr, was appreciative of a political authority that remained, at least ideologically, committed to the fulfillment of Christian ethics as described in the Sermon on the Mount. In this sense, his argument challenging a deviant government was very much Gandhian. Similar to King, Gandhi felt the necessity of an authority (not exactly government in the sense we understand today) to uniformly work for justice regardless of circumstances. Gandhi did not endorse "physical/coercive force" for justice; he considered spiritual force to be most effective. Nonetheless, the position that King held seems to have been consistent with Niebuhr's overall ideological perspective. Justifying coercion for justice, King pragmatically elaborated,

[I]f agape [selfless love which was Godly] were a historical reality in the lives of men, government, ideally would be unnecessary since forceful suasions are irrelevant wherever a love for God is perfected....Actually, however, government is very necessary, for men inevitably corrupt their potentialities of love through a lust for self-security which outruns natural needs. Men must be restrained by force, else they will swallow up their neighbours....The force of sinfulness is so stubborn a characteristic human nature that it can only be restrained when the social unit is armed with both moral and physical might.[127]

Although the government is allowed to possess adequate moral and physical strength to discharge its responsibility toward its citizens, it has to be disciplined, King forcefully argued, if it deviates from the basic norms of liberalism. In his words, "[T]he government...must never be looked upon as divine...and the reverence for government extends only as far as the purpose for which that unit was created."[128] The Christian must constantly remain vigilant toward the government, and the individual relationship with the government is thus constituted dialectically. Endorsing Niebuhr's assessment, King also saw democracy "as the most satisfactory form of collective rule [because it] arms the individual with political and constitutional power to resist the inordinate ambition of the rulers, and to check the tendency of the community to achieve order at the price of liberty."[129]

Besides his discourse on governance, King made a significant contribution in conceptualizing the dialectics between love and justice within a liberal framework of analysis, and here the ideas of Niebuhr became very critical. On the basis of his understanding of the interlinkages between love and justice in a typical Niebuhrian way, he appeared to have developed the liberal notion of justice as fairness and free from prejudices because "the essence of justice is full consideration of the claims of all parties with every system of justice resulting from compromise [since no] contending group can have all it wants or contends for, and hence must be restrained by force in its selfish aspiration."[130] Justice was "a mockery" when it was denied on the basis of artificially created and socially engineered logic, and "the system of order that results is merely the law of the ruling power which never fully considers the claims of the weaker."[131] Although King did not appear to have dealt with this issue independently, there is no doubt that this remained an important concern for him throughout his active political career. Committed to the view that love and justice were interdependent, he, like other radical theologians, including Niebuhr, criticized the white liberals' paternalistic care for the Negroes. It came out very clearly when he said that "it is not enough to say 'we love Negroes, we have many Negro friends.' They [the white liberals] must demand justice for Negroes. Love that does not satisfy justice is no love at all. It is merely a sentimental affection, little more than what [one] would have for a pet. Love at its best is justice concretized."[132] He characterized the publicized white concern for the Negro cause as "a fantasy of self-deception and comfortable vanity [given]...the apathy and disinterest in adopting legal steps to eradicate the sources of discrimination"[133] because many white men in the South "honestly believe with one side of their minds that Negroes are depraved and disease-ridden;...and they look upon any effort at equality as leading to 'mongrelization' [since] they are convinced that racial equality is a Communist idea and those who ask for it are subversive."[134] He used the same argument when he challenged the white clergymen opposing the 1963 Birmingham campaign. It was evident in his famous "Letter from Birmingham Jail" of 1963 that he was appalled at white criticism of the movement that was taking place in the city. In response, he argued that since "the whites did not express similar concern for the conditions that brought the demonstrations into being...the Negroes were left with no alternative."[135] He was thus justified in challenging the Jim Crow laws of segregation, which were "unjust because in the making of these laws, the minority who are victims had no role to play [since] they did not have the unhampered right to vote."[136] His campaign against injustice was most legitimate because he believed that "injustice anywhere is a threat to justice everywhere."[137] Like Niebuhr, who had tremendous faith in liberal legal discourse that was negatively articulated in the United States to justify discrimination against the blacks, King, while identifying the critical role of law in reconceptualizing the dialectics between love and law, said that "law cannot make a man love me, but it can keep him from lynching me."[138] In a typical Niebuhrian spirit, he further mentioned that "judicial decrees may not change the heart, but they can restrain the heartless."[139] King articulated the most clear-cut view on this complex relationship involving love, justice, and law when he defined three concepts of segregation, desegregation, and integration by saying that

[t]he word segregation represents a system that is prohibitive; it denies the Negro equal access to schools, parks, restaurants, libraries and the like. Desegregation is eliminative and negative, for it simply removes those legal and social prohibitions. Integration is creative, and is therefore more profound and far-reaching than desegregation. Integration is the positive acceptances of desegregation and the welcomed participation of Negroes into the total range of human activities.[140]

King crystallized and consolidated two important strands of his sociopolitical thought after an intellectual duel with Reinhold Niebuhr, who, despite being a product of the white cosmos of the East Coast, sought to assess the problem of racial segregation within what he considered as "objective liberalism." First, his critical reading of Niebuhr undoubtedly strengthened "his unflinching faith in liberalism" as a potentially enlightening ideology. However he believed that white liberals distorted liberalism for their selfish gain. In an identical fashion

with Gandhi, the American nonviolent activists had full faith in liberal solutions to racial discrimination, both legally and also by the sociopsychological
means of changing the prejudiced minds of whites who were unable to appreciate the core values of the Declaration of Independence, the Constitution, and
the 1863 Emancipation Proclamation. The second is a corollary of the first in the
sense that it evolved out of his effort to articulate a system of governance that
adequately fulfilled the goal of racial desegregation. Democracy, which upheld,
at least theoretically, a collective will through liberal ways of discussions, delib-
erations, and negotiations, was the form of political authority most sensitive to
his needs. If the government failed to live up to the expectations of the governed,
the citizens had every right to disobey its dictates. This is both Gandhian and
Niebuhrian in its spirit and articulation. Challenge to an unjust rule is inherently
justified to avoid further distortion in the liberal path of human governance. The
aim was not therefore to build "a separate black nation within a nation," but to
construct a true United States that was free from any kind of prejudice. As a
liberal of the Enlightenment variety, King favored the creation of a democratic
polity in which "multi-racial people are partners in power."[141] There was therefore, King argued, "no separate white path to power and fulfillment, short of
disaster, that does not share their power with black aspirations for freedom and
human dignity."[142] As it was politically useful and culturally acceptable, such a
form of government was perhaps most appropriate, King had underlined, to create a new America as it drew on the noble ideas, embodied in the Declaration of
Independence, the Constitution, and the Emancipation Proclamation. What is
unique in this dialogue between Niebuhr and King is the reconfirmation of some
of the revolutionary ideas that were rooted in the latter's faith in liberal values,
but were rearticulated in such a fashion as to gain maximum political mileage in
the context of struggles against racism in America, which historically remained
a multicultural state given the presence of the Negroes and whites.

KING'S LIBERAL CHALLENGE TO RACIAL PREJUDICES

It is true that in building a persuasive argument for his struggle against racial
discrimination, King, the activist, drew on the contributions of W. E. B. Du
Bois, Gunnar Myrdal, and Reinhold Niebuhr, among others. As will be shown
in chapter 4, his success in legally abolishing the Negroes' disenfranchisement
can be attributed to his unwavering commitment to the liberal values that created circumstances even for white Americans to oppose the Jim Crow laws. The
civil rights movement that catapulted King to the center stage was based on the
concern for social justice and basic liberal values that were critical to American
civility. For King, racial prejudice was not acceptable not because it was morally
incorrect, but because it was contrary to the fundamental liberal values that laid
the foundation for the American polity. Like Gandhi, who could not fathom the
racist nature of British colonialism, given its philosophical roots in the British
Enlightenment, King was aghast at the well-entrenched racial bias against the

American blacks since it clearly represented "a disconnect" from the exalted principles of the American Enlightenment. Besides being based on liberty, equality, and fraternity, the American Enlightment included the value of reason from the French Enlightenment tradition and also the prime social virtues of benevolence, compassion, and tolerance of the British Enlightenment.[143] The three documents that inspired King were (a) the Declaration of Independence, (b) the Constitution and (c) the 1863 Emancipation Proclamation. These documents embodied the principles and values of the natural rights tradition to which King appealed in his struggle against Jim Crow. He found in these documents profound arguments that challenged the temporal justification for racial prejudice and discrimination. He was aware that the values that informed these documents were not adequately appreciated because of specific historical circumstances; he nonetheless couched his arguments around them to draw in white compatriots who sought to correct the imbalances between these values and the system of governance that was based on these documents. While accepting them as guiding principles, what mattered to King most was "not the original intent of the founding fathers, but rather the ways in which the principles embodied in these documents could best be universalized in the present and future [which sought to project]…in his declaration that the goal of America is freedom."[144] He was not hesitant in saying that "the founding fathers of America—George Washington, Thomas Jefferson, Patrick Henry, John Quincy Adams and Abraham Lincoln were great men—but…not one of these men had a strong unequivocal belief in the equality of the black men."[145] Nonetheless, they signed "a promissory note to which every American was to fall heir [by declaring] that all men…black men as well as white men, would be guaranteed the unalienable rights of Life, Liberty and the pursuit of Happiness."[146] By challenging racial segregation and demanding racial equality King simply sought to defend his claim for social justice with reference to those fundamental principles that remained critical to the articulation of America as a nation-state.

King was able to draw white Americans to his campaign for civil rights, with its philosophical appeal to Enlightenment traditions, from which the American governance drew its sustenance. As one who was "determined to apply [his] citizenship to the fullness of its meanings,"[147] King saw himself first and foremost as an American who fought for racial equality on the basis of an understanding of American liberalism that made no distinction among the citizens on the basis of creed, color, or race. As early as 1944, he said that

"we cannot have an enlightened democracy with one great group living in ignorance. Neither could the nation be healthy with one-tenth of the people ill-nourished, sick and harbouring germs of disease, or orderly and sound with one group so ground down and thwarted that it is almost forced into unsocial attitude and crime.…We cannot come to full prosperity with one group so ill-delayed that it cannot buy goods. [And democracy] cannot succeed unless at home we give fair play and free opportunity for all people."[148]

He expressed the same concern in a letter to the editor of the *Atlanta Constitution* that he wrote in August 1946. Because the American Constitution made no distinction between races, the American Negros "are," argued King,

> entitled to the basic rights and opportunities of American citizens: the right to earn a living at work for which [they] are fitted by training and ability, equal opportunities in education, health, recreation and similar public services, the right to vote, equality before law, some of the basic courtesy and good manners that we ourselves bring to human relations.[149]

The American racial revolution, in King's view, "has been a revolution to 'get in' rather than to overthrow, [seeking] to share in the American economy, the housing market, the educational system and the social opportunities."[150] The civil rights movement that he spearheaded, along with his likeminded colleagues, was thus a serious endeavor to rearticulate the fundamental constitutional values of freedom, equality, and rights and to mobilize against a racist and deviant political authority that "dehumanized" governance to fulfill partisan aims. This was a new era of expectations that heralded efforts at reconceptualizing some of the inspiring ideals of the American independence movement by relocating their immediate socioeconomic base and ultimate philosophical roots. It was also an era of great possibilities, as old ideas endorsing racial prejudices were challenged effectively and noticeable changes in the mind-set of the significant section of the white Americans were brought about. Thus it is argued that "[t]he civil rights struggle did not consist entirely of politics and grassroots organizing, as books and documentaries on the subject have so far implied. It also implied a change in American culture, a change in what Americans thought and felt when they talked about things like freedom, equality, race and rights. It involved a change in Americans' expectations about these things, what they considered realistic as opposed to idealistic."[151] The success that King achieved in the legal abolishment of the law of segregation in 1964 was the product of sociopolitical challenges to racial discrimination as a threat to the liberal American polity. It was possible for King to at least sway the people regardless of color, creed, and clan largely because he spoke in a language that was rooted in what constituted the fundamental basis of the American system of governance.

The voice of protest that King articulated was "an inner voice," as it were, of the conscientious Americans who failed to reconcile the discriminatory laws with the high ideals of American democracy. This stance is in sharp contrast to that of another African American political activist, Malcolm X, who, despite having clearly gauged the class-related complexities of the political struggle against segregation in the Northern states, where Jim Crow laws were not operational, remained peripheral to the civil rights movement in the United States. The reasons are not difficult to comprehend, as Manning Marable elaborates in his recently published (and perhaps the most comprehensive) biography of Malcolm X.[152] The white American did not seem to be favorably disposed toward Malcolm X because he "perceived himself first and foremost as a black man, a person of African descent who happened to be a United States citizen;...he also perceived black Americans as an oppressed nation-within-a-nation, with its own culture, social institutions, and group psychology. [Hence he linked] his black consciousness to the ideological imperative of self-determination [implying that the blacks] have a natural right to decide for themselves their own destiny."[153] King's sincere commitment to liberalism was evident when he articulated his narrative of protest in the language of "nonviolence" to realize the promise of the founding fathers; Malcolm X proposed a violent path for self-defense and fulfilling the ultimate goal. In contrast with King's argument endorsing the liberal path, Malcolm X's narrative was that of "the history of structural racism— from the transatlantic slave trade to ghettoization—[and his remedy was] black reparations, compensation for the years of exploitation, blacks had endured."[154] Critical of the nonviolent challenge to a well-entrenched system of racial segregation, he saw in King's peaceful efforts "a conspiracy of the white" to weaken the radical black movements. According to him, King "is thus the best weapon that the white man who wants to brutalize Negroes, has ever gotten in this country, because he is setting up a situation where, when the white man wants to attach Negroes, they can't defend themselves because King has put this foolish philosophy out—you're not supposed to fight or you're not supposed to defend yourself."[155] He argued that the strategy of nonviolence was most suicidal in circumstances when the whites were determined "to crash the racialized minority." And, King, by pursuing a nonviolent path, provided the whites with an opportunity to fulfill their goal. That Malcolm X wanted to have nothing to do with the whites was unambiguously articulated when he stated that "[w]e want no integration with this wicked race that enslaved us. We want complete separation from this race of devils. But we should not be expected to leave America and go back to our homeland empty-handed. After four hundred years of slave labor, we have some back pay coming, a bill that owed to us that must be collected."[156] The much-hyped 1963 King-led March on Washington was not at all, according to Malcolm X, a conclusive step toward fulfilling the fundamental goal that the blacks aspired to attain. The movement was bound to fail because, as he argued, "the white liberals control the Negro and the Negro vote by controlling the Negro civil rights leaders [and] as long as they control the Negro civil rights leaders, they can also control and contain the Negro's struggle, and they can control the Negro's so-called revolt."[157] While he was convinced that the liberals' claims were vacuous, given their obvious ideological limitations, Malcolm X was also alarmed by the negative impact that the participation of whites in the march was likely to have on the African American political campaign against the racial oppression and brutality of the whites. By using the metaphor of "cream in coffee," he forcefully argued that

[i]f enough cream is poured in, eventually you don't even know that [you] had coffee in [your] cup. This is what happened with the March on Washington, led by...the Christian-Gandhian group. The whites did not integrate it; they infiltrated it. Whites joined it; they engulfed it; they

became so much a part of it, it lost its original flavour. It ceased to be a black march; it ceased to be militant; it ceased to be angry; it ceased to be impatient. In fact, it ceased to be a march; it became a picnic, an outing with a festive, circus-like-atmosphere.[158]

As is evident, both King and Malcolm X fought for black salvation, though they drew on contrasting ideologies while setting the cause of the African Americans in perspective. Like Gandhi, King largely drew on liberal values, whereas his bête-noire, Malcolm X, positioned himself differently. Unlike King, who challenged the Jim Crow laws as simply repugnant to what the founding fathers stood for to ensure liberty, equality, and fraternity, the Northern Malcolm X did not seem to appreciate the liberal method of challenging the unjust rule of the whites. For him, the only option left for the disenfranchised Negroes was to organize "an armed struggle" for self-determination that would not only settle the age-old sociopolitical imbalances in the United States but also contribute to a prejudice-free society. Despite being harshly critical of Malcolm X for his opposition to "the ideologically-reconciliatory non-violent civil rights campaign," King attributed his preference for violence to "a society that gives so many Negroes the nagging sense of 'nobodiness' and a sense of unending despair."[159] Nonetheless, true to his commitment to nonviolence, he severely criticized Malcolm X for having endorsed violence as a means to fight racial segregation, for "[f]iery demagogic oratory in the black ghettos, urging Negroes to arm themselves and prepare to engage in violence...can reap nothing but grief."[160]

THINKING ALIKE

Gandhi's and King's contextual peculiarities had a profound influence on the way each conceptualized his preferred ideological goal. British colonialism was surely a critical influence in so far as Gandhi's ideas were concerned; but the socioeconomic and political realities of India and South Africa were equally important in shaping his adoption of nonviolence as an ideology. Colonialism was surely a significant influence along with others that emerged out of the existent socioeconomic and political contexts of nineteenth and twentieth century India. King evolved his ideology in the context of the Southern states, where 70 percent of the total US African American population lived and where the Jim Crow laws were also functional. It is unclear whether King would have succeeded in the Northern states, where the blacks were not segregated (at least legally as they were in the South); but the fact that blacks were not segregated in the North does not mean that racism was absent there. The situation was far more complex in the North than in the South, where racism was clearly visible; in the North racism was more subtle and articulated in a class axis. Here the contribution of Malcolm X is immensely significant. Unlike King, who saw racism in more or less black and white terms, Malcolm X approached color prejudices not merely as a mind-set, but as inevitable in a class- divided society. King was closer to this position with the abolition of the Jim Crow laws and the promulgation of the Voting Rights Act in 1965. King approximated what Malcolm X felt by saying that "the storm...against the privileged minority...will not abate until a just distribution of the fruits of the earth enables man everywhere to live in dignity and human decency."[161] It has thus been argued that despite being located in two clearly different socioeconomic contexts, both Gandhi and King seemed to have followed the path of nonviolence because of the identical philosophical and religious dispensations that they shared. King's political language is clearly religious due to his social location as a pastor in black Christian churches in the Southern states of the United States, while Gandhi's political idioms may have had religious roots, but were always articulated in secular terms presumably because of the multiclass and religious-nationalist platform that he assiduously nurtured. King succeeded in mobilizing people for civil rights through his religious appeal, whereas Gandhi attained the nationalist goal by avoiding religious languages as far as practicable for political mobilization. Given their more or less common intellectual genealogies and ideological missions, it does not appear to be strange that both Gandhi and King came closer while conceptualizing the fundamental pillars of their respective ideologies, which are as follows:

[a] Truth and Nonviolence: Truth was God, and Gandhi always believed in envisioning the creation of Truth through nonviolence. Nonviolence and Truth were no "cloistered virtues," but were located in the human heart; hence they "seldom speak, they simply and silently act; they appeal not to the intellect," Gandhi proclaimed, "they pierce the heart." So this was not passive, but an active device for human salvation through well-designed plans and programs. Thus, Gandhi stated, [M]y ahimsa is neither maimed nor weak. It is all-powerful. Where there is ahimsa, there is Truth; and Truth is God....He is all-pervading. There is, therefore, one law for all. Wherever in the world Truth and Non-Violence reign supreme, there is peace and bliss.[162]

Nonviolence was thus a creed governed by the search for Truth. "The bravery of the non-violent," argued Gandhi, "is vastly superior to that of the violent [because] God is the shield of the non-violent."[163] While responding to a query as to how to cultivate nonviolence, the Mahatma began by saying that "the very first step in non-violence [is to] cultivate—truthfulness, humility, tolerance and loving kindness, and, above all, honesty in our daily life."[164] With all these basic human virtues, it would not be difficult even to tame the most violent persons. Nonviolence was not avoidance or

resignation from all real fighting against wickedness, [but]...is more active and more real fighting against wickedness than retaliation whose very nature is to increase wickedness. The tyrant shall be combatted not by putting up against him a sharper edged weapon, but by disappointing his expectation that there shall be no physical resistance [which] would first dazzle him, and at least compel recognition from him.[165]

The other significant ingredient of Truth-driven nonviolence was "self-suffering," which was infinitely more powerful than the law of the jungle for converting the opponent and opening his ears, which are otherwise shut to the voice of reason.[166] This was most effective because "the appeal to reason is more to the head, but the penetration of the heart comes from suffering."[167] The conviction thus rapidly grew within him that "things of fundamental importance to the people are not secured by reason alone, but have to be purchased with voluntary suffering."[168] Thus Gandhi believed that nonviolence was always a superior force because it was based on human instincts for nonviolence that became most effective in converting even the most violent person through self-suffering. This was a unique conceptualization of an equally unique method for political mobilization that Gandhi not only refined but also successfully applied in India's struggle for independence. Hence he argued that nonviolence

> is the greatest force in the world; it is the surest method of discovering the truth and it is the quickest [which] works silently, almost imperceptibly, but nonetheless surely. It is the one constructive process of Nature in the midst of incessant destruction going on about us.... There is no department of life, public or private, to which that forces cannot be applied.[169]

King's articulation was not different. As he argued, instead of combating perpetrators of violence by violence, "one of the major strengths of the nonviolent weapon is its strange power to transform and transmute the individuals who subordinate themselves to its disciplines, investing them with a cause that is larger than themselves."[170] An analysis of King's elaboration of truth and nonviolence shows that he did not differ much from Gandhi while conceptualizing these ideas in the American context, though his intellectual genealogy was different. Despite being shaped by America's rich pacifist tradition and, of course, Christian ethics, this Southern Baptist pastor reiterated some of the basic ideas that Gandhi used to defend his preference for nonviolence. He seemed to have internalized the value of nonviolence because of his uncritical faith in the Sermon on the Mount. This was evident in his statement that "he who lives by the sword will perish by the sword....we are not advocating violence. We want to love our enemies....Be good to them. Love them and let them know that you love them."[171] In the context of the 1955 Montgomery bus strike, nonviolence became an effective means of opposition, and King realized that it was more than just a method it was a specific approach to life drawing on the basic human instincts for love, compassion, and care for others. This was actually an articulation of the Sermon on the Mount, with "its sublime teaching on Jesus' love ethic."[172]

In a widely circulated note of 1957, King identified four important features of nonviolence, which are (a) nonviolence meant strict adherence to truth, which was inclusive of "honesty" and "integrity"; (b) this was an action based on "the refusal to do harm" or "renunciation of the will to kill or to damage"; (c) nonviolence was "absolute commitment to love," which was "an active out-pouring of one's whole being into the being of another"; and (d) it was based on "self-suffering," and a nonviolent protestor "resist[s] not by inflicting suffering on the opponent, but by taking suffering onto himself."[173] This was a move-ment which lifted "the love ethic of Jesus above mere interaction between indi-viduals to a powerful and effective social force on a large scale."[174] The driving force for nonviolent struggle was, for King, unconditional love. While seeking to clarify the nature of love that he had in mind, he argued that the Greek word *agape* in the New Testament approximated to his idea of love, which was "overflowing, spontaneous, unmotivated, creative and redemptive good will for all men... [whereby human beings] refuse to do anything that will defeat an individual who...does the evil deed, while hating the deed that the person does."[175] In Gandhian terms, nonviolence did not mean "meek submission to the will of the evil-doer, but it means the pitting of one's soul against the will of the tyrant."[176] In a more or less similar way, King saw nonviolence as an active method of protest that was "passive or non-aggressive in the sense that [a person clinging to nonviolence] is not physically aggressive, but strongly active spiritually."[177]

What is strikingly common between Gandhi and King was their uncritical faith in nonviolence as the key for human salvation: their conclusion was identical though their paths were different. While Gandhi drew on India's eclectic religious beliefs in support of his argument, King justified his inclination toward nonvio-lence by referring to the long-standing nonviolent traditions in Christianity.

[b] Social Justice: Integral to the sociopolitical ideas of Gandhi and King was the concern for social justice. They strongly felt that a meaningful attack on the age-old system of social discrimination was necessary to accomplish their ideological goal of human salvation. To them, the fight for political equality remained a mere "cosmetic" effort unless supplemented by an equally strong challenge against any form of injustice, visible or otherwise. Suggestive of their deep understand-ing of the social realities in which they were raised, their ideas are not only explanatory in nature, but also provide a powerful discourse challenging effectively various forms of injustice and their sources.

Both Gandhi and King were persuaded to believe that social discrimination was the outcome of prejudices seeking to justify the hegemony of one section of humanity over another. While the former challenged untouchability—which was not derivative of Hindu religious texts, but an outcome of socioeconomic processes sustaining a socioculturally divided human existence—as a social evil, King opposed racial discrimination, which was contrary to Christian ethics and also to the core values of American constitutionalism. According to Gandhi, "[N]o one can be born untouchable, as all are sparks of one and the same Fire." Untouchability was a plague [that] has to be eradicated to save Hinduism…and India.…Every Hindu, therefore who considers it a sin, should atone for it by fraternizing with untouchables, associating with them in a spirit of love and service, deeming himself purified by such acts, redressing their grievances, helping them patiently to overcome ignorance and other evil due to the slavery of ages, and inspiring other Hindus to do likewise.[178]

Untouchability was not justified in Hinduism, unless its philosophical principles were distorted with a motive. It was therefore "a curse, a blot and powerful poison that will destroy Hinduism. It is repugnant to our sense of humanity to consider a single human being as untouchable by birth."[179] Nonetheless, untouchability continued to be critical in interpersonal relationships among the Hindus, which was clearly contrary to the basic Hindu religious or ethical texts. Gandhi found neither "a warrant in reason or in the Shastras [religious texts] of untouchability [nor]…a persuasive explanation for its continuity except narrow selfish human desires."[180] Hence it had to be removed to build healthy social relationships with those who, so far, remained peripheral and also underprivileged. Mere verbal critique was not adequate to get rid of this deeply entrenched social evil; what was required of every conscious human being was "to regulate their day-to-day conduct in such a manner…to make it absolutely evident to the Harijans…that a better day has dawned for them all."[181] Gandhi believed that this was largely a matter of attitudinal change, which was possible provided the caste Hindus abdicated their prejudices toward the so-called untouchables. Untouchability "can only be removed," according to Gandhi, "when the majority of the Hindus realize that it is a crime against God and man and are ashamed of it."[182] What it required was "a process of conversion, a purification of Hindu heart."[183] Despite his serious endeavor, untouchability did not completely disappear, though Gandhi's persuasive critique remained a significant conceptual challenge to the foundation of untouchability.

A perusal of King's sociopolitical ideas also confirms that, like Gandhi, King was equally disturbed by the artificial racial segregation that challenged the very foundations of American democracy. In his "I Have a Dream" speech, he not only referred to the pernicious impact of racism on American social life, but he also set in motion a powerful movement by mobilizing the affected racialized groups. In the first part of the speech, King identifies an appalling condition in which the "manacles of segregation" and the "chains of discrimination" continue to create poverty and injustice for a segment of the population that is "languishing in the corners of American society" simply because they are "racially different." Not only was racial segregation "a blatant denial of the unity which we all have in Christ,"[184] it was also contrary to the fundamental values of American constitutional practices, as he further elaborated by saying,

When the architects of our republic wrote the magnificent words of the Constitution and the Declaration of Independence, they were signing a promissory note to which every American was to fall heir. This note was a promise that all…would be guaranteed the inalienable rights of life, liberty, and the pursuit of happiness. It is obvious today that America has defaulted on this promissory note insofar as her citizens of color are concerned.[185]

The civil rights campaign that began with Rosa Parks's refusal to give up her bus seat for a white passenger and the subsequent 1955 Montgomery bus strike finally led to the abrogation of segregation with the acceptance of the 1965 Voting Rights Act. This was a remarkable achievement, though it was not adequate to completely eradicate the sources of racial discrimination. Nonetheless, the legal sanction against racism fueled and also sustained the campaign for social justice, which was not a small achievement. As King eloquently expressed in his famous 1968 "I've Been to the Mountaintop" speech:

Like anybody, I would like to live a long life. Longevity has its place. But I am not concerned about that now. I just want to do God's will. And he has allowed me to go up to the mountain. And I've looked over. And I've seen the Promised Land. I may not get there with you. But I want you to know...that we, as a people, will get to the Promised Land.[186]

This discussion demonstrates that like Gandhi, King defended his argument for social justice with reference to Christian ethics and the values that the founding fathers held so dear. He strategically pursued this argument to accomplish the ideological goal of racial desegregation. In the case of Gandhi, the task was more difficult because his defense of the caste system contradicted his concern for the socially segregated sections among the Hindus, known as dalits in Indian parlance. This sparked off a fierce debate with his colleague, B. R. Ambedkar (described in chapter 1),[187] that caused a fissure within the nationalist political platform. For King, the situation was different since his argument was more or less endorsed by his colleagues, who also saw in his efforts a perfect strategy for mobilizing the disinherited blacks.

[c] Love and Reconciliation: Love was central to King, and truth was central to Gandhi; yet both these great men of peace spoke the language of love and drew on love and truth to organize mass movements while opposing injustices of any kind. What was unique in Gandhi and King was their ability to transform love and truth from being mere spiritual values to being instruments for political mobilization. Based on their individual beliefs, they reinvented these ideas in their specific historical context: for Gandhi, colonialism needed to be challenged because it was contrary to basic human instincts, endorsed by the core values of India's major religious communities; King saw racial segregation as an obnoxious social instrument for partisan gains, one that deviated from Christian ethics and the fundamental principles of American constitutionalism.

The Gandhian idea of ahimsa is a testimony to how love and truth are intertwined in actual human existence. Ahimsa means "both positive and active love, refraining from causing harm or destruction to living beings as well as positively promoting their well-being."[188] This suggests that by ahimsa, Gandhi did not mean merely renunciation of the will to kill or to damage, but a positive and active love and charity. Ahimsa in its positive connotation was based on the highest moral values, epitomized in "unselfish self." Gandhi thus wrote, "[A]himsa is not the crude thing it has been made to appear. Not to hurt any living things is no doubt a part of ahimsa.... [But] it is not merely a negative state of harmlessness,...it is a positive state of love, of doing good even to the evil doer."[189] For Gandhi, ahimsa was not merely a philosophical ideal, it also represented an active and energetic love leading to dedicated service to mankind. He believed that "love and active state of ahimsa requires you to resist the wrong-doer by dissociating yourself from him even though it may offend him or injure him physically."[190] It was a political weapon for the disinherited masses; as Gandhi wrote, "[A]himsa with me is a creed, the breath of life... [which] I placed before the Congress [Party] as a political weapon, to be employed for the solution of practical problems."[191]

A close look at Gandhi's concept of ahimsa shows a clear proximity with the Christian notion of charity and the Greek notion of agape, which King endorsed while mobilizing opposition against racial discrimination. Unlike Eros or *philia*, which meant love based on mutual expectation, agape referred to

> an understanding, creative, redemptive goodwill for all men. It is love that seeks nothing in return. It is an overflowing love, it's what theologians would call the love of God working in the lives of men. And when rise to love on this level, you begin to love men, not because they are likeable, but because God loves them.[192]

King's inspiration was the biblical Sermon on the Mount. He wrote that "there is power in love that our world has not discovered yet. Jesus discovered it centuries ago. Mahatma Gandhi of India discovered it a few years ago."[193] King believed that mere forgiveness of wrong-doers was not adequate and that one needed to love them. He was convinced that agape could serve as the life force of creative nonviolence because "it does not distinguish between worthy and unworthy persons; it does not distinguish between friend and enemy, but attempts to regard every man as a neighbor."[194] Hence it was possible for him to declare, "[S]end your hooded perpetrators of violence [Ku Klux Klan] into our communities at the midnight hour and drag us out on some wayside road and leave us half-dead as you beat us, and we will still love you."[195] This was further reiterated by him in his sermon entitled "The Three Dimensions of a Complete Life," in which he elaborated on the three dimensions of life in terms of "length, breadth and height"[196]: length of life was one's own concern for one's own welfare and one's desire to fulfill one's own selfish goals; breadth was about the concern for others, which was possible only after one transcended one's egocentricity; height was the driving force, because unless one had uncritical faith in God and love, one was unable to appreciate Jesus's dictum of "Love thy God with all thy heart and with all thy soul, and with all thy mind." A meaningful articulation of agape requires a fulfillment of the the second and third dimensions of life—breadth and height—because they involved "nothing in return," which held the key to Christian ethics. By referring to the oft-quoted parable of the Good Samaritan, King defended his point by saying that "unlike the priest and the Levite who passed by the wounded man, a Samaritan was a good neighbor because he was willing to help any person in distress, and he was able to look beyond external accidents to regard the stranger in need as his brother."[197]

It is now evident that Gandhi and King drew on different philosophical dispositions; nonetheless, they pursued identical aims while challenging the sources of injustice in their respective socioeconomic and political contexts. Gandhi opposed the British rule in India because "the English temperament is not responsive to a status of perfect equality with the black and brown races; then, the English must be made to retire from India."[198] True to Jesus's "universal altruism" in his magnanimous relationships with "publicans and sinners," King also saw that the increasing dehumanization in the form of discrimination, segregation, economic exploitation, and militarism "intensified the need for this kind of universal altruism" to save humanity.[199] To him, love meant devotion to Christian faith, and for a true Christian "this is at bottom the meaning of the cross."[200] It was thus possible for him to state, even in the face of a violent retaliation by the whites during the 1955 Montgomery bus strike, that "we...love our white brothers no matter what they do to us. We must make them know that we love them.... We must meet hate with love."[201] This was clearly an articulation of Christian ethics in a Gandhian way. It reinvented nonviolence not merely as a philosophical principle, but as an effective instrument to achieve a political goal in adverse circumstances.

[d] Ends and Means: Committed to nonviolence as a means, Gandhi always believed that one cannot "achieve a good end by bad means." In an identical fashion, King upheld that "means must be as pure as the end." So King's own ethical framework coincided with Gandhi's. What is fundamental here is the fact that for both Gandhi and King, the importance of ends was proportionally linked with the means: political freedom from colonialism or abolition of racial segregation was as worthy as the means of nonviolence, which could never be sacrificed under any circumstances. Gandhi's withdrawal of the 1920–22 Noncooperation Movement following the outbreak of violence in Chauri Chaura in India was a clear testimony of the extent to which he valued his faith in nonviolence. For King, it was a strategy that corresponded with the Christian ethics to which one was always committed by virtue of being a true Christian. Nonetheless, whatever may have been the etymology of their derivation, nonviolence remained supreme as a means in their endeavor at removing the sources of injustices.

In Gandhi's perception, ahimsa and truth remained integrally enmeshed. He thus argued that " without ahimsa, it is not possible to seek and find Truth. Ahimsa and Truth are so intertwined that it is practically impossible to disentangle and separate them."[202] He believed that "means to be means must always be within our reach, and so ahimsa is our supreme duty,... [and] if we take care of the means, we are bound to reach the end sooner or later.... [W]hen once we have grasped this point, final victory is beyond question."[203] His commitment to nonviolence was so deep rooted that even "harbouring uncharitable thought[s] for [one's] enemy [meant, to him] a clear departure from this doctrine."[204] In his conceptualization, conscious self-suffering remained integral to nonviolence but it never meant "meek submission to the will of the evil-doer...it [meant] the pitting of one's whole soul against the will of the tyrant: working under this law of our being, it is possible for a single individual to defy the whole might of an unjust empire."[205]

As is evident, in Gandhian perception, nonviolence and the final political goal were not dialectically linked; instead means became a crucial determinant regardless of the importance of the goal. King spoke in an identical language when he said that the first principle of the movement against racial segregation was "the idea that means must be as pure as the end [and unless]...means and ends cohere the goal shall never be accomplished." Being critical of the Machiavellian conceptualization of ends justifying the means, he further argued that "the idea of nonviolent resistance, the philosophy of nonviolent resistance, is the philosophy which says that the means must be as pure as the end, that in the long run of history, immortal destructive means cannot bring about moral and constructive ends."[206] On another occasion, he was reported to have said that "we will never have peace in the world until men everywhere recognize that ends are not cut-off from means because means represent the ideas in the making, and the end in process, and ultimately you cannot reach good ends through evil means because the means represent the seed and the end represents the tree."[207] The other significant point that came out clearly was King's endeavor at articulating the language of protest in a very Christian way. It was evident, for instance, in his sermon on November 4, 1956, when he said, "Always be sure that you struggle with Christian methods and weapons. Never succumb to the temptation of becoming bitter. As you press on for justice, be sure to move with dignity and discipline, using only the weapon of love." In this struggle against racial segregation in the land of democracy, he further exhorted,

[L]et your oppressor know that you are not attempting to defeat or humiliate him, or even to pay him back for injustices that he has heaped upon you. Let him know that you are merely seeking justice for him as well as yourself. Let him know that the festering sore of segregation debilitates the white man as well as the Negro.[208]

Only with such an attitude, would those who were fighting against racism, King felt, "be able to keep [their] struggle on high Christian standards."[209] His defence of nonviolence as a means followed the logic that Gandhi evolved though articulated in a language that had clear tilt toward Christianity. What was very striking was also King's effort at secularizing his strategy, presumably to create a broad-based sociopolitical platform. It was not therefore surprising that the goal of nonviolent resistance was not "to humiliate or defeat the opponent, but to win his friendship and his understanding" through a process of genuine reconciliation of apparently contradictory socio-economic and political forces.[210] Hence he appealed to the whites to support the campaign against racial segregation because "at the bottom,…it is a struggle not between races,…nor between seventy thousand white people and fifty thousand Negroes.…but between justice and injustice,…between the forces of light and the forces of darkness. [And], the victory in the struggle 'will not be a victory of merely sixteen million Negroes,…but a victory for justice,…a victory for goodwill,…[and] a victory for democracy."[211]

As the discussion demonstrates, two important points stand out: first, both Gandhi and King pursued a clear-cut normative point of view while presenting "the ends-means" relationships in coherent manners. Ends remained critical so long as means did not appear to deviate from the well-established principle of nonviolence. Gandhi had shown how rigid he could be in the context of the 1920–22 Noncooperation Movement; King also expressed his commitment to nonviolence in the light of massive retaliation by the white police, first in Montgomery, and later in the context of the 1963 Birmingham Movement and 1965 Selma-Montgomery March. During these events, despite being provoked by the perpetrators of violence, he remained committed to nonviolence and willingly absorbed the attack that he confronted. Secondly, it is also fair to argue that despite being committed to nonviolence, Gandhi and King seem to have drawn on rather different philosophical/ideological sources. While for Gandhi the indigenous inputs remained most critical, along with Tolstoy's religious *The Kingdom of God is within You*, which taught him the biblical Sermon on the Mount, King appreciated the biblical texts. Hence, his disquisition on the power of love as critical to nonviolence did not "draw directly from the familiar Gandhian concepts of ahimsa or satyagraha, [but]…from the Greek New Testament"[212] shaping the Christian ethics in a specific way. Gandhi was the architect of the non-violent civil resistance in India, which was built on the biblical principle of "turning the other cheek." By reiterating this principle for political mobilization against racism, King reportedly "reclaimed nonviolence for Christianity"[213]—always a critical reference for his sustained nonviolent campaign that began with the 1955 Montgomery bus strike.

[e] War and Peace: Gandhi was both a peace educator and an activist, like King. As a loyal British subject, he agreed to support the British government in South Africa in the 1906 Zulu War. He actively encouraged the recruitment of Indians for the war, which, he thought, would legitimize their claim to full citizenship.[214] The government accepted the offer to let a detachment of twenty Indians treat the wounded British soldiers. Under Gandhi's command, this corps functioned for less than two months. Nonetheless, this experience taught him how difficult it was to combat the British Empire by force—which enabled him to realize the importance of nonviolence in his fight for justice. In the First World War, he raised a nursing corps to help the wounded.

He thought that helping during the crisis would help engender support for his campaign for rights for the Indians. As he categorically
stated while defending enlisting of Indians for the war,
"[I]f we want swaraj, it is our duty to help the Empire and we shall
undoubtedly get the reward of that help. If our motive is honest, the
Government will behave honestly with us. Assuming for a moment
that it will not do so, our honesty should make us confident of our
success. It is not a mark of greatness to be good only with the good.
Greatness lies in returning good for evil."[215]

Gandhi's support for war was strategic: he assumed that assistance to the British
effort both in the 1906 Zulu War and in the First World War would help Indians
to earn their rights and that their involvement would also acquaint them with
the brutal reality of war. His position on war underwent a sea change with the
outbreak of the Second World War, when he strongly held the view that "concern for humanity is inconsistent with the recklessness with which [the war
mongers] shed their lives."[216] His letter to Hitler and also the discussion that he
had with Hitler's adviser, Ronald von Strunk, remain a clear testimony to his
well-entrenched opposition to war and uncritical acceptance of nonviolence as
perhaps the only possible means to save humanity from destruction. As he persuasively argued,

"Many of us feel that it is possible to achieve independence by non-violent
means. It would be a bad day for the whole world if we had to wade through
blood. If India gains her freedom by a class of arms, it will definitely post-
pone the day of real peace for the world....I have reasoned out the doctrine
of the sword, I have worked out its possibilities and come to the conclusion
that man's destiny is to replace the law of the jungle with the law of conscious love."[217]

The war was an evil for humanity. Gandhi was thus clear in his mind that it had
to be opposed. While questioning the use of war given its obvious pernicious
impact on human civilization, Gandhi also gave an alternative by reiterating his
uncritical faith in nonviolence. In his famous letter to Adolf Hitler, whom he
addressed as a friend, he thus firmly stated that

[w]e have found in non-violence a force, which, if organized, can without
doubt match itself against a combination of all the most violent forces in
the world. In non-violent technique,...there is no such thing as defeat; it is
all "do or die" without killing or hurting; it can be used practically without
money and obviously with the aid of science of destruction which you have
brought to such perfection.[218]

The purpose of nonviolent resistance was, according to Gandhi, not to harm or
to defeat the opponent, but to convert them. This was a positive challenge that

sought to make the British rule impossible "by nonviolent noncooperation." He felt this was sure to succeed because "it is based on the knowledge that no spoliator can compass his end without a certain degree of cooperation, willing or compulsory, of the victim."[219]

King's ideas on war and peace were articulated in the context of the Vietnam War, which he consistently opposed because it was not only contrary to his intellectual commitment to agape (the Christian notion of selfless love), but also because of the harm that it had caused to American civil life. He was appalled that "the maturity that Americans expected to display to the world" was sadly missing. He strongly felt that America was "wrong from the beginning of our adventure in Vietnam, [and] that we have been detrimental to the Vietnamese people." It was suicidal for "our great nation," King argued, if the war continued because "a nation that continues year after year to spend more money on military defense than on programs of social uplift is approaching spiritual death."[220]

As is evident, King's position on war and peace was dictated by his commitment to the love ethic of Jesus and also his appreciation for Gandhi's nonviolent resistance, which, according to him, was "the only morally and practically sound method open to the oppressed people in their struggle for freedom."[221] His opposition to the Vietnam War was thus integral to his long-drawn-out battle against violence of any kind. Besides being highly immoral, the Vietnam War had also exposed how selfish the American government was in relation to the black youths, who had been drafted for the brutal American attack in Vietnam. King argued eloquently that

[w]e were taking the black young men who had been crippled by our society and sending them eight thousand miles away to guarantee liberties in Southeast Asia which they had not found in southwest Georgia and East Harlem....The Negro and white boys...kill and die together for a nation that has been unable to seat them together in the same schools....We watch them burning the huts of a poor village, but we realize that they would never live on the same block in Detroit."[222]

What King saw in the Vietnam War was an inherent contradiction between the war and the struggle for equality at home. A discriminatory draft was draining valuable manpower from the civil rights movement and sending African American youths halfway around the world to die to protect liberties that they were denied in the South. Most of the black recruits found themselves in America's combat troops in Vietnam because of their lack of education.[223] King called this "a sordid military adventure...causing havoc with America's domestic life"[224] in which "the Negro must not allow himself to become a victim of the self-serving philosophy of those who manufacture war that the survival of the world is the white man's business alone."[225] With the draining of funds from domestic programs, King felt that "the Great Society [had become] some idle political plaything of a society gone mad on war." Appalled by the zealous support of a large section of American elites for the war, King came forward to openly oppose "the greatest purveyor of violence in the world"[226] by making people aware of the obvious adverse impact of the Vietnam conflict on the war against poverty. His attempt to link the war effort with the slow-down of the program relating to the eradication of poverty provoked a massive media attack, particularly when he compared American militarism with that of the Nazis forcing people to accept the war for an imaginary gain.[227] Instead of reacting to provocative attacks, King relentlessly carried on his campaign against the war, the main purpose of which was to initiate a revolution of values by challenging those who possessed power without compassion, who held physical might without morality, and who nurtured strength without sight.[228] King thus strongly felt that "a true revolution of values was America's only hope of conquering racism, materialism and militarism."[229]

Both Gandhi and King believed that war was detrimental to peace. Gandhi's perception of war was different because he approached the Second World War as a colonial subject and he had an obvious locational advantage since he confronted the war when he had a strong political backing from those fighting against British colonialism in India. It was easier for him to persuade his constituencies of support, presumably because of the mass opposition to colonial rule in India. It was therefore not immoral for Gandhi to launch the 1942 open rebellion against the British government when it was most vulnerable. King, however, did not have this kind of advantage, because (a) a majority of the Americans did not oppose the Vietnam War, believing that it did not affect their day-to-day life. The scene, however, changed when the number of body bags returning from Vietnam suddenly increased; and (b) the apparent split, even among those involved in the civil rights campaign, weakened King's effort at challenging the American military attack in Vietnam. Instead of opposing the war, it would have been better to support the government in crisis, as his colleagues had suggested, to fulfill the black political demands for equal voting rights and abrogation of Jim Crow in the future. King was not persuaded to do this, since he felt that his opposition to violence at home made no sense unless he raised his voice against violence perpetrated by the American state on the innocent people of Vietnam. In this sense, the point of view that King held vis-à-vis the Vietnam War was consistent with his overall ideological battle against injustice. As he argued, "Justice is indivisible....It would be rather absurd to work passionately and unrelentingly for integrated schools and not to be concerned about the survival of a world in which it was to be integrated."[230]

CONCLUDING OBSERVATIONS

This chapter revolves around two issues of tremendous theoretical significance. On the one hand, it attempts to address "the distortions" in the contemporary articulation of certain major (and also critical) liberal values shaping the sociopolitical responses toward specific groups of people. Liberalism thus became "restrictive" in its application because it was essentially a context-driven interpretation. In other words, the so-called universal of liberalism as a model of human deliberation was just cosmetic in nature. Justifying such a skewed articulation of a seemingly universal idea, the segregationists in the Southern states upheld that segregation was perhaps most appropriate for the Negroes in the long run, and hence there was nothing objectionable in such an apparently unfair system. Both Gandhi and King did not, for obvious reasons, appreciate the position taken by the segregationists to support discrimination against those who remained politically peripheral. According to them, the design of governance that defended segregation was contrary to the basic tenets of liberalism, which informed the prevalent political authority in India and the United States, respectively. It was possible for them to persuasively make the argument because of the obvious schism between the well-publicized theoretical tenets of liberalism and its articulation in reality. For Gandhi, the context of South Africa was very significant because it was in South Africa that he constructed the idea of liberal equality as an ideological goal that was equally applicable to the subjects of the British Empire. In India, the British government usually pursued "equality" among the governed by following a policy of cooption and control. This was not the case given the organic roots of racism in South Africa from which the division between blacks and whites grew. This division was an advantage for both the South African government and also its bête-noire, Gandhi: with the government becoming ruthless, it was possible for Gandhi to politically mobilize his supporters to establish "equality," or the kernel of British liberalism on which the government seemingly drew its sustenance. The situation was not very different in the case of King, who always defended his claim for racial equality by reference to the efforts, made by the architects of the republic, for the establishment of a polity drawn on the fundamental values of the liberty, equality, and fraternity. His campaign for equal treatment for the American citizens regardless of color was thus not a challenge to authority, but a serious endeavor to bring American society back to the ideological track that the founding fathers so assiduously built and nurtured.

Gandhi was also a unique intervention in liberal political philosophy for another reason: by championing the idea of secular freedom and equality, he set in motion an ideological search that was not exactly derivative of classical Western liberalism. It was an idea that was creatively interpreted in the context of the struggle for the Africans and Asians in South Africa who were denied the basic rights of freedom and equality because of the deviant nature of a so-called liberal state. Gandhi posed a clear challenge to the typical Western articulation of the basic values of liberalism that justified racial stereotypes by drawing on the Christian ideas of the value of individual, early bourgeois ideas about the transition from a state of nature to civil society, and the idea of progress that informed industrial capitalism, among others. Central to such an interpretation was a specific philosophy of history, which was endorsed by the classical exponent of liberalism, J. S. Mill. In order to justify the exclusion of the non-Europeans from the liberal framework, Mill argued that his doctrine applied "only to human beings in the maturity of their faculties" and specifically excluded "children or young

persons below the age which the law may fix as that of manhood or womanhood...who are still in a state to require being taken care of by others [and] those
backward states of society in which race itself may be considered as in its non-
age." To fulfill "this noble mission" of civilizing the backward states, Mill went
to the extent of "justifying despotism...as a legitimate mode of governance in
dealing with barbarians, provided the end be their improvement, and the means
justified by actually effecting the end."[231] The deviation from the well-defined
liberal principles was thus not a concern for alarm, but most appropriate to
meaningfully articulating liberalism in its true form! Just like children who are
disciplined by their elders, the excluded societies needed proper guidance from
those who had already attained the required level of maturity. This theoretical
argument was used to justify racial prejudices even within liberal discourse. In
other words, liberalism remained a theoretical articulation of "restrictive" freedom in the context of a growing capitalism and endorsement of racial domination by the so-called matured section of the human race at the cost of those who
were considered "racially inferior."

Gandhi and King built their critique of liberalism on the obvious logical fal-
lacy of the way exponents of exploitation viewed liberalism, based on racism and
other discriminatory designs of political nature. They also powerfully challenged
regimes that simply failed to be liberal because they clearly deviated from the
classical liberal creed. A double-edged sword, the critique not only exposed the
obvious weaknesses of the political regimes that claimed to have been drawn on
liberalism, but also enabled Gandhi and King to effectively challenge the system
of segregation which was not, at all, agreeable to the fundamental cannons of liberalism. It is true that the nature of the political challenges that Gandhi and King
spearheaded arose in radically different contexts. Nonetheless, the fundamental spirits that informed and also consolidated the protest movements in South
Africa, India, and the Southern United States were unmistakably identical: both
these great men of history found the existent political regimes arbitrary, illiberal,
and unjust within the acceptable canons of liberalism that sought to create a system of public authority. They did this not on the basis of discrimination, but by
challenging the roots of unfair rules and regulations seeking to justify artificial
segregation among human beings.

Gandhi and King built and defended their claim for racial equality by reference to the vacuous logic of classical liberalism. Human beings remained
"undifferentiated" by birth; the difference was created and sustained because of
artificially created social, psychological, and economic barriers among them to
pursue partisan goals of one group of people at the cost of the "other." Gandhi
experienced racist prejudices in their most brutal form in South Africa, and this
enabled him to creatively theorize liberalism by drawing on its undiluted spirit.
Liberalism, unless distorted, hardly allowed discrimination among human
beings on the basis of the natural biological difference of skin color. Persuaded
by this argument, King raised his voice against a state that did not live up to its
foundation, which was built on the basis of the ideas and values, enshrined in
the Declaration of Independence, the Constitution, and the 1863 Emancipation

Proclamation. Racial discrimination was simply not acceptable because it was created and also justified artificially. King thus built a powerful argument by drawing on the basic spirit of those fundamental documents that informed and also guided the republic since its formation. Not only did this argument draw the support of the victims of racism in the United States, it also considerably diluted the white opposition even in the Deep South—presumably because of the fundamentally flawed way in which it was projected as liberalism. Like Gandhi, King succeeded in challenging his opponents by creatively articulating liberalism in its true form. This caught the imagination of both his supporters and his detractors presumably because it evolved in a specific historical context that prompted evaluation of some of the fundamental tenets of the received wisdom.[232]

The second important issue relates to the conceptualization of segregation around the notion of "humiliation." The idea of segregation is directed toward deliberately humiliating others. Recently, a group of scholars focused on this dimension of human existence to meaningfully conceptualize boundaries artificially separating one section of the population from another. The effort was directed toward understanding humiliation, an almost endemic social phenomenon that "is active basically through asymmetries of intersecting sets of attitudes—arrogance and obeisance, self-respect and servility and reverence and repulsion [that] continue to survive in different forms: in the West, it is the attitude of race that is at the base of humiliation; in the East, it is the notion of untouchability that foregrounds the form and content of humiliation."[233] Untouchability is justified by canons drawn on a specific interpretation of Hinduism and sustained by sociopolitical regulations favorably disposed toward the politically dominant elites. A social segregation based on artificially created socioreligious norms is projected as normal for social equilibrium and hence is expected to not be disturbed. In the Southern states, slavery, and later segregation between the whites and blacks, remained an appropriate system simply because it was, argued forcefully by those defending discrimination, good for both the perpetrators and the victims of unjust laws of racial superiority. In the context of slavery, the inhuman treatment that was meted out to the slaves was always justified because "[t]he colored man was a prejudged culprit. The discipline of the plantation required that the difference between master and slave be never lost sight of by either. It made our master a solid mass, and fixed a common masterhood and subserviency between the ruling and the serving race. Every one of us grew up in the idea that he had, by birth and race, certain broad powers of police over any and every person of color."[234]

The sociopolitical implication of such a mind-set is devastating for it perpetuates the distinction, being justified as integral to the prevalent power-relations. It is thus argued that "[t]his perpetuation of the alien, menial relation tended to perpetuate the vices that naturally cling to servility, dense ignorance, and a hopeless separation from true liberty."[235] This is not normal, but "a paradox produced by the socially dominant elite from different societies."[236] Drawn on well-defined (but deliberately created) social norms, humiliation, involving violation of an individual's self-respect, once institutionalized, becomes a permanent source of suspicion and bitterness among the people occupying the same social space. It creates circumstances in which social institutions and practices "embody disrespect for and systematically violate the self-respect of groups of individuals."[237] Societies based on slavery, racial segregation, hierarchical status, untouchability, and the caste system are illustrative of institutionalized humiliation.

Both Gandhi and King fought for sociopolitical causes that remained integrally linked with affected groups of people subject to humiliation and suffering because of peculiar socioeconomic and political circumstances. Both figures sought to challenge the respective dominant ideological discourse since it had lost its legitimacy. It was a confluence of the context as well in the sense that both Gandhi and King launched their crusade for human salvation in circumstances where even the basic human dignity was violated for partisan reasons. It was possible for Gandhi to meaningfully challenge the political authority in South Africa and later in India simply because the context appeared to have provided him with an adequate argument demanding reform and change, if not complete overthrow. It was also not strange to find out that Gandhi, a liberal, gradually added new demands against the prevalent British state depending on what he considered most appropriate at a particular juncture of history. While constructing his model of political action, he not only drew on the Indian intellectual resources, he also relied heavily upon the Western liberal-humanist tradition. He thus displayed what Sudipta Kaviraj characterized as "a quintessentially heteronomous" mode of thought and "a particular insidious dependence" on Western categories.[238] The same appears to be true for King. Born in the segregated Southern state of Alabama, King seemed to have internalized some of the sources of racial humiliation, but never compromised with them. According to him, racial segregation was an anathema to the biblical texts and also the fundamental spirit of the American War of Independence which, by championing liberty, equality, and fraternity, never justified discrimination based on color. So, it was, as King felt, neither Christianity nor the American Enlightenment that had led to segregation, but a deliberate human design that was purposefully created to justify an artificial division among human beings. What was distinctive in both Gandhi's and King's efforts was that they built their ideological argument challenging colonial exploitation and racial segregation on the basis of an internal contradiction that appeared to have weakened the claim of liberalism as a universal ideology. They evolved a theory of political action not only on the basis of what is euphemistically called "derivative wisdom," they also tested its contemporary viability by placing it in the uncertain world of politics.[239] They were thus hardly orthodox or idea-typical, but became organic thinkers seeking to creatively conceptualize critical normative issues that seemed to have been accepted as universal. It has thus been argued that liberalism as it manifested elsewhere was "analogous and connected with Western liberalism [and yet] it was distinctly different from its classical form."[240] The significant point that emerges out of the discussion relates also to the context in which they articulated their opposition to unjust social systems and deviant political authorities; their points of view seem to have been accepted by people irrespective of class, color and creed. This is presumably because their ideas were organically connected with mind-sets that prevailed over the age-old philosophical/sociological justifications for discrimination. The ideological battle against the so-called liberals supporting discrimination and prejudices against the disinherited masses was, of course, an outcome of long-drawn processes involving both spontaneous and organized challenges and also the self-less sacrifice of human beings who never felt at ease with the artificial color line or any boundary dividing humanity for partisan gains. What made the contribution of Gandhi and King significant was their ability to comprehend liberalism in its nuanced form and also their capacity to sway the disenfranchised and underprivileged in favor of opinions challenging the prevalent power-relationship which was, so far, considered "appropriate" and also "just."

CHAPTER 3

Articulation of a New Ideology: Gandhi's Approach to Human Equality

Because he found himself virtually "a brief less" lawyer in India, Gandhi left his native country for South Africa in 1893. His South Africa sojourn not only gave him financial security, it also prepared him for a bigger role in human civilization. As a lawyer, Gandhi became a savior for the local Indians, who were being abused as coolies or "samis" by the Europeans. Gandhi gave them a voice of protest through a unique means of political action known as "satyagraha." His success in South Africa earned him the reputation of a leader who mobilized the religiously fractured Indians. By dint of sincere efforts, Hindus, Muslims, and Parsis came forward to fight against the racist government in South Africa. It was a unique achievement for an Indian who hardly knew the social characteristics of the local Indians. Within a short period, Gandhi brought them together despite differences of various kinds among them. Gandhi's political struggle in South Africa was significant in two ways: first, it enabled the Indians, who until then remained the target of racism, to fight against it under Gandhi's stewardship. Second, the protest was articulated in a unique fashion, by means of satyagraha, which was conceptualized and appeared in an embryonic form during the struggle against the racist South African regime.

Gandhi went to South Africa for a fixed assignment. But he spent twenty-one years (1893–1914) there and came back to India when he had already made a mark as a political leader who had forced the government to concede to his demands for equality for Indians in South Africa. There was no doubt that he was politically baptized in a society that saw the worst kind of racist torture by the white elites. Gandhi was persuaded to stay in South Africa by the local Indians, who found in him an able and articulate spokesman for their grievances. The South African Indians were relatively better off than the blacks, since they controlled local trade and business. Yet they were not treated on par with the whites. By joining hands with Gandhi, these local businessmen of Indian origin came together to challenge the government. So Gandhi became a symbol of protest against the humiliation of the local Indians, who were never socially recognized as equal outside the Indian fraternity. By challenging the authority, Gandhi spearheaded a campaign against the racist South African government that thrived, obviously, on various types of discrimination against the nonwhites.

His success in organizing the masses in South Africa convinced him of the importance of local issues in political mobilization. It was not, therefore, surprising that after he returned to India, Gandhi organized the peasants of Champaran (Bihar) and Kheda (Gujarat) and the workers of Ahmedabad based on their grievances against the landlords and industrialists, respectively. Gandhi launched successful campaigns against vested interests; by involving the local organizers, the strategist Gandhi sustained the movement beyond comprehension. These movements were different from those Gandhi conducted in South Africa, at least in one significant sense: these were grassroots movements seeking to redress the grievances of the peasantry and workers, who were to become major constituencies of nationalist politics. While these movements were organized against local vested interests in Champaran, Kheda, and Ahmedabad, Gandhi's campaign against the 1919 Rowlatt Act was an all-India movement that challenged the British government. The anti-Rowlatt agitation was the first movement to extend beyond the familiar domain of nationalist politics. Gandhi was anointed as the leader who mobilized the masses regardless of ethnic division. A new era of India's freedom struggle began, and new idioms of politics were articulated.

GANDHI IN SOUTH AFRICA (1893–1914)

Once in South Africa, Gandhi began confronting the racist government. Within a week of his arrival in May 1893, while he was traveling from Durban to Pretoria, he was thrown out of a first-class railway compartment despite having a genuine ticket. It was a very cold night, and he suffered terribly in the waiting room at Maritzburg station. In his words, "[D]oubt took possession of my mind. Late at night, I came to the conclusion that to run back to India would be cowardly. I must accomplish what I had undertaken."[1] He was bewildered at the outset, but was determined to fight. His experience at Charlestown, a rail terminus, was not very different. He took a stagecoach to reach Standerton. Here, too, the white officials forced him to sit on the floor, instead of on the seat for which he paid. His refusal to move out of his seat angered the officials and they physically assaulted him. He had borne the beating, but did not concede the demand. On arrival in

Standerton, he narrated his experience to his Indian friends, but was disappointed by their responses. According to them, what had happened to him was not very unusual for the Indians in the Transvaal. He reported the incident to the agent of the coach company knowing full well that no action would be taken against the assailants. He continued his journey to Pretoria. He was denied a first-class ticket by the station master of Johannesburg, who allowed Gandhi to buy a first-class railway ticket only after he defended his case by reference to railway rules and regulations. An argumentative Gandhi won the battle and began his journey for Pretoria. Here, too, he was confronted with racist white South Africans and was about to be pushed out the compartment, but for the intercession of a European fellow passenger. This lone incident of kindness was significant in shaping Gandhi's attitude toward racism. It would be wrong to dismiss the entire white population as racist, he felt. One needed to put moral pressure on the white leadership to recognize the legitimate needs and demands of the colored population.

The five-day journey from Durban to Pretoria seemed to Gandhi one of the most creative experiences of his life. He saw racism in action. He was appalled by the fate of the Indian merchants who had learned to swallow humiliation without protest. He pondered over his experience and decided not to accept injustice as part of the natural or unnatural order of South Africa. He would challenge the atrocious policies of the government simply because they had no place in the "graceful" British Empire. Racism in South Africa had been perfected by rulers who took full advantage of the Indians, who were ignorant of their rights and duties under the empire. Gandhi realized that the Indian settlers suffered largely due to the fact that they were illiterate. He felt that they needed basic English education. Moreover, Indians lost on a number of counts because they were not organized as a group and thus failed to fight the government. Gandhi translated his ideas into practice once in Pretoria. He organized a meeting of the Indians to present to them a picture of their conditions in Transvaal. It was a grand success. He broached the idea of forming an organization and volunteered to teach English to the Indian merchants.

Gandhi was preparing the Indians for a showdown with the government. However, the scene was not favorable for two reasons: (a) Transvaal, ruled by the Dutch, was a Boer state and hence was outside the orbit of the British Empire; and (b) the Boer government had already chased a large contingent of Indian settlers out of the Orange Free State. Gandhi supported the British during the Boer War because this gesture, as he thought, would strengthen the case of the Indians in South Africa to demand a fair deal in return. Hence, despite his strong opposition to the racist South African government, Gandhi articulated his bitterness during the 1890s in very mild language, which upset his colleagues who had joined him in his movement. He defended his stance as a loyal subject of the British Empire by saying that

[I]f an unflinching devotion to duty and extreme eagerness to serve our sovereign can make us of any use in the field of battle, we trust, we would not fail. . . .

The motive underlying this humble offer is to endeavour to prove that, in common with other subjects of the Queen Empress in South Africa, the Indians too, are ready to do duty for their Sovereign on the battlefield. The offer is meant to be an earnest of the Indian loyalty.[2]

... The English-speaking Indians came to the conclusion that they would offer their services unconditionally and absolutely without payment. . . in order to show the colonists that they were worthy subjects of the Queen.[3]

What is evident here is that Gandhi, who grew up in the tradition of loyalist discourse, justified his argument by reference to the duty of the subject race to the empire in crisis. But at the same time, Gandhi demanded rights for South African Indians because, as British subjects, they were entitled to rights. This is probably a watershed in Gandhi's political thinking, because it showed that he was no longer prepared to be unconditionally loyal to the British Empire. What can be argued here is that the South African experience appeared significant in identifying the limitations of a racist administration vis-à-vis the subject race. Here began Gandhi's transformation from a loyalist to a most effective political leader challenging the continuity of the Indian Raj through an organized and oppositional nonviolent mass campaign. He did this by asserting, though within the constraints of bargaining and pressure politics, the subjects' right to rebel.

His first major encounter with the colonial government came a year after his arrival in Durban, in 1894. Gandhi found out that the Natal government was pushing legislation to deprive Indians of the right to vote on grounds of race. He prepared his brief by reference to well-established British conventions and other canons of British jurisprudence. Conceding that property qualifications were not adequate to "disenfranchise" the Indians in South Africa, Gandhi argued that the denial of voting rights to the Indians was illegal and thus indefensible. He even suggested that the government might consider the scheme adopted in Cape Colony, where voting rights were granted to those possessing property worth 75 pounds and an annual income of 50 pounds. Despite the strength of the argument, Gandhi failed to persuade the Natal legislature to adopt the bill. He never conceded defeat. Gandhi decided to send a petition to the colonial secretary in London. The petition had 10,000 signatures from almost the entire population. Several copies of the petition were sent to prominent British politicians. Gandhi brought the event before the media both in Britain and in Natal. The bill was finally blocked at Westminster, and the Queen declined to give her consent. So the goal for which Gandhi fought was achieved. Two unique developments took place simultaneously. First, was the launching of the Natal Indian Congress in 1894. Despite having political goals, this was an organization that was devoted to the moral and social uplift of its members. Gradually, the Natal Congress became a lively forum for the Indian settlers, and Gandhi was undoubtedly its galvanizing force. In fact, the reduction of the annual poll tax imposed on the indentured Indian laborers from 25 pounds to 3 pounds was the first successful political achievement of the Natal Congress. The amount was enormous, given the average income of the laborers. The second development was indicative of Gandhi's rise as a strategist. Gandhi was not allowed to practice in the Supreme Court because the Bar Society of Natal prevented him from doing so. After Gandhi proved that this denial was reflective of racist bias against the Indians, the chief justice of the Supreme Court admitted him, but, in keeping with the etiquette of practicing barristers, ordered him to discard his turban in the courtroom. One could notice a change in Gandhi's attitude at this time. Just a year earlier he would have walked out of the courtroom rather than be subjected to these conditions, but now he conceded the restriction. Justifying his action as most appropriate, Gandhi thus argued,

> I saw my limitations. The turban that I had insisted on wearing in the District Magistrate's Court I took off in obedience to the order of the Supreme Court. Not that if I had resisted the order the resistance could not have been justified. But I wanted to reserve my strength for fighting bigger battles.[4]

On his return to Durban in December 1896, after a brief visit to India, Gandhi experienced another racist attack, leveled against him and those with him in the same ship. A crowd of more than 3,000 congregated to prevent him and his fellow Indian passengers from landing in the port. The crowd resolved to "burn Gandhi [since] he has vilified [white South Africans] in India and wants to flood Natal with Indians."[5] Gandhi was saved by the wife of Mr. R. C. Alexander, the "old" and "popular" superintendent of police of Durban. The scene was so inflammatory that Gandhi had "almost given up the hope of reaching home alive."[6] Finally, with the support of Mrs. Alexander, he escaped in the disguise of a constable.

The more Gandhi experienced racism, the stronger his resolve became. When in 1906, the colonial government sought to reimpose the Transvaal Asiatic Law Amendment Ordinance, which required all Indians to register with the government, Gandhi immediately resorted to action. This particular ordinance was a continuity of the 1885 Boer legislation that set up a register of Asiatics. According to this legislation, Indians were legally bound to give a "thumb-print" to obtain the right of residence. The 1906 Ordinance was more draconian than its earlier counterpart in the sense that it insisted on fingerprinting of all ten fingers; the failure to register would immediately lead to a fine, jail, or deportation. Not only was the proposed step most humiliating to the Indians, it also disillusioned Gandhi, who thought that his support of the British in the Boer War would at least change the government's attitude toward the Indians. In order to register their protest, Indians in Johannesburg gathered in the English Theatre on September 11, 1906. It was resolved that nobody would submit to this legislation. Gandhi was inspired, as he was formulating his idea of satyagraha. Interestingly, Gandhi did not lose faith in British jurisprudence as he challenged the legislation on grounds of fair play to the subjects of the crown. His statements in the September 11 meeting, moreover, also revealed his increasing sense of rebellion against colonial rule. This was evident when Gandhi welcomed imprisonment for his protest against the Immigration Restriction Act of 1907. Once the act was made a law—it came to be known as the Black Act—he launched a protest movement by refusing to register. After he was released, he went to London to persuade the government to allow at least the educated Indians to enter Transvaal. But the racist South African government would not relent. Gandhi became disillusioned, as he now saw that the empire offered slavery, not partnership.

The opposition to the Black Act contributed to Gandhi's conceptualization of satyagraha. During the Transvaal civil rights campaign (1907–1913), he had an opportunity to test and refine his unique protest movement, which had already gained momentum. Two issues figured prominently during this phase of satyagraha: (a) abolition of the Black Act and (b) removal of restrictions on the entry of Indians into Transvaal. The colonial government reacted immediately by providing verbal assurance that it would review the Black Act provided Indians registered voluntarily. Trusting the government, Gandhi thus urged his fellow Indians to register by saying that "we must register voluntarily to show that we do not intend to bring a single Indian into the Transvaal surreptitiously or by fraud."[7] Gandhi was befooled. Indians registered, but the Black Law was not outlawed. In a famous response to the government's betrayal, Gandhi led a group, on August 16, 1908, to burn thousands of registration certificates, old as well as new, outside the Haminia Mosque in Johannesburg.

A controversy arose when the Cape Supreme Court decided in 1906 to derecognize Indian marriages since they were not registered as they were in South Africa. There was no law for the registration of ordinary marriages in India, but validity of these marriages was never questioned. With Justice Malcolm Searle's judgment, Indian marriages were made null and void since they were outside the pale of legal marriages in South Africa. The judgment was disastrous because, as Gandhi argued, it "nullified in South Africa all marriages celebrated according to the Hindu, Mussalman and Zoroastrian rites."[8] The many married Indian women thus "ceased to rank as wives of their husbands and were degraded to the rank of concubines while their progeny were deprived of their right to inherit the parents' property."[9] Such an insulting judgment was bound to provoke moral outrage. As a lawyer, Gandhi petitioned the government for reconsideration of this judgment. No respite was forthcoming. The rebel Gandhi preferred satyagraha against "this unspeakable insult." Women voluntarily joined the movement against the judgment. Newcastle miners in Natal, especially indentured Indian laborers, went on strike. Gandhi's satyagraha had a new constituency. On November 6, 1913, more than two thousand protestors began their journey from Charlestown and crossed the frontier into the Transvaal to reach the Tolstoy Farm, which housed the civil resisters arrested for defying the Black Act and the immigration ban. They were arrested in Transvaal and brought back to Durban for imprisonment. This was a grand success for Gandhi's satyagraha, in which women took the leadership. So terrorized was the government that it "could not now any longer leave the Transvaal sisters," argued Gandhi, "free to pursue their activities. They too were sentenced to imprisonment for the same terms—three months—and were kept in the same prison as their male counterparts." This was a revelation to Gandhi, and prompted a radical change in his approach to gender. By agreeing to involve women in political movements as equal partners, the "orthodox" Gandhi showed appreciation for their contribution in the wider struggle against the racist government. The transformation in his views was probably due to the influence of Western feminism, given the fact that gender equality was more strongly addressed in the West than in India.[10]

Gandhian satyagraha eventually jolted the racist South African government into passing the Indian Relief Act of 1914, which abolished the requirement for the Indians to register and carry passes. It also shelved the poll tax of 3 pounds. The system of indenture was discontinued, and Indian marriages were recognized. Despite having conceded some of the principal demands of the *satyagrahis*, the racist government still stuck to its policies of immigration—both between states and into South Africa. South African experiments catapulted an unemployed barrister—as Gandhi was when he reached Durban—to the center stage of political movements among the disenfranchised.

What did Gandhi achieve in South Africa? First, there is no doubt that the South African experience made Gandhi confident and perhaps prepared him for his future struggle against British rule in India. He might not have achieved what he strove for, but he "returned home with a new method of action and a long-mediated programme for India's regeneration." Satyagraha was a new mode of protest that Gandhi crafted and tested in his struggle against racism in South Africa. The strength of satyagraha lies in human suffering. As Gandhi himself elaborated, even before satyagraha was started, satyagrahis knew that they would have to suffer even unto death, and they were ready to undergo such suffering.[11] Since the spirit of revenge was alien to satyagraha, it was best for a satyagrahi to hold his peace when he encountered extraordinary difficulties in proving the fact of his suffering. The second significant achievement was his success in mobilizing the disparate Indians in South Africa who were divided on various ethnic counts. The Indian Ambulance Corps that he created during the 1899 Boer War was illustrative of his effort in bringing the deeply divided Indians together. Given its multicultural character, the corps was characterized as "a microcosm of all classes and creeds....Hindus, Muslims, Christians and Sikhs, Madrasis and upcountrymen [sic], free Indians as well indentured labourers."[12] This tradition was firmly established in Phoenix Farm in Natal and later Tolstoy Farm in Johannesburg.[13] However, Gandhi's focus on the Indian cause prevented him from involving the non-Indian Africans as potential political allies. In defense, one can argue that Gandhi was primarily concerned with the Indians, and hence he concentrated on them. Moreover, he believed that color prejudice was something "quite contrary to the British tradition and only temporary and local."[14] He perhaps missed the serious structural implications of racism for South African society. Third, the South African experience also helped Gandhi understand the nature of Western racism in its most brutal form. By avoiding cross-cultural communications, the South African whites sought to preserve the distinct nature of their civilization. However, in Gandhi's opinion, no civilization would ever lose its dynamics simply because of contact with others; in fact, cross-cultural borrowing would enrich its contents. He was critical of the idea that "nations which do not increase their material wants are doomed to destruction."[15] This remained at the root of the Western nations' expansionist strategy. It was in pursuance of this strategy that "Western nations have settled in South Africa and subdued the numerically overwhelmingly superior races of South Africa."[16] The opposition of the Indian indentured laborers caused consternation among the white settlers who felt threatened economically by the growing importance of the Indian businessmen in trade and commerce. There was no doubt that "trade by Indians hits the British traders hard" and as a result, "the dislike of the brown races had at present become part and parcel of the mentality of the Europeans." Finally, South Africa offered a unique environment in which Gandhi made several social and political experiments which he probably could not have done in India. For instance, the Phoenix Farm that was established in Natal in 1904 translated Gandhi's vision of a society that was free from caste, clan, and ethnic prejudices. This is where Indian women were really free from patriarchal bondage; they were relatively "free" compared to their counterparts in India. Phoenix thus became

> a nursery for producing the right men [and women] and right Indians....whatever energy is put forth in Phoenix," as Gandhi wrote, "is not so much taken from India, but it is so much given to India....Phoenix is a more suitable place for making experiments and gaining proper training. Whereas in India there may be undesirable restraints, there are no such undesirable restraints in Phoenix. For instance, Indian ladies would never have come out so boldly as they are doing at Phoenix. The rest of the social customs would have been too much for them."[17]

Tolstoy Farm, which came into being in 1910, continued with the same tradition. These farms were testing grounds for Gandhi's ideas. So dear was the idea of a farm that he founded Sabarmati Ashram (near Ahmedabad) after his return to India. In India's freedom struggle, the Sabarmati Ashram continued to remain an important center of social and political activities seeking to translate Gandhi's ideas into practice.

GANDHI IN INDIA

Given his South African fame, Gandhi was already known in India even before his return. He landed in India in 1914. As a pragmatic nationalist, he decided to conduct satyagraha in a piecemeal manner in three different locations against local vested interests. While in Champaran and Kheda, he addressed peasant grievances; in Ahmedabad he mobilized the textile workers to voice their legitimate demands. Although these movements were organized around completely different issues, they were identical at least in terms of the mode of the struggle, namely satyagraha, which was being tested, for the first time, on the Indian soil.

At Champaran in Bihar, peasants raised their voice against the *tinkathia* system (according to which, European planters forced the peasants to grow indigo on three-twentieth parts of their land). This movement, which began in the 1860s, gained momentum even before the arrival of Gandhi. Led by the local middle and rich peasant leaders, the pre-Gandhian efforts failed to involve the actual cultivators. This is where Gandhi's intervention was most effective. A unique political action, the 1917 Champaran satyagraha was the first of its kind in India, and Gandhi led it in accordance with his plan and ideology. Gandhi's presence in Champaran represented hope for the *raiyats*[18] of the plantations. His act of civil disobedience and determination to endure prison convinced the peasants that the Mahatma was their savior. His extreme simplicity had brought him closer to them than all the erstwhile leaders. How he struck a chord with the peasants was surprising. Even Dr. Rajendra Prasad, who accompanied him during the Champaran movement, expressed that "it is a matter of mystery to me how these people seemed to develop the confidence that their deliverer had come."[19] His arrival in Bettiah in the Champaran region surprised not only his co-workers, but also the British sub-divisional officer, as evident in his report:

> We may look on Mr. Gandhi as an idealist, a fanatic or a revolutionary according to our particular opinions. But to the raiyats, he is their liberator, and they credit him with extraordinary powers. He moves about in the villages, asking them to lay their grievance before him, and he is daily transfiguring the imagination of masses of ignorant men with visions of an early millennium.[20]

To the masses, Gandhi meant a resurrection of hope. His nonviolent resistance provided a viable alternative in the struggle against colonialism, where force had become both illegitimate and ineffective. The Champaran satyagraha forced the government to adopt the 1918 Champaran Agricultural Act, whereby those compelled to let their land for indigo cultivation were given some relief. What Gandhi left was carried forward by local peasants, and Champaran became a strong base for nonviolent political mobilization—though the Congress leadership never allowed them to organize protests against the indigenous landlords. Despite the failure of the peasants to lead movements against the vested interests, the Champaran satyagraha articulated the neglected voice of protests. Gandhi emerged as the supreme leader, and nonviolence gained salience. This was not a subaltern protest, but one in which the subalterns were inducted into the process of political mobilization. In other words, the Champaran satyagraha represented "a battle in which many different levels of consciousness coexisted [presumably because of] the complex perspective of the participants."[21] Apart from projecting Gandhi as a perfect mobilizer, this 1917 movement also contributed to a unique multiclass political platform that prepared the clearly antagonistic classes for the battle against foreign rule. Not only did Gandhi succeed in containing the class wrath, he also created a situation in which the struggle against the exploiters coincided with the challenge against colonialism. So, Gandhian nonviolence, as the Champaran satyagraha demonstrates, provided a potent means for a legitimate and effective resistance within the new political dispensation in which the Congress was gaining in importance. The Champaran movement was a watershed in Gandhi's political life not only in terms of conceptualizing satyagraha as a device but also in terms of its application to building a political platform that transcended class.

Similar to the Champaran experiment, the 1918 Kheda satyagraha was a Gandhi-led no-revenue campaign. Rains had destroyed crops, agricultural wages had risen, there was a high rate of inflation, and there was also an outbreak of bubonic plague, all of which hit the Patidar peasants hard. They organized a movement against the government's decision not to waive land revenue. Launched by Mohanlal Pandya and Shankarlal Parikh, both of the small town of Kathlal in the district of Kheda of Gujarat, the movement gained momentum as the Gujarat Sabha, an organization under the aegis of the Congress, extended support. Once approached by the Gujarat Sabha, Gandhi arrived in Kheda in March 1918 to launch a satyagraha campaign against the government's decision to confiscate the properties of the peasants who refused to pay their land revenue. The campaign lasted for four months. In June, the government of Bombay decided not to implement the order, and the defaulters were spared. Like the Champaran satyagraha, the movement, spearheaded by the local Congress activists, continued with local support. Gandhi's presence was more symbolic than anything else. Even his lieutenants, Vallabhbhai Patel and Vitthalbhai Patel, remained insignificant in the entire movement. Instead, the local leaders were most important. Gandhi was the cementing factor, having brought the satyagrahis together for the movement, but the local leaders set the movement's agenda in their own terms. In other words, Gandhi was important in the Kheda satyagraha so long as he agreed to support the demands of local leaders. This was evident when the villagers refused Gandhi's urging for them to join the British army during the First World War.

During the Kheda satyagraha, Gandhi also participated in the Ahmedabad textile mill strike of February-March 1918. What triggered the strike was the withdrawal of plague bonuses to the workers, equivalent in some cases to 80 percent of a worker's wages. This bonus was paid to workers to dissuade them from fleeing the plague-ravaged towns. Once the epidemic was over, the mill owners decided to discontinue the practice. This decision hit workers adversely due to the spiraling rise in prices at the outbreak of the War. When the workers in Ahmedabad became restive, Gandhi was invited by Anusyya Sarabhai, a social worker who happened to be the sister of Ambalal Sarabhai, the president of the Ahmedabad Mill Owner's Association, to intervene and resolve the crisis.

Drawing on his belief that there was no major contradiction between capital and labor, Gandhi sought to defuse the crisis through dialogues with the mill owners. The mill owners appeared to be adamant and characterized Gandhi's intervention as "unwarranted." On February 22, 1918, the mill owners locked out the weavers despite Gandhi's repeated requests. With the lockout, Gandhi decided to champion the workers' cause, though he asked them to tone down their earlier demand of a 50 percent wage increase to a 35 percent increase. Although the workers agreed to Gandhi's suggestion, the mill owners did not relent, and the workers seemed to lose their morale. It was at this juncture that Gandhi began the "first" of his seventeen "fasts unto death" on March 15, 1918. This fast, which lasted for three days, forced the mill owners, who deeply respected Gandhi, to come to an agreement with the striking workers. According to the agreement suggested by the arbitration board, the workers' demand was partially fulfilled because they received a 27.5 percent wage hike. The compromise was a face-saving formula and a tactical defeat for Gandhi, though he forced the mill owners to accept the principle of arbitration in which workers' representatives, along with their employers, had a say.

A unique event in Gandhi's political life, the Ahmedabad strike added a new chapter to the Indian nationalist movement. Though critical of Gandhi's "obsession" with "passive resistance," *The Bombay Chronicle* appreciated the principle of arbitration as "a turning point in labour-employer relations in Ahmedabad" in particular and a unique system of "resolving industrial disputes" in general. *The Times* criticized Gandhi for "blackmailing" the mill owners, who admired him for his "fast unto death," though it hailed his role in articulating "arbitration" as "an effective device" to breaking the impasse between the workers and industrialists.

These three movements projected Gandhi as an emerging leader who employed different kinds of mobilizing tactics. What was common to all these movements was that (a) they were organized around local issues and (b) the importance of the local leaders couldn't be underestimated. There is no doubt that Gandhi's appearance on the scene gave a fillip to these movements. Yet if we carefully chart the movements, we will discover that Gandhi was invited to lead only after the local organizers adequately mobilized. By his involvement with these localized movements, Gandhi projected a specific kind of leadership: he was not a primary but a secondary organizer. There is no doubt that the movements attained different heights with his intervention. As was evident in Champaran and Kheda, Gandhi's intervention in elite-nationalist politics established for the first time that an authentic nationalist movement could be built upon the organized support of the peasantry, even though its political object was not what Gandhi endorsed. The peasants were meant to become "willing participants in a struggle wholly conceived and directed by others."[22] Gandhi provided "a national framework of politics in which peasants [were] mobilized but [did] not participate" in the movement's formulation. This was also true of the Ahmedabad strike, where Gandhi accommodated the interests of the mill owners even at the cost of the workers, who partially conceded their demands. Based on his belief that capital and labor are not contradictory to each other, Gandhi agreed to the negotiated settlements as probably the best solution under the circumstances, even though the workers failed to get what they had asked for. Yet Gandhi's role was most significant in articulating a form of political mobilization in which the workers were also decisive. Just like the Champaran and Kheda satyagrahas that extended the constituencies of nationalist politics by incorporating the peasantry, the Ahmedabad Textile Strike was a watershed, for it accorded a legitimate space to the workers in what was conceptualized as nationalism.

With his involvement in mass movements in Champaran, Kheda, and Ahmedabad, Gandhi forged a new language of protest for India by both building on older forms of resistance and, at the same time, accepting the colonial censure of all forms of violent protest. He emerged as a mass leader who felt the pulse of the people perhaps more keenly than anybody else during the freedom struggle. And the consequence was obvious, because it was Gandhi who transformed the struggle for freedom to a wider nationalist campaign involving various categories of people, including those who remained detached. As Jawaharlal Nehru most eloquently put it,

> [Gandhiji] attracted people. They did not agree with his philosophy of life, or even with many of his ideals. Often they did not understand him. But the action that he proposed was something tangible which could be understood and appreciated intellectually. Any action would have been welcome after the long tradition of inaction which our spineless politics had nurtured; brave and effective action with an ethical halo about it had an irresistible appeal, both to the intellect and emotions. Step by step he convinced us of the rightness of the action, and we went with him, although we did not accept his philosophy.…Gandhiji, being essentially a man of action and very sensitive to changing conditions…the road he was following was the right one thus far, and if the future meant a parting it would be folly to anticipate it.
>
> All this shows that we were by no means clear or certain in our minds. Always we had the feeling that while we might be more logical, Gandhiji knew India far better than we did, and a man who could command such tremendous devotion and loyalty must have something in him that corresponded to the needs and aspirations of the masses.[23]

GANDHI ON THE ALL-INDIA SCENE

The 1919 Rowlatt satyagraha translated Gandhian deeds into action at the pan-Indian level. Drawing on his faith in the spontaneous resistance of the masses to injustice, Gandhi was confident of the success of the campaign against the Rowlatt Act. Designed to crush the revolutionary movements in Bengal, Maharashtra, and Punjab, the 1919 Rowlatt Act authorized the British government to act sternly against those identified as terrorist groups. The act recommended (a) the amendment of the Indian Penal Code in a manner to enable the government to "check activities prejudicial to the security of the state" and also (b) to invest the ruler with the authority to short circuit "the processes of law in dealing with revolutionary crime."[24] Despite opposition by the Indian members in legislative council, the bill was adopted on March 18, 1919. Gandhi was upset with the enactment of such a draconian law and decided to challenge the government on this count. In his letter to V. S. Srinivasa Shastri, he wrote,

> I consider the Bills to be an open challenge to us. If we succumb we are done for. If we prove our word that the government will see an agitation that they have never witnessed before, we shall have proved our capacity for resistance to arbitrary or tyrannical rule....for myself if the Bills were to be proceeded with, I feel that I can no longer render peaceful obedience to the laws of a power that is capable of such a devilish legislation as these two bills, and I would not hesitate to incite those who think with me to join me in the struggle.[25]

How did Gandhi begin this movement that would catapult him to the center stage of the nationalist struggle? As a constitutionalist, he first wrote a pledge refusing to obey the act that allowed the government to act arbitrarily. He sent a telegram to the viceroy, Lord Chelmsford, explaining the reasons for his decision to launch a satyagraha against the Rowlatt Act. Finally, he addressed an open letter to "the People of India," urging them to join the satyagraha against the act.

The movement was launched on April 6, 1919. It was a watershed moment in Gandhi's political ideas in two specific ways: (a) Gandhi now realized the potential of the growing mass discontent in the anti-British struggle; and (b) this satyagraha was also a litmus test for the Mahatma, who now was confident of satyagraha as a technique for political mobilization. For Gandhi, "This retention of the Rowlatt legislation in the teeth of universal opposition is an affront to the nation. Its repeal is necessary to appease national honour." Hence he urged,

> [W]hether you are satyagrahis or not, so long as you disapprove of the Rowlatt legislation, all can join and [he was confident] that there will be such a response throughout the length and breadth of India as would convince the Government that we are alive to what is going on in our midst."[26]

The Rowlatt satyagraha was "the first country-wide" agitation against the British and it not only "transformed nationalism in India from a movement representing the classes to a movement of the masses," but it also paved the way for Gandhi's emergence as a dominant figure in Indian politics.

The movement officially began with a nationwide *hartal*[27] on April 6, 1919. It was a peaceful hartal with no reported untoward incidents. The movement, however, became violent once Gandhi was arrested on April 9. Gandhi's arrest was a preemptive measure that provoked unprecedented mass violence. For the government, it was a testing time, for it had never confronted a movement of this nature before. To contain the agitation, it therefore unleashed a reign of terror. The worst incident was the massacre of innocent people on April 13 in Jallianwallabagh in Amritsar. In order to terrorize the people participating in the movement, martial law was imposed on towns in Punjab. On this fateful day, a peaceful unarmed crowd, consisting mainly of villagers who came for a fair and had not been told of the ban on meetings, was brutally gunned down by Reginald Edward Harry Dyer, who was a British Indian army officer.[28] The killings provoked mass outrage. But Dyer's only regret before the Hunter Commission[29] was that he ran out of bullets and the narrow lanes prevented him from bringing an armored car, for "it was no longer a question of merely dispersing the crowd, but one of producing a moral effect not only on those present but more specifically throughout the Punjab."[30]

The unprecedented scale of the British response seems to have quelled the situation, and the movement showed signs of dissipation. Yet the movement caused concern to the British authority for two reasons: first, it put the British authority, for the first time, on the defensive. Second, the movement did not seem to have run out of steam even after Gandhi's arrest. Defending the spontaneous outburst against the brutal authority as "natural," a pamphlet was circulated, especially in the cities, that exhorted the people to participate in the movement against the Black Bill (the nationalists' term for the Rowlatt Act). Urging the people not to sit "idle" because

the Black Bill has been set in motion [and] the leader of the Satyagraha and a great man of action—Mahatma Gandhi—has been arrested....Now is the time to show how much inherent power the Indian possess. When man has got power to avert his own calamity, then what difficulty can there be in abrogating the Black Bill....[S]o long as the Rowlatt Bill is not repealed, every Indians should take the vow of satyagraha...and be ready to sacrifice for the cause.[31]

The movement was stronger in cities and larger towns than in rural areas. The April 6 hartal was observed most enthusiastically in almost all the Indian provinces. But the places where the movement took off were Amritsar, Gujranwala, and a number of smaller towns in Punjab; in Ahmedabad, Viramgam, and Nadiad in Gujarat; and in Delhi, Bombay, and, to a lesser extent, Calcutta. What surprised the government most was the relative tranquility in Calcutta, which was always the epicenter of the nationalist assault on the British. In a communication to the secretary to the Government of India, the chief secretary of Bengal, J. H. Kerr, wrote,

The main features of the recent disturbances have been the insignificant part played by the Bengali element, the intervention of the Marwaris, and the fraternalization of Muhammadans and Hindus, of which the most striking illustration in Calcutta was the attendance of Hindus at the meeting in the Nakhoda Mosque. [The evolution] of the Movement point[s] to the existence of some general organization...but the indications seem to be that the disturbances were organized from outside Bengal, and the attempts to rouse the mass of people against Government have certainly been less successful here than elsewhere.[32]

How did Gandhi mobilize people? Gandhi gave the Indian masses a new mantra—the mantra of satyagraha. While challenging the British during the Rowlatt satyagraha, he was supported by the Home Rule League, founded by Annie Besant and Bal Gangadhar Tilak and their followers. He also drew upon the support extended by his Muslim friends. Nevertheless, before embarking on action, Gandhi set up his own organization. The Satyagraha Sabha was constituted with its head office in Bombay on February 28, 1919. The Sabha was vested with the responsibility of conducting the campaign against the Black Bill. Yet the success of the Rowlatt satyagraha in those selective areas was largely attributed to the enthusiastic participation of the local leaders. In Bihar, Bengal, and Delhi, prominent local leaders were involved from the very beginning. Without Hasan Imam's participation in Bihar, the movement would not have gained momentum; similarly, the role of C. R. Das and Byomkesh Chakrabarti in Bengal was most significant in sustaining the momentum of the satyagraha. In Delhi, Swami Shraddhananda played a crucial role in political mobilization during the campaign. Apart from these lieutenants, who had organic links with the locals, Gandhi's success in galvanizing the masses could be attributed to his skillful exploitation of popular religious symbols. But this does not conclusively explain Gandhi's surge in popularity, for Tilak in Maharashtra and Aurobindo in Bengal before him had resorted to religious symbols for political mileage, but with limited success. What was distinctive about Gandhi was his intelligent application of symbols, religious and otherwise, that were meaningful to a cross-section of the Indian population, located at various levels of social hierarchy. Moreover, instead of endorsing the much-hyped idea of a "composite culture," Gandhi always believed that Muslims were a distinct social community. Since religion was the dominant key to loyalty among Indians, he believed that it would be politically inappropriate to dismiss it as "divisive." This is what explains the increasing participation of the Muslim leaders and their followers in the Rowlatt satyagraha and other Gandhi-led pan-Indian movements that followed. Muslims joined the movements spontaneously in Bengal, Bihar, and Punjab largely because the local Muslim leaders urged them to do so. As is evident, Gandhi emerged as an effective strategist. Not only did the campaign spread the nationalist message across the country, it was illustrative of Gandhi's capacity to draw the masses, irrespective of caste, community, and religion.

THE RISE OF GANDHI AS A PAN-INDIAN LEADER: THE NONCOOPERATION AND CIVIL DISOBEDIENCE MOVEMENTS

Gandhi inaugurated a new era in India's freedom struggle by involving people from various level of society. He was also instrumental in transforming the Indian National Congress from an urban-based organization dominated by lawyers mainly from the metropolitan cities of Calcutta and Bombay into a political party with an organizational network that reached even into villages. Gandhi's democratization of the Congress lay in extending its influence into the villages, which was essential for revitalizing the nationalist movement. The Congress, which was at first just a platform for the ventilation of grievances, became a mass organization to challenge the British government. There is no doubt that it was only under the aegis of Gandhi that the Congress metamorphosed into a giant organization whose tentacles reached all over the country. As Jawaharlal Nehru most eloquently put it,

> The whole look of the Congress changed; European clothes vanished and soon only *khadi* was to be seen; a new class of delegate, chiefly drawn from the lower middle classes, became the type of Congressmen; the language used became increasingly Hindustani, or sometimes the language of the province where the session was held, as many of the delegates did not understand English, and there was also a growing prejudice against using a foreign language in national work; and a new life and enthusiasm and earnestness became evident in Congress gatherings.[33]

The freedom struggle thus acquired a mass base in an unprecedented way. Furthermore, despite internal ideological divisions within the Congress, its nationalist goal was never compromised. Gandhi became the supreme leader, and satyagraha emerged as an effective mode of nationalist protest.

THE NONCOOPERATION MOVEMENT (1920-22)

The mobilization of the masses during the Rowlatt satyagraha was unprecedented and convinced Gandhi of the growing popular discontent against the British rule. It was not, therefore, surprising that he launched another anti-government campaign in 1920, which lasted for two years. Known as the Noncooperation Movement, it was inspired by the brilliantly simple but politically dangerous idea that, since the colonial state in India owed its sustenance to the cooperation of Indians, it would disintegrate if they withdrew support and set up alternative institutions to replace the existing ones. Following his usual style, Gandhi began the Noncooperation Movement with advance notice to the viceroy. The movement had several stages. Participants initially resigned from government services and refused to use the institutions of government and schools. Later they refused to pay taxes or serve the armed forces, and they burned foreign clothes. Gandhi was forced to adopt such stern measures as a last resort. "I can retain," argued Gandhi, "neither respect nor affection for a Government which has been moving from wrong to wrong to defend its immorality."[34] Gandhi was electric. Thousands of people, whether formally associated with the Congress or not, plunged into action against "the satanic" government. Gandhi was hailed as "a saviour" even by Rabindranath Tagore, who, despite critiquing Gandhi's strategy of burning foreign clothes, admired "the Mahatma," the title that he coined for Gandhi. Tagore said that "it is fortunate that this movement is headed by a man like Gandhi whose saintly life has made him adored all over India. As long as he is at the helm I am not doubtful of the safe arrival of the ship at the port of destination."[35]

Gandhi promised swaraj (independence) within a year if noncooperation was total and widespread. Was Gandhi unrealistic in making such a promise, as many apprehended? It was a hollow and utopian promise if we interpret it literally, as the British remained firm and strong in every respect as they had during the period of agitation against the Black Act. What was the message then? With this slogan, Gandhi sought to articulate his dream of a strong India that was capable of winning independence. For him noncooperation was (a) a way of demonstrating the hollowness of the colonial state without the cooperation of the average Indians and (b) proof that Indians were capable of managing their business with ease and comfort. There was another dimension as well. His assurance of swaraj within a year also inspired the masses to involve themselves in the anti-British movement despite the adverse consequences. He injected "freedom from fear." A new zeal of the masses was evident. Not cowed by the brutalities of the British government, the masses ventured into a "world of imagined communities" to attain the goal of independence. "The essence of his teaching was," argued Jawaharlal Nehru, "fearlessness and truth, and action allied to these, always keeping the welfare of the masses in view.... It was a psychological change, almost as if some expert in psycho-analytical methods had probed deep into the patient's past, found out the origins of his complexes, exposed them to his view, and thus rid him of that burden."[36]

The campaign began in June 1920. The first step was a *hartal* (strike) on August 1. The strike was successful, as it coincided with the death of Tilak. The Congress had, by then, a well-laid-out organizational network in the country. The Muslims had also emerged as a separate block in Indian politics. By 1920, Gandhi executed a masterstroke in going for an alliance with the Muslim leaders to strengthen the nationalist platform. The three stance that he adopted was: Punjab wrong, Khilafat wrong, and attainment of swaraj in one year. Punjab had become an emotive issue, especially after the killing of innocent people in the Jallianwalla Bagh massacre; the Khilafat issue also gained momentum because of the decision of the British government to dismantle the Ottoman Empire and to undermine the spiritual and temporal authority of the Ottoman sultan as caliph of Islam. Finally, swaraj, though ill-defined, created hopes among those fighting the British in response to Gandhi's call.

The Nocooperation-Khilafat merger was testimony to Gandhi's ability to temper rivalries and to secure cooperation among the Hindu-Muslim political leadership. As he himself explained,

I hope by my "alliance" with the Mohamedans [sic] to achieve a threefold end—to obtain justice in the face of odds with the method of Satyagraha and to show its efficacy over all other methods, to secure Mohamedans' friendship for the Hindus and thereby internal peace also, and last but not least to transform ill-will into affection for the British and their constitution which in spite of its imperfections has weathered many a storm.[37]

This statement clearly suggests the growing importance of elite Muslims as an important constituency of nationalist politics. As a true liberal, Gandhi expressed his unflinching faith in the British constitution and in the peaceful methods of satyagraha. He also realized that Hindu-Muslim unity was a prerequisite for India's future as a nation. Muslims joined hands with Gandhi to gain political mileage. Once they were recognized as a critical minority in India, neither the British nor the Congress could afford to ignore them in any negotiation for future India. Realizing the politics of "presence," Muslims also agreed to extend support to the Congress agenda that included satyagraha against the British government for "Punjab wrongs." So, for both Gandhi and the Ali brothers,[38] the brains behind the merger, the Nocooperation Movement was a master strategy for uniting Hindus and Muslims for a nationalist cause. The unity was, however, short-lived because the nucleus of politics shifted with the growing mass participation in movements against the British.

While the association with the Khilafat Movement was strategic, Gandhi's arguments against the "wrongs" in Punjab were emotionally charged. Hurt by the brutalities perpetrated in Punjab at the behest of General Dyer, he was pushed toward noncooperation as possibly the most appropriate means to challenge the government. He was appalled by the rapid deterioration of British rule, which had once epitomized fair play and justice. In 1919, he "pleaded...for cooperation with the Government" and he did so because he

honestly believed that new era was about to begin, and that the old spirit of fear, distrust and consequent terrorism was about to give place to the new spirit of respect, trust and goodwill. [He sincerely] believed that the officers that had misbehaved during the martial law regime in the Punjab would be at least dismissed and the people would be otherwise made to feel that a Government that had always been found quick (and rightly) to punish popular excesses would not fail to punish its agents' misdeeds.[39]

However, his optimism was in vain, as it soon became clear that the British government did not find the massacre in Amritsar unjustified. He minced no words while condemning the ruling authority in terms of basic human values. Defending his decision to go ahead with the noncooperation agenda even without the support of his colleagues, he argued,

Government be a source of an insufferable wrong, if the report of Lord Hunter's Committee and the two dispatches be a greater wrong by reason of their grievous [condoning] of these acts, it is clear that we must refuse to submit to this official violence. Appeal to the Parliament by all means if necessary, but if the Parliament fails us and if we are worthy to call ourselves a

nation, we must refuse to uphold the Government by withdrawing cooperation from it.[40]

On another occasion, he expressed his disillusionment with the government
for having lost the moral authority to rule. He unambiguously condemned the
British government when he stated,

> But to my amazement and dismay, I have discovered that the present rep-
> resentatives of the Empire have become dishonest and unscrupulous. They
> have no real regard for the wishes of the people of India and they count
> Indian honour as of little consequence. I can [thus] no longer retain affec-
> tion for a Government so evilly manned as it is now-a-days.[41]

Gandhi was thus persuaded to believe that the British government in India was
brutal and had "no intention of enacting the ideals of [the British] constitution."[42] He was a constitutionalist only in a limited sense: he made a representation to the government before he embarked on the campaign. In this sense,
there was continuity between the style he adopted in South Africa and the one
he used in India in the context of the Rowlatt satyagraha. But the comparison
ends there because the aim of the Noncooperation Movement in India was to
harm the British socially, economically, and politically. Gandhi had reasons to
be confident that he would succeed for four reasons. First, the Indian masses
had supported him in his campaign against the Black Act. Despite his failure
to repeal the act, Gandhi emerged as an undisputed leader who involved the
masses in the movement against the ruler. What separated Gandhi from his
erstwhile nationalist colleagues was his success in setting a common political
agenda for the people at large and thus expanding the constituencies of nationalist politics. Second, although it was a strange coincidence, Gandhi drew
political capital out of the Muslim grievances against the British for demean-
ing the caliph. By appreciating the Khilafat cause, the Mahatma created conditions for Hindu-Muslim amity, at least for a political goal. There is no doubt
that the Khilafat campaign gained significance through its merger with the
Noncooperation Movement and also by Gandhi's endorsement of the Khilafat
cause. Third, by the time the noncooperation movement was to be launched,
Gandhi had already become a nationalist leader with a considerable following
across the country. The people had followed the wide publicity that he received
after successful satyagrahas in Champaran, Kheda, and Ahmedabad. These
experiments also drew to Gandhi a group of local leaders who were inspired
by and committed to Gandhi's political ideology. Not only did they provide
Gandhi with adequate organizational support, they also created conditions for
Gandhian values to strike roots even in areas where Gandhi had hardly visited.
Fourth, by revitalizing the Congress, Gandhi had prepared a strong organizational network to pursue the nationalist goal. From a mere political platform, active only on the occasion of the annual sessions, the Congress became
a movement organized around well-defined principles and strategies. It would

not be wrong to suggest that by the time the Noncooperation Movement was launched, the Congress became Gandhian in the sense that other competitive ideologies were either peripheral or extinct for all practical purposes. It is true that the Congress translated the nationalist vision into practice by undertaking various programs in which the role of the masses was significant, but Gandhi always remained its steward.

THE NONCOOPERATION MOVEMENT: CONSOLIDATION OF GANDHI

What alarmed the administration was the impact of the boycott slogan on the government institutions as a whole; almost 80 percent of them were seriously affected between 1919 and 1921. While explaining this phenomenon, an official report admitted,

There was something in the movement that appealed to most diverse types of minds....Imagination has been fired and a spiritual uplift initiated. Something that had been wanting in our college life had been supplied....the situation presented possibilities of romance and adventure that irradiated [otherwise sterile] student life. Picketing and procession were [therefore] as irresistible to such minds as a bump supper and a "rag" to Oxford undergraduates. [Students] became for the first time conscious that they were wasting time over a kind of education not suited to their needs and leading them to an office stool.[43]

Compared with the erstwhile Congress campaign, the NonCooperation Movement demonstrated that the old closed shop of limited politics had been thrown wide open. Far greater numbers than before, from all parts of India, were participating in an overt political campaign, using a far wider range of techniques than earlier politicians had ever used simultaneously. The political nation was thus expanded to accommodate various kinds of interests that had been peripheral in the past.

An important dimension of nationalist politics unfolded with its incorporation of the working-class struggle. In 1921, there were 396 strikes involving 600,351 workers and a loss of 6,994,426 man days. Postwar recession had forced factory owners to cut production to four days a week, provoking the strikes. The C. R. Das–led Bengal Congress immediately took up the cause of the workers to sharpen its attack on the colonial state. The chain of strikes in Bengal that followed the Chandpur firing was partly attributable to the involvement of leading Congressmen like C. R. Das and J. M. Sengupta and partly due to a spontaneous uprising of the entire population, especially the lower classes, who expressed through the strikes their acute sense of economic exploitation and racial abasement under white rule. A disturbed Ronaldshay, who appeared panic stricken in view of the widespread nature of the strike, wrote,

The most disquieting feature is the extent of the hold which events have shown they have already acquired over large classes of people. They have been able to call strikes in the inland steamer lines and the Assam-Bengal Railway, and they have been able to call *hartals* in a number of east Bengal towns simultaneously.[44]

The "strike fever," as it was characterized in the official discourse, was endemic and affected primarily the industries of eastern India. Part of the reason for this lay in the fact that the leadership succeeded in attributing workers' misery principally to the European and American ownership.[45] The fact that they were generally insensitive to the grievances of the Indian workers made them an easy target for the nationalist protest. Besides, the local Congressional leadership was crucial in organizing the disparate workers, providing both ideological direction and material help. For leaders like C. R. Das and J. M. Sengupta, labor was increasingly becoming an important constituency of nationalist politics, recognized later in the 1922 Gaya Congress; and thus by championing the workers' cause, they initiated a process that signaled and articulated various contradictions in the Gandhi-led movement and widened the social base of the freedom struggle. Because strikes did not fit within his plan of nonviolent noncooperation, Gandhi, while condemning the strike fever, argued,

In India we want no political strikes....we must gain control over the unruly and disturbing elements....we seek not to destroy capital or capitalists, but to regulate the relations between capital and labour. We want to harness capital to our side. *It would be folly to encourage sympathetic strikes.*[46] (emphasis added)

The Noncooperation Movement also brought the peasants to the forefront of nationalist politics. By prioritizing village reconstruction through self-help, Gandhi articulated his plan for an economic revival "through spinning wheel and hand-woven cloth *(charkha and khadi)*, panchayats or arbitration courts, national schools and campaign for Hindu-Muslim unity and against the evils of liquor and untouchability."[47] Although these programs may not have been uniformly effective as strategies for political mobilization, they nonetheless unfolded a new process by involving a hitherto neglected section of society in a struggle that, despite its pronounced political content, was equally a battle against well-entrenched vested interests in the localities. It was not therefore surprising that the peasants of Kanika in Orissa challenged the local *zamindars*[48] for having demanded extra rent. Invoking Gandhi, the militant section of the Orissa Congress leaders organized the peasants for the establishment of "Gandhi Raj," when no one would have to pay rent; so convinced were the peasants that they boycotted and intimidated, on occasions, those who were inclined to pay rent to the zamindars. The movement, though led by the Orissa Congress, did not receive Gandhi's approval, and it was later unconditionally revoked. Gandhi was, however, inclined to encourage a no-revenue campaign in a rayatwari settlement area like Bardoil and not in any zamindari region, where it would inevitably involve "no rent." By trying to contain "no rent" campaigns, Gandhi projected a specific type of leadership that mobilized peasants exclusively and on the basis of the so-called unifying issues that transcended even well-defined boundaries among the antagonistic classes. So it was logical that Gandhi deprecated all attempts to create discord between landlords and tenants and advised the tenants to suffer rather than fight. The peasants had to join forces to fight the most powerful zamindar, namely, the government.

THE CIVIL DISOBEDIENCE MOVEMENT (1930–32)

Gandhi launched the civil disobedience movement in 1930 to challenge both British rule, which appeared to him "a perfect personification of violence," and the growing hatred toward the agents of this rule, which took the form of casual assassination' "The call of 1920," he further wrote, "was a call for preparation. The call in 1930 is for engaging in the final conflict."[49] Gandhi launched the civil disobedience movement by sending a charter of demands to the viceroy on March 2, 1930, which was as follows:

(1) total prohibition; (2) reduction of the rupee ration to Is 4d; (3) reduction of land revenue by at least 50 percent and making it subject to legislative control; (4) abolition of the salt tax; (5) reduction of military expenditure by at least 50 percent; (6) reduction of the salaries of the highest grade service to one half or less so as to suit the reduced revenue; (7) imposition of protective tariff on foreign cloth; (8) passage of the Coastal Tariff Reservation Bill; (9) discharge of all political prisoners save those condemned for murder, withdrawal of all political prosecutions and abrogation of Section 124-A, Regulation III of 1818 and the like and permission of all Indian exiles to return; (10) abolition of the CID or its popular control; and (11) issue of licenses to use firearms for self-defence, subject to popular control.

Gandhi's eleven-point ultimatum to the viceroy disappointed many leading Congressmen, including Nehru, since it contained no demand for any change in the political structure, not even the dominion status. "Bewildered" at Gandhi's charter of demands, which ultimately boiled down to a campaign for salt preparation, Nehru thought that it was a sad climb down from the *Purna Swaraj* resolution.[50] As Nehru argued, "Salt suddenly became a mysterious word, a word of power. The Salt Tax was to be attacked, the salt laws were to be broken. We were bewildered and could not quite fit in a national struggle."[51] Irwin, the viceroy, was not perturbed at all: in a letter to the secretary of state, Wedgewood Benn, he wrote, "At present the prospect of a salt campaign does not keep me awake at night."

Gandhi's eleven points incorporated the demands of almost every section of Indian society. By choosing salt as the central issue, he strove to organize

144   CONFLUENCE OF THOUGHT

an anti-British campaign in which the participation of a majority of the people was ensured, since salt was essential for everyday survival. He also included the boycott of foreign cloth as a strategy because of its effectiveness in the earlier Congressional campaigns. Hence the civil disobedience movement revolved primarily around attacks on the government salt monopoly and the boycott of foreign cloth.

On March 12, 1930, Gandhi's Salt Satyagraha began with a carefully organized month-long march covering 240 miles from Sabarmati Ashram in Ahmedabad to Dandi on the west coast of Gujarat. The Dandi March lasted until April 5 and included seventy-eight chosen volunteers. It was a campaign for freedom, following from the 1929 Lahore Congress's adoption of the complete independence resolution and authorization of the All-India Congress Committee (AICC) to launch civil disobedience. For deciding to breach the Salt Act, the government saw Gandhi as "a laughing stock involved in a kindergarten state of political revolution."[52] Salt could never become, the government was emphatic, "an issue of concern."[53] The most that could happen was that small quantities of inferior salt would be sporadically produced in some coastal areas and consumed locally—which would neither threaten the government nor affect the price of salt adversely. Nevertheless, the movement gained momentum. As Subhas Chandra Bose commented, "At every step the Mahatma received an unexpectedly warm welcome and that made the Government realize that the coming campaign would be a much more serious affair than they had thought at first."[54] Gandhi reached Dandi on April 5. With "the consummate showmanship of a great political artist,"[55] he picked up a palmful of salt in open defiance of the government and signaled his opposition to the unlawful Salt Act. In order "to cope with the emergency," the government finally arrested Gandhi on May 5 under the archaic Bombay Regulation xxv of 1827 that legalized detention without trial. Instead of dampening the enthusiasm of the participants, the arrest of the Mahatma stimulated the resistance against the government. The Congress Working Committee left with the local leadership to decide the course of action once the Mahatma was interned. In order to sustain the spirit of civil disobedience, the newspaper *Young India* thus exhorted,

Each town, each village may have…to become its own battle field. The strategy of the battle must then come to be determined by local circumstances and change with them from day to day. The sooner the workers prepare for this state of things, the earlier shall we reach the goal. They should need little guidance from outside. They know that there must be no deviation from the principles of civil disobedience as laid down by Mahatma Gandhi or from the main programme of action as fixed by the Congress.[56]

It has been argued that there was no all-India blueprint for civil disobedience in 1930-1 as there had been in the 1920–22 Noncooperation-Khilafat campaign, and as a result, the movement in practice became a series of loosely coordinated local conflicts. There is no doubt that the success of the civil disobedience campaign was largely due to the importance of salt as an emotive issue. Once the scope of the movement was extended to the breach of forest laws, the nonpayment of taxes to *ryotwari* areas, and the boycott of foreign clothes, banks, shipping and insurance companies, it took the form of a well-orchestrated campaign against British rule. No part of British India escaped, though the intensity differed widely in proportion to which the campaign addressed the local grievances.

Although the 1930 civil disobedience movement began with the breach of the salt laws, civil resistance spread to other fields. As the Mahatma marched in the villages, an intense propaganda was carried on by those involved in the campaign, who asked the people to give up service under the British government and to prepare for nonpayment of tax as well. It was not therefore surprising that the violation of the Salt Act soon became just one activity, and resistance to the government took various forms. Jawaharlal Nehru attributed this to

the promulgation of various ordinances by the Viceroy prohibiting a number of activities. As these ordinances and prohibitions grew, the opportunities for breaking them also grew and civil resistance took the form of doing the very thing that the ordinance was intended to stop.[57]

At every village where Gandhi stopped he spoke briefly. On one occasion, while reiterating the famous eleven points, he attacked the Salt Act by saying,

Who can help liking this poor man's battle? The cruel tax is not respecter of persons. It is therefore as much the interest of the Mussalmans as of the Hindu to secure its abolition. This is a fight undertaken in the name of God and for the sake of millions of paupers of this country.[58]

Besides highlighting the inhuman nature of the British government, Gandhi, in his speeches, always couched his arguments with issues relevant to village life, such as khadi,[59] cow protection, hygiene, and untouchability. He also appealed to those serving the government. By the time the Dandi March came to an end, about one-third of the 760 village headmen had resigned. This might not have seriously affected the British administration, but it was symbolically significant in the face of a seemingly strong governmental authority.

As a strategist, Gandhi succeeded in infusing popular misery with political content by attributing such misery to the oppressive nature of the Raj. Astonished by the immense popularity of the civil disobedience campaign, the moderate Tejbahadur Sapru candidly admitted,

The Congress has undoubtedly acquired a great hold on popular imaginations. On the roadside stations where until a few months ago I could hardly have suspected that people had any politics. I have seen with my eyes demonstrations and heard with my ears the usual Congress slogans. The popular feeling is one of excitement. It is fed from day to day by continuous and persistent propaganda on the part of the Congressmen—by lectures, delivered by their volunteers in running trains and similar activities....There is no doubt whatever in my mind that *there is the most intense distrust of the Government and its professions.* Indeed I have little doubt in my mind that racial feeling has been fanned to a very dangerous extent....It seems to me that the Congress is really fighting for its own supremacy in the country.[60] (emphasis added)

With a gradual expansion of its organizational network, the Congress certainly became stronger than before. For Gandhi, the violation of the salt law was the last throw of a gambler,[61] and he insisted that the risk of violence was worth it. The movement appeared inevitable given the government's refusal to concede the most humane demands of its subjects. This was unfortunate, as Gandhi himself said, because "on bended knees I asked for bread and received stones instead." Hence he repudiated the salt law and regarded it as his "sacred duty to break the mournful mandatory of compulsory peace that is choking the heart of the Nation for want of free vent."[62]

DO OR DIE: GANDHI'S ARTICULATION OF FREEDOM

The Quit India Movement was not merely another instance of the civil disobedience campaign; it was also "an open rebellion." All the past satyagraha movements, wrote the *Harijan*, were protests against "the unwanted or unapproved acts" of the Raj, the authority of which was, however, conceded. Hence, the Congress "registered protests by breaking the salt laws, forest regulations, the enforcement of section 144 Indian Penal Code, curfew orders, executive bans on meetings etc. and [we] bowed our heads to lathis of the police who represented the collective self of the people—the government, or underwent sentences of imprisonment as model prisoners etc."[63] The situation, however, changed, for as soon as "even the tacit recognition of the government by the people is consciously withdrawn, a government ceases to have any sanction and persons who attempt to exercise governmental authority are usurpers and no obedience is due to them and any punishment meted out having no sanction became the acts of ruffian."[64] The AICC resolution of August 8, 1942, demanding, in Gandhi's words, "that the British authority should end completely irrespective of the wishes or demands of various parties"[65] is certainly a significant departure from the earlier practices, when the authority of the government had political sanctions to carry out the laws such as they are, and hence was legitimate. With .the onset of the Quit India Movement, the political equation between the government and Congress underwent a radical change, with the Raj being identified as "a usurper of authority and power."[66]

The final countdown began, and the Congress leadership, including Gandhi, appealed to the provincial Congress committees to remain united in the context of the last battle for freedom. Nehru, after his trip to the United Provinces, was convinced that the forthcoming campaign was likely to attain the goal in view of the emotional attachment of the people to the cause of "independence" and the role of Gandhi in galvanizing the masses into action. In his words,

The mood of the country had changed, and from a sullen passivity it rose to a pitch of excitement and expectation. Events were not waiting for a Congress decision or resolution; they had been pushed forward by Gandhiji's utterances and now they were moving onwards with their momentum. It was clear that, whether Gandhiji was right or wrong, he had crystallised the prevailing mood of the people. There was a desperateness in it, and emotional urge which gave second place to logic and reason and a calm consideration of the consequences of action.[67]

On August 8, 1942, the AICC met in Bombay and approved what became famous as the Quit India Resolution. Harping on the familiar theme of the final British withdrawal from India, the resolution runs thus:

The perils of today. . . necessitates the independence of India and the ending of British domination. No future promises or grievances can affect the present situation or meet that peril. They cannot produce the needed psychological effect on the mind of the masses. Only the glow of freedom now can release that energy and enthusiasm of millions of people which will immediately transform the nature of the war.

The AICC therefore repeats with all emphasis the demand for the withdrawal of the British power from India....The Committee appeals to the people of India to face the dangers and hardships that will fall to their lot with courage and endurance and to hold them together under the leadership of Gandhi and carry out his instructions as disciplined soldiers of Indian freedom. They must remember that non-violence is the basis of this movement.[68]

For the Congress, India's independence was contingent on British withdrawal. What was, however, different from the past movements that the Congress had led was the Congress asking the participants to act independently in the forthcoming struggle in case the leaders were arrested. The AICC thus exhorted,

A time may come when it may not be possible to issue instructions or for instructions to reach our people and when no Congress committees can function. When this happens, every man and woman who is participating in this movement must function for himself or herself within the four corners of the general instructions issued. Every Indian who desires freedom and strives for it must be his guide urging him on along the hard road where there is no resting place and which leads ultimately to the independence and deliverance of India.[69]

The message the resolution conveyed was categorical in the sense that the AICC urged the people to take part in what was identified as "the last battle for freedom." For Gandhi, "this [was] the last struggle of [his] life" and he did not want to wait any longer because "delay is injurious and waiting any further would be humiliation for us."[70] He thus appealed to the people to follow the mantra "Do or Die":

We shall either free India or die in the attempt; we shall not live to see the perpetuation of our slavery. Every true Congressmen or [Congress] women will join the struggle with an inflexible determination not to remain alive to see the country in bondage and slavery.[71]

In a message to the nation just before his arrest, Gandhi described the task more precisely. Reiterating his faith in nonviolence, he elaborated,

Everyone is free to go the fullest length under ahimsa; complete deadlock by strikes and other non-violent means; satyagrahees must go out to die not to live; they must seek and face death; it is only when individuals go out to die that the nation will survive. *KarengeYa Marenge* [We will do or die].[72]

Neither the AICC resolution nor Gandhi's last message was allowed to be reported in the press. So there was less trouble, especially immediately after the incarceration of the entire Congress leadership, including Gandhi, than there otherwise might have been. The government strategy seemed to have worked in snatching the wind away from the Congress's sail, as Tottenham, secretary to the Government of India (Home-Political) 1942–3, prevented the Congress's message from getting across to the people. Although there were protest marches in Bombay, Gujarat, and Bengal following the adoption of the resolution, they did not pose a serious threat to the British administration. In other words, the decision to gag the press paid off at least initially and a confident viceroy sought the secretary of state's permission to deport Gandhi to save India from further crisis. When Linlithgow, India's viceroy from 1936 to 1943, put the matter before the Executive Council for discussion, the council unanimously and vigorously opposed Gandhi's deportation, which would have caused bad reactions in India and resulted in Gandhi staging a fast abroad. This would have led to a consequent crop of speculation, rumors about his ill-treatment, and so on. In view of the strong opposition of the majority of the Executive Council members, L. S. Amery, the secretary of state, did not press the issue. There were also differences of opinion at the highest level of the British administration as to whether Gandhi should be released if he undertook a fast unto death. The viceroy held the view that Gandhi should not be set free "even if he fasted to death." All the governors, except that of Sind, opposed the viceroy vehemently. R. Lumley, the Bombay governor, for instance, was "certain that it would be [the] gravest political blunder to allow him to die in detention." The governor of the Central Provinces was "emphatically of the opinion that local reactions would be most unfavourable. . . . We would be left with no friends in India and even some of the Indian members of the Superior Services will turn against us." Hence, he suggested to the viceroy "that Gandhi should be released and restricted to Sevagram if he embarks on a fast."[73]Apprehending the disastrous consequences of Gandhi's death during imprisonment, Churchill's war cabinet appeared inclined to shift Gandhi to his ashram in case of a fast, provided "he could still be isolated from the outside world at Sevagram." As there was no categorical support for his view at the highest level of the Raj, Linlithgow had no alternative but to accept that "we must be prepared in the event of a fast to set Gandhi at liberty (leaving it to himself to decide where he wants to go or whether he prefers to remain in Aga Khan's house at Poona) once [the] fast begins to endanger his life and I feel, in the circumstances, this is the best alternative."[74]

THE AUGUST REVOLUTION: A RADICAL MOVEMENT

The August movement was probably most radical in its attitude toward the British and in terms of the methods it employed. Gandhi's "Do or Die" slogan was an ultimatum to the British, leaving no space for negotiation at all. Such an attitude was absent in the noncooperation and civil disobedience movements, as the Congress leadership was always keen to settle the disputes through some kind of compromise. Gandhi, too, agreed to accept compromise even at the cost of undermining the cause he fought for; the consequences of this attitude were farreaching. On the one hand, the masses who took part in the anti-British campaign felt betrayed—something that was likely to adversely affect the future Congress mobilization. Just as Gandhi opposed radical social movements that tended to disrupt social equilibrium, he was identified as a conservative political activist who declined to disturb the foreign rule. On the other hand, both the failure of Gandhi's previous Congress movements and his success in containing them at his will strengthened the Raj in two ways: (a) due to Gandhi's commitment to nonviolence, he steered the political agitation in such a way as not to cause severe disruption in the British rule; and (b) once the political force of the movements was neutralized, the British administration was able to concentrate on controlling other radical sociopolitical movements challenging the continuity of colonialism. So, despite the apparent threat to the Raj, both the noncooperation and the civil disobedience movements let loose a political process that was conducive to the maintaining British rule. This, in turn, shaped, to a large extent, the anti-imperial movement before the onset of the open rebellion.

Whatever the implications of the past Congress-led political movements, their significance in gradually radicalizing the Congress cannot be denied. The Congress had anticipated that the nature of the August movement would be different from previous ones and hence, it was not surprising that Congress workers were instructed to capture the heightened mass radicalism. In fact, the Congress volunteers resorted to open violence in a number of cases. It is debatable whether Gandhi would have allowed such a movement to continue in view of his strong antipathy to violence. The movement became violent gradually, and British provocation played a significant role. In fact, this violence introduced another dimension to the structure of politics during the open rebellion. The movement's deviation from a true Gandhian path highlighted the autonomous path that it had taken in its articulation of aims and mobilization. These were carried out through different idioms and in the context of a completely different ideological perception. It followed a unique pattern and demonstrated new dimensions of the structure of grassroots politics. This argument seems convincing in light of the August 8 resolution and the transformation of the movement after the incarceration of the top Congress leadership.

CONCLUDING OBSERVATIONS

Gandhi's South African experience was remarkable in the way that it transformed him from a loyalist to a rebel. Once he returned to India, his strategy was different. In Champaran and Kheda, he championed the peasant causes. Supported by the local leaders, Gandhi mobilized the affected peasants against revenue remission. Similarly, in Kheda, he supported the movement of those peasants affected by the decision of the Bombay government to confiscate their property for their failure to pay tax. The Ahmedabad textile strike provided Gandhi with an opportunity to deal with the workers who were struggling for a "plague bonus." Here, the adversaries were the Gujarati mill owners, who happened to be close to him. He faced a dilemma for obvious reasons. The strategist Gandhi persuaded the workers to slash down their demand for an increase in bonuses and convinced the mill owners to accept the increase. The strike came to an end, and Gandhi gained tremendous nationwide popularity.

By the time the Rowlatt satyagraha was launched, Gandhi was totally transformed. He certainly became a rebel. He challenged the British government in India not because of the draconian nature of the Rowlatt Act, but because it would prevent Indians from seeking legal aid against governmental atrocities in the name of "fair play and justice." There is no doubt that Gandhi truly built a multiclass platform in which opposition to the British government seemed to have prevailed over other considerations. Satyagraha also became organic to his ideology of nonviolence. A new era began in which Gandhi not only wrote the script for the national freedom struggle, but also became its sole guide, if not arbiter, in the movements that followed the 1919 Rowlatt satyagraha.

The noncooperation and civil disobedience movements confirmed the growing popularity of the technique and also the acceptability of its creator. So far confined to the educated middle class, the freedom struggle percolated down to the villages during the noncooperation campaign, and Gandhi remained its supreme leader. The period 1920–32 was most significant in Gandhi's evolution for a variety of obvious reasons. He became the Mahatma and rose to prominence not merely as a nationalist leader, but also as "a great soul" of India. Based on civilizational resources, his ideology of ahimsa breathed fresh life into a nationalist movement that had become fractured due to ideological rivalries among its participants. So the emergence of Gandhi as the undisputed leader of the Congress marked a radical break with the past. Almost all the pre-Gandhian nationalist leaders were skeptical of Gandhi. By involving the masses in the anti-British campaign, Gandhi articulated a qualitatively different ideology that translated the popular grievances into action against the alien state. A new era dawned in Indian politics. N. C. Chaudhuri has commented,

The victory of Gandhism, which was the victory of a new kind of nationalism over all previous forms of rational nationalism, preached and practiced
in modern India, forces the men of all schools not only into silence but into
incomprehension.[75]

The 1942 open rebellion, or the Quit India Movement, was a confrontation of
a different type, for the Congress clung to violence as necessary to counter the
British attack. It was a mismatched battle, though, because the unarmed Congress
volunteers fought British forces that were equipped with modern weapons. This,
inter alia, is indicative of the spontaneity of the participants, who rose in revolt
against the British despite adverse consequences. For the Mahatma, the open
rebellion was a novel experiment. As shown, he launched it, but he did not guide
it, as he was incarcerated once the movement was declared. However, the course
of the movement confirms three important points that are linked with the evolution of Gandhi as a mass leader. First, despite his absence from the scene, the
movement continued unabated by drawing ideological inspiration from ahimsa.
On occasions, there were violent eruptions that too were defended in the name
of the Mahatma. This suggests the hegemonic influence of the Mahatma over
those participating in "the last war against imperialism." Second, as evident in
the earlier pan-India movements, the open rebellion was sustained by the local
Gandhians, who remained most critical in both interpreting Gandhi's message
to the Congress volunteers and then executing it. Their role was thus most crucial
in popularizing Gandhi at the grassroots level. Finally, the Quit India Movement
was a failure for the Mahatma. The withdrawal of a large section of Muslims,
especially those championing the 1940 Lahore Resolution for a separate Muslim
state, undoubtedly weakened the nationalist platform. Gandhi failed to defuse
Jinnah's separatist campaign. It would therefore not be ahistorical to suggest
that the Quit India Movement made a dent in the Mahatma's nationalist image
because Muslims preferred to support the British government during the open
rebellion.

Nonviolence, which was so far a guiding force in the Congress-led freedom
struggle, seems to have been largely undermined in the wake of the 1942 Quit
India Movement[76] due to circumstances that went beyond Gandhi's control.
Although the movement had shown symptoms of a mass upheaval, it collapsed
under a fierce imperial retaliation, owing to the military preparedness of the
British following the Second World War. In the absence of the major Congress
leaders, including Gandhi, the movement, though shortlived, took a violent turn,
which inter alia provoked ruthless military intervention by the British.[77]

The British administration seemed perplexed by the rather quick dissemination of Gandhian ideas in the remote areas, subsequently taking note of the tremendous influence of Gandhi in shaping the popular psyche. That Gandhi was
identified as a savior of the poverty-stricken masses was evident in a police report
mentioning that "the real power of his name is perhaps to be traced back to the
ideal that he who got *bedakhli* (illegal exaction) stopped in Pratapgarh in UP."[78]
Accordingly, the UP peasants were reported to have believed that Gandhi would

"provide holdings for them through ahimsa."[79] These illustrations indicate and probably justify the role of rumor in underscoring the institutionalized form of politics in the context of a transitional society like India. Underlying this is probably the explanation as to why the Gandhi-type leadership, exemplified, for instance, in Swami Prajnananda in Bengal, Swami Darshanananda in Bihar, or Baba Ramchandra in Pratapgarh, had strong religious overtones. Besides arguing that these outsiders established the crucial link between the upper and lower courses of the nationalist struggle, which had its manifestation in both the organized and unorganized worlds of politics,[80] they brought out another interesting dimension of the Gandhi-led freedom movement: the peasants, experiencing a unique period of acute strain and tension, still needed an outsider to organize themselves.

Moreover, the fact that Gandhi, unlike his predecessors, swayed the masses with his well-entrenched Indianness (in his lifestyle and political vocabulary) demonstrated an ability to translate the popular grievances into political action in the face of imperial oppression and atrocities. This is a part of the story narrating the rise of Gandhi in the context of the freedom struggle. In order to grasp the quintessence of the Mahatma as an organic leader of the nationalist movement, one needs to pay attention to the process projecting Gandhism as an ideology developed through a dialogue with rapidly changing socioeconomic and political arrangements. What is noticeable in such a construct is the absence of familiar Gandhian ideas which are justified, in turn, as being in tune with nonviolence and its concomitant value system. So what had happened in Chauri Chaura in 1922 and during the Quit India Movement in 1942, which defied the fundamental precepts of Gandhism, seems to be an offshoot of a peculiar interpenetration between ideology and reality. That Gandhism had a firm grip over the mass psyche despite tendencies otherwise was evident in the unconditional submission of those, believing in violence, to the Mahatma in both the cases. Therefore the eclipse of nonviolence and its subsequent triumph merely identify the relative weakness of the contesting ideologies which, though they posed a serious threat to nonviolence in Punjab, Maharashtra, and Bengal, appeared peripheral at the national level. Hence the historical impact of Gandhism on the evolution of nationalism was immensely significant.

By sincerely championing ahimsa, the Mahatma provided a format for articulating the anti-British sentiments in the form of satyagraha, which was probably the most appropriate strategic method of struggle at that particular juncture of India's nation-building.[81] Unlike other prevalent ideologies, Gandhism thus succeeded in providing, for the first time in nationalist politics, an ideological basis for including the whole people, irrespective of caste, class, and creed, into an imaginary construct called "political nation." In other words, not only did Gandhian nonviolence put up an effective challenge to the British domination, it also created conditions for the inclusion of the largest segment of the nation, namely the peasantry, into the Indian state that was to emerge with the eclipse of imperialism. Gandhism, with its concomitant value system, however, appropriated the, peasantry only in so far as it contributed to the nationalist struggle, conceived and directed by the Indian National Congress. Although Gandhi introduced new constituencies in the anti-British political campaign by including both the peasantry and the workers, his endeavor in an otherwise elite-dominated freedom struggle did not aim to train the masses in self-conscious attainment of power by themselves, but to solicit their cooperation in the Congress-led struggle for swaraj. That Gandhi succeeded in reinvigorating the "otherwise sterile" nationalist movement despite the ideological limitations of what he offered through nonviolence indicated the extent to which "national democracy" triumphed and other ideologies were marginalized. Notwithstanding the anti-Gandhi wave in independent India, Gandhi appeared invincible in whatever he undertook between 1920 and 1942, primarily because of the Mahatma's physical and mental affinity with the traditions and temperament of the Indian masses, which yielded results in the context of a volatile socioeconomic and political order.

CHAPTER 4

Challenging Jim Crow: King's Approach to Racial Discrimination

Despite being born in two completely different locations, both Gandhi and King confronted racial discrimination in its most brutal form—Gandhi in South Africa, where it was clearly contrary to philosophically justified British liberalism, and King in the United States, the country of liberty, fraternity, and equality. The Jim Crow laws of segregation were, for King, clearly at variance with the Declaration of Independence, the Constitution, and the 1863 Emancipation Proclamation. For King, the continuity of the legally sanctioned discriminatory practices not only threatened the foundational basis of the state in America, it also considerably weakened its claim of being liberal. It was thus natural for King, just like Gandhi, to oppose the system of segregation because it was hardly justified in the light of the basic canons of American democracy.

King had a very protected life when he was young. He was nurtured by a family that instilled in him the finer values of love, compassion, and empathy for others. As he elaborated in his *Autobiography*,

[I]t was quite easy for me to think of a God of love mainly because I grew up in a family where love was central and where lovely relationships were ever present. It is quite easy for me to think of the universe as basically friendly mainly because of my uplifting hereditary and environmental circumstances. It is quite easy for me to lean more toward optimism than pessimism about human nature mainly because of my childhood experiences.[1]

He was influenced by his father, who was a pastor of the Ebenezer Baptist Church. As the president of the National Association for the Advancement of Colored People (NAACP) in Atlanta, he led a campaign in Atlanta "to equalize teachers' salary" and was also instrumental "in the elimination of Jim Crow elevators in the courthouse."[2]

At the same time, King also faced many adversities. When he was six, he was slapped by a white lady in Atlanta's downtown because, as the lady shouted at him, he was "that nigger that stepped on her foot." He absorbed the shock because that was "instinctive of the blacks, raised in the atmosphere of segregation."[3] He experienced the pang of racial discrimination while traveling to Booker T. Washington School as he was not allowed to sit in the front of the bus, which was reserved for the white students. He felt miserable, though helpless, because of the circumstances in which blacks tended to accept humiliation as part of their being. Unable to accept racial segregation, the fourteen-year-old King thus wrote in an essay—"The Negro and the Constitution"—that

we cannot have an enlightened democracy with one great group living in ignorance. We cannot have a healthy nation with one-tenth of the people ill-nourished, sick, harbouring germs of disease which recognize no color lines—obey no Jim Crow laws....Let us see to it that increasingly at home we give fair play and free opportunity [so that] the spirit of the Thirteenth, Fourteenth and Fifteenth Amendments [is] translated into actuality.[4]

This was King's first articulated response to the Jim Crow laws of discrimination. Both Gandhi and King suffered humiliation because of color prejudices. What is striking is the fact that the systemic humiliation to which they were subjected left an indelible imprint in their minds. It would not be an exaggeration to suggest that these incidents made them strong in their determination to fight against racism and injustice. Gandhi graphically illustrated how he was insulted while he was traveling in a train in South Africa:

The train reached Maritzburg, the capital of Natal....A passenger came and looked at me up and down. He saw that I was "a coloured man." That disturbed him. Out he went and came in again with one or two officials. They all kept quiet, when another official came to me and said, "come along, you must go to the van compartment." "But I have a first class ticket," said I. "That does not matter," rejoined the other. "I tell you, you must go to the van compartment." "I tell you [Gandhi added], I was permitted to travel in this compartment at Durban, and I insist on going on in it." "No, you won't," said the official. "You must leave this compartment, or else I shall have to call a police constable to push you out." "Yes, you may. I refuse to get out voluntarily," [said Gandhi]. The constable came. He took me by the hand and pushed me out. My luggage was also taken out. I refused to go to the other compartment and the train steamed away. I went and sat in the waiting room keeping my hand-bag with me leaving the other luggage where it was. The railway authorities had taken charge of it.

It was winter, and winter in the higher regions of South Africa is severely cold. Maritzburg being at a high altitude, the cold was extremely bitter. My overcoat was in my luggage, but I did not dare to ask for it lest I should be insulted again, so I sat and shivered.[5]

This incident was a watershed moment in Gandhi's political life. Out of such humiliation emerged a different Gandhi, one resolved to plunge into action as perhaps the only option to eradicate the evils of racism. As he argued, while he was in the cold waiting room in Maritzburg,

I began to think of my duty. Should I fight for my rights or go back to India or should I go on to Pretoria without minding the insults, and return to India after finishing the case. It would be cowardice to run back to India without fulfilling my obligation. The hardship to which I was subjected was superficial—only a symptom of the deep disease of colour prejudice. I should try, if possible, to root out the disease and suffer hardships in the process. Redress for wrongs I should seek only to the extent that would be necessary for the removal of the colour prejudice.[6]

The Maritzburg incident brought before Gandhi the devastating nature of racism, which was ruthlessly practised by a section of humanity at the cost of a majority. This led to the rise of the rebel Gandhi, who failed to fathom why he was discriminated against despite being a subject of the same empire as the South Africans. Instead of absorbing the shock, he decided to combat the color prejudices politically "to root out the disease of color prejudice" completely.

King faced the same plight in his home state of Georgia, which was racially segregated. While Gandhi suffered the humiliation of color prejudices at the age of twenty-four years, King was only fourteen when he, returning home from a Negro Elks-sponsored oratorical contest with his teacher, Mrs. Bradley, was subjected to such an inhuman ordeal. He won the contest for his speech, ironically entitled "The Negro and the Constitution." He was applauded by the judges for his lucid language and the strength of the argument. The joy ended with his experience on the bus, as he graphically illustrated:

Anyway, that night, Mrs. Bradley and I were on a bus returning to Atlanta, and at a small town along the way, some white passengers boarded the bus, and the white driver ordered us to get up and give the whites our seats. We didn't move quickly enough to suit for him, so he began cursing us, calling us black sons of bitches. I intended to stay right in that seat, but Mrs. Bradley finally urged me up saying we had to obey the law. And, so we stood up in the aisle for the ninety miles to Atlanta. That night will never leave my memory. It was the angriest I have ever been in my life.[7]

On another occasion, an incident involving bigotry and public transportation came even closer to Gandhi's first experience in South Africa. King had passed the entrance examination to Atlanta's prestigious Morehouse College, enrolling at the age of fifteen without graduating from high school. To earn money for his college tuition he worked summers on a tobacco farm in Connecticut. He was very happy because of the personal and social freedom that he enjoyed in New England. He had no problem entering by the front doors or sitting wherever he wished in restaurants and theaters, just like the white folks. But the train trip back to Atlanta at the end of the summer drove home to him once more the terrible reality of his situation as a Negro. On this occasion, as the train entered Virginia, King made his way to the dining car to select his seating, as he had done on the way through New York and New Jersey. But the train was in Dixie now, and the waiter led him to a rear table and pulled a curtain down to shield the white passengers from his presence. He sat there staring at that curtain, unable to believe that others could find him so offensive. "I felt," he mentioned to his friend, "as though the curtain had dropped on my selfhood."[8]

Such incidents remained constant references in both Gandhi's and King's later lives, as is evident from the way they articulated their sociopolitical ideas. For them, the systemic color prejudices were rooted in a specific mind-set that needed to be combated by nonviolent means. Gandhi never reconciled to the racial abuse to which the Indians in South Africa were subjected. He raised his voice in the *Indian Opinion* against the way Europeans dubbed Indians as "coolies." The term "coolie" means porter; Europeans displayed "deliberate contempt" by describing every Indian as a coolie regardless of profession, even referring to "coolie lawyers and coolie traders."[9] On one occasion, a police officer thrashed Gandhi because he mistakenly used the pavement surrounding the Presidential Place in Pretoria for his regular walk.[10] Although it was a clear case of racial prejudice as Gandhi was aware that the policeman "no doubt treats Negros as he [treated] me,"[11] he decided not to pursue legal redressal because he made it "a rule not to go to court in respect of any personal grievance" despite the assurance of his white companion to stand by him as a witness.[12]

Gandhi did not have comparable experiences of racism in India, presumably because of the peculiar way in which the British system accommodated educated Indians within its governance. There were segregated areas for the whites in major metropolitan cities and also small towns; but segregation never became a serious individual issue to those fighting for liberation from colonialism. The situation was different for King, who suffered day in and day out because of legally endorsed segregation between blacks and whites in the Southern states. Segregation, as King illustrated, generated "a sense of nobodiness" among the Negros. The color prejudices were so strong that the blacks were not treated as human beings, and there was no alternative but to fight the unjust law. The situation in which the Southern blacks were forced to remain was so appalling that it was impossible for them not to resort to action, because "[t]here comes a time when the cup of endurance runs over, and men are no longer willing to be plunged into an abyss of injustice where they experience the blackness of corroding despair."[13]

Two fundamental points come out of King's graphic illustrations of racist torture: first, racial segregation gained sustenance, as a legitimate attitude, from
a racially based mind-set that had grown in America since the days of slavery,
when slave parents and plantation owners regarded childhood as a time to prepare African American youngsters for the lives they faced as slaves. While whites
saw it as a time to teach "efficient work habits and discipline to ensure that black
children would grow into 'good hands,' slave parents aimed to impart the skills
needed to survive enslavement."[14] It was natural for those constrained by the
existing racial hierarchy to have accepted racism as part of their being. Racial
supremacy was thus politically convenient for the whites, who desired to maintain the existing power relationships. Second, while identifying the roots of racial
segregation in a mentality, King became convinced of the natural outbursts of the
outcastes because "oppressed people cannot remain oppressed forever [and] the
urge for freedom will eventually come."[15] This realization is what put King a class
by himself. Not only did he conceptualize the problem of racial hierarchy, he, like
Gandhi, also put forward a probable course of action for redemption. As was true
of Gandhi, it was King's mother who had instilled in him tremendous confidence
and self-belief. His mother, reminisced King, "taught [him] that [he] should feel a
sense of 'somebodiness' to face a system" that was inherently structured to make
the African Americans feel "less than and not equal to" the whites.[16]

By focusing on four major movements in which King was involved—the 1955
Montgomery bus strike, the 1963 March on Washington, the 1963 Birmingham
campaign, and the 1965 Selma-Montgomery March—this chapter seeks to bring
out the distinctive nonviolent nature of the black civil rights campaign in America.
It is true that King's charismatic leadership worked miracles in these movements,
though it was not at all effective in King's campaign in Albany, Georgia, where he
failed to rouse mass support even among the blacks. What complemented King's
leadership was the organizational support of the Southern Christian Leadership
Conference (SCLC), which King and his colleagues had founded in 1957 to guide
the movement against racial discrimination. As a true liberal, King justified his
demands for racial equality as most appropriate because of their cultural roots in
African American Christian faith in love and justice and also the American democratic tradition. "We the disinherited of this land," argued King, "...are tired of
going through the long night of captivity....We are reaching out for the daybreak
of freedom, justice and equality."[17] According to him, the protest for desegregation was completely congruent with the American constitutional and religious
traditions, and he thus reiterated, on another occasion, that "no one can scorn
non-violent direct action of civil disobedience without canceling out American
history."[18]

THE 1955 MONTGOMERY BUS STRIKE

One of the most decisive moments in the history of the civil rights movements
happened to be the 1955 Montgomery bus strike. The strike was an outcome

of resentments of the African American community due to racial oppression. As a natural outburst against the Montgomery ordinance, which was adopted in November 1900 and dictated segregation in public transportation,[19] the bus strike always remained nonviolent and clearly Gandhian, despite provocation. The protestors' resolve to remain nonviolent even when confronted with violent harassment drew international attention and catapulted the civil rights movement onto the world stage. In other words, the 1955 bus strike was a watershed moment in the entire struggle against Jim Crow. For the protestors, the discriminatory seating arrangements in public transport were contrary to the core values of American democracy and hence needed to be done away with. What was unique about the movement was its nonviolent nature and the support that it had following Rosa Parks's arrest for refusing to abide by the discriminatory seating arrangement. By challenging the prevalent rules and regulations, the local African Americans articulated a new form of protest for themselves. It was perhaps one of the few successful efforts with a clear agenda and goal. With mass support for the cause, the Montgomery bus strike firmly established nonviolence as an effective strategy for mobilizing the unarmed blacks. The fact that the protest was legitimate and also constitutional seemed to have created and consolidated a base for the campaign that the local African Americans organized.

The Montgomery bus strike began on December 1, 1955, when a local resident, Rosa Parks, was arrested because of her refusal to follow the law of segregation in public transport.[20] It was an incident that ignited the fire of protest in a unique way among the blacks and later among a section of local whites, presumably because they viewed the protest as genuine and humane. As an NAACP activist, Parks had suffered humiliation earlier, but was determined to fight at an opportune moment. It is perhaps most natural for victims to raise their voices when faced with unbearable torture, as Parks mentioned in her interviews with the local press after her arrest. She referred to an incident that infuriated her long before the famous Montgomery refusal. In early 1943, while attempting to register to vote, she discovered that "exercising her right as an American meant surmounting a series of deliberate bureaucratic obstacles."[21] For instance, it was deliberate on the part of the council not to leave sufficient time before announcing the schedule of voter registration. The goal was to discourage blacks, who had less access to such information, from registering. Furthermore, registration was scheduled between 10 a.m. and noon, when white employers refused to let their black workers off work. It was also evident that registration officers usually took longer to complete the paperwork for blacks, limiting the number who could register on any given day. Parks failed to register after making two attempts. As a devoted Christian, she always prayed to God for courage and mental strength to withstand humiliation. On her second attempt, in November 1943, she experienced a vexatious ordeal in public transport involving a bus driver named James F. Blake, who would play an even larger role in her life a dozen years later in Montgomery. Although the Jim Crow laws provided for clearly demarcated public areas for whites and colored people, the bus system in the South seemed to follow "a byzantine set of rules, made more confusing by the bus of the individual drivers." In Montgomery, out of thirty-six seats in the bus, the ten seats farthest toward the back of the buses were unofficially designated for blacks—unless there were white passengers to occupy them. As for the sixteen seats in the middle of the bus, individual drivers imposed their own segregation rules at random and enforced them "with the threat of the pistols they always carried."[22] Though clearly unfair, the system persisted in Montgomery because the blacks "learned to forego the middle seats or at least to give them up to any white person on board." Many drivers made blacks pay their fares tat the front door, then get-off and re-enter the bus through the back door. It was, Parks mentioned, "a form of everyday public humiliation in apartheid Montgomery." She further stated that "some bus drivers were meaner than others [though] not all of them were hateful." Nonetheless, "segregation itself is vicious, and…there was no way you could make segregation decent or nice or acceptable."[23]

In this fateful journey for voter registration, Rosa Parks confronted James F. Blake, who derived tremendous pleasure from spitting tobacco juice out of his bus window and cursing at "niggers" just for the fun of it. His favorite sport was, Parks remembered, "making African-Americans pay in the front of the bus and walk back to board in the rear, then leaving them with a face full of exhaust as he [sped] the bus away before they could get-in."[24] On that November afternoon, she boarded the bus through the front door and refused to exit as Blake requested because the rear door was jammed with African American passengers. Blake fumed and shouted at her saying that if she was unable to re-enter by the back door she should leave the bus entirely. Her defiance annoyed him so much that he held Parks's coat sleeve to push her physically from the bus. She remained quiet and asked him not to hit, assuring him that she would leave of her own accord. In response to his abusive instruction—"get off my bus"—Rosa responded "by intentionally dropping her handbag then plopping [it] down on whites-only seats to retrieve it on her way out, further infuriating the driver."[25]

The November encounter was resolved in a peaceful manner when Rosa capitulated to Blake's demands, though the manner in which she protested reflected nonviolent passive resistance. This incident seems to have charted a course of future action for Rosa Parks and the NAACP. It was a strange coincidence that Blake confronted Rosa Parks again, in December 1955, twelve years after this November encounter. Though Blake drove buses in Montgomery, Parks avoided getting onto any bus that he was driving. It has been argued that the momentous December incident took place when Parks "absentmindedly" boarded Blake's bus, and that her act of civil disobedience was "partly the result of her personal revulsion of a particular driver."[26]

On that fateful afternoon of December 1, 1955, Rosa Parks boarded the bus, which had just one empty seat in the row immediately behind the section reserved for whites. The rear seats, meant for the blacks, were already taken. Rosa therefore took the seat that was available. At a later stop, several other passengers boarded and one white passenger was left standing in the aisle. The driver, in order to provide a seat to the white man, asked those seated behind the white section to give up their seats; three of them immediately heeded the instruction while Rosa Parks refused. As she recollected, "I remained where I was. When the driver saw that I was still sitting there, he asked if I was going to stand-up. I told him, no. I wasn't. He then said, well if you don't stand up, I am going to have you arrested. I told him to go on and have me arrested."[27] The driver asked the police for intervention, and Parks was arrested, even though she had paid the fare and hence had a legitimate right to the seat. Her arrest started an unprecedented nonviolent movement in Montgomery.

The arrest had a snowball effect on the community of blacks. Once the Montgomery women's council resolved to go ahead with a bus boycott as a protest against such humiliation, E. D. Nixon[28] and his colleagues in the local NAACP joined. Nixon was very popular and he persuaded his colleagues to support the campaign, particularly as the city was small enough that one could avoid needing to use public transport. He sought to make it a national issue and contacted black ministers of national reputation elsewhere; he approached Martin Luther King Jr., though he was not as quick to extend his support as colleagues including Ralph D. Abernathy and H. H. Hubbard. King's involvement radically altered the complexion of the movement. When King joined the movement instantly became a national campaign. The strike brought the city of Montgomery to a standstill with its circular requesting Montgomery blacks "not to ride the bus to work, to town, to school, to any-place."[29] As true liberals, the NAACP leadership "offered to send a delegation to discuss blacks' grievances with the bus company, and specifically abjured the use of any unlawful means or any intimidation to persuade persons not to ride the buses."[30] Protestors joined the strike spontaneously. King, when he cruised down every major street and examined every passing bus, found that most of the buses were empty except for a few white passengers. A zealous King thus pronounced that "instead of the 60 percent cooperation we had hoped for, it was becoming apparent that we had reached almost 100 percent. A miracle had taken place: the once dormant and quiescent Negro community was now fully awake."[31] It was a complete boycott because every Negro taxi community in Montgomery had also agreed to support the protest. The success was largely an outcome of mass resentment against the age-old and oppressive system of segregation.

The 1955 Montgomery bus strike was one of those efforts in which King successfully mobilized the victims of racism against the visible forms of oppression. In his *Stride Toward Freedom: The Montgomery Story*,[32] which is "an account of a few years that changed the life of Southern community," King put on record his own views on this movement by saying that

> ... it is the chronicle of 50,000 Negroes who took to heart the principles of non-violence, who learned to fight for rights with the weapon of love, and who, in the process, acquired a new estimate of their human worth....It is the story of the Negro leaders of many faiths and divided allegiances, who came together in the bond of a cause they knew was right. And, of the Negro followers, many of them beyond middle age, who walked to work and

home again, as much as twelve miles a day for a year rather than submit to the discourtesies and humiliation of segregated buses.[33]

According to King, the movement was spontaneous, and people participated to register their protest over the deliberate distortions of the liberal values that the founding fathers held so dear. The majority of the Negroes who, argued King, "took part in the year-long boycott of Montgomery's buses were poor and untutored, but they understood the essence of the Montgomery movement."[34] He defined Rosa Parks's defiance as "an individual expression of a timeless longing for human dignity and freedom." She was not planted, he further argued, "by the NAACP or any other organization, she was planted there by her personal sense of dignity and self-respect; she was anchored to that seat by the accumulated indignities of days gone and boundless aspirations of generations yet unborn. She was a victim of both the forces of history and destiny, backed by the Zeitgeist, or the spirit of time."[35] As one who employed religion for political mobilization, King also underlined the Christian identity of Rosa Parks, who became a strong voice of protest because of her "Christian commitment and devotion to Jesus,"[36] which naturally attracted people of the same religious denomination.

Like Gandhi's satyagraha in South Africa, King's "stride toward freedom" represented a serious effort not only to put on record the entire event, but also to articulate meaningfully and to reiterate some of the major ideological strands of nonviolent civil resistance that it launched. Both redefined prevalent modes of the struggle against injustice, to which the participation of victims had remained peripheral in the past. Montgomery was strategically important since, as Bayard Rustin pointed out, without a victory at Montgomery, "the southern protest movement, then showing its first signs of life, would [have] die[d] stillborn."[37]

As a result of the Montgomery bus strike, the US Supreme Court affirmed a decision of a special three-judge US district court that segregation on buses was unconstitutional. The bus strike made six things clear. First, the movement was a natural reaction to the well-entrenched racial prejudices confronting African Americans in America. It had grown out of many experiences that "have often been humiliating and have led to deep resentment." The Negroes constituted about 75 percent of bus riders in Montgomery. Yet they faced conditions that caused "a great deal of embarrassment [including] the very humiliating experience of being arrested for refusing to give up seats to a white passenger."[38] Second, the Montgomery bus strike translated King's conceptualization of nonviolent civil resistance into reality. Despite provocation, even to the extent where detractors bombed King's house, the campaign remained nonviolent, since "love is," declared King, "our great instrument and our great weapon, and that alone." While challenging violence, which "creates many more problems than it solves," he further stated that "he who lives by the sword will perish by the sword."[39] Third, the Montgomery bus strike confirmed King's undiluted faith in nonviolence. It was at this time that the Gandhian emphasis "on love and non-violence" became most effective in King's campaign against racial segregation. The protest, which was absolutely nonviolent, was articulated in a democratic fashion.

It was never allowed to phase out, since King and his colleagues "sought relief for the complaints within the framework of law." Instead of attacking the laws, they requested that the government consider their demand sympathetically. By denying Negroes even the right to be heard, the bus segregation was contrary to democracy, which guaranteed each citizen "equal opportunity and privileges to enjoy the benefits of what service he is able to pay for, so long as he does not infringe upon the rights of others."[40] Fourth, the bus strike was the last option under the circumstances since "the rights of the Negroes have been infringed upon repeatedly." So, the strike was a legitimate form of protest to achieve " a fair, just and honorable settlement of a contentious issue."[41] Fifth, for the Negroes, the Montgomery strike was not at all an outcome of racial bitterness against the whites. As King elaborated, "[T]he tension in Montgomery is not between seventy thousand whites and fifty thousand Negroes; the tension is at bottom a tension between justice and injustice....If there is a victory for integration in America, it will not merely be a victory for sixteen million Negroes, but it will be a victory for justice, a victory for good will, a victory for democracy."[42] What is evident here is King's unflinching faith in American democracy and political liberalism. He was thus persuaded to believe that a solution to the race imbroglio was likely to be found within the available liberal parameters. Finally, despite being critical of the white Christians, King did not appear to have lost faith in Christianity. He was a true Christian seeking to address race relations from a Christian point of view. Hence he confidently stated that "we must keep...God in the forefront. Let us be Christian in all of our actions [and only then] we can realize the true meaning of love and justice, the kernel of Christianity."[43] So committed was King to biblical values that he, on another occasion, declared that "we live in a Christian community in which brotherhood and neighborliness should prevail among all the people. We can rely on these principles to guide those in authority and other people of influence to see that the Christian way is the only way of reaching a satisfactory solution to the problem."[44] Unlike Gandhi, who employed religion strategically because of India's peculiar sociological complexion, King utilized religious affiliation to build and consolidate among blacks the campaign against racial discrimination. It was therefore not odd for King to highlight the religious identity of Rosa Parks or the citizens of Montgomery while appreciating their contribution to the movement against racial segregation.

The 1955 Montgomery bus strike was a watershed moment in King's political career not only because it gave him a chance to articulate his ideology of nonviolence, but also because it allowed him to project an alternative discourse by drawing upon Christian ethics and the Gandhian method of civil disobedience. Also, much like Gandhi, who established the Natal Congress as an organization to challenge the state, King founded the Montgomery Improvement Association (MIA) in 1955 to pursue his ideological goal. It was an intelligent step on his part to involve the local people whose support was most critical in sustaining the movement. King pursued two alternative methods of spreading the movement and engaging with the cause and those who held it high: he not only attacked segregation through a series of mass meetings and rallies, he also sought to inspire the local African Americans by reference to their contribution to America's growth as a nation. While evolving such a technique, he was indebted to the evangelist Billy Graham, who helped King prepare the groundwork for the movement by compiling mailing lists, enlisting church sponsors and volunteer groups, arranging publicity campaigns, and creating special bus routes.[45]

Notwithstanding MIA's role in Montgomery, King attributed the success of the bus strike to "the rise of a new Negro with a new sense of dignity and destiny. Montgomery had broken the spell of Negroes being unworthy [and was] ushering in concrete manifestations of the thinking and action of the new Negro."[46] As King himself explained,

> The story of Montgomery is the story of 50,000 Negroes who are tired of injustices and oppression, and who are willing to substitute tired feet for tired souls, and walk and walk until the walls of injustice are crushed by the battering rams of historical necessity. This is the new Negro[47]. . . ready to sacrifice his life to challenge segregation...which is a cancer in the body politic [that] must be removed before our democratic health can be realized.[48]

While the protests in Montgomery marked a resurgence of the Negroes as a community willing to challenge racial discrimination in the Southern states, the US Supreme Court seemed to have been favorably disposed toward the Negroes as well. In its famous *Brown vs. Board of Education* ruling of 1954, the Supreme Court reversed the equally famous 1896 verdict of *Plessy vs. Ferguson*, which established the doctrine of separate-but-equal as the law of the land. Under this doctrine, equality of treatment was accorded when the races are provided substantial equal facilities, even though these facilities remain separate. The 1954 *Brown* case challenged the doctrine by arguing that "segregation with the sanction of law has a tendency to [retard] the educational and mental development of Negro children and to deprive them of some of the benefits they would receive in a racial[ly] integrated school system."[49] The Supreme Court, felt King, "gave a death blow to the old Plessy doctrine, insisting that separate facilities are inherently unequal and to segregate a child because of his race is to deny him the equal protection of the law."[50] The Supreme Court ruled that segregation was contrary to the Fourteenth Amendment to the Constitution. This amendment reiterated the 1866 Civil Rights Act by endorsing that "all persons born in the United States [regardless of race]...were citizens and were to be given full and equal benefit of all laws."[51] The institutions of power thus created circumstances conducive to the Negro cause of racial equality.

The Montgomery movement attained success partly because of King's charismatic leadership, which swayed African Americans to support the bus boycott, and partly because of his colleagues, who worked from behind the scenes to sustain the daily momentum for more than a year. While dwelling on the Montgomery bus strike, Bayard Rustin provided perhaps the most persuasive description by focusing on the specific nature of the movement, which was a class by itself given its historical and sociological roots and the psychological involvement of its participants. It became a monumental event in the history of the civil rights movement because, as Rustin viewed, following the Montgomery bus strike, "the centre of gravity and the centre of activity for the whole civil rights movement was [sic] the church people and ministers of the south."[52] In his communication of December 23, 1956, with King, Rustin attributed the success of the movement to the following three factors: first, the movement involved all social strata of blacks, who came forward because the boycott not only gave them an instrument of empowerment, it also created the possibility of a bright future with the removal of the Jim Crow laws of segregation. "The fellowship, the ideals, the joy of sacrifice for others and other varied features of the movement have," argued Rustin, the most prominent force behind the MIA, "given people something to belong to which had the inspiring power of the Minute Men, the Sons of Liberty, and other organized forms which were products of an earlier American era of fundamental change."[53] Second, the nonviolent nature of the movement, in which the enemy was treated with equal respect, won the heart of the opponents. What was critical in the success of the Montgomery strike was a combination of factors, including unity among the blacks, intelligent planning, and a high level of moral and ethical motivation. That the strikers had no "hatred" or "ill-feeling" toward the perpetrators of racism seemed to have radically altered the perception of the whites who participated and appeared to have learned "the value of being together." Montgomery remained an important event in America's social life, which, felt Rustin, "contributed to the mental health and growth of the white man's mental health, and thus to the entire nation."[54] Finally, the success of the Montgomery strike would not have been possible without the active participation of the local inhabitants who, with their commitment and dedication to the cause, never allowed the movement to die down. This was unique because the role of leadership was confined to providing ideological direction, while local activists provided perhaps the most useful services to the campaign and its cause by sustaining the momentum in the day-to-day struggle.

Besides catapulting King onto the center stage, the Montgomery bus strike is also remembered for "[t]he strong sense of unity and purpose exhibited by the Negro community, the ability of the black citizens to sustain the boycott through month after weary month [and] their renewed determination in the face of violence."[55] With mass participation in the boycott of public transport, the Montgomery bus strike set in motion a completely different kind of mass movement, argued Rustin, since "the fight of the Negro for integration and equality is a vital component in the fight for common man, Negro and white alike, to realize higher living standards, higher education, and culture and a deeper commitment to moral and ethical principles."[56] The Montgomery movement was thus historically most significant because it had not only given a well-defined sense of identity to the African Americans, it had also "contributed to the movement of America to achieve a nation capable of utilizing impressive industrial might for the benefit of all."[57] It was true that Montgomery heralded a new era in the history of the black political campaign for self-dignity, which remained a casualty so long as the Jim Crow laws were effective. According to an eyewitness, the Montgomery protest not only "repudiated the violent machismo of America, it also stirred to awakening another America—the America of Emerson, Thoreau, of the Quakers, of the abolitionists, the America of principle and compassion. A new America was born."[58]

It is also true that the 1955 bus strike initiated several new socioeconomic and political processes in America challenging the fundamental issue of discrimination, which was not merely a problem of racism, but one of a specific mind-set supporting the exploitation of human beings by human beings. It is thus argued that during the movement, "the city slipped into a surreal dimension…in which the moderate white opinion was tragically silenced … and any hint of deviation from the white supremacist orthodoxy [invited immediate retaliation] in the form of active harassment and social ostracism."[59] Not only did the whites institutionalize their views through the formation of an organization called Citizens' Council, they also sought to fulfill their ideological goal by adopting a militant stance that was clearly articulated in a 1959 resolution stating that

> we believe that any person who speaks, writes or in any way advocates or works for anything short of total and complete segregation will be ostracized, and will earn and receive the condemnation of the public....we feel sure that an aroused and informed public will make it unprofitable and uncomfortable for any person to remain in our community if he is not willing to support the will of the community in this matter."[60]

Nonetheless, in the changed socioeconomic environment, the white opposition, however strong, was never effective, suggesting perhaps the rise and consolidation of an alternative ideology seeking to champion both Christian ethics and fundamental constitutional principles. With the rescinding of segregation in public transport, the MIA-led Montgomery movement thus proved, beyond doubt, the extent to which the core humane values of Christianity remained adequate in mobilizing people of identical religious allegiance for a common cause. The movement that began with the arrest of Rosa Parks in December 1955 thus articulated a voice that was previously peripheral, but gained momentum with the spontaneous participation of the racially segregated and socioeconomically underprivileged African Americans in campaigns against artificially maintained racist discrimination.

There was another dimension that surfaced with the formation of the SCLC and when the black protest movements against segregation became more organized and well-directed. Although King was projected as its leader, his colleagues, especially Bayard Rustin and A. Philip Randolph, appeared to have provided the required organizational skill to sustain the organization and consolidate its support base among the blacks and white sympathizers. The first meaningful protest movement under SCLC guidance, the 1955 Montgomery bus strike, actually affected the prevalent social, economic, and political order supporting racial discrimination. It was Rustin who was the main pillar behind the SCLC in the context of the bus strike. To continue the movement against the Jim Crow laws in the aftermath of the Montgomery strike, Rustin suggested two specific methods: voting power and mass direct action. It was not easy to augment Negro power through the first method, given the obvious resistance by the whites, who still held substantial authority. Instances abound showing how the Negroes were denied registration as voters on flimsy grounds. At the same time, many blacks lacked interest in voting, which was a further constraint on challenging the white hegemony through liberal means. Hence Rustin submitted that "so long as Negro voters remained too insignificant to influence the outcome of elections, we shall have to rely more and more on mass direct action as the one realistic weapon."[61] They became confident that their success in the 1955 Montgomery bus strike had demonstrated that "the center of gravity ha[d] shifted from the courts to the community action and the leaders should now realize that the people, and not simply their lawyers, could win their own freedom."[62] King seemed persuaded, as his 1957 address to the NAACP revealed, when he echoed Rustin's concerns by saying that there was a

need to expand the struggle on all fronts. Up to now we have thought of the color question as something which could be solved in and of itself. We know now that while it [is] necessary to say "No" to racial injustice, this must be followed by a positive programme of action: the struggle for the right to vote, for economic uplift of the people. A part of this is the realization that men are truly brothers, that, the Negro cannot be free so long as there are poor and underprivileged people....Equality for Negroes is related to the greater problem of economic uplift for Negroes and white men, They share a common problem and have a common interest in working together for economic and social uplift, They can and must work together.[63]

A clear change in King's perception was thus visible in the aftermath of the 1955 Montgomery bus strike. Despite being critical of racial segregation, he was aware that declaring segregation in public transport illegal was not adequate as long as the majority of the Negroes reeled under severe poverty and remained ignorant of their rights (and also duties) within the liberal democratic framework of American constitutionalism. In order to expand his political horizon, King also talked about the plight of poor whites, who were as oppressed as their black counterparts. Here the influence of labor activists such as Randolph and Rustin was evident. The campaign for civil rights was thus no longer confined to the demands for racial desegregation; it became a movement for radical socio economic changes in which class issues were equally important.

THE 1941 MARCH ON WASHINGTON

The idea of rallies for political purposes was nothing new. A. Philip Randolph, a trade union leader, planned the famous March on Washington of July 1941 when America was getting ready to involve itself in World War II. The purpose of the July march to the capital was to force the government to stop racial segregation in the military. This was a strategic moment for Randolph to raise the issue of racial discrimination on behalf of those in the American army. Black veterans of World War I, despite their service, were tormented by Jim Crow laws once they went back to their homes in the Dixie states. The plight of the Negro soldiers remained unchanged because "employers and unions denied them jobs, real estate agents and politicians confined them to ghettoes, and a vast number of whites treated them with deep-rooted antagonism and generally did their best to keep them in permanent misery."[64] This was an immediate source of provocation to the black leadership, which found in this instance another illustration of racial discrimination. The proposed march was to be a challenge to the age-old practices of racial discrimination that had become "lived experiences" of the blacks. Reflecting the black sentiments, the manifesto that Randolph and his colleagues prepared to justify such a confrontation with the Roosevelt government was nothing but a list of demands for racial equality. They are as follows:

1. We demand in the interest of national unity, the abrogation of every law which makes a distinction in treatment between citizens based on religion, creed, color or national origin. This means an end to Jim Crow in education, in housing, in transportation, and in every other social, economic and political privilege; and especially, we demand, in the capital of the nation, an end to all segregation in public places and in public institutions.

2. We demand legislation to enforce the Fifth and Fourteenth Amendment guaranteeing that no person shall be deprived of life, liberty or property without due process of law, so that the full weight of the national government may be used for the protection of life and thereby may end the disgrace of lynching.

3. We demand the enforcement of Fourteenth and Fifteenth Amendments and the enactment of the Pepper Poll Tax so that all barriers in the exercise of suffrage are eliminated.

4. We demand the abolition of segregation and discrimination in the Army, Navy, Marine Corps, Air Corps and all other branches of national defense.

5. We demand an end to discrimination in jobs and job training. Further, we demand that the Fair Employment Practices Commission (FEPC) be made a permanent administrative agency of the US government and that it be given power to enforce its decisions, based on its findings.

6. We demand that federal funds be withheld from any agency which practices discrimination in the use of such funds.

7. We demand colored and minority representation on all administrative agencies so that these groups may have recognition of their democratic right to participate in formulating policies.

8. We demand representation for the colored and minority racial groups on all missions, political and technical, which will be sent to the peace conference so that the interests of all people everywhere may be fully recognized and justly provided for in the postwar settlement.[65]

Although the March on Washington was called off, the Randolph manifesto still achieved a remarkable victory in the sense that a presidential decree was issued establishing a Fair Employment Practices Committee. This move signaled perhaps the first serious federal involvement in the economic interests of the African American community, although the other main issues of racial discrimination—including discrimination in the military—were shelved. It took almost seven years before the Truman Executive Order, in 1948, upheld "equal treatment and opportunity for all persons in the armed forces without regard to race, color, religion or national origin."[66] These orders were hardly adequate to meaningfully combat the well-entrenched structure of exclusion and discrimination that drew sustenance from the Jim Crow laws. Hence Randolph, despite having withdrawn the March on Washington in 1941, carried forward his crusade against the racial othering of the blacks in a series of meetings and rallies in various US cities because "vested political interests in race prejudice are so deeply entrenched that to them winning the war against Hitler is secondary to preventing Negroes from winning democracy for themselves."[67]

The March on Washington set in motion a new type of politics that gained momentum over time. Both the March on Washington and the FEPC set out to "rally African-Americans to challenge racial discrimination and generate sufficient political pressure for social change"[68] among whites as the legal stipulations proved more cosmetic than effective. In order to fulfill his ideological goal, Randolph held ecumenical and interracial prayer meetings, especially to attract the white, as well as black, religious leaders of Catholic, Jewish, and Protestant faiths. The purpose was "to stir the white American community's public conscience, showing how hatred endangered American democratic and Christian institutions."[69] The other important contribution that Randolph made to the civil rights movement derived from his internalization of the Gandhian philosophy of nonviolence. He always believed that nonviolent demonstrations were the only means by which the disenfranchised African Americans could exert their influence on a government that, in its pursuit of a policy of segregation, was unfair to an integral section of the population. Nonviolent demonstration also provided psychological benefits: participation in movements against racism would provide "an outlet for the frustrations of southern blacks and thus minimize the possibility of violence [which would, Randolph feared] dissipate the reservoir of good will, built by the non-violent nature of the southern struggle."[70]

THE 1963 MARCH ON WASHINGTON

The second March on Washington, in 1963, was a historic occasion in the civil rights movement in the United States for two important reasons: first, like the first one, which was later withdrawn with the acceptance of some of the demands, the 1963 march attained the goals that it had set out to accomplish. Two major acts—the 1964 Civil Rights Act and the 1965 Voting Rights Act—were approved, thoroughly challenging segregation and outlawing discrimination based on race in education, public accommodations, employment, and any federally funded program. Second, the march remained a historical moment for King, who, through his "I Have a Dream" speech, evolved an ideologically persuasive and politically meaningful conceptual model to challenge racism in particular and sources of human oppression more generally. What is significant in his conceptualization was his sincere commitment to liberalism and nonviolence, which he initially derived from Christian ethics and later from Gandhi.

The story of the second March on Washington followed the same trajectory in the sense that it was Randolph who suggested, to King, the idea of a mass rally early in 1963. King was persuaded to accept the suggestion given the success that the first march had attained even before it was undertaken. The plan was to hold a two-day gathering in Washington, DC, to highlight the economic subordination of the Negroes. As sketched out by Randolph's close aide and the main pillar of his mammoth organization, Bayard Rustin, the fundamental objective of the 1963 March on Washington was to get rid of racial segregation and to establish economic justice for African Americans. With the disappearance of economic inequality along racist lines and integration in the fields of education, housing, transportation and, public accommodation, racial segregation was likely to melt away.[71] The aim was to establish equality. Thus, argued Rustin,

> our feet are set in the path of equality—economic, political, social and racial. Equality is the heart and, essence of democracy, freedom and justice. Without equality of opportunity in industry, in labor unions, schools and colleges, government, politics and before law, without equality in social relations and in all phases of human endeavor, the Negro is certain to be consigned to an inferior status. There must be no dual standards of justice, no dual rights, privileges, duties or responsibilities of citizens. No dual forms of freedom.[72]

Ideologically, this march was thus not different from earlier efforts that had challenged the Jim Crow discrimination. Organizationally, it was, however, different in the sense that the 1963 March on Washington represented a coalition of several civil rights organizations, all of which had different approaches and different agendas—though on this occasion they came together for a common cause, seemingly by underplaying their differences. The Big Six organizers were James Farmer of the Congress of Racial Equality (CORE), Martin Luther King Jr. of the Southern Christian Leadership Conference (SCLC), John Lewis of the Student Nonviolent Coordination Committee (SNCC), A. Philip Randolph of the Brotherhood of Sleeping Car Porters, Roy Wilkins of the National Association for the Advancement of Colored People (NAACP) and Whitney Young Jr., of the National Urban League (NUL). Supported by a strong coalition of organizations with more or less identical ideological aims, the organizers of the march set out specific demands, which included the passage of meaningful civil rights legislation, the elimination of racial segregation in public schools, protection for demonstrators against police brutality, a major public-works program to provide jobs regardless of race and color, the passage of a law prohibiting racial discrimination in public and private hiring, a $2 per hour minimum wage, and self-government for the District of Columbia, which had a black majority.[73]

It is true that several organizations came together for a common cause, although the differences of opinion surfaced once their respective leaders addressed the gathering of almost 250,000 people. The tone was certainly not Gandhian or nonviolent, because "the Negroes, the victims of racism over centuries, have become impatient," as John Lewis of the SNCC declared. He said,

> The revolution is at hand, and we must free ourselves of the chains of political and economic slavery. The non-violent revolution is saying [that] we will not wait for the courts to act, for we have been waiting hundreds of years. We will not wait for the President, nor the Justice Department, nor Congress, but we will take matters into our own hands, and assure us victory. For those who have said, be patient and wait, we must say [that] patience is a dirty and nasty word. We cannot be patient, we do not want to be free gradually, we want our freedom, and we want it now. We cannot depend on any political party, for Democrats and the Republicans have betrayed the basic principles of the Declaration of Independence."[74]

Lewis further charged that American politics was "dominated by politicians who build their careers on immoral compromises and ally themselves with open forms of political, economic and social exploitation."[75] This radical speech caused a fissure among those who took a lead in organizing the March on Washington. Roy Wilkins of the NAACP threatened to quit unless his request not to allow John Lewis to speak was conceded. Randolph defused the crisis by persuading Lewis to tone down his statements.[76] There was another serious charge against the organizers: no women leader was invited to address the congregation, which probably hinted at the organizers being patriarchal in their strategy, as the feminist author Pauli Murray charged. According to her, "[I]t is indefensible to call a national March on Washington and send a Call which contains the name of not a single woman leader. Nor can this glaring omission be glossed over by several Negro women to appear on the 28 August program.... [T]he tokenism is as offensive," she angrily added, "when applied to women as when applied to Negroes, and that I have not devoted the greater part of my adult life to the implementation of human rights to condone any policy which is not inclusive."[77] Nonetheless, the march was a huge success presumably because of the astute Randolph and his younger colleague Rustin, who never allowed the bond to be disrupted by internal feud.

After preliminaries of singing and benediction, Randolph delivered the afternoon keynote address, in which he announced the ideological aims and objectives of the August march. He said that they were in the midst of

> a massive moral revolution [which] reverberates throughout the land, touching every city, every town, every village where [blacks] are segregated,

oppressed and exploited. But this civil rights demonstration is not confined to the Negro; nor is it confined to civil rights; for our white allies knew that they cannot be free while we are not. And we know that we have no future in which six million black and white people are unemployed, and millions more live in poverty.... Those who deplore our militancy, who exhort patience in the name of a false peace, are in fact supporting segregation and exploitation. They would have social peace at the expense of social and racial justice. They are more concerned with easing racial tensions than enforcing racial democracy.[78]

In his address, Randolph reiterated some of the major points of the manifesto that he had prepared for the 1941 march. According to Randolph, the American military attack on Hitler, which was justified as appropriate to protect democracy in the world, was paradoxical given the denial of basic democratic rights to the Negroes in the country. "Negroes in Uncle Sam's uniform," he further added in his address,

are being put down, mobbed, sometimes even shot down by the civilian and military police, and on occasion, lynched. Vested political interests in race prejudice are so deeply entrenched that to them winning the war against Hitler is secondary to preventing Negroes from winning democracy for themselves....[Unless] the humblest and weakest person can enjoy the highest civil, economic and social rights that the biggest and most powerful possesses...democracy makes no sense.[79]

What ran through these efforts was his concern for racial equality, which yet remained a distant goal. For real democracy to strike roots in America, what was required, suggested Randolph, was a complete abnegation of the Jim Crow laws. Such a move would make "America a moral and spiritual arsenal of democracy."[80]

Martin Luther King Jr. was the last speaker, and Randolph introduced him as "the moral leader of our nation." For Randolph, King was the face of the civil rights movement, for not only did he "epitomize the emergence of a new militant black church, something that he had hoped for since his radical activism before World War I," but he could also "stir the imagination of the black irrespective of age and socio-economic locations."[81] King's effort contributed, as Randolph had conceptualized, to the rise of the black militant church with "a social gospel." Characterizing the August 28 march "as the greatest demonstration for freedom in the history of our nation," King's famous "I Have a Dream" speech became the signature touchstone of the march. Unlike any of the speakers, he avoided attacking the administration for being racially biased, though he charged the American leaders with not being attentive to the fundamental values of American constitutionalism. Reflecting his sincere commitment to liberalism, the speech was a reiteration of the values that the founding fathers held so dear. While strongly arguing against artificially created racism, King advanced three arguments in his defense: first, the white

Americans had fulfilled their partisan designs by simply bypassing Abraham Lincoln's 1863 Emancipation Proclamation, which "came as a great beacon light of hope to millions of Negro slaves who had been scared in the flames of withering injustice." So the continuity of the Jim Crow laws was not only a challenge to Lincoln's vision, it was also a threat to the values enshrined in the Declaration of Independence and the Constitution. The march was organized to demonstrate that "the Negro is still languishing in the corners of American society, and finds himself in exile in his own land." The second point in his speech relates to the growing resentment of the Negroes in response to centuries of oppression. When the architects of the republic, argued King, wrote "the magnificent words of the Constitution and the Declaration of Independence, they were signing a promissory note [guaranteeing] to all men, the inalienable rights of life, liberty and the pursuit of happiness." Speaking metaphorically, he compared these promises to "a bad check" that the American authority should now respect by honoring the vision that the founding fathers of this great nation had espoused and nurtured. Now was the time "to rise from the dark and desolate valley of segregation to the sunlit path of racial justice... [and also to] lift our nation from the quicksand of racial injustice to the solid rock of brotherhood." According to King, the demands were legitimate, because the Negroes, as much as their white counterparts, remained historically integral to American society. The victims of racist discrimination seemed to have run out of patience. As King articulated, "[W]e cannot be satisfied as long as the Negro's basic mobility is from a smaller ghetto to a larger one. We can never be satisfied as long as a Negro in Mississippi cannot vote and a Negro in New York believes he has nothing for which to vote.... We will not be satisfied until justice rolls down like water and righteousness like a mighty stream. There will be neither rest nor tranquility in America," warned King, "until the Negro is granted his citizenship rights, and unless this is conceded, the whirlwind of revolt will continue to shake the foundations of our nation." Finally, King understood the revolt as a natural outcome of century-old Negro resentments. But he true to his commitment to the Sermon on the Mount and Gandhian nonviolence, never endorsed violence or any deviation from what he sincerely believed. Aware of the devastating impact of being violent, he insisted on conducting the struggle "on the high plane of dignity and discipline." In order to fulfill this goal, he suggested two concrete steps: he asked those involved in struggle against racism not "to allow our creative protest to degenerate into physical violence [and also to] rise to the majestic heights of meeting physical force with soul force." While being committed to nonviolence, King was also aware that adherence to vengeful violence was likely to alienate the whites who also participated in the August march. It would be strategically suicidal if the Negroes failed to earn respect from their "white brothers," who also realized that "their destiny is tied-up with our destiny and their freedom is inextricably bound to our freedom." Contemporary America, felt King, was neither true to the American creed of "all men are created equal" nor was adequately equipped to realize liberty, equality and fraternity in their true manifestations.[82]

The "I Have a Dream" speech was the signature touchstone of the August 28 March: not only was it reflective of King's optimism, it was also a fine example of a liberal exposition of human protests. Besides contributing to a successful protest march that was certainly a show of strength, King and his colleagues also forced the government to legally endorse their demands. Ten months later, President John F. Kennedy's civil rights bill, championed in Congress by the new president, Lyndon B. Johnson, was signed into law as the landmark Civil Rights Act of 1964. One year after that the other bookend legislative achievement of the Southern civil rights struggle, the Voting Rights Act of 1965, also became law. So, politically, the March on Washington was a successful effort; ideologically, it reconfirmed King's unflinching commitment to nonviolence, and, organizationally, it represented a rare occasion when major civil rights organizations, irrespective of their ideological differences, came forward to fight for a common cause. Besides the civil rights organizations, the participation of the white churches seemed to have strengthened the movement beyond recognition, as King argued by saying that "no single factor...gave so much momentum [as] the decision of the religious leaders of this country to defy tradition and become an integral part of the quest of the Negro for his rights."[83]

THE BIRMINGHAM CAMPAIGN, 1963

The fall of 1962 was a difficult time for King and his colleagues because of the failure of the nonviolent campaign in Albany, Georgia, and the increasing questioning of nonviolence as a strategy vis-à-vis the segregationists. It was a defeat that considerably weakened the civil rights movement in the Dixie states. What made King slightly defensive was the criticism that he had faced because of his uncritical faith in the strategy of nonviolence. Questions were raised as to whether nonviolence was an appropriate strategy to combat racial segregation. The differences among the major civil rights organizations—SNCC, SCLC, and CORE—came to the surface during the movement in Albany, an old slave-trading center in the Deep South. The growing confidence of SNCC activists in Albany, in particular,

> led to their open criticism of the approaches of other civil rights groups,
> especially the SCLC, and their decision to expand the work into rural areas;
> but they also learned in Albany that even massive, sustained and generally
> disciplined protests based on moral principles did not necessarily ensure
> immediate success and efficient police action against demonstrators could
> seriously hamper their struggle.[84]

King was aware of the situation and he tried to accommodate their views without abandoning the idea of nonviolence. Regardless of their respect for King, the SNCC activists sought "opportunities to dispute his position, thereby expressing the black anger, discontent and disillusionment that could not be conveyed through King's moderate rhetoric."[85] So it was a testing time for King, who now felt the need for another campaign to sustain the spirit of his followers, to prove the viability of nonviolence, and to revive the mass tempo of the civil rights movement. For King, defeat and victory were both sides of the same coin, and as a political activist he always learned from defeat. "If I had to do it again," he mentioned, "I would guide the community's leadership differently than I did."[86] It was a temporary setback for the people of Albany, but King noted that "[t]he atmosphere of despair and defeat was replaced by the sense of strength of people who had dared to defy tyrants and discovered that tyrants could be defeated....Albany would never be the same again. We had won a partial victory in Albany and a partial victory to us was not an end but a beginning."[87]

So the stage was ready. As regards King's involvement in the campaign, the pattern was the same: he joined the movement after it already had begun. In the 1950s, Fred Shuttlesworth[88] and his colleagues started a movement against segregation in Birmingham at the behest of the Alabama Christian Movement for Human Rights (ACMHR), which was one of the eighty-five affiliates of the SCLC. The city of Birmingham was notorious for its ruthless implementation of racial segregation and equally ruthless commissioner of police, Eugene Bull Conner, "a racist who prided himself on knowing how to handle the Negro and keep him in his place." Bull Conner held this key position for many years and displayed "as much contempt for the rights of the Negroes as he did defiance for the authority of the federal government." An atmosphere of violence and brutality prevailed in the city in which "local racists intimidated, mobbed and even killed Negroes with impunity."[89] The SLCC agreed to get involved in the campaign in Birmingham because King believed that the movement could, if successful, "break the back of segregation all over the nation [since] the city had been the country's chief symbol of racial intolerance. A victory there shall [therefore] set forces in motion to change the entire course of the drive for freedom and justice."[90] It was therefore decided to thoroughly plan the movement well in advance to avoid its derailment under any circumstances. Christened as Project C—the C for Birmingham's confrontation—a detailed blueprint was prepared to steer the campaign toward its goal. Led by King, the Birmingham campaign resorted to nonviolent direct action to defy laws supporting segregation. King summarized the philosophy of the Birmingham campaign when he said that "[t]he purpose of...direct action is to create a situation so crisis-packed that it will inevitably open the door to negotiation."[91]

One of the unique features of Project C was to be a Negro economic boycott of the local businesses. It was a Gandhian strategy of "omission" that yielded positive results, as King stated, because "the Negro population had sufficient buying power so that its withdrawal could make the difference between profit and loss for many businesses."[92] In addition to the economic boycott, which was not appreciated by a large number of black businessmen and ministers,[93] the first few days were confined to sit-ins at lunch counters in the downtown department stores and drug stores; the demonstrators were arrested under the local "trespass after warning" ordinance. The first week passed by smoothly, making the local authority confident of its ability to contain the movement quickly. This feeling soon disappeared as the movement gained momentum. The economic boycott was most effective, and most of the shops lost considerable earnings. With the increasing number of volunteers, the SCLC expanded its sphere of operation with several other tactics: kneel-ins at churches, sit-ins at the library, a march on the county building to mark the opening of a voter registration drive. The local police remained calm but made the demonstrators stand behind bars in public places in accordance with segregation laws. In order not to allow the movement to spread, the city government obtained a court injunction directing the demonstrators to cease all activities until approved by the court. The Alabama courts were "notoriously famous for sitting on cases of this nature," and so the injunction was "a maliciously effective pseudo-legal way of breaking the back of legitimate moral protest. [The] injunction method [was] a leading instrument of the South to block the direct action civil rights drive and to prevent Negro citizens and their white allies from engaging in peaceful assembly, a right guaranteed by the First Amendment Act."[94] Since the injunction was issued to thwart a genuine movement, it was morally correct for the demonstrators, felt King and his colleagues, to disobey the court order. The order surprised many, as the civil rights movement had an overt liberal character, and many within it possessed an unflinching faith in the liberal institutions of justice, like the courts. For his part, King justified his action on the grounds that the authority had played foul. As a Gandhian, he found it morally appropriate to counter an immoral authority pushing people to the wall by hook or crook. It was therefore not a violation of constitutional principles but a challenge to "a draconian authority [that] had misused the judicial process in order to perpetuate injustice and segregation."[95]

King was arrested, and the movement entered its most critical phase: not only did white moderates join the campaign, but high school students began participating in the resistance movement as well. They were "eager to get involved and also hungry for participation in a significant social effort."[96] The victory of the Birmingham campaign was shaped, to a significant extent, by the emotional attachment these teenagers felt to the cause of racial equality. Serious as they were about what they were doing, these teenagers, argued King,

had that marvelous humor that arms the unarmed in the face of danger. Under their leaders, they took delight in confusing the police. A small decoy group would gather at one exit of the church, bringing policemen streaming in cars and on motorcycles. Before the officers knew what was happening, other groups, by the scores, would pour out of other exits and move, two by two, toward [the place in downtown where we were scheduled to congregate]. Many arrived at their destination before the police could confront and arrest them.... The police ran out of paddy wagons and had [to requisition] sheriff's cars and school buses [to transport them to the jail]."[97]

As in other campaigns, King was always open for dialogue and negotiation with the city authority. There were four major issues that figured in his list of demands to get out of this imbroglio:

1. The desegregation of lunch counters, rest rooms, fitting rooms, and drinking fountains in variety and department stores.
2. The upgrading and hiring of Negroes on a nondiscriminatory basis throughout the business and industrial community in Birmingham.
3. The dropping of all charges against jailed demonstrators
4. The creation of a biracial committee to work out a timetable for desegregation in other areas of Birmingham life.

Despite having expressed willingness to open a dialogue with the protesters, the Birmingham local authority and police commissioner, Bull Conner, left no stone unturned to crash the campaign. Even the local businessmen preferred to incur losses rather than capitulate to the demands of the protestors, who also failed to mobilize the media in their favor, unlike in the case of Montgomery bus strike. The scene, however, underwent a radical change when national pressure began to mount on the White House, forcing the administration to act. On May 4, 1963, the attorney general sent two of his emissaries to seek a truce in the tense racial situation in Birmingham. With their intervention, the local authority agreed to sit for a discussion to resolve the crisis. An agreement was signed on May 10, and the month-long campaign was withdrawn once the major demands were met, as the terms and conditions of the agreement show:

1. The desegregation of lunch counters, rest rooms, fitting rooms and drinking foundation, in planned stages within ninety days.
2. The upgrading and hiring of Negroes on a non-discriminatory basis throughout the industrial community of Birmingham.
3. Official cooperation with the movement's legal representatives in working out the release of all jailed persons on bond or on their personal recognizance.
4. Through the Senior Citizens Committee or Chamber of Commerce, communication between Negro and white to be publicly established within two weeks in order to sort-out issues of differences and confrontation between the two racial communities.[98]

The May 10 agreement added another feather to the cap of the civil rights movement. Although it was a micro movement, it had national ramifications—which perhaps explains the intervention by the White House. Reflective of a new wave of politics, the Birmingham campaign became "a model in southern race relations [suggesting] that the sins of a dark yesterday will be redeemed in the achievements of a bright future."[99] While the Montgomery bus strike had accorded King national prominence, the Birmingham boycott placed him in a very prominent position within the entire civil rights movement in the United

States. He rose to fame due to his "Letter from a Birmingham Jail," in which he clearly articulated his views on racism and racial segregation. His letter was also a challenge to an open letter written by Alabama's leading clergy, in which they disparaged the entire campaign as "destructive" to civil tranquility and likely to foment violence and racial hatred. In the letter, he said that segregation had completely lost its legitimacy in the changed socioeconomic and political milieu. The language King used in his letter drew on the liberal ideas of the leading proponents of the fight against injustice. In order to be persuasive, King put himself into a great tradition of protests starting with Socrates, extending down through primarily Christian history, "from the early prophets to Christ himself, to Paul, to Aquinas, Augustine, Martin Luther and Bunyan [in addition to] Reinhold Niebuhr, Martin Buber and Paul Tillich, leading modern spokesmen from both the Christian and Jewish faiths."[100] Instead of defending his position with reference to Gandhi or Thoreau, King, as an effective strategist, invoked the patriarchal figures and imageries that would instantly link the local habitants with the movement. He also referred to the architect of the Declaration of Independence, Thomas Jefferson who, by declaring that "all men are created equal," was also an extremist in the context of a segregated America.

There are three important dimensions of King's refutation of the arguments[101] made by the white clergy in trying to undermine the civil disobedience in the city of Birmingham. First, one of the serious charges against King was his violation of the court's injunction in the light of his continuous exhortation to the public to obey the Supreme Court's 1954 decision outlawing segregation in public schools. His response was based on the fundamental assumption that laws were not ends in themselves, but means of achieving justice. Besides pursuing this fundamental distinction between means and ends, he also categorized laws as just and unjust: while the former needed to be respected, the latter had no place in a civilized society. In order to substantiate his argument, he thus stated that "[t]here are two types of laws: there are just laws and there are unjust laws....What is the difference between the two?...A just law is a man-made code that squares with the moral law or law of God. An unjust law is a code that is out of harmony with the moral law." Seeking to strengthen his argument by drawing on an authentic voice in Christianity, he further elaborated that "Paul Tillich has said that sin is separation. Isn't segregation an existential expression of man's tragic separation, an expression of his estrangement, his terrible sinfulness?...Obey the 1954 decision of the Supreme Court because it is morally right...and disobey segregation ordinances because they are morally wrong."[102] He was morally justified in challenging the unjust legal embargo because it was directed at preserving racial segregation and thus denying citizens the First Amendment privilege of peaceful assembly and protest.

The second dimension relates to King's persuasive efforts at drawing on Christianity to defend civil disobedience as a natural outcome of those suffering due to another's whims. According to him, "true" Christians always resisted "fallen" regimes in history—whether it was Hebrew resistance by the exiled Shadrach, Meshach, and Abednego against Nebuchadnezzar in ancient Babylon or the opposition of the early Christians against the edicts of the Roman Empire. One was committed to the highest moral laws regardless of consequences, and that was what a true Christian was expected to do. Hence he failed to appreciate why "everything Hitler did was legal and everything Hungarian freedom fighters did in Hungary was illegal. It was illegal to aid and comfort a Jew in Hitler's Germany. But I am sure that if I had lived in Germany during that time, I would have aided and comforted my Jewish brothers [and sisters] even though it was illegal. If I lived in a communist country...I would advocate disobeying...anti-religious laws."[103] What King revealed here was his uncompromising stance vis-à-vis unjust laws since they were contrary to the highest moral laws.

The final dimension was about King's unequivocal support for direct action as perhaps the only alternative left under the circumstances. Disappointed with the white church and its leadership because of its reluctance to aid the civil resistors, he was persuaded to accept open peaceful defiance as most appropriate in Birmingham by saying that

[w]e had no alternative except that of preparing for direct action, whereby we would present our very bodies as a means of laying our case before the conscience of the local and national community.... You may well ask, why direct action? Why sit-ins, marches etc.? Isn't negotiation a better path? You are exactly right in your call for negotiation. Indeed, this is the purpose of direct action. Nonviolent direct action seeks to create such a crisis and establish such creative tension that a community that has constantly refused to negotiate is forced to confront the issue. It seeks so to dramatize the issue that it can no longer be ignored.... I am not afraid of the word tension. I have earnestly worked and preached against violent tension, and there is a type of constructive tension that is necessary for growth.[104]

The alternative that King had opted for seemed to have built a solid organization given the absence of any effective mechanism to resolve the impasse. For King, it was not a confrontation between "good" and "bad," but one that, by championing the fundamental values of the American dream became critical in the articulation of what "this great nation" stood for. As he eloquently put it, "When these disinherited children of God [Negroes of Birmingham] sat down at lunch counters they were in reality standing up for the best in the American dream and the most sacred values in our Judeo-Christian heritage."[105] It was not therefore surprising that those who joined the movement had to take a pledge in the name of God and Christianity that ran as follows:-

"(1) Meditate daily on the life of teachings of Jesus;
(2) Remember always that the non-violent movement seeks justice and reconciliation—not victory;
(3) Walk and talk in the manner of love for God is love
(4) Pray daily to be used by God in order that all men might be free."[106]

Besides its distinctive religious fervor, the 1963 Birmingham campaign was a historic occasion in the series of movement against racial segregation in at least two fundamental ways: first, it was a local movement that became national with King's involvement in the campaign, which followed the formation of the ACMHR in Birmingham. The movement was remarkable if judged from the point of view of its organizational base: not only did the blacks participate, the white moderates also came forward to willingly endorse the ideological goal of the civil rights movement. With the growing interest of the high school students in the sit-ins at lunch counters, the Birmingham campaign introduced a dimension, hitherto unknown, in the African American campaign for racial equality. Second, the Birmingham campaign reconfirmed King's unflinching commitment to nonviolence and also the core values of American constitutionalism. He fought against segregation since it clearly contradicted Christian ethics and values enshrined in the Declaration of Independence, the Constitution, and the 1863 Emancipation Proclamation. He drew on these fundamental documents to inspire the participants who should not have suffered by virtue of being American citizens. According to him, Bull Conner was a product of circumstances in which these documents were conveniently bypassed to fulfill partisan goals and aims of a selected group of people. Such an argument acted miraculously in bringing the white moderates to King's cause. Although the civil rights advocates proclaimed to disobey "evil laws," they also remained committed to nonviolence, ruling out "retaliation" of any kind. As King mentioned, "[W]e will wear [those supporting segregation] down by our capacity to suffer [and] in winning the victory, we will not only win our freedom, we will also appeal to your heart and conscience that we will win in the process."[107] His basic concern was thus not merely to remove segregation but to create a beloved community that was free from artificially created racial prejudices. It was a difficult task to accomplish, although King, as a true apostle of nonviolence, always believed that "the dark clouds of racial prejudice will soon pass away and the deep fog of misunderstanding will be lifted from our fear-drenched communities."[108] By successfully courting violence while restraining violence in his followers, King and the SCLC projected the Birmingham struggle as one between good and evil forces. This easily gained him credibility among the blacks because of their faith in Christian ethics. Such a dramatic and also ritualized confrontation "proved irresistible to the media and, in turn, to audiences at home and abroad."[109] King's appeal thus turned out to be relevant to all Americans. Just as King was speaking to the clergymen and laymen alike, he spoke with them both as "a Christian and as an American."[110]

THE SELMA-TO-MONTGOMERY MARCH, 1965

What followed the Birmingham campaign was the Selma-to-Montgomery March of 1965, in which several civil rights organizations participated. The Selma campaign was the last sustained Southern protest movement that attracted whites as well. Unlike the 1963 Birmingham campaign, in which the King-led SCLC remained the nodal organization, the movement in Selma was reported to have been initiated by the Student Nonviolent Coordinating Committee (SNCC), the radical student organization. It has been shown that the SNCC was not at all happy with the SCLC's "more cautious leadership over the protest associated with the Selma to Montgomery march,"[111] although none of its key members were in a position to replace the SCLC's supremo, Martin Luther King Jr. For King, however, the association of the SNCC with the campaign was very useful in building and also sustaining the momentum of the movement. Given the emotional attachment of the committed SNCC members to the cause for racial equality, it was also easier for them to associate with the campaign, which had, surely, pursued a radical goal by seeking to guarantee voting rights to the blacks. The Selma campaign was led by King, who became not only a national hero because of his sustained role in the civil rights campaign, but also a global entity by 1965 when he won the Nobel Prize for Peace. So King's involvement with the Selma March immediately attracted international attention once the movement took off in early 1965.

The aim of the campaign was to achieve voting rights for Negroes in Selma, which would mean "ensuring a voice in their destiny."[112] The goal of the demonstrations was "to dramatize the existence of injustice"[113] being perpetuated in the name of obvious natural differences between the whites and their black counterparts. The reasons for the protest at Selma are not therefore difficult to seek, if judged in the light of the well-entrenched racist bias of the majority of the whites in the Dixie states. What allowed such an institutionalized racism was certainly "fear." The racist history of the blacks in the Deep South dictated that the black people could come together to do only three things: sing, pray, and dance; they were simply incapable of doing anything else, the argument goes, and if they tried to get involved in any other activity, they "were threatened or intimidated." For centuries, blacks had been taught to believe that "voting politics...is white folks' business [which] they monopolized by methods [ranging from] economic intimidation to murder."[114] It has been historically true that the blacks who held positions of power and respect in the Dixie towns were always at the mercy of the whites; the power that they had "was delegated to them by the white community [and] what the master giveth, the master can take away."[115] So they hardly held substantial power to address the racial imbalance in society not merely because of white domination, but also because of the "inferiority complex" that they were suffering from. From this perspective, the fight for voting rights was empowering, and King and, before him, the SNCC activists, agreed to be part of the demonstration since it would give the blacks a sense of being.[116] The second difficulty faced by the protestors related to the so-called parade ordinances, which prevented processions and also congregations without the approval of the city council. Given their "natural" submissiveness, the local blacks were restrained from undertaking any activity that was likely to provoke white retaliation. It was their "fear" that always surfaced whenever efforts were made to violate the "white-made and sponsored laws and conventions,"[117] despite blacks being the majority in Selma. The third link in the chain of denial was "the slow pace of the register and the limited number of days and hours for registration as voters."[118] This was a strategy that was consistently applied to restrict the black voters, as shown in the context of the Montgomery bus strike. Rosa Parks was denied registration by the same technique, which provoked protest from among the blacks in Montgomery. As a contemporary report shows, out of 15,000 Negroes, only 350 of them managed to register themselves. Besides taking these deliberate steps to prevent blacks from registering to vote, the officials in the council asked the applicants "abstruse, and in some cases, even fanciful questions to have pronounced their education inadequate when they could not answer."[119] This was an artificial barrier to voters' registration and was clearly unconstitutional according to the 1901 Alabama Constitution, which required, in addition to age, residence, sanity, and absence of a criminal record, lawful employment and the ability to read and write English or the ownership of property worth $ 300 or more. The prospective voters were also expected to pay $1.50 as a poll tax per year. As literacy had become widespread and the amount of the poll tax was so meager, it was almost impossible for the local authority to deny registration to the blacks. Hence, the segregationists devised newer techniques every day to scuttle the efforts of the blacks in registering to vote, evn though they were violating the categorical principles of the Constitution. One tactic involved the administration of a questionnaire to prospective voters to test their knowledge of the Constitution and the government. As the civil rights movement gained momentum, the questionnaire was used not to acquaint the voters with the basic ideas of American political life, but to test their knowledge before allowing registration—which was, again, unconstitutional. Black applicants—and occasionally their white counterparts—were denied registration for "the most minor and insignificant errors."[120] If a person made any mistake at all in filling out the form, the local authority could altogether reject the application. Such a rejection was "justified" even in cases where the interviewee failed to convince the authority about his character. This was the situation in Dallas County, of which Selma was a part. Here, the practice of denying voter applications was common, and the segregationists defended it as "a mere rule-based decision."[121] The final instrument of denial was the so-called literacy test. The board of registers introduced a new test in 1964 to examine whether applicants were well-enough acquainted with the Constitution and the system of governance. As a contemporary study demonstrates, during the three-year period before the 1965 approval of the legislation for voting rights, the proportion of registered black voters never crossed beyond 15 percent. The available statistics would thus seem to indicate that "the conduct of the board of registers was in fact vastly more significant than the content of the test in determining the number of blacks and whites who were added to the rolls [and] it was evident in the fact that regardless of the changes in the registration requirements, the board always managed to find the overwhelming majority of whites qualified and the overwhelming majority of black unqualified."[122]

The denial of registration to the blacks was institutionalized by various legal and extralegal stipulations that gained an easy acceptance among the segregationists for obvious reasons. Disregard for the constitutional principles was always paternalistically justified. As it was most eloquently put by King,

> Clearly the heart of the voting problem lay in the fact that the machinery for enforcing this basic right was in the hands of state-appointed officials answerable to the very people who believed they could continue to wield power in the South only so long as the Negro was disenfranchised. No matter how many loopholes were plugged, no matter how many irregularities were exposed, it was plain that difficulties were to remain so long as the segregationist mind-set continued to exist."[123]

Besides manipulating the rules and regulations, the local segregationists were determined not to disrupt the existing status quo in race relations for purely selfish reasons. It was therefore obvious that the SNCC, in its efforts to establish racial equality in Dallas County, was likely to face severe opposition. The situation became worse with King's arrival in January 1965. During the Selma campaign, violent segregationists "turned to terror tactics to prevent the Dallas County's blacks from following the example of the blacks in Montgomery and elsewhere."[124] The newly formed Citizens' Council came to their aid. Founded on racial prejudices, the council lamented the failure of the blacks "to realize that the Constitution was not written for them or any other colored race [and also proclaimed] that it was God's intention that whites should lead and black should follow."[125] Segregation, the council further added, was "a modus vivendi [that] has been worked out through the centuries in the South whereby two highly diverse races of people may live in the same community in peace and mutual achievement, freed of daily and constant irritations and conflicts that are inherent in a bi-racial society."[126] Hence the white moderates were warned by the council when they supported King on his arrival because not only would the movement disrupt social tranquility in the area, it would also weaken the foundational basis of racial co-existence in Selma. This worked both ways: the white moderates' fear of "negative publicity and also disturbance in the area" produced in them "a hostility to the King effort fully equal to that of the segregationists"; at the same time, the black moderates who were still uncertain as to whether they should support the movement rallied behind King and the SCLC. It is thus argued that "the initial effect of King's advent was to polarize the town completely along its racial division, by throwing the white moderates into the arms of the segregationists and the black moderates into the arms of those fighting for racial equality."[127] There is no doubt that King, with his remarkable charismatic quality and ability to pull together a crowd and supporters, galvanized the blacks in Selma to participate in a movement that was, of course, crystalized and consolidated by the radical SNCC. It was difficult for its radical members to completely ignore the nonviolent strategy that King and his colleagues adopted, given the widespread admiration of King and his zeal for leadership. Not only did the leading activists of the SNCC confront a dilemma over the leadership that King had projected, they were also "torn between their

desire to encourage mass militancy among southern blacks and their conflicting desire to avoid actions that would disrupt ongoing projects and interfere
with the developments of long term programs."[128] King also faced a dilemma.
He was reported to have been reluctant to choose Selma, which was considered
to be the SNCC's stronghold, "for fear that [the] SNCC would regard an SCLC
campaign as an invasion of SNCC territory."[129] The dilemma was resolved in
the context of the Selma campaign when the SNCC, or at least a majority of its
leading proponents, agreed to accept nonviolence given the mass support in
its favor. It was thus a strategic calculation that appeared to have provided the
SNCC with a great opportunity to remain critical in the Selma protest against
racial segregation.[130]

The situation was hardly nonviolent, especially when the segregationists began
retaliating against the protestors. A black youth, Jimmie Lee Jackson, died on
February 26 when he was shot while trying to protect his mother and grandmother
from a police beating. On March 7, police attacked, tear-gassed, and beat merci-
lessly a group of nonviolent marchers, and later, on March 11, a white Unitarian
minister, Reverend James Rebb, was beaten to death. This final incident seemed to
have electrified the entire atmosphere, and more than 400 ministers, rabbis, priests,
and nuns marched along with King in Selma.[131] Ten days after Rebb's death, the
proposed 54-mile Selma-Montgomery March resumed under the protection of the
Alabama National Guard, which was placed under federal control by order from
President Johnson. With the completion of the march, King had simultaneously
achieved two goals: on the one hand, he had succeeded in persuading the country's
highest political authority to seriously look into the issue of segregation; on the
other hand, he was able to argue that racism was a national issue affecting the rise
of America and the vision of the founding fathers. He assured white moderates that
they should not fear black backlash. By being committed to nonviolence despite
provocation otherwise, it was possible for King to retain the support of moderate
whites and also to expand his influence among those white moderates who were
fence sitters. What was remarkable was his capacity to articulate his ideology in
those terms that automatically built a base for the campaign for racial desegregation regardless of socioeconomic and political barriers. His aim was not merely to
protect the Negroes in America, but to fulfill the American dream as articulated by
the founding fathers through the Declaration of Independence, the Constitution,
and the 1863 Emancipation Proclamation. His was not a racist goal, but a national
goal, which, once attained, would truly translate the fundamental values of the
American Enlightenment into practice.

After the Selma imbroglio was resolved, King proclaimed,

Let us therefore continue our triumph and march to the realization of the
American dream. Let us march on segregated housing until every ghetto
of social and economic depression dissolves and Negroes and whites live
side by side in decent, safe and sanitary housing....Let us march on poverty until no American parent has to skip a meal so that their children
may eat. March on poverty until no starved man walks the streets of our

cities and towns in search of jobs that do not exist....Let us march on ballot boxes until we send to our city councils, state legislatures, and the United States Congress men who will not fear to do justice, love mercy and walk humbly with their God. Let us march on ballot boxes until all over Alabama's God's children will be able to walk the earth in decency and honor.[132]

One of the reasons for King's political success was certainly his ability to couch his ideological preferences for nonviolence within the overall liberal paradigm. He fought against racial segregation simply because it was highly un-American and was not rooted in the values of American constitutionalism. He was Gandhian in his outlook but did not justify nonviolence solely in Gandhian terms, but in terms of Christian ethics. This tactic immediately struck an emotional chord with the African Americans because of their religious affiliation with Christianity. The other significant point explaining the Selma success related to King's strategic sense: he agreed to lead the campaign, which was also organized and built by the militant SNCC, among others. It was possible for him to sustain the coalition because of his remarkable capacity to resolve differences through dialogue and discussion even with adversaries. Furthermore, his willingness to engage in dialogue always left room for discussion. It was thus not a strange coincidence that King was readily acceptable to the White House and that whenever there was a crisis in race relations, the Baptist pastor was invariably invited to find a respectable solution. Like Gandhi, he, by being receptive to other viewpoints, always sought to create a consensus among diverse opinions.

The result of King's efforts was obvious: one of the profound achievements of the 1965 Selma-Montgomery March was the August 1965 passage of the Voting Rights Act, which essentially killed, at least legally, the Jim Crow laws. The Voting Rights Act allowed the hitherto disenfranchised blacks to utilize their recently acquired rights to participate in the political processes, which had a significant impact on the electoral politics in the South. Many white officials who had earlier supported segregation were voted out of office, and those who wished to remain in office changed their attitude toward segregation and racial minorities. Even George Wallace, the Alabama governor and notoriously rabid segregationist, was also found "courting black voters for fear of being voted out of office."[133]

CONCLUDING OBSERVATIONS

An era of sustained mass militancy over civil rights issues came to an end with the acceptance of the 1965 Voting Rights Act. Two Alabama cities— Birmingham and Selma—created history: while the 1963 Birmingham campaign led to the 1964 Civil Rights Act, the Selma upsurge culminated in the outlawing of discriminatory voting practices with regard to the hitherto disenfranchised Negroes of the South. Both these important pieces of legislation ushered in a new era in which racial segregation was, at least legally, abolished.

By forcing the state to accept universal franchise, the movements that King and other civil rights organizations led appeared to have realized the core values of American constitutionalism, enshrined in the Declaration of Independence, the Constitution, and the Emancipation Proclamation. Both these acts deflated the Jim Crow system through their constitutional acceptance of racial desegregation, and amounted to "the second Reconstruction of the South restoring to black Southerners rights that had been formally granted" with the Emancipation Proclamation.[134] In this sense, the greatest contribution that King made was to give a sense of justice and honor to the socioeconomically peripheral and racially segregated blacks in the Dixie states. This had obvious ramifications elsewhere in the United States. There is no doubt that these movements and also the ensuing legislation became the basis of affirmative action in later years, whereby the underprivileged African Americans were given access to those facilities that were denied to them because of the Jim Crow laws. Undoubtedly, these revolutionary legislations initiated a process of change, though not adequate to radically alter the mind-set that endorsed various kinds of discrimination. Nevertheless, one cannot undermine the contribution of the struggle that King and his colleagues undertook to create a structure of governance based on the Jeffersonian dictum that "all should be treated equally." In this sense, the state has a responsibility to create conditions in which the American dream of creating a free and equal society is allowed to remain an inspiring ideal, as President Johnson underlined while defending the argument for universal franchise. As he stated,

> All Americans...should be indignant when one American is denied the right to vote. The loss of that right to a single citizen undermines the freedom of every citizen. This is why all of us should be concerned with the efforts of our fellow Americans to register to vote in Alabama....I hope that all Americans will join with me in expressing their concern over the loss of any American's right to vote....I intend to see that the right is secured for all our citizens.[135]

It is therefore not an exaggeration that the federal government appeared to have been favorably disposed toward the campaign for securing voting rights for the blacks in 1965. The visible change of attitude can be explained partly by the growing momentum of the civil rights movement across the state—a momentum that the ruling party could not afford to ignore—and partly by the increasing media publicity at home and abroad that threatened to seriously harm the global image of America as a democracy. Although desegregation disappeared, at least legally, with the adoption of the Civil Rights Acts, there was a paradoxical resurgence of Jim Crow in a different garb in the context of the changed environment of global capitalism. The African Americans, like their underprivileged counterparts elsewhere in the globe, continue to remain in racially segregated communities with inferior housing, public schools, and health care facilities.[136]

In the context of the movements that finally culminated in the acceptance of the Civil Rights Act in 1965, the 1963 March on Washington was the last nail in the coffin. Built on the spontaneous resentment of the blacks, the march was perhaps the most significant event in the rise of an America that finally abdicated, at least legally, the Jim Crow system of governance. Racial segregation was abolished by implementing the true spirit of the Fourteenth Amendment. This amendment had been, until this point, an abortive effort at constructing a racially equal society in America, presumably because of a well-entrenched racially prejudiced mind-set that was too strong to be overturned at that historical moment. Not only did the march inspire the blacks in the Dixie states, it became a source of congregation for the blacks and also white liberals elsewhere in the United States. Although the march was made possible because of sustained efforts by various African American organizations, it was a historical milestone in the consolidation of a nation-state that was free from, at least legally, racial prejudices. This was one of those rare campaigns for racial equality in which King was involved from the very outset, along with his colleagues, including Bayard Rustin, A. Philip Randolph, and others.

From the civil rights point of view, the March on Washington remained most significant not only because it represented a concerted effort on the part of the victims of racism but also because it was an occasion when King reaffirmed his faith in American liberalism by making his demands for racial desegregation in the language of the architects of the Constitution. The famous speech—"I Have a Dream"—is a clear testimony of how committed King was to liberalism. The idea of holding a mass rally came to him from Gandhi, who had, through the famous 1930 Dandi March in opposition to the salt tax, demonstrated the critical significance of mass rallies in political mobilization. According to Gandhi, the benefit of such a tactic was obvious because the Dandi March, while passing through several Indian villages during those 240 miles, acquainted the local people with the nationalist cause as well as with the devilish political design of the British government. Gandhi immediately struck an emotional bond with the people, who, to a significant extent, helped him mobilize for the nationalist cause. The British administration was alarmed, and it was admitted that "the personal influence of Gandhi threaten[ed] to create a position of real embarrassment to the [government]....In some areas, he ha[d] already achieved a considerable measure of success in undermining the authority of the government."[137]

While the Montgomery bus strike was a micro experiment, the 1963 March on Washington was its macro manifestation. One can thus draw a parallel between the King-led transport boycott in Montgomery and the Gandhi-led nonviolent resistance in Champaran, Kheda, and Ahmedabad. Gandhi led these movements at the local level before applying his lesson at the pan-Indian level in the context of the 1920–22 Noncooperation Movement. In terms of ideological aims, those of the March on Washington were similar to those of the 240-mile Dandi March in 1930. Besides mobilizing blacks and white moderates around issues of racism, the March on Washington put direct pressure on the Kennedy government to rearticulate its responses toward one-tenth of the American populace. In a similar way, Gandhi attained a political victory in the Dandi March by forcing the British government to withdraw the salt tax. While this move had no effect on the financial health of the empire given the tax's meager contribution to the annual budget, the withdrawal of salt tax was however a testimony to British weakness in the face of the nationalist challenge, which was certainly a strategic victory for Gandhi and his colleagues. The selection of Dandi was strategic and aimed to gain maximum political mileage. Dandi was a small and extremely poor hamlet, and it was thus inadequate to accommodate the large contingent of people who accompanied Gandhi. Since it was given wide publicity, several journalists from all over the world came to witness the occasion. Not only did these journalists publicize the violation of government decree by nonviolent means, they also wrote about the poverty that the Indians were subjected to because of the failure of the British government to take care of their basic needs. The Dandi March was thus a magic stroke that blended "the strong political message with a human interest story that caught the imagination of millions in India and abroad."[138]

In conceptual terms, the Montgomery bus strike was an act of omission, while the March on Washington and the Selma-Montgomery March were acts of commission, just like Gandhi's Noncooperation Movement was illustrative of the former whereas the Dandi March represented the latter. This is a conceptual distinction that Gene Sharp makes while explaining the nature of nonviolent resistance. According to Sharp, acts of omission are those where people may refuse to perform acts that they usually perform, are expected, by custom, to perform, or are required by law or regulation to perform; acts of commission, contrarily, involve those acts that people do not usually perform, are not expected by custom to perform, or are forbidden by law or regulation to perform.[139] Following Sharp's distinction, one can broadly classify the nonviolent movements that Gandhi and King launched in their respective domain: the 1955 Montgomery bus strike largely remained an act of omission because boycott of public transport, or avoidance of acts that people of Montgomery usually performed, was the main agenda. Gandhi's first pan-Indian movement of noncooperation with the British belonged to this category. The Dandi March and the rallies that King undertook were identical in nature because both had the aim of forcing the respective governments to accept the demands that, despite being "legitimate" from the participants' point of view, did not receive serious attention from the administration. The distinction may not always be appropriate to comprehend the complexities of movements, as these two forms of acts remain interwoven in an equally complex way. But its analytical utility is beyond question.

Conclusion

Confluence of Thought seeks to support the argument that the moral politics of redemptive love and nonviolence that Gandhi and King consistently pursued represents an appealing vision for the present century. Their commitment to non-violence and their desire for social justice shine forth in the darkness of an age of nuclear weapons and genocide. They thus remain an inspiration to each new generation of thinkers and activists in the political tradition of nonviolence that bears their names. In the light of the detailed discussion in the preceding chapters one can safely deduce that Gandhi and King were perhaps the best examples of individuals who successfully combined instinctive ideology (religion) with its derived counterpart from the great texts into a dynamic synthesis. Gandhi evolved his model of nonviolent struggle by blending together his personal religious faith with deep social commitment. In his perception, service to humanity was the path to "self-actualization" and thus spiritually most fulfilling. In an identical way, King sought a similar blend of religion with social involvement. Religion without a clear social purpose was futile since King believed that "God is both finite and personal—a loving Father who strives for good against the evil that exists in the universe [and mortal human beings] are his instruments in that glorious struggle."[1]

By pursuing religion-driven social action, both Gandhi and King articulated their political mission at enormous personal sacrifice; they treaded the same pathway at the ends of their lives. Assassins' bullets silenced each of them, and their missions remained unfulfilled. Gandhi was marginalized in the Indian political scene after independence, which occurred just a few months before his death. Following Britain's withdrawal in 1947, India was partitioned into two independent countries, India and Pakistan, despite Gandhi's vehement opposition, which he expressed by saying that India would be partitioned "on his dead body."[2] King's untimely demise at the age of thirty-nine likewise robbed him of the chance to fulfill his ultimate sociopolitical mission, and life, to him, thus became "a continual story of shattered dreams."[3] Nonetheless, he stood in a class by himself by organizing successful political campaigns against racial segregation, starting with the 1955 Montgomery bus strike that finally culminated in the acceptance of the 1965 Voting Rights Act and political equality. Despite being the pivot of the civil rights campaign, it would not have been possible for him to attain the goal without the unflinching support of his equally committed colleagues and supporters. These supporters were hardly bothered about the adverse consequences of their participation in the movement, as they sought to translate into reality the basic values of American liberalism, manifested in the Declaration of Independence, the Constitution, and the 1863 Emancipation Proclamation.

II

By drawing on the ideas of Gandhi and King, the aim of this book is also to provide a critique of Benedict Anderson's conceptualization of "modular forms."[4] An idea borrowed from mathematics, modular forms refer to those equations that can easily be applied to identical circumstances. Modular forms are considered to be a stepping stone to further advancement in mathematical research. While seeking to explain the sociological roots of nationalism as a unifying category, Benedict Anderson, in his *Imagined Communities* (1983), forcefully argued that the form of nationalism that had emerged in Europe and North America seemed to have provided a modular form that was emulated elsewhere in the world. His assessment is based on his argument that given the complementarity of nationalism and capitalism, it was obvious that favorable socioeconomic and political circumstances would emerge to support the articulation of nationalism in these areas. This further means that nationalism preexists in a modular form and hence the basic tenets of one form of nationalism (i.e., pan-European and North American) can easily be exported to other countries (i.e., non-European and non-American circumstances). According to Anderson, nations are not so much the product of specific sociological circumstances such as language, race, religion, and so on but are imagined into existence. Nations seen as "imagined communities" appear to be a useful construct in underlining the homogeneity of interests of various sections of society in any struggle against colonial powers. His theorization is totalizing—a universal history of the modern world that fails completely to consider the dynamics of anticolonial nationalisms in Afro-Asian countries. The conceptualization of modular forms is a theoretical attempt to redefine "anticolonial resistance" within a predetermined framework of analysis that tends to bypass, if not undermine, the creative articulation of nationalism in struggles for political freedom from colonialism elsewhere. Partha Chatterjee, in his *The Nation and its Fragments*,[5] takes issue with Anderson's conception of "modular" forms of nationalism. According to Chatterjee, such a concept hardly explains the nationalism that emerged in the context of anticolonial political mobilization in India. He accepts Anderson's basic premise about the essentially "invented" nature of national identities and the importance of such factors as "print capitalism" in their spread and consolidation. He however challenges Anderson's assumption concerning "modular forms" of nationalist intervention since it ignores the point that if modular forms are completely fashioned and exported, nothing is left to be imagined.

My study of the confluence of Gandhi's and King's thought confirms the obvious limitations of Benedict Anderson's "universalized" claim of modular forms of nation, nationalism, and national identity. Since Anderson seeks to provide a universal design for nationalism (or "one size fits all"), he appears to have underplayed, if not ignored, the critical role that context plays in shaping a particular idea. For Anderson, the nation is an imagined community, but if it exists as a modular form, there is nothing to be imagined. Furthermore, the imagined community cannot be divorced from the socioeconomic milieu in which it is conceptualized. Hence, applied to another circumstance, any modular form is likely to deviate from its original incarnation. Anderson's argument does not leave any scope for the creative articulation of the community since his theorization is totalizing, seeking to build a universal history of the modern world that fails completely to consider the dynamics of a community with reference to its prevalent circumstances.

Despite having been inspired by the Western Enlightenment, Gandhi articulated his language of "nationalism" in a way that was both context driven and intellectually innovative, since India was hardly "a nation" in the conventional Western sense. Likewise, King was hardly persuaded by the conventional interpretation of Christianity, which appeared to have justified segregation by "distorting" the messages of the New Testament. Here he found the ideas of Reinhold Niebuhr, Walter Rauschenbush, Howard Thurman, Benjamin E. Mays, and Mordecai Johnson, among others, very pertinent in reconceptualizing the fundamental tenets of Christianity. He found it possible to argue that "segregation is an existential expression of man's tragic separation, an expression of his awful estrangement, his terrible sinfulness."[6] So challenging the segregation ordinances was justified because they were morally wrong. Howard Thurman's *Jesus and the Disinherited* (1949) reinforced King's perception of Christianity as a liberating ideology. The distinction that Thurman made between "Christianity" and the "religion of Jesus" enabled King to reinterpret Christianity as a set of rejuvenating socioeconomic ideals. According to Thurman, Jesus was a true genius "who was so conditioned and organized within himself that he became a perfect instrument for the embodiment of a set of ideals—ideals of such dramatic potency that they were capable of changing the calendar, rechanneling the thought of the world, and placing a new sense of the rhythm of life in a weary, nerve-snapped civilization."[7] Like Gandhi, who reinvented the nationalist discourse so that it was not derivative or heteronymous but based on "difference,"[8] King, by emphasizing the Sermon on the Mount, reinterpreted Christianity. His followers readily accepted him as an authentic voice, presumably because of his recognized role as a pastor. Gandhi gave him the instrument of nonviolence which, King argued, was an articulation of Jesus's ethics. King's conceptualization of civil resistance was also creative in that it drew its sustenance from nonviolence. And, while King was indebted to Gandhi for the concept of nonviolence, he redefined its foundational basis by drawing attention to Christianity, especially the Sermon on the Mount.

The preceding argument follows from the way that both Gandhi and King reinvented traditions in accordance with their own theoretical inclination and also their perception of the reality that they had confronted while organizing protest movements for genuine socioeconomic and political causes. Benedict Anderson's theoretical formulation of "modular forms," despite being intellectually conceivable, does not seem to provide any scope to articulate ideas or conceptualizations that are not exactly "derivative" in their theoretical content. Hence it can safely be argued that Anderson's model has a limited application presumably because of its ethnocentric roots. The theoretical intervention made by Gandhi and King is refreshing in three distinct ways: (a) it enables us to conceptualize a situation that is not exactly derivative of European or American sociopolitical circumstances; (b) it also provides a persuasive argument to creatively understand context-driven ideas by reference to their specific socioeconomic roots; and (c) it also exposes the inherent limitations of the argument defending a "one-size-fits-all" syndrome.

III

Gandhi was a religious seeker, and his interests and experiments were far more extensive and thorough than King ever gave him credit for. As the nationalist movement unfolded, Gandhi introduced several new ideas that hardly figured when he first conceptualized and launched it. The political movement was not insulated from his personal life, and his commitment to nonviolence was total to the extent of being "rigid." The withdrawal of the 1920–22 Noncooperation Movement, which followed the violence during the anti-British protest in Chauri Chaura in the United Provinces, was an example of this.

Gandhi never abdicated asceticism while pursuing his political goals because he believed that asceticism and nonviolence complemented each other. He preferred ascetic life because of its obvious strategic advantage in the Indian context, in which asceticism was usually preferred—presumably because families inculcated religious values in children at a very young age. Gandhi had his personal reasons too: he regarded asceticism as necessary for his self-purification and the fulfillment of spiritual goals that remained distant otherwise. Asceticism also contributed to and strengthened concern for others because only through an ascetic life and self-denial could one easily give up bodily comfort. As long as individuals remained attached to worldly comfort and pleasure, the sources of violence would remain, and people would find it difficult to be completely nonviolent, as Gandhi argued. His main concern was to establish self-control over mind, body, and spirit. He inherited this concern from the great Hindu saint Patanjali, who taught five major ingredients of discipline: noninjury, truth, nontheft, continence, and noncovetousness.[9] Throughout his political career, in pursuit of rigid self-discipline, Gandhi, as King pointed out, "adhered to austere diets, undertook prolonged fasts, pursued the ideal of non-possession or voluntary poverty, wore a loin cloth, took a vow of sexual abstinence at the age of thirty-six, chose for his home a very poor village where untouchables predominated, and for more than a total of six years endured the privations of prison life."[10] King felt that these experiences helped Gandhi to achieve "not only the capacity to avoid the commission of external violence but also the strength to preserve non-violence of the spirit."[11] King might not have had an ascetic life in the sense Gandhi had, but in his desire to be a true Christian, he also endured sacrifice and suffering. By challenging the Jim Crow laws of segregation, he lent a powerful voice to the disinherited blacks of America, even though his actions put his life in constant danger. His decision to take a minimum salary from the Southern Christian Leadership Conference (SCLC) and willingness to live with his family in a shack in Chicago during the 1966 Chicago Housing Struggle also reflect the extent to which King was agreeable to a simple life. Coretta King, his wife, confirmed this by reminiscing that "Martin always tried to eliminate from our own lives all things that we could do without."[12] He was totally convinced that much of the corruption in America "stems from the desire to acquire material things—houses, land and cars." After his trip to India, he became far more devoted than ever to the Gandhian "simplicity of living," which was, according to him, not conceivable in "the mechanized complexity of American life."[13] He even considered the idea of changing his "style of dress to a simpler one," but did not pursue this route as "unusual dress might even tend to alienate followers."[14] As Coretta King recollected, King always faced a dilemma since he was not as "ascetic" as Gandhi was, though he came to terms with this apparent deviation by saying that

in our civilization, a man who has to travel a lot will do his job more efficiently with a car; he could not function without having a place to live, and would have great difficulty without a telephone. [King] thus accepted that in the conditions prevailing in America, we had to have certain things and that he must strive to be more like Gandhi spiritually.[15]

Over the course of time, King seemed to have realized the importance of self-introspection, which Gandhi found most useful in thinking through the miseries of existence and myopic ideological vision. Immediately after the 1965 Selma-to-Montgomery March, he expressed his thoughts by saying, "I subject myself to self-purification and to endless self-analysis; I question and soul-search constantly into myself to be as certain as I can that I am fulfilling my sense of purpose, that I am holding fast to my ideals, that I am guiding my people in the right direction."[16]

Thomas Weber, in *Gandhi as Disciple and Mentor*,[17] addresses the differences between Gandhi and King in their approach to nonviolent civil resistance by making a distinction between "whole Gandhi" and "political Gandhi."[18] This book is attentive to this distinction while pursuing the argument of "the confluence of thought" between Gandhi and King. The African Americans did not appear to have appreciated Gandhi's ascetic life or esoteric practices; they were not inspired by Gandhi's vegetarianism, celibacy, or naturopathy, presumably because they never considered them relevant to their struggle. King may not have been exactly spiritually inclined in the sense Gandhi was, but he was persuaded to accept Gandhi's strategy of nonviolence as perhaps the best instrument to fight against racial prejudices. In this sense he tilted toward the "political Gandhi." African Americans brought the message of nonviolence to the United States long before King emerged on the political scene, and this message seemed to have been received favorably by the black churches in the Southern states because of its compatibility with Christian ethics. The Gandhian method of resistance—satyagraha—attracted black attention rather easily because it "demands courageous resistance [and also] humane attitude toward adversaries."[19] The Christian notion of *agape* was most clearly articulated by Gandhi's focus on "disinterested love" as an organizing principle; agape "brings Gandhi's spirit of inclusiveness into an American context."[20] As King meaningfully articulated, "[I]n our struggle against racial segregation, I came to see at a very early stage that a synthesis of Gandhi's method of nonviolence and the Christian ethics of love is the best weapon available to Negroes for their struggle for freedom and human dignity."[21] This perhaps explains why King readily accepted nonviolence as "a political technique," while he ignored other significant aspects of Gandhi's spiritually endorsed sociopolitical ideas. For instance, fasting was an important dimension in Gandhi's nonviolent civil resistance. It was also an important aspect of his existence as a human being because fasting was, as Gandhi characterized, "the spiritual medicine that he applies from time to time for diseases that yield to that particular treatment."[22] He even believed that political violence or the breakdown of satyagraha was but a reflection of the satyagrahi's failure to exercise swaraj in the sense of controlling one's basic instincts.[23]

King did not appear to have been persuaded by such a Gandhian mode of asceticism. He also did not find Gandhi's ruthless critique of Western industrialization persuasive though, by 1967–68, he had taken a stronger position against American capitalism, suggesting that the removal of racial segregation also involved a radical restructuring of the prevalent socioeconomic entitlements. This means that African Americans were drawn to Gandhi's belief system because it provided a clear voice—the voice of nonviolence—to those opposing repression and torture. They found in Gandhi a clear articulation of the

Christian traditions of renunciation; they were also "tethered to the pragmatism of a Gandhian grammar of dissent in its everyday operations against regimes of foreign and native oppression."[24] One thus gets inspired to fight for justice without necessarily being persuaded by Gandhi's spiritual quest and ideas about the unity of life.[25] Although "the political Gandhi" became "prominent" in King's *weltanschauung*, it will be conceptually restrictive if we undermine the philosophical underpinnings behind its making. There is hardly a situation where the "whole Gandhi" is likely to be articulated, given its specific socioeconomic roots in colonial India and South Africa.

What is thus most intellectually challenging in grasping the confluence of ideas between Gandhi and King is understanding the roots and articulation of their ideas in the context of their different socioeconomic circumstances. In this sense, the confluence of thought argument seems appropriate for conceptualizing the interesting trajectory of sociopolitical ideas that were rooted in two entirely different socioeconomic and political circumstances, as the argument draws upon basic human values that are "universal" in character. Likewise, by defending Christianity in the spirit of the Sermon on the Mount, King clearly showed that he had drawn on different traditions. He was therefore not exactly imitating Gandhi but utilized the Gandhian technique in the American context. His account of the Montgomery bus strike, *Stride toward Freedom*, clearly "privileges the Sermon on the Mount: it was Jesus of Nazareth that stirred the Negroes to protest with the creative weapon of love," while Gandhi offered "merely technical assistance."[26] This was also evident in his repeated assertion that the civil rights campaign was a synthesis of the Gandhian method with the ethic of Christian love. It was not therefore surprising that his admonitions to followers "drew upon the Bible more often than upon the pages of the *Indian Opinion* [by drawing the attention of the participants to the Christian dictum that] they that take the sword will perish by the sword."[27] Gandhi gave him the instrument of nonviolence. In turn, King argued that nonviolence was an articulation of Jesus's ethics. This was a creative conceptualization of civil resistance that drew its sustenance from nonviolence. King was thus indebted to Gandhi though he redefined the foundational basis of nonviolence by drawing attention to Christian ethics, as articulated in the Sermon on the Mount.

IV

There is no doubt that Gandhi was the supreme leader in India's freedom struggle. As shown in chapter 1, his nationalist colleagues, despite being critical of his fascination with nonviolence and his reluctance to challenge Hindu orthodoxy, never pursued their respective ideological goals to the extent of damaging the anti-British political platform. The Indian National Congress, which Gandhi led and revamped, provided him with institutional support during India's freedom struggle. At the same time, it is also true that Gandhi failed to instill confidence in the Muslims in India, who found a more reliable and gratifying voice in M. A.

Jinnah. While Gandhi had opposed the two-nation theory from the day it was conceptualized in Lahore in 1940, India was partitioned in 1947, marring the freedom movement.

In the United States, the black church played a fundamental role in the making of Martin Luther King Jr. Not only did it provide a readily available institutional platform, it also placed him in direct contact with the black believers and allowed him to gradually build his image as a crusader. This was a great opportunity that King utilized to the fullest possible extent to pursue his ideological goal of racial desegregation. In this sense, the role that the Indian National Congress played for Gandhi is the role that the black Baptist church played for King. Nonetheless, the black church was not always a help in the struggle against Jim Crow racial restrictions, and it is a myth that it was the central institution providing essential resources and leadership. Still, a section of the African American clergy, including King, C. T. Vivian, James Lawson, Andrew Young, Ralph David Abernathy, Fred Shuttlesworth, and others, played a crucial role in the entire struggle, while the black church, as an institution, was "deeply divided over the protest strategies and tactics of the de-segregation campaigns."[28] It is true that a sizeable section of the black clergies allowed their churches to be utilized "as freedom schools, sites for political meetings and voter registration training,"[29] but a large majority did not appear to be very enthusiastic. In fact, the largest African American congregation, the National Baptist Convention, remained aloof from the King-steered SCLC movement. Besides general apathy and also dislike for King and his colleagues, especially Bayard Rustin and A. Philip Randolph because of their alleged communist leanings, many ministers were reluctant to take part in the campaign for racial equality presumably because they "for years had been on the private payroll of white political and business elites [and thus] had a financial interest in maintaining the Jim Crow status quo."[30] Besides these contextual reasons, the blacks were internally divided due to socioeconomic differences. The concept of black unity was "illusory," argued Rustin, and it is therefore wrong to assume that "blacks think monolithically."[31] In fact, Rustin was not in favor of racial unity; instead he felt strongly that "it is far more important for blacks to form alliances with other forces of society which share common needs and common goals and which are in general agreement over the means to achieve them."[32]

There was even division among NAACP (National Association for the Advancement of Colored People) activists over King's strategy of nonviolence. Some felt that nonviolence would not work in the United States. William Pickens of the NAACP raised, for instance, serious questions about the feasibility of nonviolent civil resistance against a well-entrenched state in his columns in *New York Amsterdam News*. He argued that the Gandhian method was not workable simply because it originated in circumstances that were radically different from those in the United States. Charging those who were in favor of Gandhian nonviolence as people "who reason in shallow analogies," Pickens argued that "mere prayer shall not solve the race problem [unless]...it is coupled with, as the Christian Bible clearly mentions, work, with suffering, paying with courage of performance."[33] He also offered a second, far more contemplative, argument. Gandhi led a domestic majority against minority foreigners, while African Americans found themselves a minority in relation to their fellow citizens, who constituted a majority in the United States. In the latter instance, civil disobedience or boycott would have been suicidal. If the Negroes had started "a boycott against working for and trading with white people, or against buying any of the facilities, owned and controlled by whites, [they] would [have been] the first to freeze and starve."[34] The whites would have been "crippled," but the blacks would have been "utterly ruined."[35] Similarly, nonpayment of taxes or resignation from government offices would never have been appropriate simply because nonpayment of tax would lead to seizure of property, and withdrawal from official position was of no consequence as such positions could easily be replaced. So, as Pickens argued, the Gandhian model had limited application in the context of the US socioeconomic structure.[36]

Despite uncertainty regarding the feasibility of nonviolence as a strategy to challenge racial segregation, the idea, which cohered with a fundamental biblical message, appeared to have swayed even a large section of white Americans. There were thus clear divisions even among the Southerners, who generally endorsed and supported racial hierarchy. The South was, argued DuBois,

> not solid [because]…the attitude of the Southern whites toward the blacks is not, as so many assume, in all cases the same; the ignorant Southerner hates the Negro, the workingmen fear his competition, the money-makers wish to use him as a laborer, some of the educated see a menace in his upward development, while others—usually sons of the masters—wish to help him to rise.[37]

DuBois's description of the situation was quite accurate: over the course of time a sizeable section of Southerners emerged who, without any moral commitment, found themselves compelled to break with the segregationists in order "to restore social peace, a good business climate or the good name of their city in the national headlines."[38] As contemporary studies show, these middle-of-the-road Southerners "sought a quiet role for themselves, and when exposed, they were accused of violating the southern way of life and betraying their race; [nonetheless], by their sheer numbers and standing in the community, they undermined the credibility of their attackers."[39]

As shown by David Chappell in his work on the civil rights campaign,[40] white drivers shuttled blacks and whites to MIA (Montgomery Improvement Association) meetings in various parts of the city during the 1955 Montgomery bus strike. This act annoyed segregationists, but it undoubtedly ensured a critical mass of participation in the meetings. White Southerners gave financial contributions to support the movement for racial desegregation, and the MIA records confirm that the amount that the protestors raised from the whites was quite substantial. Such contributions were testimony to the fact that "there were many white people in Montgomery who were willing to see the system change [because they felt that] a segregated society was not some abstract, alien thing to the black participants in the movement but a form of degradation and insult, maintained by a particular group of white people in the name of all white people."[41] Persuaded by the moral argument that racial discrimination was contrary to Christianity and also the American Constitution, the white clergy seemed to have endorsed the King-led campaign since "it would help the South through a peaceful and orderly transitional period toward the integration that is inevitable [and] if King...who has been working on the guilty conscience of the South...can bring us contrition, that is our hope."[42] So the motives of the whites for supporting the civil rights agitation were, as the available research shows, "varied and complex—a mixture of altruism, pragmatism, paternalism, guilt and numerous other idiosyncratic sentiments."[43]

V

During the nationalist movement in India, several images were projected around the human Gandhi. In a peculiar unfolding of the freedom struggle, Gandhi redefined "politics" as being not confined to "a defined sphere" but invading everyday life. Gandhi was not merely a leader; he also became a part of the masses. His simple attire, use of colloquial Hindi, and reference to the popular allegory of *Ramrajya* "made him comprehensible to the common people." In popular myths, he was invested with a supernatural power that could heal pain and deliver common people from their day-to-day miseries. The masses interpreted Gandhi in their own ways, drawing meanings from their own lived experiences, and made him a symbol of power for the weak and underprivileged. As evident on various occasions, the masses "crossed the boundaries of Gandhian politics and deviated from his ideals of non-violence, ... while believing at the same time that they were following their messiah into a new utopian world of Gandhi raj."[44]

The British government expressed surprise at Gandhi's growing popularity during the Noncooperation Movement, a time when he was still not so well known to the Indian masses. An intelligence report of 1921 underlined the unprecedented quality of his appeal among the people in a small town in Uttar Pradesh while describing their reaction to news of a probable visit. The report says that as soon as the announcement was made that he was coming,

Hindu and Moslem villagers [came] from long distances—on foot, with their bedding on their heads and shoulders, on bullock carts, on horseback, as if a great pilgrimage was going on, and the estimate that nearly a lakh of persons [100,000] had come and gone back disappointed. It was simply touching to see how eagerly they inquired if there was any hope of his coming. Never before has any political leader, or perhaps even a religious leader, in his own lifetime stirred the masses to their very depths throughout the country and received the homage of so many people....His influence is certainly phenomenal and quite unprecedented."[45]

While explaining Gandhi's role in galvanizing the masses into action in the 1920–22 Noncooperation Movement it has thus been argued that "there was no single authorized version of the Mahatma to which [the participants of the Noncooperation Movement] may be said to have subscribed in 1921. Indeed, their ideas about Gandhi's 'orders' and 'powers' were often at variance with those of the local Congress-Khilafat leadership and clashed with the basic tenets of Gandhism itself. The violence of Chauri Chaura was rooted in this paradox"[46] The events during the Quit India movement demonstrate that on various occasions, Gandhi, the person, appeared insignificant in comparison with "the image of Mahatma," which was constantly reworked in popular vision. Arguably, neither Gandhi nor the Congress High Command would have approved of such co-optation. For instance, during the height of the Quit India movement, several images of Gandhi gained currency. To the people of Contai, West Bengal, the Mahatma, endowed with divine power, could never be killed; people believed that Gandhi was not "hurt" even when the British police fired bullets at him. Gandhi could not be kept in jail since, according to a rumor, he, with his power, could escape the prison as soon as he wanted. People in the small Bengal hamlet of Tamluk believed that "if you uttered the name, Gandhi, before the British police they would lose the capacity to fire."[47] The mass confidence in Gandhi spread across the country, and it was not surprising that people in far-flung Gorakhpur believed that "bullets ha[d] turned into water by the grace of Gandhiji."[48] Thus it was not merely coincidental that the slogan "Gandhiji ki jai" (victory to the Mahatma) became very popular in the course of the movement. The British administration, taking note of the tremendous influence of Gandhi in shaping the popular psyche, seemed perplexed at the rapid dissemination of his ideas in remote areas of the district. What probably drew people to Gandhi's ideas was his image as "a savior" of the poverty-stricken masses. A contemporary police report[49] mentioned that "the real power of [Gandhi's] name is perhaps to be traced back to the ideal" that the Mahtama devoted his life to the cause of the poor Indians. The Congress mobilization during the nationalist phase demonstrated the effectiveness of Gandhi's image, which significantly contributed to the consolidation of anti-British sentiments at the grassroots level. The Congress's success thus lay in its ability to meaningfully explain and translate Gandhi's agenda. Although the Quit India Movement was launched by the Congress, its success can be attributed largely to the role of a new group of political activists across India. By translating Gandhian ideas in such a way as to gain maximum mileage, the local leaders articulated their political agenda by attributing the popular grievances to imperialism. Furthermore, the interpretation of Gandhi's ideas also varied in accordance with the preferences of the leadership involved in the mobilization for the anti-British offensive. Thus, for instance, one type of leadership exemplified in Swami Prajnananda in Bengal, Swami Darshanananda in Bihar, or Baba Ramchandra in Pratapgarh invested the Gandhian message with particularly strong religious overtones. The critical role of outsiders reveals a significant theoretical gap in the spontaneity thesis by highlighting the role of the leadership in realizing the revolutionary potential of the rural masses in accordance with a specific political goal.

Gandhi emerged as the supreme leader of the nationalist movement presumably because of his capacity to mobilize people regardless of caste, creed, and clan. His appeal was universal and was interpreted differently by different sections of society. As Judith Brown argues,

> To the really poor and illiterate Gandhi's message and appeal was social and religious. To the more prosperous peasants and the traders and the professional men of small towns his appeal became more overtly political; while at the highest level of political participation he could couch demands in the language of legislature and constitution.[50]

As a leader, he was most appealing perhaps due to his success in addressing several social constituencies at the same time. The issues that he raised were not always exactly political, but social and religious as well, which probably helped Gandhi expand his constituencies of support. By linking the political struggle with the fight against various kinds of injustice, meted out to the underprivileged to defend structural inequalities, Gandhi fused the nationalist campaign with the struggle for social justice. His appeal was thus twofold. Apart from resisting foreign rule, he also undertook several steps to fight against well-entrenched social evils, justified in the name of religion and religious prejudices. This is where the Gandhian charisma is located.

It was not possible for the British administration to gauge Gandhi's appeal when he first appeared on the scene. Recognizing the "unusual" significance of Gandhi in nationalist political mobilization in the context of the Noncooperation Movement, Lord Willingdon, the tough Madras governor who had little appreciation for what Gandhi was pursuing, thus commented, "Gandhi is here with the whole of his gang. It is amazing what an influence this man is getting. One of my ADCs came from Calcutta with them in the train and was tremendously impressed with the huge crowds at every station, their orderliness, and absolute devotion to their leader....Now I admit [that] the position is becoming one of extraordinary difficulty. There is no doubt that Gandhi has got a tremendous hold on the public imagination."[51]

Jawaharlal Nehru described Gandhi as "a powerful current of fresh air that made us stretch ourselves and take deep breaths; a beam of light that pierced the darkness and removed the scales from our eyes; a whirlwind that upset many things, but most of all the working of people's minds."[52] The essence of his teaching was "fearlessness and truth, and action allied to these always keeping the welfare of the masses in view."[53] Unless "the system that produces misery and poverty of peasants and workers" was totally removed, freedom appeared futile. Nehru attributed the meteoric rise of Gandhi on the national scene to his capacity to identify with the masses, "speaking their language and incessantly drawing attention to them and their appalling conditions." Gandhi was never an outsider. He seemed to have emerged from millions of Indian citizens. Organically

linked with the mass psyche, ahimsa acquired a different connotation when it
became an ideological weapon in the nationalist struggle. Similarly, satyagraha,
a technique with roots in the Indian tradition, appeared most devastating to the
colonial rulers when endorsed by the masses. Unable to gauge the effectiveness
of ahimsa and love as political weapons, Lord Reading, the viceroy, dismissed
the Gandhi-led anti-British Noncooperation Movement by saying that Gandhi's
views bordered on "fanaticism that non-violence and love will give India its
independence and enable it to withstand the British government."[54] Hence he
found it difficult to understand his practice of them in politics. That the viceroy misread Gandhi was proved beyond a doubt as the nationalist movement in
India had unambiguously demonstrated the fact that "the gospel of love" was far
more effective than hatred and the fragility of "brute force" against "soul force"
that informed Gandhi's technique of satyagraha. There is no doubt that Gandhi
reinvented India's freedom struggle by introducing the ideology of nonviolence
in the anti-British campaign. However he failed to transcend, in the early stages
of the new dispensation, the limitation of his environment. It was thus stated in
a confidential report from the American Embassy in Madras that "far off indeed
yet is the day when non-violence or love will be the ruling factor in determining
the relations between man and man and nation and nation, the day that signifies
unalloyed love for living beings."[55]

To the British government, Gandhi remained an explosive force, and to the
people of India, he was perhaps the most effective political leader—a person who
swayed the masses with his persona as an ideological messiah. His charisma had
a cultural referent. Gandhi's effectiveness as "a peripatetic teacher was related
less to his oratorical or theatrical skills," argue Lloyd and Susan Hoeber Rudolph,
"than to the reputation that preceded him and the ideal that he embodied."[56]
While underlining Gandhi's popularity and magical capacity in defusing tension between Hindus and Muslims, even during the height of the 1946 Calcutta
riots, the Calcutta-based counselor of the American Embassy stated that

> he is constantly besieged in his temporary home [in Calcutta] by people
> seeking his advice on all sorts of political and personal problems. The
> assembled crowd always insisted on his appearing at a window briefly
> to speak to them. The noise and clamor caused him to hold his ears: in
> explaining his action, he remarked that he hoped that brain was still young
> but that his ears were getting old.[57]

Gandhi was also widely credited "with being the wizard responsible for the
magical transformation of Calcutta." The peace rallies that were organized at
Gandhi's behest attracted people from various sections of the city. There was no
doubt that Gandhi's presence in the riot-torn city of Calcutta, as the report suggests, quelled the tension between Hindus and Muslims in the city.

In India's freedom struggle, Gandhi played an undeniably critical role: his
ideological belief in nonviolence inspired the participants in the anticolonial
struggle despite adverse consequences. The Mahatma always remained a referent

even when he was not on the scene, as was the case during the 1942 open rebellion. It is therefore not surprising that local activists built and consolidated the nationalist movement in accordance with their interpretation of the Gandhian message of nonviolence.

King played a similarly critical role in the movements in which he was involved. Following the 1955 Montgomery bus strike, King was consistently projected as the face of the civil rights agitation, as he was nationally and internationally acclaimed for his involvement in the movement. Nonetheless, his role in organizing the campaign was not so critical outside of his massive appeal among Americans irrespective of color. One King colleague who steadfastly contributed to the civil rights movement by building and consolidating an organization to support the campaign was Bayard Rustin. Beginning with the Montgomery agitation, it was Rustin who exerted "a strong behind-the-scene influence on King and later protestors."[58] He was well known as an active member of the Communist Youth League before he joined the civil rights campaign, but he left the league out of his disillusionment over his colleagues' level of commitment to the cause of the underprivileged. He joined the Fellowship of Reconciliation (FOR) in 1940; he and his colleagues from FOR were arrested for their opposition to the draft during the war. After his release, he was again arrested in 1942 for his individual protest against the Jim Crow laws in Tennessee.

Like Gandhi, King was aided by able colleagues who were able to sustain the campaign through a focus on local issues. But rather than remaining within the ideological confines of King's concern for integration, it has been argued that "the local movements displayed a wide range of ideologies and proto-ideologies, involving militant racial and class consciousness."[59] The leaders of these movements clearly acted independently of King or the SCLC despite having upheld nonviolence as an appropriate political weapon rather than a philosophy of life. This argument challenges the assumption that King was central to various local movements during the civil rights era; instead the movements flourished because indigenous leaders who felt ideologically connected to King handled the local issues efficiently. This was the case presumably because King and these local leaders held an identical aim: to remove the root cause of social disequilibrium in Southern states. One of the revealing examples was the 1955 Montgomery bus strike, which followed an unplanned defiance by a local inhabitant, Rosa Parks. Not only did the protestors form the MIA to bolster the boycott of public transport, they also approached the national black leaders, including King, who did not seem enthusiastic when first approached. It is true that King's involvement drew national and international attention to the movement and helped build a support base for the cause across the country. Nonetheless, one cannot deny that the Montgomery struggle was "an extension of previous civil reform efforts [though] it began as an outgrowth of local institutional networks rather than a project of any national civil rights organization."[60] Even in Albany, where the agitation fizzled out because of ruthless oppression perpetrated by people like Bull Connor and the Georgia governor, King did not join the protestors until the movement was already widespread and involved various strata of the black population. The scene was no different in Birmingham or Selma, where the King-steered SCLC waited until the movement had attracted mass support before plunging into action. What this reveals is that King remained a secondary organizer in the movements that comprised the overall civil rights campaign. In this sense, King approximated the role that Gandhi played in the three initial 1918 movements in Champaran, Kheda, and Ahmedabad. Gandhi's involvement gave the movements the momentum they needed to force the authorities to concede at least part of the protestors' demands. So, Gandhi was a useful instrument not only in expanding the movement's base and strengthening it to an extent that alarmed the ruling authority, but also in creating circumstances for an amicable solution through dialogue and negotiation. Like Gandhi, who was always a source of inspiration in the struggle against injustice whether or not as an active presence, King was seen by many black activists as "a source of inspiration rather than of tactical direction."[61]

Gandhi and King represented two different types of leadership, and yet their approach to their leadership role was unmistakably similar: ideologically, both of them upheld nonviolence and attacked the source—as opposed to the perpetrators—of oppression. They were thus readily acceptable to the authorities despite being opposed to them. Presumably this acceptance stemmed from Gandhi's and King's unflinching faith in the basic liberal mode of conflict resolution. And yet they were more radical than their colleagues who preceded them in social justice movements. Before Gandhi rose to prominence in the Indian political scene in the first quarter of the twentieth century, the anti-British campaign was divided into the moderate and extremist camps. Neither of these varieties had any mass base: the former was too mild a form of protest, confined to a very small section of the Indian population, while the latter failed to attract mass support, for two reasons. The first was that extremism, as an ideology, was hardly appreciated by the Indians at large presumably because of the well-entrenched pacifist tradition in India. The second was that despite their selfless sacrifice for the nationalist cause, the extremist camp alienated the Muslims because of their visible anti-Muslims bias. Gandhi's arrival on the nationalist scene radically altered the complexion of the anti-British struggle, which no longer remained confined to specific sectors of Indian society, but expanded its reach ideologically and geographically. Although the Gandhi-led movement was nonviolent, it was not passive, as the protestors were goal driven.

One can draw a historical parallel with the type of change that King brought about in the civil rights campaign. It is evident that mass activism of the 1950s and 1960s grew out of previous, less-organized movements against racial injustice. The new activism, moved "beyond the once dominant NAACP tactics of litigation, lobbying and propagandizing [by crafting] a new tactic within a familiar strategy based on appeals to power."[62] Moreover, it created an atmosphere of hope for a discontented racialized minority that had represented "an amorphous source of social energy [that] the leaders of national civil rights organizations [meaningfully] directed to pursue the ideological goal of racial de-segregation."[63]

King appeared at a very interesting historical juncture in American history. Notwithstanding its local roots, with his involvement, the campaign against racial segregation no longer remained confined to the disinherited blacks; it spread across the country, attracting the attention of the whites in the areas where the movements were organized and elsewhere in the country. King's success was attributed to his ability to serve as "a conciliatory force in a diverse social movement," which grew out of his unique combination of contrasting qualities: on the one hand, his "cosmopolitan awareness of the modern currents of theological and political thought," and on the other hand, his "lifetime experience in the black Baptist church, the largest African-American religious denomination."[64] King was undoubtedly one of the dominant forces that infused the endeavor with a new spirit and commitment.

There is a parallel here with Gandhi. Before Gandhi's arrival on the political scene, the Indian nationalist movement, as mentioned earlier, was plagued by two mutually contradictory ideological formations of moderate and extremist factions. These failed to link the masses with the nationalist goal presumably because of their fears about uncontrolled mass movements.[65] By being accommodative of conflicting socioeconomic interests, Gandhi evolved a model of resistance that was acceptable to business interests, the relatively well-off, and the socially dominant in rural areas. These groups stood to lose if "the political struggle turned into uninhibited and violent social revolution."[66] Gandhi gave them confidence by providing an ideological model that certainly sought political changes, but without affecting the prevalent class relations in any substantial way. It has been argued that the Gandhian doctrine of nonviolence "lay at the heart of the essentially unifying, umbrella-type role assumed by Gandhi and the Gandhian Congress, mediating internal social conflicts, contributing greatly to joint national struggle against foreign rule, but also leading to periodic retreats and major reversals."[67]

Nonviolence based on the Gandhian methods of "investigation, communication/negotiation, confrontation and reconciliation"[68] offered the participants of the civil rights movement a new philosophical and tactical basis and rallied the African Americans around a discipline and a sense of moral imperative that hardly existed in the past. An activist and close aide to King reminisced,

> The clear and shining example of Gandhi's campaign in India against colonialism [contributed to] fostering a new togetherness, a new communion among those who were willing to accept the burdens of protest. No more were there the feeling that lonely, individual, uncoordinated modest protest actions or voter registration drives in out-of-the-way towns would only bring about reprisals or violence to a greater end. Now even when such protests were carried out by individuals, those individuals felt part of a larger whole that was moving—thus the deeper connotation of the term movement."[69]

Like Gandhi, King emerged as a mediator of conflicting social, economic, and political interests. His wide range of skills and sense of pragmatism prepared him to comprehend the internal and external demands of the movement. King allowed his colleagues to make their points even when they disagreed with him,[70] hearing out various points of view and acquainting himself with different dimensions of the issues that were placed for discussion.

King understood the black world differently, presumably because of his relatively privileged social background, having grown up in a stable family with a fairly good public image.[71] Having been intimately connected with the church, King gradually learnt how to make persuasive arguments based on the biblical texts. His privileged background also helped make him acceptable to liberal whites, a majority of whom remained otherwise indifferent to the black cause, as the civil rights campaign was perceived to be an exclusively black affair. Among the major civil rights leaders, King was perhaps the only leader who built a bridge between the two racially segregated communities of blacks and whites. He was not only able to "articulate black concerns to white audiences," but was also able to convey a general sense of goodness of the whites to the blacks.[72] His defense of the fundamental values of the American Enlightenment persuaded white liberals to his cause, while his focus on ethical insights from the Sermon on the Mount easily convinced African Americans and white Americans alike that nonviolence was not, at all, an alien idea, but integrally linked with the Judeo-Christian heritage. So, through his advocacy of nonviolence, King, like Gandhi, articulated a dissenting ideology, bringing together racially divided communities as compatible partners presumably because of their uniform religious denominations. Through his persuasive oratory skills, accompanied by his day-to-day involvement in community activities, King put across the point that racial prejudice, segregation, and discrimination were not "merely un-American [and] undemocratic...but [also a] moral sin against God."[73] For the religious Christians, King's argument surely made them feel guilty over racial segregation and automatically created a favorable social atmosphere in which they could appear to readily accept King's argument for change. As David Chappell has shown, King's skillful application of the valued American democratic ethos and emotionally defended Christian ethics dissipated, to a significant extent, the white fear of social, economic, and political displacement.[74] Nonetheless, his effectiveness as a protest leader stemmed from his ability to mobilize the black community's resources through his day-to-day involvement in black community institutions, including the regional and national institutional network of black churches. The distinctiveness of King's ideas of justice, love, and hope was largely attributed to his vocation as pastor of Dexter and Ebenezer Baptist churches and as president of the SCLC, an organization mainly of preachers. His ideology was derived from his belief that "non-violence and unearned suffering [are] redemptive."[75] What made his appeal penetrating was his skill in linking Christian ethics with American constitutional values. In the context of the Montgomery boycott of public transport, he thus emphatically declared that "we believe in the Christian religion. We believe in the teachings of Jesus. We believe in American democracy with its deep-seated idea of all are created equal."[76] By focusing on "justice, love and hope, all grounded in the black church's faith in Jesus Christ,"[77] King had evolved an ideology in which the presence of God was most vital, as he reiterated in one of his morning addresses just on the eve of the Montgomery boycott by saying,

> I am here to say to you this morning that some things are right and some things are wrong. Eternally so, absolutely so. It's wrong to hate. It has always been wrong and always will be wrong! It's wrong in America, it's wrong in Germany, it's wrong in Russia, it's wrong in China. It was wrong in two thousand BC, and it's wrong in nineteen-fifty-four AD! It always has been wrong and it always will be wrong!...Some things in the universe are absolute. The God of the universe has made it so."[78]

What is striking about Gandhi and King was that both of them had built their ideological attack on human atrocities by reference to the visible distortions of the fundamental values on which the system of governance was supposedly based. Whether in South Africa or later in India, Gandhi convinced his detractors by couching his argument in a liberal fashion. He showed that racism or colonial exploitation was contrary to what the British Enlightenment stood for. His ideological response also took into account other important sources, including his idiosyncratic interpretation of major Indian religions and Western intellectual sources. His nonviolent civil resistance was undoubtedly influenced by his ideological belief in liberalism which was shared by his colleagues in the nationalist struggle. Like Gandhi, King spearheaded his campaign for racial desegregation by drawing on the fundamental tenets of Chrisitian ethics, especially the Sermon on the Mount and also the humanitarian appeal of the American constitution reflected through the Jeffersonian declaration that "all men are created equal" which was constitutionally reinforced by the 1863 Emancipation Proclamation.

The growth of the Gandhi-led struggle and its eventual success in attaining India's political freedom from British rule in 1947 was possible because of the critical role that the local political activists played in wresting power from the colonial rulers. The same dynamic worked in the movements that King steered in two ways. On the one hand, the civil rights movement had clear local roots— whether in Montgomery, Birmingham, or Selma—organized around localized issues of segregation—that is, of public transport, housing segregation, and denial of voting registration, respectively. While local organizers started each movement, they all certainly gained significant momentum with King's involvement. On the other hand, King, by adhering to his Christian faith, also constructed a meaningful ideological response with strict reference to the biblical texts, especially the New Testament. As his involvement in the movements against racism deepened and he began to accentuate his appeal to white support, his approach turned to the Christian idea of love. He did this to eradicate the fears of both black and whites regarding violence. Love was a driving force and an effective strategy in the context of the deeply rooted social schism between racially segregated communities.[79] King reiterated this in his address to the protestors in Montgomery where he stated that in the first days of the protest...the phrase most often heard was Christian love. It was the Sermon on the Mount, rather than a doctrine of passive resistance, that initially inspired the Negroes of Montgomery to dignified social action. It was Jesus of Nazareth that stirred the Negroes with the creative weapon of love.[80]

It was here that King accepted nonviolence as an instrument for political mobilization rather than a philosophy of action. But he was not a Gandhian during the initial stages of his involvement in the civil rights campaign in Montgomery. His wavering faith in nonviolence was evident in the fact that he applied for a gun when white violence threatened his life, following his participation in the Montgomery bus strike. He did not even greatly appreciate the Christian idea of love at this time, presumably because of the threat of upsurges and violent repercussions in the Black Belt regions of Mississippi, Alabama, and Georgia. This fear came out very clearly in his statement at his first meeting in Montgomery: "[H]ow could I make a speech that would be militant enough to keep my people aroused to positive action and yet moderate enough to keep this fever within controllable and Christian bounds."[81] King's attitude changed as he became intimately involved with the movement, beginning with the Montgomery bus strike. The Montgomery protestors' victory in legally overcoming segregation in public transport convinced him of the effectiveness and credibility of nonviolence in political mobilization, regardless of the circumstances.

The Montgomery movement also owed its success to the organizational support that Bayard Rustin provided from its beginning. A Gandhian to the core, Rustin believed that "next to A. Philip Randolph, Gandhi had a more direct influence on the development of the civil rights strategy than any other individual."[82] The civil rights movement remained nonviolent largely because of Rustin's firm grip over the campaign, which he never allowed to deviate from the path of nonviolence. While Rustin played a critical role in couching the protest strictly in the Gandhian way, grassroots activists played an equally significant role in sustaining the momentum. It is thus evident that the strength and durability of the civil rights campaign was largely due to the involvement of the grassroots leaders who gradually and integrally became linked through thousands of mass meetings, workshops, citizenship classes, freedom schools, and informal discussions. Rather than merely accepting guidance from above, the Southern black protestors were, argued Clayborne Carson, "resocialized as a result of their movement experiences."[83]

King was certainly Gandhian, but with a difference in the sense that he articulated the Gandhian message through the lens of Christian ethics and in relation to the American socioeconomic milieu. As a close aide of King reminisced, "[T]he discipline of prayer and Bible study had instilled a sense of togetherness [among the participants who]...saw religion providing support to challenge injustice in this lifetime, not just making promises for the next."[84] In the same way that India's freedom struggle was nonviolent in the Gandhian sense but also drew on other important ideological strands, the American civil rights movement provided King with an opportunity to creatively blend Christian ethics with what he learned from other ideological sources, including Gandhian nonviolence and the inputs from the grassroots activists. It was thus a unique ideological package based on "ideas disseminated from the bottom as well from the top down."[85]

Gandhi and King had similar ideological responses against injustice despite being located in completely-different socioeconomic and political circumstances. In two significant ways, they were identical in their approach to political mobilization: on the one hand, they opposed artificially created racial hierarchy and discrimination on the basis of an understanding that such discrimination was a partisan distortion of the Enlightenment tradition. In their struggle for the exploited, they, on the other hand, drew on what they had derived from their colleagues and those unknown figures who fought against discrimination and inequality at the grassroots level. Besides being dialectically linked with the prevalent socioeconomic and political milieu, Gandhi and King continuously reinvented what they instinctively acquired and what they learnt from other sources, including their colleagues and critics. Gandhi's and King's distinctive ideological points of view emerged from such a complex interplay of factors, and put them in classes by themselves. What is most striking is that they each skillfully applied social, political, and economic idioms to easily sway the people at particular junctures of history: just when colonial exploitation in India and racial segregation in America reached a point of no return, being sources of agony and distress for the majority in each case. Historically conditioned and politically challenging, the ideological response that Gandhi and King evolved was not only contextual but also transcendental in its application and appreciation; they thus continue to remain inspirational, even decades after their deaths, to generations of people seeking to correct social imbalances under adverse circumstances.

NOTES

INTRODUCTION

1. The word "Dixie" refers to a currency, issued by the Citizens State Bank (located in the French Quarter of New Orleans). The ten-dollar note was known as a "Dixie" because it had on one side the French word—Dixie. In course of time, Dixie became an acceptable term for most of the Southern states. As a definite geographical location within the United States, Dixie is usually associated with eleven Southern states that flocked together to form the Confederate States of America, which included South Carolina, Mississippi, Florida, Alabama, Georgia, Louisiana, Texas, Virginia, Arkansas, North Carolina, and Tennessee. This expression gradually acquired a clear ideological meaning in the context of racial segregation.
2. Martin Luther King Jr., "The Strength to Love," in *A Testament of Hope: The Essential Writings and Speeches of Martin Luther King Jr.*, ed. James M. Washington (New York: HarperOne, 1986), p. 506.
3. This is based on the text available in Catherine M. Lewis and J. Richard Lewis, ed., *Jim Crow America: A Documentary History* (Fayetteville: University of Arkansas Press, 2009), pp. 1, 6–8.
4. Coretta King, *My Life with Martin Luther King Jr.* (Chicago: Holt, Rinehart and Winston, 1969), p. 24.
5. John W. Cell, "Race Relations," in *Encyclopedia of Southern Culture*, ed. Charles Reagan Wilson and William Ferries (Chapel Hill: University of North Carolina Press, 1989), p. 189.
6. C. Vann Woodward, *The Strange Career of Jim Crow*, Commemorative Edition (New York: Oxford University Press, 2002), p. 7.
7. Michelle Alexander, *The New Jim Crow: Mass Incarceration in the Age of Colorblindness* (New York: The New Press, 2010), p. 34.
8. Martin Luther King's statement—quoted in Woodward, *Strange Career*, p. 232.
9. Ray Sprigle, *In the Land of Jim Crow* (New York: Simon and Schuster, 1949), p. 10.
10. Ibid., p. 59.
11. Ibid., pp. 59–60.
12. Randall Kennedy, Nigger: *The Strange Career of a Troublesome Word* (New York: Vintage Books, 2003) (reprint), p. 7.
13. Ibid., p. 8.

14. Martin Luther King Jr., "Letter from Birmingham Jail, 1963," in *I Have a Dream: Writings and Speeches That Changed the World*, ed. James M. Washington (San Francisco: Harper, 1992) (reprint), p. 88.
15. Martin Luther King Jr., *Where Do We Go from Here?* (Boston, MA: Beacon Press, 1967), p. 97.
16. *The Autobiography of Malcolm X*, as told to Alex Haley (New York: Random House, 1973) (reprint), p. 43.
17. Jeniffer Ritterhouse, *Growing up Jim Crow: How Black and White Southern Children Learned Race* (Chapel Hill: The University of North Carolina Press, 2006), p. 17.
18. Ibid., p. 18.
19. Martin Luther King Jr., "The Montgomery Story: Address Delivered at the Forty-Seventh Annual NAACP Convention," in *Papers of Martin Luther King Jr.*, ed. Clayborne Carson, vol. 3 (Berkeley: University of California Press, 1992), p. 301.
20. Ibid.
21. Ibid.
22. Document 49, Letter and Address, Black Ministers of Washington, "Doomed to Destruction," August 13, 1910, in Lewis and Lewis, *Jim Crow America*, p. 144.
23. Washington, *Essential Writings and Speeches of Martin Luther King Jr.*, p. 374.
24. Jabari Asim, *The N Word: Who Can Say It, Who Shouldn't, and Why* (Boston, MA: Houghton Mifflin, 2007), p. 119.
25. Manning Marable, *The Great Wells of Democracy: The Meaning of Race in American Life* (New York: Basic Ovitas Books, 2002), p. 162.
26. The data available in the report was prepared by The Pew Charitable Trust, Washington, DC, February 2012, p. 6.
27. Alexander, *The New Jim Crow*, p. 248.
28. Ibid., p. 248
29. Gerald McNight, *The Last Crusade: Martin Luther King Jr., the FBI, and the Poor People's Campaign* (Boulder, CO: Westview Press, 1998), p. 83.
30. Martin Luther King Jr. "Where Do We Go from Here?" in *"A Testament of Hope": The Essential Writings and Speeches of Martin Luther King Jr.*, ed. James M. Washington (New York: HarperOne, 1986), p. 586.
31. Martin Luther King Jr., "A Testament of Hope" (a posthumous article), in Washington, *Testament of Hope*, p. 314.
32. Marable, *The Great Wells of Democracy*, p. 162.
33. Alexander, *The New Jim Crow*, p. 241.
34. Martin Luther King Jr., *Strength to Love* (Philadelphia, PA: Fortress Press, 1963), pp. 45–8.
35. David Gallen, ed., *Malcolm X as They Knew Him* (New York: Carroll & Graf, 1992), p. 129.
36. Robert Friedman, "Institutional Racism: How to Discriminate without Really Trying," in *Racial Discrimination in the United States*, ed. Thomas F. Pettigrew (New York: Harper & Row, 1975), p. 406.
37. Andrew Young, *An Easy Burden: The Civil Rights Movement and the Transformation of America* (New York: HarperCollins, 1996), p. 114.
38. Friedman, "Institutional Racism," p. 406.

39. Warren E. Steinkraus, "Martin Luther King's Personalism and Non-Violence," *Journal of the History of Ideas* 34, no.1 (January-March 1973): p. 105.

40. Martin Luther King Jr., *The Trumpet of Conscience* (New York: Harper & Row, 1967), p. 54.

41. Ibid., p. 8.

42. Young, *An Easy Burden* (New York: HarperCollins, 1996), p. 447.

43. King's statement is quoted in Young, *An Easy Burden*, p. 523.

44. Young, *An Easy Burden*, p. 529.

45. Gandhi's dialogue with the Americans is well explored in (a) Sudarshan Kapur, *Raising up a Prophet: The African-American Encounter with Gandhi* (Boston, MA: Beacon Press, 1992); (b) Leonard A. Gordon, "Mahatma Gandhi's Dialogues with Americans,"*Economic and Political Weekly*, January 26, 2002; (c) Lloyd Rudolph, "Gandhi in the Mind of America," *Economic and Political Weekly*, November 20, 2010.

46. Ira Chernus, *American Nonviolence: The History of an Idea*, (New York: Orbis Books, 2004), p. 85.

47. Ibid., p. 86.

48. Kapur, *Raising up a Prophet*, p. 17.

49. Marcus Garvey, "Speech," March 12, 1922, *The Negro World*, May 6, 1922—quoted in Kapur, *Raising up a Prophet*, p. 21.

50. W. E. B. DuBois, "Gandhi and India," *The Crisis*, March 1922, p. 207—quoted in Vinay Lal, "Gandhi's West, the West's Gandhi," *New Literary History* 40, no. 2 (2009): p. 296.

51. Ibid., p. 296.

52. M. K. Gandhi, "A Little Love Message," reproduced in *The Correspondence of W. E. B. DuBois, 1877–1934*, Vol. 1, ed. Herbert Apthekar (Amherst: University of Massachusetts Press, 1973), p. 403.

53. W. E. B. DuBois, "The Wide, Wide World," *New York Amsterdam News*, October 28, 1931, p. 8, quoted in Kapur, *Raising up a Prophet*, p. 56.

54. Drusilla Dunjee Houston, "The Little Man Gandhi," *Chicago Defender*, December 12, 1931, quoted in Kapur, *Raising up a Prophet*, p. 55.

55. "Will a Gandhi Arise?," *Chicago Defender*, November 5, 1932, quoted in Kapur, *Raising up a Prophet*, p. 66.

56. Reinhold Niebuhr, *Moral Man and Immoral Society: A Study in Ethics and Politics* (New York: Charles Scribner's Sons, 1932), p. 255.

57. Ibid., p. 241.

58. Ibid.

59. Ibid., p. 244.

60. Martin Luther King Jr., "My Pilgrimage to Non-Violence," in Carson, *Papers of MLK*,vol. 4, p. 479.

61. M. K. Gandhi, "Requisite Qualifications," in *Collected Works of Mahatma Gandhi*, Vol. 75, p. 196.

62. Niebuhr, *Moral Man and Immoral Society*, p. 243.

63. Karuna Mantena, "*Another Realism: The Politics of Gandhian Non-Violence*," *American Political Science Review* 16, no. 2 (May 2012): p. 457.

64. C. Seshachari, *Gandhi and the American Scene: An Intellectual History and Enquiry* (Bombay: Nachiketa Publications Limited, 1969), p. 135.

65. Joseph Kip Kosek, "Reichard Gregg, Mohandas Gandhi and the Strategy of Non-Violence," *Journal of American History* 92, no. 1 (March 2005): 1325.
66. Richard B. Gregg, *The Power of Non-Violence* (London: J. B. Lippincott Company, 1934), p. 60.
67. Gregg, *The Power of Non-Violence*, p. 89.
68. Leonard A. Gordon, "Mahatma Gandhi's Dialogues with Americans," *Economic and Political Weekly*, January 26, 2002, 340.
69. Gregg, *The Power of Non-Violence*, p. 43.
70. Ibid., p. 54.
71. Ibid., p. 239.
72. Ibid., p. 240.
73. Ibid., *The Power of Non-Violence*, p. 241.
74. King to Gregg, May 1, 1956, in Carson, *Papers of MLK*, vol. 3, pp. 244-5.
75. Kosek, "Reichard Gregg," p. 1344.
76. Martin Luther King Jr., "My Pilgrimage to Non-Violence," in Carson, *Papers of MLK*, vol. 4, pp. 473-81.
77. Gregg to King, April 2, 1956, in Carson, *Papers of MLK*, vol. 3, pp. 211-12.
78. Kosek, "Reichard Gregg," p. 1348.
79. Krishnalal J. Sridharani, *War without Violence: A Study of Gandhi's Method and Its Accomplishment* (New York: Harcourt Brace & Co., 1939), p. 13.
80. Ibid., p. 19.
81. James Farmer, *Freedom... When?* (New York: Random House, 1965), p. 55.
82. James Weldon, Executive Secretary, NAACP, was reported to have said this at the annual meeting of the NAACP in 1922—quoted in George M. Frederickson, *Black Liberation: A Comparative History of Black Ideologies in the United States and South Africa* (New York: Oxford University Press, 1995), p. 222.
83. Howard Thurman, *With Head and Heart: The Autobiography of Howard Thurman* (New York: Harcourt Brace & Co., 1979), pp. 132-3.
84. Ibid., p. 132
85. Ibid., p. 132
86. These statements and expressions are quoted from Benjamin E. Mays, *Born to Rebel: An Autobiography of Benjamin E. Mays* (New York: Charles Scribner's Sons, 1971), pp. 155-6.
87. Benjamin E. Mays, "What Are the Differences between Gandhi and Nehru?" *Norfolk Journal & Guide*, June 5, 1937—quoted in Kapur, *Raising Up a Prophet*, p. 97.
88. Benjamin E. Mays, "The Color Line around the World," *Journal of Negro Education*, April 6, 1937—quoted in Kapur, *Raising Up a Prophet*, p. 66.
89. Mays, "The Color Line around the World," in Kapur, *Raising Up a Prophet*, p. 66.
90. Clayborne Carson, ed., *The Autobiography of Martin Luther King Jr.* (New York: International Properties Management Inc., in association with Warner Books, 1998), p. 23.
91. Martin Luther King Jr. "My Pilgrimage to Nonviolence," p. 478.
92. Ibid.
93. Ibid.
94. A. J. Muste, *Non-Violence in an Aggressive World* (New York: Harper, 1972) (reprint), p. 175.
95. Ibid., p. 176.

96. Jervis Anderson, *A. Philip Randolph: A Biographical Portrait* (New York: Harcourt, 1973), p. 278.

97. A. Philip Randolph, "Rise and Fight," *Black Worker*, June 1960, p. 14—quoted in Paula F. Pfeffer, *A. Philip Randolph: Pioneer of the Civil Rights Movement* (Baton Rouge and London: Louisiana State University Press, 1990), p. 203.

98. A. Philip Randolph, "Keynote Address to the Policy Conference of the March on Washington Movement," September 26, 1942—quoted in Vinay Lal, "Gandhi's West, the West's Gandhi," *New Literary History* 40, no. 2 (Spring 2009): p. 299.

99. James Farmer, *Lay Bare the Heart: An Autobiography of the Civil Rights Movement* (New York: New American Library, 1985), p. 74.

100. Ibid., p. 74

101. John D'Emilio, *Lost Prophet: The Life and Times of Bayard Rustin* (New York: Free Press, 2003), p. 52.

102. Bayard Rustin, *Strategies for Freedom: The Changing Patterns of Black Protest* (New York: Columbia University Press, 1976), p. 24.

103. Ibid.

104. Bayard Rustin, "The Negro and Nonviolence," in *Down the Line: The Collected Writings of Bayard Rustin* (Chicago: Quadrangle Books, 1971), pp. 10–11.

105. Bayard Rustin's assessment of the civil rights movement in America, June 27, 1960—quoted in Jervis Anderson, *Bayard Rustin: The Troubles I Have Seen: A Biography* (New York: HarperCollins, 1997), p. 197.

106. Lal, "Gandhi's West, West's Gandhi," 301.

107. Kapur, *Raising Up a Prophet*, p. 165.

108. Sean Scalmer, *Gandhi in the West: The Mahatma and the Rise of Radical Protest* (Cambridge, UK: Cambridge University Press, 2011), p. 104.

109. Ibid.

110. Quoted in Harvard Sitkoff, *King: Pilgrimage to the Mountaintop* (New York: Hill and Wang, 2008), p. 44.

Chapter 1

1. Daddy King is quoted in Benjamin Mays and Martin Luther King Sr., "The Old Men: Two Who Knew Him Well," in *My Soul Is Rested: Movement Days in the Deep South Remembered*, ed. Howell Raines (New York: G. P. Putnam's Sons, 1977), pp. 460–61—reproduced in Mary King, *Mahatma Gandhi and Martin Luther King Jr: The Power of Non-Violent Action, Cultures of Peace Studies* (Paris: UNESCO Publishing, 1999), p. 90.

2. He articulated his view that colonialism came along with Western industrialism in *Hind Swaraj* (Ahmedabad: Navjivan Publications, 1909).

3. M. K. Gandhi, *An Autobiography, or the Story of My Experiments with Truth* (Ahmedabad: Navjivan Publishing House, 2008) (reprint), p. 127.

4. Ibid., pp. 274–5.

5. Ibid., p. 4.

6. Ibid., p. 83.

7. Ibid., p. 83.

8. Leo Tolstoy, "A Letter to a Hindu," 1908, Project Gutenberg, http://www.gutenberg.org/ebooks/7176.

9. Margaret Chatterjee, *Gandhi's Religious Thought* (Notre Dame, IN: University of Notre Dame Press, 1983), p. 51.

10. Ibid.
11. Gandhi, *An Autobiography*, p. 274.
12. Gandhi, *An Autobiography*, p. 275.
13. M. K. Gandhi, "Henry David Thoreau and Civil Disobedience," *Young India*, March 3, 1926, in *Collected Works of Mahatma Gandhi* (*CWMG* hereafter), Vol. 34, p. 347.
14. Edward Carpenter, *Civilization: Its Cause and Cure and Other Essays* (London: Swan Sonneschein & Co, 1889), p. 33
15. Roughly speaking, *swaraj* was Gandhi's synonym for freedom, which meant both political freedom and self-rule.
16. Carpenter, *Civilization*, p. 49.
17. Gandhi, *An Autobiography*, p. 31.
18. Ibid., p. 63.
19. Ibid., p. 31.
20. C. F. Andrews, *Mahatma Gandhi's Ideas* (New York: The Macmillan Company, 1930), p. 87.
21. Ibid., p. 17.
22. Ibid., p. 87.
23. In reconceptualizing some of the fundamental values of Christianity, Gandhi owed a great deal to his colleagues and friends in South Africa, especially Reverend J. J. Doke and C. F. Andrews, who also participated in the nationalist struggle that Gandhi led in India after his return from South Africa in 1914.
24. Gandhi's letter to the press, May 26, 1909, *CWMG*, Vol. 9, p. 337.
25. M. N. Roy, *India in Transition*, chapter 8, reproduced *Selected Works of M. N. Roy, 1917–1922*, ed. Sibnarayan Ray, vol. 1 (New Delhi: Oxford University Press, 2000), p. 346.
26. Ibid., pp. 348–9.
27. Amalesh Tripathy, *The Extremist Challenge: India between 1890 and 1910* (Bombay: Orient Longman, 1967).
28. Roy, *India in Transition*, in Ray, *Selected Works of M. N. Roy*, vol. 1, p. 368.
29. M. N. Roy, "The Cult of Non-Violence: Its Socio-Economic Background"—reproduced in *Selected Works of M. N. Roy, 1923–1927*, ed. Sibnarayan Ray, vol. 2 (New Delhi: Oxford University Press, 2000), p. 156.
30. Ibid.
31. Ibid., p. 154.
32. M. N. Roy, "The Release of Gandhi," in *Selected Works of M. N. Roy (1923–1927)*, ed. Sibnarayan Ray, vol. 2 (New Delhi: Oxford University Press, 2000), pp. 182–3.
33. Ibid., p. 182
34. Ibid., p. 183
35. M. N. Roy, "Appeal to the Nationalists"—reproduced in *Selected Works of M. N. Roy, 1923—1927*, ed. Sibnarayan Ray, vol. 2 (New Delhi: Oxford University Press, 2000), p. 324.
36. M. N. Roy, "Definition of Swaraj," in *The Vanguard of Indian Independence*, vol. 2, reproduced in *Selected Works of M. N. Roy, 1923–1927*, ed. Sibnarayan Ray, vol. 2 (New Delhi: Oxford University Press, 2000), p. 101.
37. MN Roy, "India's Problem and Its Solution," reproduced in *Selected Works of M. N, Roy, 1917–1922*, ed. Sibnarayan Ray, vol. 1 (New Delhi: Oxford University Press, 2000), p. 555.

38. Sudipta Kaviraj thus argues, "Gandhi's politics were not wholly mystical; rather, even its mysticism was often deliberate, its irrationalities carefully thought-out." Sudipta Kaviraj, "The Heteronomous Radicalism of M. N. Roy," in *Political Thought in Modern India*, ed. Thomas Pantham and Kenneth L Deutsch(New Delhi: Sage, 1986), p. 229.

39. With remarkable clarity of vision, Rabindranath Tagore succinctly wrote about his views on nation in a rather small piece, entitled *Nation Ki* (Bengali). During his lecture tour in America, 1916–17, he elaborated some of these points, including his views on nationalism in India. See Rabindranath Tagore, *Nationalism* (New Delhi: Rupa, 1994) (rpt., originally published in 1917), pp. 77–99.

40. Ibid, p. 89.

41. Rabindranath Tagore to Amiya Chakraborty, no date, in *The Mahatma and the Poet: Letters and Debates between Gandhi and Tagore, 1915–1941*, ed. and comp. Sabyasachi Bhattacharya (New Delhi: National Book Trust, 1997), p. 172.

42. Ashis Nandy, *The Illegitimacy of Nationalism*, (New Delhi: Oxford University Press, 1994), p. 89.

43. Tagore, *Nationalism*, p. 90.

44. The Congress dismissed Jinnah's demand for parity because "in numerical terms this meant the equation of minority with majority which was both absurd and politically impossible." To this Jinnah retorted that "the debate was not about numbers nor even about communities but about Nations. Nations were equal irrespective of the size." For details of Jinnah's argument, see Diana Mansergh, ed., *Independence Years: The Selected Indian and Commonwealth Papers of Nicholas Mansergh* (New Delhi: Oxford University Press, 1999), pp. 227—30.

45. Jinnah's Presidential Address in the 1940 Lahore Session of the All-India Muslim League. See S. S. Pirzada, ed., *Foundations of Pakistan*, Vol. 2 (Karachi: 1970), p. 337.

46. Jinnah always insisted that "there are two major nations in India. This is the root cause and essence of our troubles. When there are two major nations[,] how can you talk of democracy[,] which means that one nation['s] majority will decide everything for the other nation although it may be unanimous in its opposition....These two nations cannot be judged by western democracy. But they should be treated as equals and attempts should be made to solve the difficulties by acknowledging this fact." Jinnah's press statement, *The Dawn*, August 1, 1946.

47. Ayesha Jalal, "Nation, Reason and Religion; Punjab's Role in the Partition of India," *Economic and Political Weekly*, August 8, 1998, 2185.

48. Paul Brass, *Ethnicity and Nationalism: Theory and Comparison* (New Delhi: Sage, 1991), p. 94.

49. N. K. Bose and P. H. Patwardhan, *Gandhi in Indian Politics* (Bombay: Asian Publishing House, 1967), p. 7.

50. Rabindranath Tagore, "The Call of Truth," reproduced in *The Mahatma and the Poet: Letters and Debates between Gandhi and Tagore, 1915–1941*, ed. and comp. Sabyasachi Bhattacharya (New Delhi: National Book Trust, 1997), pp. 83–4.

51. Rabindranath Tagore's reflections on non-cooperation and cooperation, in *The Mahatma and the Poet: Letters and Debates between Gandhi and Tagore, 1915–1941*, ed. and comp. Sabyasachi Bhattacharya (New Delhi: National Book Trust, 1997), p. 58.

52. Rabindranath Tagore, "Reflections on Non-Cooperation and Cooperation," *Modern Review*, May 1921—reproduced in Bhattacharya, *The Mahatma and the Poet*, pp. 58, 62.
53. Ranajit Guha, *Dominance without Hegemony: History and Power in Colonial India* (New Delhi: Oxford University Press, 1998), p. 121.
54. Ibid.
55. Tagore, "The Call of Truth,"in Bhattacharya, *The Mahatma and the Poet*, p. 79.
56. *Charkha* is the spinning wheel while *khaddar* is home-spun cloth. In ideological terms, Gandhi used these two expressions to build his defence for a self-reliant economy which, in Gandhi's parlance, was "swaraj."
57. Rabindranath Tagore, "The Cult of Charkha," *Modern Review*, September 1925—reproduced in Bhattacharya, *The Mahatma and the Poet*, pp. 101–2.
58. Rabindranath Tagore, "Striving for Swaraj," *Modern Review*, September 1925—reproduced in Bhattacharya, *The Mahatma and the Poet*, p. 115.
59. Ibid., p. 118.
60. Ibid., p. 121.
61. Ibid.
62. M. K. Gandhi, "The Poet and the Charkha," *Young India*, November 5, 1925—reproduced in Bhattacharya, *The Mahatma and the Poet*, p. 123.
63. Ibid., p. 125.
64. Ibid., p. 124.
65. M. K. Gandhi, *Young India*, March 11, 1926, *CWMG*, Vol. 34, pp. 372–73.
66. According to Gandhi, "Khadi should be linked with liberty. All the time you are spinning, you would not think in terms of your own requirements, but in terms of the requirements of the nation. You will say, 'I want to clothe the whole nation that is naked and I must do it non-violently.' Each time you draw a thread, say to yourselves, 'we are drawing the thread of swaraj.' Multiply this picture million-fold and you have freedom knocking at your door." *Harijan*, January 28, 1939, in *CWMG*, vol. 68, p. 133.
67. Gandhi's press statement, *Harijan*, February 16, 1934, in *CWMG*, vol. 63, p. 238. "Harijans" (or God's children) was how Gandhi characterized the untouchables.
68. Tagore's statement to the press, *Amrita Bazar Patrika*, March 24, 1934.
69. Tagore to Mahatma Gandhi, January 28, 1934—reproduced in Bhattacharya, *The Mahatma and the Poet*, p. 156.
70. Tagore's statement to the press, *Amrita Bazar Patrika*, February 24, 1934.
71. Gandhi, "Superstition vs. Faith," *Harijan*, February 28, 1934, in *CWMG*, vol. 63, p. 261.
72. B.R.Ambedkar,"Gandhism," reproduced in *The Essential Writings of B. R. Ambedkar*, ed. Valerian Rodrigues (New Delhi: Oxford University Press, 2002), p. 165.
73. M. K. Gandhi, *Young India*, January 19, 1921—reproduced in Mahatma Gandhi, *What is Hinduism?* (New Delhi: National Book Trust, 2001) (reprint), p. 115.
74. B. R. Ambedkar, "Outside the Fold," in Rodrigues, *The Essential Writings of B. R. Ambedkar*, p. 331.
75. Gandhi's idea of village swaraj is that "it is completely republic, independent of its neighbours for its own vital wants, and yet interdependent for many others in which dependence is a necessity. Thus every villager's first concern will be to grow its own food crops and cotton for its cloth....The government of the village will

be conducted by a panchayat of five persons, annually elected by the adult villagers, male and female, possessing minimum prescribed qualifications." Gandhi, *Harijan*, July 7, 1942, *in CWMG*, vol. 83, pp. 308–9.

76. B. R. Ambedkar, *The Untouchables: Who Were They and Why They Became Untouchables?* (New Delhi: Amrit Book Company, 1948), pp. 21–2.

77. Judith Brown, "The Mahatma and Modern India," *Modern Asian Studies* 3, no. 4 (July 1969): p. 331.

78. Upendra Baxi, "Emancipation as Justice: Babasaheb Ambedkar's Legacy and Vision," unpublished paper presented at the inaugural oration at the Babasaheb Ambedkar Centenary Celebration, University of Madras, March 5, 1991, p. 17.

79. B. R. Ambedkar, *Mr. Gandhi and the Emancipation of Untouchables* (Jalandhar: Bheem Patrika Publications, 1943), pp. 196–7.

80. Bhikhu Parekh, *Gandhi* (Oxford: Oxford University Press, 1997), p. 18.

81. C. B. Khairmode, *Dr. Bhimrao Ramji Ambedkar* (in Marathi), vol. 4 (Pune: Sugava Prakashan, 1989), p. 42—quoted in M. S. Gore, *The Social Context of an Ideology: Ambedkar's Political and Social Thought*, (New Delhi: Sage, 1993), p. 137.

82. Ainslie T. Embree, *Imagining India: Essays on Indian History* (New Delhi: Oxford University Press 1989), p. 171.

83. The head-on collision was thus avoided, and Gandhi succeeded. As a biographer noted, "At Yerawada, the politician in Gandhi became successful and the Mahatma was defeated. So effective and crushing was the victory of Gandhi that he deprived Ambedkar of all his life-saving weapons and made him a powerless man as did Indra in the case of Karna." Dhananjoy Keer, *Dr. Ambedkar: Life and Mission*, (Bombay: Popular Prakashan, 1962), pp. 215–16.

84. Gauri Viswanathan, *Outside the Fold: Conversion, Modernity and Belief* (New Delhi: Oxford University Press, 1998), p. 213.

85. B. R. Ambedkar, "Ranade, Gandhi, and Jinnah," lecture given on the occasion of the 101st birthday celebration of M. G. Ranade on January 18, 1943, at Poona.

86. M. G. Ranade (1842–1901) was a liberal politician who also became a member of the House of Commons. He was known for his critique of Hindu society, based on his understanding of the practices of Hinduism in contemporary India. Born in 1842 at Biphad in Nasik district of Bombay presidency in a Chitpavan Brahmin family, Ranade was influenced by the pure monotheism of the *Upanishads*. He was famous for his views deprecating the caste system and untouchability. As a true liberal, he championed the cause of women and favored widow remarriage. He was an ardent supporter of industrialization, emancipation of the *ryot* (cultivators holding land from the landlord on certain conditions) from the moneylender. As an editor of an Anglo-Marathi daily from Bombay, *Induprakash* (1864–71), Ranade published his views on social reform. A founding member of the Indian National Congress, Ranade was characterized as a "modern *rishi*" (saint) by his Congress colleagues. S .P. Sen, *Dictionary of National Biography*, vol. 3 (Calcutta: Institute of Historical Studies, 1973–74), pp. 479–81.

87. Khairmode, *Dr. Bhimrao Ramaji Ambedkar*,Vol. 5, p. 198—quoted in Gore, *Social Context*, p. 166.

88. B. R. Ambedkar, "Ranade, Gandhi and Jinnah," reproduced in Rodrigues, *The Essential Writings of B. R. Ambedkar*, p. 124.

89. Ibid., p. 129

90. Baxi, "Babasaheb Ambedkar's Legacy and Vision," pp. 35–7.
91. Clayborne Carson, ed., *The Autobiography of Martin Luther King Jr.* (New York: Intellectual Properties Management, Inc. (IPM) in association with Warner Books, 1998), p. 5.
92. Ibid.
93. Clayborne Carson, "Introduction" to *Papers of MLK Jr* (*The MLK Papers* hereafter), vol. 2 (Berkeley: University of California Press, 1994), p. 22.
94. Benjamin E. Mays, *The Negro's God*, (Boston, MA: Chapman and Grimes, 1938), p. vii.
95. Mikleson, Thomas Jarl Sheppart, Th.D, "The Negro's God in the Theology of Martin Luther King Jr.: Social Community and Theological Discourses," PhD diss., Harvard University, 1988, pp. 6–7.
96. A. L. Herman, *Community, Violence and Peace*, (Albany, NY: State University of New York Press, 1999), p. 124.
97. Henry David Thoreau, *Civil Disobedience and Other Essays* (New York: Dover Publications, 1993, Rpt.), p. 7.
98. Martin Luther King, "I Have a Dream," in *I Have a Dream: Writings and Speeches That Changed the World*, ed. James M. Washington (San Francisco and New York: Harper 1992), p. 82.
99. Henry David Thoreau, *Civil Disobedience and Other Essays*, (New York: Dover Publications, 1993) (reprint), p. 7.
100. Ibid., p. 8.
101. Ibid., p. 18.
102. Ibid., p. 9.
103. Martin Luther King, "Pilgrimage to Non-Violence," in *"A Testament of Hope": The Essential Writings and Speeches of Martin Luther King Jr.*, ed. James M. Washington (New York: HarperOne, 1986), p. 40.
104. Martin Luther King Jr., speech before the National Conference on Religion and Race, Chicago, IL, January 17, 1963—quoted in David J. Garrow, *Bearing the Cross: Martin Luther King Jr. and the Southern Christian Leadership Conference* (New York: William Morrow, 1986), p. i.
105. Ibid.
106. Walter Rauschenbush, *The Social Principles of Jesus*, (New York: Association Press, 1920), p. 75.
107. Ibid., p. 76.
108. Ibid., p. 106.
109. Ibid., p. 161.
110. Ibid., p. 162.
111. Walter Rauschenbush, *Christianity and the Social Crisis*, (London: The Macmillan Company, 1913), p. 249.
112. Ibid., p. 253.
113. Ibid., p. 357.
114. Martin Luther King, "I Have a Dream," p. 58.
115. Ibid.
116. Ibid.
117. Martin Luther King Jr., "My Pilgrimage to Non-Violence," in Carson, *Papers of MLK*, vol. 4, p. 474.

118. Reinhold Niebuhr, *Moral Man and Immoral Society*, (New York: Charles Scribner's Sons, 1932), p. 118.

119. Garrow, *Bearing the Cross*, p. 42

120. Martin Luther King Jr., "Reinhold Niebuhr's Ethical Dualism," in Carson, *Papers of MLK*, vol. 2, p.142.

121. Reinhold Niebuhr, "The Preservation of Moral Values in Politics," in *Non-Violence in America: A Documentary History*, ed. Staughton Lynd (New York: The Bobbs-Merrill Company, 1966), p. 517.

122. Washington, *"A Testament of Hope,"* p. 295.

123. Howard Thurman, *Jesus and the Disinherited*, (New York: Abington Press, 1949), p. 16.

124. Ibid., p. 34.

125. Ibid., p. 77.

126. Ibid., p. 21.

127. Howard Thurman, *With Head and Heart: The Autobiography of Howard Thurman* (New York: Harcourt Brace & Company, 1979), pp. 216–17.

128. Martin Luther King Jr., "The Strength to Love," in Washington, *A Testament of Hope*, p. 511.

129. Ibid., p. 513.

130. King's statement—quoted in Garrow, *Martin Luther King Jr.*, p. 47.

131. Martin Luther King Jr., "My Pilgrimage to Non-Violence," in Carson, *Papers of MLK*, vol. 4, pp. 474–5.

132. W. E. B. DuBois, *The Souls of Black Folk*, (Oxford: Oxford University Press, 2007), p. 32.

133. W. E. B. DuBois, *The Souls of Black Folk*, (Oxford: Oxford University Press, 2007), p. 208.

134. Niebuhr, *Moral Man and Immoral Society*, pp. 247–8.

135. Ibid., pp. 275–6.

136. Ibid., p. 279.

137. Carson, *The Autobiography of Martin Luther King Jr.*, pp. 23–4.

138. David J. Garrow elaborated on how King became drawn to nonviolence and also the role of Bayard Rustin in this process in his *Bearing the Cross*, pp. 72–3.

139. All these statements are quoted from Carson, *The Autobiography of Martin Luther King Jr.*, p. 26.

140. Ibid., p. 26.

141. Ibid., p. 7.

142. Martin Luther King Jr., *Stride toward Freedom*, (New York: Harper & Brothers, 1958), p. 149.

143. Martin Luther King Jr., "Pilgrimage to Non-Violence," in Carson, *Papers of MLK*, vol. 5, p. 423.

144. Martin Luther King, "Letter from Birmingham Jail (1963)," in Washington, *I Have a Dream*, p. 94.

145. Martin Luther King Jr., "Nobel Prize Acceptance Speech (1964)," in Washington, *"I Have a Dream"*, p. 109.

146. Martin Luther King, Jr. "A Comparison of the Conception of God in Tillich and Wieman," p. 216—quoted in Hans Walton Jr., *The Political Philosophy of Martin Luther King, Jr.*, (Westport, CT: Greenwood Publishing, 1972), p. 57.

147. M. K. Gandhi, *Young India*, August 11, 1920, reproduced in M. K. Gandhi, *Non-Violence in Peace and War* (Ahmedabad: Navjivan Publishing House, 1942), vol. 1, p. 2.

148. Martin Luther King Jr., "A Christmas Sermon on Peace," *The Trumpet of Conscience* (New York: Harper & Row, 1967), p. 74.

149. Ibid., p. 77.

150. "A Talk with Martin Luther King," Ithaca, NY, December 1960 in Carson, *Papers of MLK*, vol. 5, p. 569.

151. Martin Luther King's address, September 16, 1962, in Carson, *Papers of MLK*, vol. 6, p. 444.

152. Martin Luther King Jr., "An Autobiography of Religious Development," November 22, 1950, in Carson, *Papers of MLK*, vol. 1, p. 363.

153. Martin Luther King Jr., "My Pilgrimage to Non-Violence," in Carson, *Papers of MLK*, vol. 5, p. 423.

154. Martin Luther King Jr., "His Influence Speaks to World Conscience," in Carson, *Papers of MLK*, vol. 4, p. 355.

155. Ibid.

156. Ibid.

157. Martin Luther King Jr., "*I Have a Dream*," p. 59.

158. Martin Luther King Jr., *Stride toward Freedom*, (New York: Harper and Brothers, 1958), p. 97.

159. Ibid., p. 98.

160. Ibid., p. 99.

161. Martin Luther King Jr., *Why We Can't Wait* (New York: Harper and Row, 1964), p. 14

162. Walton, *The Political Philosophy of Martin Luther King, Jr.*, p. 65. The discussion draws on this text unless otherwise stated.

163. James Hanigan, *Martin Luther King Jr. and the Foundations of Nonviolence*, (Boston, MA: University of America Press, 1984), p. 196.

164. King's address of September 30, 1962, in Carson, *Papers of MLK*, vol. 6, p. 442.

165. Martin Luther King Jr., "*Stride toward Freedom*," p. 104.

166. Martin Luther King Jr., "*I Have a Dream*," p. 80.

167. This argument is based on David J. Garrow, "The Intellectual Development of Martin Luther King Jr.: Influences and Commentaries," *Union Seminary Quarterly Review* 40, no. 1 (1986): pp. 5–20.

168. Martin Luther King Jr., *Strength to Love*, (New York: Pocket Books, 1964), p. 11—quoted in Walton, *The Political Philosophy of Martin Luther King, Jr.*, pp. 47–8.

169. Martin Luther King Jr., address of February 10, 1957, in Carson, (*Papers of MLK*, vol. 4, p. 124.

170. Carson, *The Autobiography of Martin Luther King, Jr.*, p. 60.

171. Gandhi, *An Autobiography*, p. 31.

172. Martin Luther King Jr., "A View of the Cross Possessing Biblical and Spiritual Justification," in Carson, *Papers of MLK*, vol. 1, p. 285.

173. The preamble to the SCLC Constitution—quoted in Hanigan, *Martin Luther King Jr*, pp. 293–4.

174. Garrow, "The Intellectual Development," p. 15.

175. Martin Luther King Jr., "Man in a Revolutionary World, p. 240—quoted in John J. Ansbro, *Martin Luther King Jr.: The Making of a Mind*, (New York: Orbis Books, 1983), p. 176.

176. Martin Luther King Jr., "A View of the Cross," in Carson, *Papers of MLK*, vol. 1, p. 285.
177. Ibid.
178. William Robert Miller, *Martin Luther King Jr.: His Life, Martyrdom and the Meaning for the World* (New York: Weybright and Talley, 1968), p. 286—quoted in Hanigan, *Martin Luther King Jr.*, p. 273.
179. Martin Luther King Jr., *Strength to Love*, p. 29.
180. Martin Luther King Jr., *Stride toward Freedom*, p. 139.
181. King's statement to Judge Eugene, September 5, 1958—Ansbro, *Martin Luther King Jr.*, p. 139.
182. Martin Luther King Jr., "Love, Law and Civil Disobedience," in *A Testament of Hope*, p. 47.
183. Martin Luther King Jr., *Stride toward Freedom*, p. 102.
184. Martin Luther King Jr., "Love, Law and Civil Disobedience," in *A Testament of Hope*, p. 47.
185. Martin Luther King Jr., *Stride toward Freedom*, pp. 171–2.
186. Gandhi, *Harijan*, January 13, 1940, in *CWMG*, vol. 77, p. 201.
187. Gandhi, *Young India*, April 3, 1930, *CWMG*, vol. 49, p. 2.

CHAPTER 2

1. Farah Godrej, *Cosmopolitan Political Thought: Method, Practice, Discipline* (New York: Oxford University Press, 2011), p. 143.
2. Gyan Pandey, *A History of Prejudice: Caste and Difference in India and USA*, Mimeograph, 2012, p. 26.
3. Ibid., p. 16.
4. Walter White, *A Man Called White: The Autobiography of Walter White*, (New York: Viking Press, 1948), p. 11—quoted in Pandey, *A History of Prejudice*, p. 14.
5. Iris Marion Young, "Structural Injustice and the Politics of Difference," in Kwame Anthony Appiah and Engelbert Habekost, ed., *Justice, Governance, Cosmopolitanism and the Politics of Difference: Reconfigurations in a Transnational World*, Humboldt University, 2004/2005, p. 89
6. Ibid.
7. Ibid., p. 90
8. Ibid., p. 90.
9. Viola Andrews's private papers, available at Emory University Manuscripts and Rare Book Library—quoted in Gyanendra Pandey, "Unarchived Histories: The 'Mad' and 'Trifling,'" *Economic and Political Weekly*, January 7, 2012, 39.
10. I reproduce the argument made by Iris Marion Young unless otherwise stated. See Iris Marion Young, *Justice and the Politics of Difference* (Princeton, NJ: Princeton University Press, 1990).
11. Adam James Tebble, "What Is the Politics of Difference," *Political Theory* 30, no. 2 (April 2002); 262.
12. Anshuman Mondal, "Gandhi, Utopianism and the Construction of Colonial Difference," *Interventions* 3, no. 3 (2001): 419.
13. The 1891 Age of Consent Bill raised the marriageable age of girls from ten to twelve years. Tilak opposed the bill because it was, according to him, a clear interference with Hinduism and would thus set a dangerous precedent.

14. While making this argument, I have drawn on Partha Chatterjee, *The Nation and Its Fragments: Colonial and Post-Colonial Histories* (New Delhi: Oxford University Press, 1994), pp. 4–7.

15. James M. Washington, ed., *I Have a Dream: Writings and Speeches That Changed the World* (San Francisco and New York: Harper, 1992) (reprint), p. 5.

16. Martin Luther King Jr., "The Montgomery Story: Address Delivered at the Forty-Seventh NAACP Convention," June 27, 1956, in *Papers of Martin Luther King*, ed. Clayborne Carson, vol. 3 (Berkeley: University of California Press, 1997), p. 301.

17. Washington, *I Have a Dream*, p. 88.

18. The Jim Crow laws were state and local laws in the United States enacted between 1876 and 1965. They mandated de jure racial segregation in all public facilities for black Americans. In reality, this led to treatment and accommodations that were usually inferior to those provided for white Americans, systematizing a number of economic, educational, and social disadvantages. The origin of the phrase "Jim Crow" has often been attributed to "Jump Jim Crow," a song-and-dance caricature of African Americans performed by white actor Thomas D. Rice in blackface.

19. He languished for as many as 2238 days in prison in South Africa and India; he had worked for not less than 21 years for the emancipation of Indian immigrants in South Africa. Graham Turner, *Catching up with Gandhi* (New Delhi: Penguin, p. 83).

20. M. K. Gandhi, *An Autobiography, or the Story of My Experiments with Truth* (Ahmedabad: Navjivan Publishing House, 2008) (reprint), p. 35.

21. Ibid., p. 36

22. Judith Brown, "The Making of a Critical Outsider," in *Gandhi and South Africa*, ed. Judith Brown and Martin Prozesky (Pietermaritzburg: University of Natal Press, 1996), p. 22.

23. Gandhi, *An Autobiography*, p. 158.

24. Reproduced from Manfred B. Stegar, *Gandhi's Dilemma: Nonviolent Principles and Nationalist Power* (New York: St. Martin's Press, 2000), p. 18.

25. Ibid., p. 27

26. Ibid., p. 29

27. Judith M. Brown, *Gandhi: The Prisoner of Hope*, (New Delhi: Oxford University Press, 1990), pp. 63–4.

28. *Indian Opinion*, March 31, 1906—quoted in Brown, *Gandhi*, p. 64.

29. M. K. Gandhi, *Satyagraha in South Africa* (Ahmedabad: Navjivan Publishing House, 2006) (reprint), p. 67.

30. Ibid.

31. Ibid., p. 66.

32. Stegar, *Gandhi's Dilemma*, p. 29.

33. Stegar, p. 30.

34. Brown, *Gandhi*, p. 63.

35. The fact that Gandhi did not fight for the blacks in South Africa, who also suffered due to racism, may appear to have indicated his personal prejudices. John Lelyveld, *Great Soul: Mahatma Gandhi and His Struggle with India*, (New York: Alfred A. Knopf, 2011.

36. B. R. Nanda, *In Search of Gandhi: Essays and Reflections* (New Delhi: Oxford University Press2002), p. 39.

37. *Collected Works of Mahatma Gandhi*, Vol. 1, p. 367.

38. Gandhi's petition of September 26, 1896, in *CWMG*, Vol. 2, pp. 74, 105.

39. Gandhi's statement of February 29, 1908, in *CWMG*, Vol. 8, p. 167.
40. Gandhi's statement of March 7, 1908, in *CWMG*, Vol. 8, p. 199.
41. Gandhi's statement of April 9, 1904, in *CWMG*, Vol. 3, p. 429.
42. Gandhi's statement of December 24, 1903, in *CWMG*, Vol. 3, p. 379.
43. M. K. Gandhi, "My Second Experience in Gaol," *Indian Opinion*, January 16, 1909, in *CWMG*, Vol. 9, p. 257.
44. *Indian Opinion*, December 24, 1903, in *CWMG*, Vol. 3, p. 379.
45. *Indian Opinion*, October 31, 1908, in *CWMG*, Vol. 9, p. 487.
46. This point is persuasively argued by James D. Hunt in his "Gandhi and the Black People in South Africa," *Gandhi Marg*, April-June 1989, pp. 7–24.
47. Gandhi provided a vivid account of his involvement in the medical corps in his *Satyagraha in South Africa*For an interpretation, see Brian M. Du Toit, "The Mahatma Gandhi and South Africa," *Journal of Modern African Studies* 34, no. 4 (December 1996): pp. 643–60.
48. Gandhi, *Satyagraha in South Africa*, p. 9.
49. Ibid.
50. Gandhi, *Satyagraha in South Africa*, p. 11
51. Ibid.
52. I have elaborated this argument in my *Social and Political Thought of Mahatma Gandhi* (London: Routledge, 2006).
53. Bhikhu Parekh pursues this argument in in his *Colonialism, Tradition and Reform*, (New Delhi: Sage, 1999).
54. Gandhi, *Satyagraha in South Africa*, p. 97.
55. Ibid.
56. Ania Loomba, *Colonialism/Postcolonialism*, (London: Routledge,1998), pp. 67–9, 173—quoted in Stegar, *Gandhi's Dilemma*, p. 46.
57. Stegar, *Gandhi's Dilemma*, pp. 49–50.
58. Stegar, *Gandhi's Dilemma*, p. 61.
59. Clayborne Carson,ed., *The Autobiography of Martin Luther King Jr.*, New York: International Properties Management Inc., in association with Warner Books, 1998), p. 1.
60. Coretta Scott King, *My Life with Martin Luther King Jr.*, (Chicago, IL: Holt, Rinehart and Winston, 1969), p. 84.
61. David L. Chappell, *A Stone of Hope: Prophetic Religion and the Death of Jim Crow*, (Chapel Hill: The University of North Carolina Press, 2004), p. 3
62. Booker T. Washington, *Up from Slavery* (New York: Bantam Books, 1977) (reprint).
63. Ibid., p. 226.
64. Ibid., p. 54.
65. Louis R. Harlan, ed., *The Booker T. Washington Papers*, vol. 1, (Urbana: University of Illinois Press, 1972), p. 416.
66. W. E. B DuBois, *The Souls of Black Folk*, (Oxford: Oxford University Press, 2008) (reprint), p. 38.
67. Ibid., p. 39.
68. Ibid., p. 39.
69. The Atlanta Compromise was the nickname of a famous speech given by Booker T. Washington in 1895 in Atlanta when he assured whites that he would not do anything to challenge white supremacy. He believed that white supremacy was a

system where whites got the best and had most of the power to run things. He also further held that they deserved it because they were somehow better because they were white.

70. DuBois, *The Souls of Black Folk*, p. 39.

71. Ibid., pp. 39–40.

72. Ibid., p. 40.

73. Ibid., p. 44.

74. Ibid., p. 44.

75. W. E. B. DuBois, "On Being Black" (1920), in *W. E. B. Du Bois: A Reader*, ed. Meyer Weinberg (New York: Harper & Row, 1970), p. 4.

76. Racism expresses itself in three basic ways. First, it is a violent act of imposition. As a mode of domination, racism is defined above all by its violent character, its disruption and progressive destruction of a people's life whether it is called colonialism, imperialism, the holocaust of enslavement, neocolonialism, settlerism, occupation, or globalization. Second, racism expresses itself as an ideology or, more precisely, as an ideology of justification of the imposition. It is an ideology that ranges from the rawest of biological, religious, and cultural absurdities to elaborate intellectual and pseudointellectual projects masquerading as social science. Finally, racism expresses itself as institutional arrangement, as structures and processes that promote and perpetuate the imposition and ideology. The educational system, the media, the courts, the legislative bodies, and the economic structures from small businesses to transnational corporations all contribute to the promotion and perpetuation of systemic racism. See Maulana Karenga, "Du Bois and the Question of the Color Line: Race and Class in the Age of Globalization," *Journal of Socialism and Democracy* (online) 57, no. 25 (33) (2012), http://sdonline.org/33/du-bois-and-the-question-of-the-color-line-race-and-class-in-the-age-of-globalization/.

77. W. E. B. DuBois, "The Conservation of Races," 1897 address before the American Negro Academy, reproduced in his *The Souls of Black Folk*, p. 184.

78. WEB DuBois, "White Co-Workers," *Crisis*, May 18, 1920—reproduced in Weinberg, *WEB Du Bois*, p. 324.

79. Manning Marable, *The Great Wells of Democracy: The Meaning Of Race In American Life* (New York: Basic Civitas Books, 2002), p. 321.

80. W. E. B. DuBois, "The Souls of the White Folk," *Independent*, August 18, 1920—reproduced in Weinberg, *W.E.B. Du Bois*, p. 304.

81. W. E. B. DuBois, "Three Centuries of Discrimination," in *Racial Discrimination in the United States*, ed. Thomas Pettigrew (New York: Harper & Row, 1975), pp. 8–9.

82. W. E. B. DuBois, "Prejudice," *Crisis*, November 1927—reproduced in Weinberg, *WEB Du Bois*, p. 326.

83. W. E. B. DuBois, "The Present Outlook for the Darker Races of Mankind" (1900), reproduced in *The Oxford W.E.B. Du Bois Reader*, ed. Eric Sundquist (Oxford: Oxford University Press, 1996), 47–54.

84. Philip S. Foner, *W. E. B. Du Bois Speaks: Speeches and Addresses, 1890–1919* (New York: Pathfinder Press, 1970), p. 125.

85. DuBois, *The Souls of Black Folk*), p. 8

86. All the statements with inverted commas are taken from W. E. B. DuBois, *An Autobiography: A Soliloquy on Viewing My Life from the Last Decade of Its First*

Century, ed. Herbert Aptheker (New York: International Publishers, 1968), pp. 21, 398–401.

87. Howard Winant, "Dialectics of the Veil," in *The New Politics of Race: Globalism, Difference, Justice* (Minneapolis: University of Minnesota Press, 2004), p. 78.

88. Du Bois's analysis of race and racism, explored through the concept of the veil, retains its explanatory power. The idea helps explain the vast importance of racial identity, racial oppression, and resistance and racialized social structure in the creation and organization of the modern world. As a theoretical framework that addresses and links "the micro" and "macro" social meanings of race; that illuminates the continuity and transformation of racial conflict from the historical past to the unresolved racial present; and that illustrates the connections between the racial contradictions with the human soul and those of national (and global) society, the concept of the veil transcends all other attempts to thematize and analyze racial dynamics. For details, see Winant, *The New Politics of Race,* pp. 79–81.

89. W. E. B. DuBois, "Address to the Nations of the World" (1900), reproduced in Foner, *W. E. B. Du Bois Speaks,* pp. 124–7.

90. W. E.B. DuBois, "The African Roots of War" (1915), reproduced in Weinberg, *W.E.B. Du Bois,* pp.60–71.

91. This argument is pursued by Karenga in *"Du Bois and the Question of the Color Line."*

92. Appendix III in DuBois, *The Souls of Black Folk,* p. 208

93. Alex M. Rogers, "On the Color Line: The Early Ideologies and Methodologies of Dr. W. E. B. DuBois," *Colonial Academic Alliance Undergraduate Research Journal* 2, no. 1 (2011): 2.

94. Ibid., p. 3.

95. W. E. B. DuBois, "On Being Ashamed of Oneself" in Weinberg, *WEB Du Bois,* p. 16.

96. King's argument is reproduced from his tribute to Du Bois, published in Foner, *WEB Du Bois Speaks,* pp. 12–20.

97. Rogers, "On the Color Line 4.

98. David L. Chappell, *Inside Agitators: White Southerners in the Civil Rights Movement,* (Baltimore and London: John Hopkins University Press, 1994), p. ix.

99. Ibid., p. xxii.

100. Clayborne Carson, "Foreword," Chappell, *Inside Agitators,* p. xi.

101. David Gallen and Peter Skutches, ed., *Malcolm X As They Knew Him* (New York: Carroll & Graf, 1992), p. 268.

102. David W. Southern, *Gunnar Myrdal and Black-White Relations: The Use and Abuse of an American Dilemma, 1944–1969* (Baton Rouge and London: Louisiana State University Press, 1987), p. 55.

103. Ibid.

104. Junfu Zhang, "Black-White Relations: The American Dilemma," *Perspectives* 1, no. 4 (February 2000), http://www.oycf.org/Perspectives2/4_022900/black_ white.htm.

105. Southern, *Gunnar Myrdal and Black-White Relations,* p. 57

106. Gene Roberts and Hank Klibanoff, *The Race Beat: The Press, the Civil Rights Struggle and the Awakening of a Nation* (New York: Alfred A. Knopf, 2006).

107. Gunnar Myrdal, *An American Dilemma: the Negro Problem and Modern Democracy* (New York: Harper & Row, New 1962) (reprint), p. 3.

108. Ibid., p. 526.

109. Ibid., p. 525.

110. Ibid., p. 526–7.

111. Martin Luther King, Jr, "The Christian Pertinence for Eschatological Hope," in Carson, *Papers of MLK*, vol. 3, pp. 124–5.

112. By this, King meant the application of the principle of equality before law, which included the abrogation of all the legal, social, economic, and political restrictions for African Americans that were rooted in the Jim Crow system of racial segregation.

113. Myrdal, *An American Dilemma*, p. 521.

114. Southern, *Gunnar Myrdal and Black-White Relations*, p. 225.

115. Reinhold Niebuhr, *Moral Man and Immoral Society* (New York: Charles Scribner's Sons, p. 123.

116. Ibid., pp. 119, 118.

117. Ibid., p. 14.

118. Ibid., pp. 15–16.

119. Ibid., p. 119.

120. Carson, ed., *Autobiography of Martin Luther King Jr.*, p. 27.

121. Ibid.

122. Ibid.

123. Martin Luther King Jr., "On Niebuhr," May 9, 1952, in Carson, *Papers of MLK*, vol. II, p. 141.

124. Marin Luther King Jr., "Our Struggle," April 1956, in Carson, *Papers of MLK*, vol. 3, p. 237.

125. Samuel DuBois Cook, "Review of *The Negro of America* by Arnold Rose," *Journal of Negro History* 49 (1964): 209.

126. Martin Luther King Jr., "Reinhold Niebuhr's Ethical Dualism" May 9, 1952, in Carson, *Papers of MLK*, vol. 2, p. 146.

127. Ibid., p. 147.

128. Ibid.

129. Ibid.

130. Ibid., p. 149.

131. Ibid., p. 150.

132. Martin Luther King Jr., *Where Do We Go from Here? Chaos or Community* (Boston, MA: Beacon Press, 1968), pp. 89–90.

133. Martin Luther King Jr., "Where Do We Go From Here? Chaos or Community" (abridged) in *The Essential Writings and Speeches of Martin Luther King Jr.*, ed. James M. Washington (New York: Harper One, 1986), p. 557.

134. King, "Our Struggle," in Carson, *Papers of MLK*, vol. 3, p. 240.

135. Martin Luther King Jr., "Letter from Birmingham Jail," in Washington, *I Have a Dream*, p. 85.

136. Ibid., p. 90.

137. Ibid., p. 85.

138. Martin Luther King Jr., "The American Dream" *The Negro History Bulletin* 31, no. 5 (May 1968): p. 14.

139. Martin Luther King Jr., "Strength to Love," in *A Testament of Hope*, ed. James M. Washington (New York: HarperOne, 1986), p. 500.

140. Martin Luther King Jr., "The Ethical Demands of Integration," *Religion and Labour*, May 1963, p. 4—quoted in Kenneth L. Smith and G. Zapp Jr., *Search for the Beloved Community: The Thinking of Martin Luther King Jr.*, (Valley Forge, PA: Judson Press, 1974), p. 88.

141. Martin Luther King, Jr., "Where Do We Go From Here?" in Washington, *Testament of Hope:* p. 589.

142. Ibid., p. 588.

143. In pursuing this argument, I have drawn on Gertrude Himmelfarb, *The Roads to Modernity: The British, French and American Enlightenments* (New York: Alfred A. Knopf, 2004), (reprint).

144. Lewis V. Baldwin, "American Political Traditions and the Christian Faith: King's Thought and Praxis," in Lewis V. Baldwin, Rufus Burrow Jr., Barbara A. Holmes, and Susan Holmes Winfield, *The Legacy of Martin Luther King, Jr.: The Boundaries of Law, Politics and Religion* (Notre Dame: University of Notre Dame Press, 2002), p. 126.

145. King, *Where Do We Go from Here?*, pp. 75–6.

146. Washington, *A Testament of Hope*, p. 217.

147. King's address at the MIA mass meeting at Holt Street Baptist Church, December 5, 1955 (at Montgomery)—reproduced in Carson, *Papers of MLK*, vol. 3, p. 71.

148. Martin Luther King Jr., "The Negro and the Constitution," in Carson, *Papers of MLK*, vol. 1, p. 110.

149. Martin Luther King Jr., "Kick up the Dust," Letter to the editor, *Atlanta Constitution*, August 6, 1946, in Carson, *Papers of MLK*, vol. 1, p. 121.

150. Martin Luther King Jr., "Non-Violence: The Only Road to Freedom," in Washington, *A Testament of Hope*, p. 58.

151. David L. Chappell, *A Stone of Hope*, p. 3.

152. Manning Marable, *Malcolm X: A Life of Reinvention* (New York: Penguin Books, 2011).

153. Ibid., p. 482.

154. Ibid., p. 483.

155. Gallen and Skutches, *Malcolm X*, p. 139.

156. Malcolm X, "The Chickens Come Home to Roost," in *The African-American Experience: Black History and Culture through Speeches, Letters, Editorials, Poems, Songs and Stories*, ed. Kai Wright (New York: Black Dog & Leventhal Publishers, 2009) (reprint), p. 540.

157. Ibid., p. 537.

158. Ibid., p. 538.

159. Carson, *The Autobiography of Martin Luther King Jr.*, p. 266.

160. Carson, *The Autobiography of Martin Luther King Jr.*, p. 266.

161. Martin Luther King Jr., *Where Do We Go from Here?*, p. 189.

162. M. K. Gandhi, "Ahimsa," *Harijan*, September 29, 1946, in *The Selected Works of Mahatma Gandhi*, Vol. 5, ed. Shriman Narayan (Ahmedabad: Navjivan Publishing House, 1969), pp. 166–7.

163. M. K. Gandhi, "Non-Violence," *Harijan*, September 1, 1940, in Narayan, *Selected Works of Mahatma Gandhi*, p. 171.

164. Ibid., p. 167.
165. M. K. Gandhi, "What is Satyagraha?" *Harijan*, October 8, 1925, in Narayan, *Selected Works of Mahatma Gandhi*, p. 178.
166. M. K. Gandhi, *India's Case for Swaraj* (Bombay: Yeshanand & Co., 1932), p. 369—quoted in Raghavan Iyer, *The Moral and Political Thought of Mahatma Gandhi* (New York: Oxford University Press, 1973), p. 287.
167. Ibid.
168. Iyer, *Moral and Political Thought of Mahatma Gandhi*, p. 288.
169. Gandhi's letter to "the world tomorrow" November 14, 1924, in *CWMG*, Vol. 29, p. 340.
170. Martin Luther King Jr., *Playboy* Interview, in Carson, *A Testament of Hope*, p. 349.
171. King, "My Pilgrimage to Non-Violence," in Carson, *Papers of MLK*, vol. 4, p. 477.
172. Ibid., p. 481.
173. These inputs are drawn on the private papers of Martin Luther King Jr., kept in the Mugar Library, Boston University—quoted from Mary King, *Mahatma Gandhi and Martin Luther King Jr.: The Power of Non-Violent Action,* (Paris: UNESCO Publishing 1999), p. 247.
174. King, "My Pilgrimage to Non-Violence," in Carson, *Papers of MLK*, vol. 4, p. 478.
175. Martin Luther King Jr., "Love Your Enemies," Sermon delivered at Dexter Baptist Church, November 17, 1957, in Carson, *Papers of MLK*, vol. 4, pp. 319–20.
176. Gandhi's discussion with Christian missionaries, December 12, 1938, in *CWMG*, Vol. 74, pp. 307–8.
177. Martin Luther King Jr., "Non-Violence and Racial Justice," *Christian Century*, February 6, 1957.
178. M. K. Gandhi, "From Yeravda Mandir," in Narayan, *The Selected Works of Mahatma Gandhi*, p. 236.
179. Gandhi to a Harijan worker, June 27, 1936, in *CWMG*, Vol. 69, pp. 176–7.
180. M. K. Gandhi, "Implications of Constructive Programme," *Harijan*, August 18, 1940, *CWMG*, Vol. 79, p. 378.
181. M. K. Gandhi, "Untouchability," *Harijan*, June 20, 1936, *CWMG*, Vol. 69, pp. 168–9.
182. M. K. Gandhi, "The Role of Law" in Mah*atma Gandhi: The Essential Writing*s, ed. Judith Brown (Oxford: Oxford University Press, 2008), p. 218.
183. Ibid.
184. Martin Luther King's sermon in Ebenezer Church, February 10, 1957, in Carson, *Papers of MLK*, vol. 4, p. 124.
185. Martin Luther King Jr., "I Have a Dream," in *"I Have a Dream": Writings and Speeches That Changed the World,* ed. James M. Washington (San Francisco and New York: Harper, 1992), p. 102.
186. Martin Luther King Jr., "I See the Promised Land," in Washington, *"I Have a Dream,"* p. 203.
187. Chakrabarty, *Social and Political Thought*, pp. 84–115.
188. Parekh, *Colonialism, Tradition and Reform*, p. 130.
189. M. K. Gandhi, *Young India*, January 19, 1921, *CWMG*, vol. 23, pp. 33–5.

190. Ibid., pp. 35.
191. M. K. Gandhi, *Ethical Religion* (Madras: S. Ganesan, 1922), p. 30.
192. King, "Love Your Enemies, in Carson, *Papers of MLK*, vol. 4, p. 319.
193. Ibid., p. 322
194. John J. Ansbro, *Martin Luther King Jr.: The Making of a Man* (New York: Orbis Books, 1983), p. 9.
195. Martin Luther King Jr., "A Christmas Sermon on Peace," in King, *The Trumpet of Conscience* (New York: Harper & Row, 1967), p. 74.
196. Martin Luther King Jr., "Three Dimensions of a Complete Life," in King, *Strength to Love*, (New York: Harper & Row, 1963), p. 69.
197. Ibid., p. 19.
198. Gandhi to C. F. Andrews, November 23, 1920, *CWMG*, vol. 22, p. 1.
199. Ansbro, *Martin Luther King Jr.*, p. 30.
200. Martin Luther King Jr., "Paul's Letter to American Christians: A Sermon Delivered at Dexter Avenue Baptist Church," November 4, 1956, in Carson, *Papers of MLK*, vol. 3, p. 420.
201. Martin Luther King Jr., *Stride toward Freedom: The Montgomery Story*, (New York: Harper & Row, 1958), pp. 137–8.
202. Gandhi, "From Yeravda Mandir," in Narayan, *Selected Works of Mahatma Gandhi*, vol. 4, p. 216.
203. Ibid., p. 219
204. M. K. Gandhi's address to the YMCA (Madras), February 16, 1916, *CWMG*, vol. 15, p. 168.
205. M. K. Gandhi, "The Doctrine of the Sword," *Young India*, August 11, 1920, *CWMG*, vol. 21, p. 135.
206. Martin Luther King Jr., "Love, Law and Civil Disobedience," in Washington, *A Testament of Hope*, p. 45.
207. Martin Luther King Jr. "A Time to Break Silence," in Washington, *A Testament of Hope*, p. 231.
208. Martin Luther King Jr., "Paul's Letter to American Christians," in Carson, *Papers of MLK*, vol. 3, p. 418.
209. Ibid.
210. Martin Luther King Jr., "Non-Aggression Procedures to Interracial Harmony: Address, Delivered at the American Baptist Assembly and American Home Mission Agencies Conference," July 23, 1956, in Carson, *Papers of MLK*, vol. 3, p. 326.
211. Ibid.
212. Scan Scalmer, *Gandhi in the West: The Mahatma and the Rise of Radical Protest*, (Cambridge: Cambridge University Press, 2011), p. 171.
213. The report on the American Baptist Convention was published in *Crusader*, New York, April 1957—quoted in Scalmer, *Gandhi in the West*, p. 171
214. M .K. Gandhi, *Satyagraha in South Africa* (Ahmedabad: Navjivan Publishing House, 1928), p. 67.
215. M. K. Gandhi, "Appeal for Enlistment," June 22, 1918, *CWMG*, vol. 17, p. 83.
216. M. K. Gandhi's interview with Captain Strunk, July 3, 1937, *CWMG*, vol. 71, p. 405.
217. Ibid., p. 404.

218. M. K. Gandhi, "Letter to Adolf Hitler," December 24, 1940, *CWMG*, vol. 79, p. 455.

219. Ibid., p. 454.

220. King, "A Time to Break Silence," in Washington, *A Testament of Hope*, p. 235.

221. King, *Stride toward Freedom*, p. 97.

222. King, "A Time to Break Silence," in Washington, *A Testament of Hope*, p. 233

223. This point figures prominently in Russell Eugene Dowdy, "Nonviolence Vs. Nonexistence: the Vietnam War and Martin Luther King Jr.," MA thesis, Department of History, North Carolina State University, 1983, pp. 172–84.

224. Martin Luther King Jr., press statement, *The Times*, April 14, 1966.

225. Martin Luther King Jr., press statement, *Chicago Defender*, January 7, 1966.

226. King, "A Time to Break Silence," in Washington, *A Testament of Hope*, p. 233.

227. "Dr. King's Error," *New York Times*, April 7, 1936.

228. King, "A Time to Break Silence," in Washington, *A Testament of Hope*, p. 241.

229. Dowdy, "Nonviolence Vs. Nonexistence," p. 142.

230. King, *The Trumpet of Conscience*, p. 24

231. H. B. Acton, ed., *Utilitarianism, Liberty and Representative Government by J. S. Mill*, (London: J. B. Dent, 1972), p. 73.

232. While developing the entire argument, I have drawn on Andrew Nash, "Gandhi in South Africa: An Interpretation," paper presented at a seminar of the Department of History, University of Kwa-Zulu-Natal, August 11, 2004.

233. Gopal Guru, ed., *Humiliation: Claims and Content* (New Delhi: Oxford University Press, 2009), p. 1.

234. Arlin Turner, ed., *The Negro Question: A Selection of Writings on Civil Rights in the South by George W. Cable*, (New York: Doubleday Anchor Books, 1958), pp. 62–3.

235. Ibid., pp. 62.

236. Guru, *Humiliation*, p. 1.

237. Bhikhu Parekh, "Logic of Humiliation" in Guru, *Humiliation*, p. 31.

238. Sudipta Kaviraj, "The Heteronomous Radicalism of M. N. Roy," in *Political Thought in Modern India*, ed. Thomas Pantham and Kenneth Deutsch (New Delhi: Sage, 1986), p. 235.

239. Farah Godrej pursues this argument in the context of Gandhi's sociopolitical ideas in *Cosmopolitan Political Thought*, pp. 107–10.

240. C. A. Bayly, *Recovering Liberties: Indian Thought in the Age of Liberalism and Empire* (Cambridge: Cambridge University Press, 2012), p. 357.

CHAPTER 3

1. M. K. Gandhi, *Satyagraha in South Africa* (Ahmedabad: Navjivan Publishing House, 1928). This discussion is drawn on this tract unless otherwise stated.

2. MK Gandhi, 'The Indian Question', 23 February, 1901, *CWMG*, vol. 3. pp. 113–14.

3. MK Gandhi to the Colonial Secretary, 1 August, 1903, *CWMG*, vol. 3. p. 129.

4. Quoted in Krishna Kripalani, *Gandhi: A Life* (New Delhi: National Book Trust, 2000), p. 32.

5. M. K. Gandhi, *An Autobiography, or the Story of My Experiments with Truth* (Ahmedabad: Navjivan Publishing House, 1927), p. 177.

6. Ibid.

7. Gandhi, *Satyagraha in South Africa,* p. 145.

8. Ibid., p. 252.

9. Ibid.

10. Gandhi, *Satyagraha in South Africa,* pp. 258–9.

11. Judith Brown, *Gandhi: Prisoner of Hope* (New Delhi: Oxford University Press, 1990), p. 26.

12. Surnedra Bhana and Goolam Vahed, *The Making of a Political Reformer: Gandhi in South Africa* (New Delhi: Manohar Books, 2005), p. 95.

13. The Phoenix Farm in Natal (1904) and the Tolstoy Farm in Johannesburg (1910) were Gandhian experiments of communal living that sought to
    (a) train new passive resisters
    (b) experiment in communal living
    (c) take care of the family of prisoners involved in passive resistance
    (d) evolve a mind-set for multicultural existence.

14. Gandhi's interview to *The Natal Advertiser,* January 13, 1897, *CWMG,* vol. 2, p. 6.

15. Gandhi's letter to Dadabhai Naoroji, January 30, 1903, *CWMG,* vol. 3, p. 21.

16. Ibid., p. 23

17. M. K. Gandhi, "Note on Ourselves," *Indian Opinion,* December 24, 1904, *CWMG,* vol. 4, pp. 144–46.

18. In the Indian agrarian context, a *raiyat* was someone who had acquired a right to hold land for purpose of cultivating it, whether alone or by members of his family, hired laborers or partners.

19. Rajendra Prasad, *At the Feet of Mahatma Gandhi* (Bombay: Asia Publishing House, 1961), p. 7.

20. A report of the subdivisional officer, Bettiah, on September 23, 1917—quoted in Jacques Pouchepadass, *Champaran and Gandhi: Planters, Peasants and Gandhian Politics* (New Delhi: Oxford University Press, 1999), pp. 217–18.

21. Ibid., p. 234.

22. Partha Chatterjee, "Gandhi and the Critique of Civil Society," in *Subaltern Studies,* ed. Ranajit Guha, vol. 3, (New Delhi: Oxford University Press, 1984), p. 189.

23. Jawaharlal Nehru, *An Autobiography* (London: The Bodley Head, 1941), pp. 254–55.

24. M. V. Pylee, *Constitutional Government in India* (London: Asia Publishing House, 1965), p. 29.

25. Gandhi to V. S. Srinivasa Shastri, February 9, 1919, *CWMG,* vol. 15, pp. 87–8.

26. Gandhi's speech on the satyagraha movement, Trichinopoly, March 25, 1919, *CWMG,* vol. 15, p. 155.

27. *Hartal* in Indian parlance means "strike."

28. Dyer commanded the Jallianwala Bagh massacre in the Punjab in 1919, killing several thousands of people who gathered there to protest against the imposition of the draconian 1918 Rowlatt Act.

29. Headed by Lord William Hunter, the purpose of the Hunter Commission (appointed on October 14, 1919) was to investigate the political disturbances in Bombay, Delhi, and Punjab and to find out the causes for them. It also sought to study the effectiveness of the administrative steps that were taken to cope with them.

30. Editorial in *Amrita Bazar Patrika*, October 18, 1919.

31. "An Appeal to the Public: Mahatma Gandhi Arrested—Friends Wake Up"—quoted in *Essays on Gandhian Politics: The Rowlatt Satyagraha of 1919*, ed. Ravinder Kumar (Oxford: Clarendon Press, 1971), pp. 337–8.

32. J. H. Kerr to the Secretary of State, Government of India, April 14, 1919—quoted in Kumar, *Essays on Gandhian Politics*, p. 328.

33. Nehru, *An Autobiography*, pp. 65–6.

34. M. K. Gandhi to the Viceroy, Lord Chelmsford, June 22, 1920, *CWMG*, Vol. 20, p. 415.

35. *Amrita Bazar Patrika*, July 18, 1920.

36. Jawaharlal Nehru, *The Discovery of India* (New Delhi: Oxford University Press, 1989), p. 358–9.

37. M. K. Gandhi, "The Khilafat Question," *Young India*, April 28, 1920, *CWMG*, vol. 21, p. 114.

38. Maulana Mohammad Ali and Maulana Shaukat Ali—two brothers who worked hard for the merger of the noncooperation movement with the Khilafat movement.

39. *Young India*, July 28, 1920, *CWMG*, vol. 18. p. 89.

40. *Young India*, June 9, 1920, *CWMG*, vol. 17, p. 483.

41. *Young India*, July 28, 1920, *CWMG*, vol. 18. p. 89.

42. Judith Brown, *Gandhi's Rise to Power*, (Cambridge: Cambridge University Press, 1972), p. 246.

43. P. C. Bamford, *Histories of the Non-Cooperation and Khilafat Movements* (New Delhi: Government of India, 1925; rpt. New Delhi: Imprint, 1974), pp. 102–3.

44. Ronaldshay to Montague, June 15, 1921, Indian Office Records (IOR), Mss. Eur. D 609(2) Zetland Collection.

45. The jute industry was controlled by both the Europeans and Americans, which was not the case in other industries in colonial India.

46. M. K. Gandhi, "The Lesson of Assam," *Young India*, June 15, 1921. Gandhi reiterated his argument in a meeting in Calcutta on September 11, 1921, by condemning the strike fever that tended to disrupt unnecessarily the amicable relationship between the industrialists and the workers. See *The Statesman*, September 22, 1921.

47. Gandhi's address to the special session of the All-India Congress Committee, September 4–9, 1920, *CWMG*, Vol. 21, p. 257.

48. *Zamindar* means "landlord."

49. *Young India*, March 11, 1930, *CWMG*, vol. 43, pp. 117.

50. The Purna Swaraj declaration, or declaration of the independence of India, was made by the Indian National Congress on Janaury 26, 1930, resolving to fight for complete self-rule independent of the British Empire.

51. Nehru, *An Autobiography*, p. 210.

52. A note by H. Haig, the Home Member, Government of India, December 23, 1930, National Archives of India, New Delhi, Hope-Poll 257/V and KW/1930.

53. Lord Irwin, the Viceroy, to Wedgewood Benn, Home Member, December 28, 1930, India Office Records, London, Halifax Papers, Mss. Eur. C 152 (6).

54. Subhas Chandra Bose, *The Indian Struggle, 1920–42* (London: Asia Publishing House, 1964), p. 179.

55. Claude Markovits, *The Un-Gandhian Gandhi: The Life and Afterlife of the Mahatma*, (New Delhi: Permanent Black, 2003), p. 77.

56. *Young India*, July 17, 1930, *CWMG*, vol. 43, p. 358.

57. Nehru, *An Autobiography*, p. 215.

58. Gandhi's speech at Broach, March 26, 1930, *Young India*, April 4, 1930, *CWMG*, vol. 23, p. 127.

59. *Khadi* in Indian parlance refers to home-spun clothes.

60. Tejbahadur Sapru to Irwin, September 19, 1930, IOR, Halifax Papers, Mss. Eur. C 152 (25).

61. *The Times of India*, May 5, 1930.

62. Gandhi's letter to H. S. L. Polak, July 13, 1930, *CWMG*, vol. 49, p. 363.

63. Jawaharlal Nehru's speech at the All-India Congress Committee meeting while moving "the Quit India" resolution on August 8, 1942 in Bombay, Nehru Memorial Museum and Library, New Delhi, All India Congress Committee Papers, G22/1942.

64. R. Tottenham, Additional Secretary to F Puckle, Secretary, Information and Broadcasting, Government of India, August 24, 1942, National Archives of India, New Delhi, KW to HPF (1) 3/7/42.

65. Nicholas Mansergh, E.X.R Lumby, and Penderel Moon, eds., *The Transfer of Power*, Vol. II, Her Majesty's Stationery Office, London, 1971, p. 622.

66. Gandhi's speech at the All-India Congress Committee just before his arrest, August 8, 1942, *CWMG*, vol. 83, p. 203.

67. Nehru, *Discovery of India* (New Delhi: Oxford University Press, 1989) (reprint), p. 475.

68. Quotations are from Nicholas Mansergh, E. W. R. Lumby, and Penderel Moon, ed., *The Transfer of Power 1942-1947* (London: Her Majesty's Stationery Office, 1971) unless otherwise stated. See Vol. II, *The Quit India Resolution*, p. 622.

69. Ibid., p. 624.

70. Gandhi's press interview of August 6, 1942, quoted in R. Tottenham, *Congress Responsibility* (Delhi: Government of India, 1943), p. 62.

71. Gandhi's speech at the AICC meeting, August 8, 1942, *CWMG*, vol. 76, p. 392.

72. Ibid., p. 403.

73. Viceroy to the Secretary of State, August 9, 1942, reporting the view of the Governors on the question of Gandhi's fast, IOR, L/PO/6/102A Tgm.

74. Lord Linlithgow (India's Viceroy) to Lord Amery (Secretary of State), 28 August 28, 1942, IOR, L/PO/6/102A Telegram.

75. N.C. Chaudhuri, *The Autobiography of an Unknown Indian* (Berkeley and Los Angeles: University of California Press, 1968), p. 400.

76. For details, see Amba Prasad, *Indian Revolt of 1942*, (Delhi: Impex, 1958); F. Hutchinson, *Spontaneous Revolution: The Quit India Movement*, (New Delhi: Manohar Books, 1971); G. Pandeyed., *The Indian Nation in 1942* (Calcutta: K. P. Bagchi & Company, 1982); N. Mitra, ed., *The Indian Annual Register*, July-December 1942 (this volume contains the government document entitled "Congress Responsibility for Disturbances").

77. Bidyut Chakrabarty, "Political Mobilization in the Localities, 1942," *Modern Asian Studies* 26, no. 4 (December 1992).

78. Fortnightly Report for the first half of February 1928, IOR, L/PJ/12/1.

79. Viceroy to the Secretary of State, October 13, 1921, IOR, Mss Eur E 238/10, Reading Papers.

80. A detailed discussion has been pursued in my *Subhas Chandra Bose and Middle-Class Radicalism* (New Delhi: Oxford University Press, 1990), chapter 1.

81. As the Mahatma himself admitted, it was not necessary for everyone joining the political campaign to accept ahimsa as a creed. It was possible to accept it merely as a political strategy, without its religious core. In his words, "[A]himsa with me is a creed, the breath of life. But it is never as a creed that I placed before India or, for that matter, before anyone except in casual or informal talks. I placed it before the Congress as political weapon, to be employed for the solution of practical problems." Quoted in Partha Chatterjee, "Gandhi Please Stand Up?" *Illustrated Weekly of India*, January 15-21, 1984, p. 29.

CHAPTER 4

1. Clayborne Carson, ed., *The Autobiography of Martin Luther King Jr.* (New York: Intellectual Properties Management in association with Warner Books, 1998), pp. 2-3.

2. Ibid., p. 5.

3. Ibid., p. 9.

4. Ibid., pp. 9-10.

5. M. K. Gandhi, *An Autobiography, or the Story of My Experiments with Truth* (Ahmedabad: Navjivan Publishing House, 2008) (reprint), pp. 103-4.

6. Ibid., p. 104.

7. Carson, *The Autobiography of Martin Luther King Jr.*, p. 10.

8. Ibid., p. 11.

9. M. K. Gandhi, *Satyagraha in South Africa* (Ahmedabad: Navjivan Publishing House, 2006) (reprint), p. 36.

10. Gandhi, *An Autobiography*, p. 120.

11. Ibid., p. 121.

12. Ibid.

13. James M. Washington, *I Have a Dream: Writings and Speeches That Changed the World* (New York and San Francisco: Harper, 1992), p. 89.

14. Statement engraved in the American History Museum, Washington, DC.

15. Martin Luther King Jr., "Letter from Birmingham Jail," in *A Testament of Hope*, ed. James M. Washington (New York: HarperOne, 1986), p. 297.

16. Carson, *The Autobiography of Martin Luther King Jr.*, p. 3.

17. King's statement of December 5, 1955—quoted in Mary King, *Mahatma Gandhi and Martin Luther King Jr.: The Power of Non-Violent Action* (Paris: UNESCO Publishing, 1999), p. 333.

18. King's address to the American Jewish Committee, March 9, 1965—quoted in Michael J. Nojeim, *Gandhi and King: The Power of Non-Violent Resistance*, (Westport, CT: Praeger, 2004), p. 223.

19. J. Mills Thornton III, *Dividing Lines: Municipal Politics and the Struggle for Civil Rights in Montgomery, Birmingham and Selma*, (Tuscaloosa: University of Alabama Press,2002), pp. 42-6.

20. For details on the involvement of Rosa Parks in the bus strike at Montgomery, see Thornton, *Dividing Lines*, pp. 57-61.

21. Douglas Brinkley, *Rosa Parks: A Life*, (New York: Penguin, 2000), p. 55.

22. Ibid., p. 57.

23. Ibid.

24. Ibid., p. 58.

25. Ibid., p. 59.

26. Ibid.

27. Rosa L. Parks, "Interviews," in *My Soul Is Rested: The Story of the Civil Rights Movement in the Deep South*, ed. Howell Raines (New York: Penguin, 1977), p. 41.

28. E. D. Nixon (1899–1987) was an active leader of the civil rights movement in Alabama. He was the one who endeavored hard to increase the number of registered black voters in Montgomery and was one of the key members of Montgomery Improvement Association and the Montgomery Bus Boycott.

29. Carson, *The Autobiography of Martin Luther King Jr.*, p. 52.

30. Thornton, *Dividing Lines*, p. 64.

31. Carson, *The Autobiography of Martin Luther King Jr.*, p. 55.

32. Martin Luther King Jr., *Stride toward Freedom: The Montgomery story*, (New York: Harper & Brothers, 1958).

33. Ibid., p. 9.

34. Ibid.

35. King's speech of December 5, 1955—reproduced in Brinkley, *Rosa Parks*, p. 141.

36. Kai Wright, ed., *The African-American Experience: Black History and Culture through Speeches, Letters, Editorials, Poems, Songs and Stories* (New York: Black Dog & Leventhal Publishers, 2009), p.486.

37. Bayard Rustin, *Strategies for Freedom: The Changing Patterns of Black Protest* (New York: Columbia University Press, 1976), p. 38.

38. Martin Luther King Jr., "Walk for Freedom," May 1956 in *The Papers of MLK of Martin Luther King Jr.*, ed. Clayborne Carson, vol. 3 (Berkeley: University of California Press, 1997), p. 277.

39. Ibid., pp. 278–9.

40. King, "To the Citizens of Montgomery," January 27, 1956, in Carson, *Papers of MLK*, vol. 3, p. 107.

41. King, "Walk for Freedom," in Carson, *Papers of MLK*, vol. 3, p. 107.

42. King, "Non-Aggression Procedures to Interracial Harmony," address delivered at the American Baptist Assembly and American Home Mission Agencies Conference, July 23, 1956, in Carson, *Papers of MLK*, vol. 3, p. 326.

43. Carson, *The Autobiography of Martin Luther King Jr.*, p. 60.

44. King, "To the Citizens of Democracy," January 27, 1956, in Carson, *Papers of MLK*, vol. 3, p. 108

45. Taylor Branch, *Parting the Waters: America in the King Years, 1954–1963*, (New York: Simon & Schuster 1988), pp. 227–8.

46. Martin Luther King Jr., "Our Struggle," in Carson, *Papers of MLK*, vol. 3, p. 237.

47. King, "The New Negro of the South: Behind the Montgomery Story," June 1956, in Carson, *Papers of MLK*, vol. 3, p. 283.

48. King's address of June 27, in Carson, *Papers of MLK*, vol. 3, p. 308.

49. Deirdre Mullane, ed., *Crossing the Danger Water: Three Hundred Years of African-American Writing* (New York: Anchor Books, 1993), p. 629.

50. King, "The Meaning of Montgomery," June 1956, in Carson, *Papers of MLK*, vol. 3, p. 283.

51. James Farmer, *Lay Bare the Heart: An Autobiography of the Civil Rights Movement*, (New York: New American Library, 1985), p. 11.
52. "Bayard Rustin Reminisces," transcript of an interview by Ed. Edwin—quoted in Cynthia Taylor, *A. Philip Randolph: The Religious Journey of an African-American Labor Leader* (New York: New York University Press, 2006), p. 178.
53. Bayard Rustin to King, December 23, 1956 in Carson, *Papers of MLK*, vol. 3, p. 492.
54. Ibid.
55. Rustin, *Strategies for Freedom*, p. 37.
56. Bayard Rustin to King, December 23, 1956, in Carson, *Papers of MLK*, vol. 3, p. 494.
57. Ibid.
58. Farmer, *Lay Bare the Heart*, p. 186.
59. Thornton, *Dividing Lines*, p. 96.
60. The January 1959 resolution of the Citizens' Council is reproduced from Thornton, *Dividing Lines*, p. 97.
61. David J. Garrow, *Bearing the Cross: Martin Luther King Jr., and Southern Christian Leadership Conference* (New York: William Morrow and Company, 1986), p. 86.
62. Ibid., p. 87.
63. King's address—quoted in Garrow, *Bearing the Cross*, pp. 94–5.
64. Jerrold M. Packard, *American Nightmare: The History of Jim Crow* (New York: St. Martin's Press, 2002), p. 176.
65. Reproduced from Mullane, *Crossing the Danger Water*, pp. 569–70.
66. Ibid., pp. 577
67. A. Philip Randolph's statement, quoted in Ibid., pp. 568.
68. Cornelius L. Bynum, *A. Philip Randolph and the Struggle for Civil Rights* (Urbana: University of Illinois Press, 2010), p. 180.
69. Taylor, *A. Philip Randolph*, p. 154.
70. Paula F. Pfeffer, *A. Philip Randolph, The Pioneer of the Civil Rights Movement* (Baton Rouge and London: Louisiana State University Press, 1990), p. 177.
71. Jervis Anderson, *Bayard Rustin: Troubles I've Seen*, (New York: HarperCollins, 1997), pp. 51–2.
72. Ibid., p. 48.
73. Drawn from Shmuel Ross, "Civil Rights March on Washington," *Infoplease.com*, http://www.infoplease.com/spot/marchonwashington.html#ixzz1ul7YEPAi.
74. Ibid.
75. John Lewis quoted in Clayborne Carson, *In Struggle: SNCC and the Black Awakening of the 1960s* (Cambridge, MA: Harvard University Press, 1981), p. 94.
76. Anderson, *Bayard Rustin*, pp. 260–1.
77. Pauli Murray's letter to A. Philip Randolph is quoted in Anderson, *Bayard Rustin*, p. 259.
78. Randolph's statement is quoted in Anderson, *Bayard Rustin*, p. 257.
79. A. Philip Randolph, "Why Should We March?" *Survey Graphic*, no. 31, (November 1942), pp. 488–9.
80. Ibid., pp. 489.
81. Taylor, *A. Philip Randolph*, p. 199.
82. King's "I Have a Dream" speech is quoted from Wright, *The African-American Experience*, pp. 531–3.

83. Carson, *The Autobiography of Martin Luther King, Jr.* p. 222

84. Clayborne Carson, "SNCC and the Albany Movement," *Journal of Southwest Georgia* 2 (Fall 1984), p. 15.

85. Carson, *In Struggle*, p. 208.

86. Martin Luther King Jr., "Why We Can't Wait," in *A Testament of Hope: The Essential Writings and Speeches of Martin Luther King Jr.*, ed. James M Washington (New York: Harper One, 1986), p. 541.

87. Carson, *The Autobiography of Martin Luther King*, pp. 168–9.

88. Reverend Fred Shuttlesworth (1922–2011) was a minister in Birmingham, Alabama, and a civil rights activist who led the campaign against racial segregation and other forms of discrimination based on color. He was also associated with the formation of the Southern Christian Leadership Conference (SCLC) and was one of the primary organizers of the 1963 Birmingham campaign along with Martin Luther King Jr.

89. Washington, *A Testament of Hope*, p. 527.

90. Ibid., p. 530.

91. Garrow, *Bearing the Cross*, p. 246.

92. Carson, ed., *The Autobiography of Martin Luther King Jr.*, p. 174.

93. Thornton, *Dividing Lines*, p. 299.

94. Washington, *A Testament of Hope*, p. 542.

95. Ibid.

96. Ibid., p. 546.

97. Ibid., pp. 547–8.

98. Ibid., p. 552.

99. Ibid., p. 554.

100. Richard P. Fulkerson, "The Public Letter as a Rhetorical Form: Structure, Logic and Style in King's 'Letter from Birmingham Jail,'" *The Quarterly Journal of Speech* 65, no. 2 (1965): pp. 130–1.

101. "Letter from Birmingham Jail" was not merely directed to the eight clergymen critical of King's civil disobedience in Birmingham. It was not directed only to the Negros of the community who were being asked by the clergymen to withdraw support for the civil rights demonstrations. It was addressed primarily to the moderate and laymen, black and white, in both North and South. Haig Bosmajian, "The Letter from Birmingham Jail," in *Martin Luther King Jr.: A Profile*, ed. C. Eric Lincoln (New York: Hill and Wang, 1970), pp. 128–43.

102. Washington, *I Have a Dream*, p. 89.

103. Ibid., pp. 89–90.

104. Ibid., pp. 86–7.

105. Ibid., p. 100.

106. Andrew Young, *An Easy Burden: The Civil Rights Movement and the Transformation of America*, (New York: HarperCollins, 1996), p. 238.

107. King's statement—quoted in Nojeim, *Gandhi and King*, p. 240.

108. Washington, *I Have a Dream*, p. 100.

109. Doug AcAdam, "The US Civil Rights Movement: Power from Below and Above, 1945–70," in *Civil Resistance and Power Politics: The Experience of Non-Violent Action From Gandhi to the Present*, ed. Adam Roberts and Timothy Garton Ash (Oxford: Oxford University Press, 2009), p. 70.

110. Bosmajian, "The Letter from Birmingham Jail" in Lincoln, *Martin Luther King Jr.*, p. 129.
111. Carson, *In Struggle*, p. 153.
112. Carson, *The Autobiography of Martin Luther King Jr.*, p. 271.
113. Martin Luther King Jr., "Behind the Selma March," in Washington, *A Testament of Hope*, p. 127.
114. Kwame Tour and Charles V. Hamilton, *Black Power: The Politics of Liberatin* (New York: Vintage Books, p. 100).
115. Ibid., p. 101.
116. Washington, *A Testament of Hope*, pp. 128–31.
117. Carson, *The Autobiography of Martin Luther King Jr.*, p. 272.
118. Ibid.
119. Thornton, *Dividing Lines*, p. 436.
120. Ibid., p. 438
121. Tour and Hamilton, *Black Power*, p. 104.
122. Thornton, *Dividing Lines*, p. 461.
123. Carson, *The Autobiography of Martin Luther King Jr.*, p. 272.
124. Thornton, *Dividing Lines*, p. 393.
125. Ibid., p. 401.
126. Ibid.
127. Ibid., p. 473.
128. Carson, *In Struggle*, p. 161.
129. Thornton, *Dividing Lines*, p. 476.
130. Tour and Hamilton, *Black Power*, pp. 101–5.
131. Stephen B. Oates, *Let the Trumpet Sound: The Life of Martin Luther King, Jr.*, (New York: Harper & Row, 1982), p. 349.
132. Carson, *The Autobiography of Martin Luther King Jr.*, p. 285.
133. Oates, *Let the Trumpet Sound*, p. 371.
134. Adam Fairclough, "Martin Luther King, Jr. and the Quest for Nonviolent Social Change," *Phylon, The Atlanta University Review of Race and Culture* 47, no. 1 (Spring 1986): 1—reproduced in *Martin Luther King Jr.: Civil Rights Leader, Theologian, Orator*, ed. David Garrow (New York: Carlson Publishing Inc., 1989), p. 333.
135. Johnson's statement—quoted in Garrow, *Bearing the Cross*, p. 385.
136. Clayborne Carson, "Civil Rights Movement: An Overview" (personal correspondence), March 3, 2011.
137. Viceroy to the Secretary of State, London, April 24, 1930, India Office Records, London, Sykes Papers, Mss. Eur F 130 (2).
138. J. Krishnalal Sridharani, *War without Violence: A Study of Gandhi's Method and Its Accomplishment* (New York: Harcourt Brace & Co., 1939), p. 131.
139. Gene Sharp, *The Politics of Non-Violent Action* (Boston, MA: Peter Sargent, 1972), p. 68.

CONCLUSION

1. Coretta King, *My Life with Martin Luther King Jr.* (Chicago, IL: Holt, Rinehart and Winston, 1969), p. 92.
2. In his prayer meeting in June 1947, Gandhi thus lamented, "Pakistan is a bad thing....What is there to rejoice over it? Our country has been divided; does it

mean that we should divide our hearts? How can the people of a country become two people? India can have only one people."

3. As King elaborated, " [O]ne of the agonies of life is that we are constantly trying to finish that which is unfinishable. We are commanded to do that. And, so we...find ourselves in so many instances having to face the fact that our dreams are not fulfilled." Clayborne Carson, ed., *The Autobiography of Martin Luther King Jr.*, (New York: International Properties Management Inc., in association with Warner Books, 1998), p. 356.

4. Benedict Anderson, *Imagined Communities: Reflections on the Origin and Spread of Nationalism* (London and New York: Verso, 1983).

5. Partha Chatterjee, *The Nation and its Fragments: Colonial and Post-Colonial Histories* (New Delhi: Oxford University Press, 1994).

6. Martin Luther King Jr., "Twelve Suggestions For Action," in *The Papers of Martin Luther King Jr.*, ed. Clayborne Carson, vol. 4 (Berkeley: University of California Press, 2000), p. 124.

7. Howard Thurman, *Jesus and the Disinherited*, Abingdon Press, New York, 1949, p. 93.

8. This argument is based on Partha Chatterjee's *Nationalist Thought and Colonial World: A Derivative Discourse*, (New Delhi: Oxford University Press, 1986) and *The Nation and its Fragments*.

9. William Cenkner, "Gandhi and Creative Conflict," *Thought* 45, no. 178 (Autumn 1970): 427, quoted Martin Luther King Jr., "Man in a Revolutionary World," p. 240—quoted in John J. Ansbro, *Martin Luther King Jr.: The Making of a Mind* (New York: Orbis Books, 1983), p. 145.

10. Martin Luther King Jr., "Man in a Revolutionary World," p. 240—quoted in John J. Ansbro, *Martin Luther King Jr.: The Making of a Mind* (New York: Orbis Books, 1983), p. 146.

11. Ibid.

12. Coretta Scott King, *My Life with Martin Luther King Jr.*, p. 161.

13. Ibid., p. 178.

14. Ibid.

15. Ibid., p. 179.

16. Martin Luther King, *Playboy* Interview, in Carson, *A Testament of Hope*, p. 376.

17. Thomas Weber, *Gandhi as Disciple and Mentor*, (Cambridge: Cambridge University Press, 2004).

18. Ibid., pp. 249–50.

19. Denis Dalton, *Non-Violence in Action: Gandhi's Power* (New Delhi: Oxford University Press, 1998), p. 183.

20. Ibid.

21. Martin Luther King Jr., "His Influence Speaks to the World," in *Papers of MLK of Martin Luther King Jr.*, ed. Clayborne Carson, vol. 4 (Berkeley: University of California Press, 2000), p. 355.

22. Gandhi to Mira Behn, December 8, 1932 in *The Selected Works of Mahatma Gandhi*, ed. Shriman Narayan, vol. 5, (Ahmedabad: Navjivan Publishers, 1969), p. 403.

23. Vinay Lal, "Gandhi's West and West's Gandhi," *New Literary History*, 40, no. 2 (Spring 2009): p. 302.

24. Ibid.

25. Thomas Weber persuasively makes this point while assessing Gandhi's philosophy in action. According to Weber, while "a narrow reading would certainly give us a political technique with which to challenge repressive power, a wider reading shows that Gandhi's spiritual quest and ideas about the unity of life are not necessarily irrelevant or confusing to many." Weber, *Gandhi as Disciple and Mentor*, pp. 249–52.

26. Sean Scalmer, *Gandhi in the West: The Mahatma and the Rise of Radical Protest*, (Cambridge: Cambridge University Press, 2011), p. 169.

27. Ibid., p. 170.

28. Manning Marable, *The Great Wells of Democracy: The Meaning of Race in American Life* (New York: Basic Civitas Books, 2002), p. 283.

29. Ibid.

30. Ibid, p. 283.

31. Bayard Rustin, *Strategies for Freedom: The Changing Patterns of Black Protest*, (New York: Columbia University Press, 1976), p. 65.

32. Ibid.

33. William Pickens, "Gandhism and Prayer Will Not Solve the Negro's Problem," *New York Amsterdam News*, February 10, 1932, quoted in Sudarshan Kapur, *Raising Up a Prophet: The African-American Encounter with Gandhi* (Boston, MA: Beacon Press, 1992), p. 57.

34. Ibid., p. 58.

35. Ibid.

36. Ibid., p. 59.

37. W. E. B. DuBois, *The Souls of Black Folk* (New York: Oxford University Press, 2008) (reprint), pp. 42–3.

38. David L. Chappell, *Inside Agitators: White Southerners in the Civil Rights Movement* (Baltimore and London: Johns Hopkins University, 1994), p. xxii.

39. Ibid.

40. Ibid., xxii.

41. Ibid., p. 69.

42. Ibid., p. 81.

43. Clayborne Carson, "Foreword," in Chappell, *Inside Agitators*, p. xxi.

44. Shahid Amin, *Event, Metaphor, Memory: Chauri-Chaura, 1922-1992* (New Delhi: Oxford University Press, 1995), pp. 170–71.

45. Weekly Report of Director, Intelligence Bureau, March 10, 1921, National Archives of India (NAI), Home-Poll 53/1921,quoted in Judith M. Brown, *Gandhi: Prisoner of Hope* (New Delhi: Oxford University Press, 1990), p. 168.

46. Shahid Amin, "Gandhi as Mahatma: Gorakhpur District, Eastern Uttar Pradesh," in *Subaltern Studies*, ed. Ranajit Guha, vol. 3 (New Delhi: Oxford University Press, 1984), p. 55.

47. Author's personal interview with Sushil Dhara, one of the major nationalist activists during the 1942 Quit India Movement in Midnapore, Bengal, July 9, 1985.

48. Shahid Amin, *Event, Metaphor, Memory: Chauri Chaura, 1922-1992*, (New Delhi: Oxford University Press, 1995), p. 16.

49. Deputy Commissioner of Police, Calcutta, to M. O. Carter, Governor of Bengal, September 28, 1942, IOR, London, R/3/2/33.

50. Judith M. Brown, "The Mahatma and Modern India," *Modern Asian Studies* 3, no. 4 (1969): p. 337.
51. Willingdon, the Madras Governor, to Reading, the Viceroy, April 3, 1921, IOR, Mss. Eur. F 93(5).
52. Jawaharlal Nehru, *The Discovery of India* (New Delhi: Oxford University Press, 1989), p. 358.
53. Ibid.
54. Viceroy to Montague, the Secretary of State, May 19, 1921, IOR, London, Mss. Eur. F238/3 Reading Collection, Reading.
55. Monash University Library, Melbourne, microfilm collection of declassified State Department documents, classified report, prepared by the American Intelligence, August 18, 1942.
56. Susanne Hoeber Rudolph and Lloyd I. Rudolph, *Gandhi: The Traditional Roots of Charisma* (Delhi: Orient Longman, 1987), p. 5.
57. Monash University Library, Melbourne, microfilm collection of declassified State Department documents, Counselor, American Embassy in Calcutta, to the Secretary of State, August 27, 1947.
58. David L. Chappell, *A Stone of Hope: Prophetic Religion and The Death of Jim Crow* (Chapel Hill and London: University of North Carolina Press, 2004), p. 55.
59. Clayborne Carson, "Civil Rights Reform and the Black Freedom Struggle," in *The Civil Rights Movement in America*, ed. Charles W. Eagles (Jackson: University Press of Mississippi, 1986), p. 24.
60. Ibid., p. 25.
61. Ibid., p. 26.
62. Ibid., p. 22.
63. Ibid.
64. Clayborne Carson, "Between Contending Forces: Martin Luther King Jr. and the African-American Freedom Struggle,"*O[rganization] of A[merican] H[istorians] Magazine of History* 19, no. 1 (January 2005), p. 18.
65. I have pursued this argument in my "Radicalism in Modern Indian Social and Political Thought: Nationalist Creativity in the Colonial Era," in *Political Ideas in Modern India*, ed. V. R. Mehta and Thomas Pantham, vol. 10 (7) (New Delhi: Sage, 2006), pp. 3–25.
66. Sumit Sarkar, *Modern India, 1885–1947* (New Delhi: Macmillan India, 1983), p. 180
67. Sumit Sarkar, *Modern India, 1885–1947* (New Delhi: Macmillan India, 1983), p. 180.
68. Andrew Young, *An Easy Burden: The Civil Rights Movement and the Transformation of America* (New York: HarperCollins, 1996), pp. 189–90.
69. Ibid., p. 156.
70. Ibid., p. 382.
71. Carson, *The Autobiography of Martin Luther King*, p. 1.
72. Clayborne Carson, "Martin Luther King Jr.: Charismatic Leadership in a Mass Struggle," *Journal of American History* 74 (September 1987): 449.
73. Howard Thurman, *With Head and Heart: The Autobiography of Howard Thurman* (San Diego, CA: Harcourt & Brace Company, 1979), p. 223.
74. Chappell, *Inside Agitators*, p. 138.

75. Martin Luther King Jr., *Stride toward Freedom* (New York: Harper & Brothers, 1958), p. 179.
76. Ibid., p. 183.
77. James H. Cone, "The Theology of Martin Luther King Jr.," *Union Seminary Quarterly Review* 40, no. 4 (1986): pp. 21–39.
78. Martin Luther King's statement of 1954—quoted in Clayborne Carson, "Martin Luther King Jr. and the African-American Social Gospel" in *African-American Christianity*, ed. Paul E. Johnson (Berkeley: University of California Press, 1994), p. 175.
79. This argument is pursued by Cone, "The Theology of Martin Luther King Jr.," pp. 21–39.
80. King, *Stride toward Freedom*, p. 84.
81. Ibid., pp. 59–60.
82. Bayard Rustin, *Strategies for Freedom: The Changing Contours of Black Protest* (New York: Columbia University Press, 1976), p. 20.
83. Carson, "Martin Luther King Jr.," p. 453.
84. Young, *An Easy Burden*, p. 238.
85. Clayborne Carson, "Martin Luther King Jr.," p. 453.

BIBLIOGRAPHICAL NOTES AND
SELECT BIBLIOGRAPHY

Texts on Gandhi and Martin Luther King Jr. can be classified into three segments: in the first segment, the focus is on tracts written by Gandhi and King. These published texts provide very useful inputs for the work. The second segment contains published collected works, which are very exhaustive. In the case of Gandhi, most of his written texts have already been incorporated into the collected works that have been published by the Government of India and are also available online. King's collected works are not complete yet; nonetheless, six volumes of King texts published so far are very pertinent to any scholarly work on King. The literature in the final segment includes the scholarly works on the sociopolitical ideas of Gandhi and King. Since this book is also a contextual study of the history of ideas, the books, articles, and other relevant written tracts focusing on the contexts have also been included in this segment. Judith Brown's *Gandhi's Rise to Power: Indian Politics, 1915–1922* (Cambridge: Cambridge University Press, 1972) and *Gandhi and Civil Disobedience: The Mahatma in Indian Politics, 1928–1934* (Cambridge: Cambridge University Press, 2008) provide a very useful contextual study of the rise of Gandhi as an unquestionable leader of India's freedom struggle. In the same fashion, two books on the American civil rights movement deserve mention. These are David J. Garrow, *Bearing the Cross: Martin Luther King Jr. and the Christian Leadership Conference* (New York: William Morrow and Company, 1986) and Taylor Branch, *Parting the Waters: America in the King Years, 1954–1963* (New York: Simon & Schuster, 1988).

Both Gandhi and King left an enormous number of written texts for posterity. One can thus easily identify specific sociopolitical ideas that are integral to their views. Gandhi wrote a partial autobiography (*My Experiments with Truth*), a political treatise (*Hind Swaraj*), a movement book (*Satyagraha in South Africa*), a few pamphlets, a very large number of articles in the two weeklies that he edited, namely, *Indian Opinion* (South Africa) and *Young India* (India), and an even larger number of letters to viceroys, fellow politicians, and disciples. Besides these, he delivered speeches at conferences, congresses, and at his regular prayer meetings. King also left a large body of writings for posterity. *The Autobiography of Martin Luther King Jr.*, (New York: IPM in association with Warner Books,

1998), edited by Clayborne Carson, is a balanced account of King's life that provides useful insights into the period and also describes the evolution of King's sociopolitical ideas. Other than this autobiography, King published six books. These included two collection of sermons, *The Measure of a Man* (1959) and *Strength to Love* (1963); a collection of radio addresses entitled *The Trumpet of Conscience* (1968); and three books that are "movement books." The first movement book, *Stride toward Freedom* (1958), is a philosophical account of the Montgomery bus boycott, including a general outline and defense of the method of direct nonviolent protest. The second movement book, *Why We Can't Wait* (1964), is a philosophical account of the 1963 Birmingham campaign for jobs and freedom. This text includes the famous "Letter from Birmingham Jail," in which King offers a philosophical defence of nonviolence, addressed to the moderate white clergy. The last movement book was published in 1967 in anticipation of a national campaign against poverty. Entitled *Where Do We Go from Here? Chaos of Community* (1968), this posthumous publication is a complex interweaving of ideas and thoughts that evolved during the course of King's struggle for equality and justice.

Besides their own writings, the other significant sources happen to be the compilation of their texts in the form of collected works. Available online, *The Collected Works of Mahatma Gandhi* (New Delhi: Publication Division, Government of India, (1958–1998)), are an important source of the Gandhian texts that I have used extensively in my work. Besides this official publication, Navjivan Publishing House published a six-volume set called *Mahatma Gandhi: Selected Works* in the centenary year of Gandhi's birthday. Similarly, six volumes edited by Clayborne Carson, *The Papers of Martin Luther King Jr.* (Berkeley: University of California Press, 1992–2007), contain a minefield of information that is very useful in comprehending the complex nuances of the sociopolitical ideas of Martin Luther King Jr. with reference to the volatile American socioeconomic contexts.

Select Bibliography

Acton, H. B., ed., *Utilitarianism, Liberty and Representative Government by J. S. Mill.* London: J. B. Dent, 1972.

Alavi, Hamza. "Misreading Partition Road Signs." *Economic and Political Weekly,* November 2–9, 2002, 4515–23.

——. "Social Forces and Ideology in the Making of Pakistan." *Economic and Political Weekly,* October 21, 2002, 4313–20.

Alexander, Michelle. *The New Jim Crow: Mass Incarceration in the Age of Colorblindness.* New York: The New Press, 2010.

Ali Chaudhuri, Muhammad. *The Emergence of Pakistan.* New York: Columbia University Press, 1967.

Ambedkar, B. R., "Thoughts on Pakistan." In *Inventing Boundaries: gender, politics and partition of India,* edited by Mushirul Hasan. New Delhi: Oxford University Press, 2000.

——. *What Congress and Gandhi Have Done to the Untouchables.* Bombay: Thacker & Co., 1946.

Amin, Shahid. *Event, Metaphor, Memory: Chauri Chaura, 1922–92.* New Delhi: Oxford University Press, 1995.

——. "Gandhi as Mahatma: Gorakhpur District, Eastern UP, 1921–22." *Subaltern Studies: Writings on South Asian Studies,* edited by Ranajit Guha, vol. 3. New Delhi: Oxford University Press, 1984.

Ananthanathan, A. K., "The Significance of Gandhi's Interpretation of Gita." *Gandhi Marg* 13, no. 3 (October 1991).

Anderson, Benedict. *Imagined Communities: Reflections on the Origin and Spread of Nationalism.* London and New York: Verso, 1983.

Anderson, Jervis. *Bayard Rustin: Troubles I Have Seen: A Biography,* New York: Harper Collins, 1997.

Andrews, C. F. *Mahatma Gandhi's Ideas.* New York: The Macmillan Company, 1930.

Ansbro, John J., *Martin Luther King Jr.: The Making of a Mind.* New York: Orbis Books, 1983.

Appiah, Kwame Anthony, Seyla Benhabib, Iris Marion Young, and Nancy Fraser, *Justice, Governance, Cosmopolitanism and the Politics of Difference: Reconfigurations in a Transnational World.* Berlin: Humboldt University, 2004/2005.

Asim, Jabari, *The N word: Who Can Say It, Who Shouldn't, And Why.* Boston, MA: Houghton Mifflin Company, 2007.

Bagchi, Amiya. *Private Investment in India, 1900–39.* Cambridge: Cambridge University Press, 1972.

Bakshi, Rajni, *Bapu Kuti: Journeys in Rediscovery of Gandhi.* New Delhi: Penguin, 1998.

Baldwin, Lewis V. "American Political Traditions and the Christian faith: King's Thought and Praxis." In *The Legacy of Martin Luther King, Jr.: The Boundaries of Law, Politics and Religion,* edited by Lewis V. Burrow Baldwin Rufus Jr., Barbara A Holmes, and Susan Holmes Winfield. Notre Dame, IN: University of Notre Dame Press, 2002.

Bandyopadhyaya, Jayantuja. *Social and Political Thought of Gandhi.* Bombay: Allied Publishers, 1969.

Bandyopadhyay, Sekhar. *From Plassey to Partition: A History of Modern India.* New Delhi: Orient Longman, 2004.

Bayly, C. A. *Recovering Liberties: Indian Thought in the Age of Liberalism and Empire.* Cambridge: Cambridge University Press, 2012.

Bhalla, Alok, ed. *Stories about the Partition of India.* New Delhi: Penguin, 1994.

Bhattacharyya, Buddhadeva. *Evolution of the Political Philosophy of Gandhi.* Calcutta: Calcutta Book House, 1969.

Bhattacharya, Sabyasachi, ed. and comp. *The Mahatma and the Poet: Letters and Debates between Gandhi and Tagore, 1915-1941.* New Delhi: National Book Trust, 1997.

——. *Vande Mataram: The Biography of a Song.* New Delhi: Penguin, 2003.

Bilgrami, Akeel. "Gandhi, the Philosopher." *Economic and Political Weekly,* September 23, 2003, 4159–65.

Birla, G. D. *In the Shadow of the Mahatma: A Personal Memoir,* Calcutta: Orient Longman, 1964.

Bloom, Harold. *W. E. B. Du Bois.* Philadelphia, PA: Chelsea House Publishers, 2001.

Bondurant Joan V. *Conquest of Violence: The Gandhian Philosophy of Conflict.* Princeton, NJ: Princeton University Press, 1958.

Bose, Nirmal Kumar. *My Days with Gandhi*. Calcutta: Orient Longman, 1974.
——. *Studies in Gandhism*. Calcutta: India Associated Publishing Co., 1962.
Bose, Subhas Chandra. *The Indian Struggle, 1920–42*. London: Asia Publishing House, 1964.
Bose, Sugata. "Nation, Reason and Religion: India's Independence in International Perspective." *Economic and Political Weekly*, August 1, 1998.
Bose, Sugata, and Ayesha Jalal. *Modern South Asia, History, Culture, Political Economy.* New Delhi: Oxford University Press, 1998.
Bosmajian, Haig, "The Letter from Birmingham Jail." In *Martin Luther King Jr.: A Profile*, edited by C. Eric Lincoln. New York: Hill and Wang, 1970.
Branch, Taylor, *Parting the Waters: America in the King Years, 1954-1963*, New York: Simon & Schuster 1988.
Brinkley, Douglas, *Rosa Parks: A Life*, New York: Penguin, 2000.
Brown, Judith M. *Gandhi and Civil Disobedience: The Mahatma in Indian Politics, 1928-1934*. Cambridge: Cambridge University Press, 1977.
——. *Gandhi: Prisoner of Hope*. New Delhi: Oxford University Press, 1990.
——. *Gandhi's Rise to Power: Indian Politics, 1915-1922*. Cambridge: Cambridge University Press, 1972.
——. "The Mahatma and Modern India." *Modern Asian Studies* 3, no. 4 (1969).
——. "The Making of a Critical Outsider." In *Gandhi and South Africa*, edited by Judith Brown and Martin Prozesky. Pietermaritzburg: University of Natal Press, 1996.
——. *Modern India: The Origins of an Asian Democracy.* New
Delhi: Oxford University Press, 1985.
——. *Nehru: Political Life*. New Delhi: Oxford University Press, 2004.
Brown, Judith M., and Anthony Parel. *The Cambridge Companion to Gandhi*, Cambridge: Cambridge University Press, 2011.
Bynum, Cornelius L., *A. Philip Randolph and the Struggle for Civil Rights*. Urbana: University of Illinois Press,2010.
Carpenter, Edward. *Civilization: Its Cause and Cure and Other Essays*. London: Swan Sonneschein & Co., 1889.
Carson, Clayborne. "Between Contending Forces: Martin Luther King Jr.and the African-American Freedom Struggle." *O[rganization] of A[merican] H[istorians] Magazine of History* 19, no. 1 (January 2005).
——. "Civil Rights Reform and the Black Freedom Struggle." In *The Civil Rights Movement in America*, edited by Charles W. Eagles. Jackson: University Press of Mississippi, 1986.
——. *In Struggle: SNCC and the Black Awakening of the 1960s*, Cambridge, MA: Harvard University Press, 1981.
——. "Martin Luther King Jr. and the African-American Social Gospel." In *African-American Christianity*, edited by Paul E. Johnson. Berkeley: University of California Press, 1994.
——. "Martin Luther King Jr.: Charismatic Leadership in a Mass Struggle." *Journal of American History* 74 (September 1987).
——. "Paradoxes of King Historiography." *O[rganization] A[merican] H[istorians] Magazine of History* 19, no. 1 (January 2005).
——, ed. *The Papers of Martin Luther King Jr.* 6 vols. Berkeley: University of California Press, 1992-2007.

Cell, John W. "Race Relations." In *Encyclopedia of Southern Culture*, edited by Charles Reagan Wilson and William Ferries. Chapel Hill: University of North Carolina Press, 1989.

Chakrabarty, Bidyut. *Biplabi: A Journal of the 1942 Open Rebellion*. Calcutta: K. P. Bagchi, 2002.

——. *Local Politics and Indian Nationalism: Midnapur, 1919-1944*. Delhi: Manohar, 1997.

——. *The Partition of Bengal and Assam, 1932-47: Contour of Freedom*. London and New York: Routledge Curzon, 2004.

——. "Peasants and the Bengal Congress, 1928-38," *South Asia Research* 5, no. 1 (May 1985).

——. "Religion, Colonialism and Modernity: Relocating 'Self' and 'Collectivity.'" *Gandhi Marg* 23, no. 3 (2002).

——. *Subhas Chandra Bose and Middle Class Radicalism: A Study in Indian Nationalism, 1928-40*. New Delhi: Oxford University Press, 1990.

——, ed. *Communal Identity in India: Its Construction and Articulation in the Twentieth Century*. New Delhi: Oxford University Press, 2003.

Chakrabarty, Dipesh. "Nation and Imagination." *Studies in History* 15, no. 2, New Series 1999.

Chappell, David L. *Inside Agitators: White Southerners in the Civil Rights Movement*. Baltimore and London: Johns Hopkins University Press, 1994.

——. *A Stone of Hope: Prophetic Religion and the Death of Jim Crow*. Chapel Hill and London: University of North Carolina Press.

Chatterjee, Margaret. *Gandhi's Religious Thought*. Notre Dame, IN: University of Notre Dame Press, 1983.

Chatterjee, Partha. "Gandhi and the Critique of Civil Society." In *Subaltern Studies: Writings on South Asian Studies*, edited by Ranajit Guha. Vol. 3. New Delhi: Oxford University Press, 1984.

——. "Gandhi Please Stand Up?" *Illustrated Weekly of India*, January 15-21, 1984.

——. *The Nation and Its Fragments: Colonial and Post-Colonial Histories*. New Delhi: Oxford University Press, 1994.

——. "The Nation in Heterogeneous Time." *Indian Economic and Social History Review* 38, no. 4 (2001).

——. *Nationalist Thought and the Colonial World: A Derivative Discourse*. New Delhi: Oxford University Press, 1986.

——. *The Politics of the Governed: Reflections on Popular Politics in Most of the World*. New Delhi: Permanent Black, 2004.

——. *A Princely Impostor? The Kumar of Bhawal and the Secret History of Indian Nationalism*. New Delhi: Permanent Black, 2002.

Chaudhuri, Nirad C. *The Autobiography of an Unknown Indian*. Berkeley: University of California Press, 1968.

——. *Thy Hand Great Anarch: India, 1921-52*. London: Chatto and Windus, 1987.

Chernus, Ira. *American Nonviolence: The History of an Idea*. New York: Orbis Books, 2004.

Choudhury, Khaliquzzaman. *Pathway to Pakistan*. Lahore: Longmans, 1961.

Cohn, B., *Colonialism and Its Forms of Knowledge: The British in India*. Princeton, NJ: Princeton University Press, 1996.

Cone, James H., "The Theology of Martin Luther King Jr." *Union Seminary Quarterly Review* 40, no. 4 (1986).

Copley, Anthony *Gandhi against the Tide*. New Delhi: Oxford University Press, 1993.

D'Emilio, John. *Lost Prophet: The Life and Times of Bayard Rustin*. New York: Free Press, 2003.

Dalton, Dennis. *Non-Violence in Action: Gandhi's Power*. New Delhi: Oxford University Press, 1998.

Darling, Malcolm Lyall. *At Freedom's Dawn*. Oxford: Oxford University Press, 1949.

Das, Durga, ed. *Vallabhbhai Patel Correspondence, 1945–50*. Vol. 4. New Delhi: Konark Publishers, 1990.

Dasgupta, Ajit K. *Gandhi's Economic Thought*. London and New York: Routledge, 1996.

Datta, V. N. "Iqbal, Jinnah and India's Partition." *Economic and Political Weekly*, December, 14–20, 2002.

Doke, Joseph J. *MK Gandhi: An Indian Patriot in South Africa*. London: Indian Chronicle, 1909. Republished by the Ministry of Information, Government of India, New Delhi, 1967.

Dowdy, Russell Eugene. "Nonviolence Vs. Nonexistence: The Vietnam War and Martin Luther King Jr." MA thesis, Department of History, North Carolina State University, 1983.

DuBois, W. E. B. "The African Roots of War" (1915). Reproduced in *W.E.B. DuBois: A Reader*, edited by Meyer Weinberg. New York: Harper & Row, 1970.

——. *An Autobiography: A Soliloquy on Viewing My Life from the Last Decade of Its First Century*. Edited by Herbert Apthekar. New York: International Publishers, 1968.

——. *The Souls of Black Folk*. Oxford: Oxford University Press, 2008 (reprint).

——. "The Wide, Wide World." *New York Amsterdam News*, October 28, 1931.

Dutt, R. Palme. *India Today*. London: Victor Gollancz Ltd., 1940.

Erickson E. *Gandhi's Truth: On the Origins of Militant Non-Violence*. New York: Faber & Faber, 1970.

Fairclough, Adam, "Martin Luther King, Jr. and the Quest for Nonviolent Social Change." *Phylon, the Atlanta University Review of Race and Culture* 47, no. 1 (Spring 1986).

Farmer, James. *Lay Bare the Heart: An Autobiography of The Civil Rights Movement*. New York: New American Library, 1985.

Ferguson, Niall. *Empire: The Rise and Demise of the British World Order and the Lessons for Global Power*. New York: Basic Books, 2002.

Fisher, Louis. *Gandhi: His Life and Message for the World*. New York: New American Library, 1982

——.*The Life of Mahatma Gandhi*. New York: Harper and Row, 1981.

Foner, Philip S., ed. *W.E.B. Du Bois Speaks: Speeches and Addresses, 1890–1919*. N ew York: Pathfinder Press, 1970.

Fox, Richard. *Gandhian Utopia: Experiments with Culture*. Boston, MA: Beacon Press, 1989.

Frederickson, George M., *Black Liberation: A Comparative History of Black Ideologies in the United States and South Africa*. New York: Oxford University Press, 1995.

Freitag, Sandria B., *Collective Action and Community: Public Arenas and the Emergence of Communalism in North India*. New Delhi: Oxford University Press, 1990.

Friedman, Robert. "Institutional Racism: How to Discriminate without Really Trying." In *Racial Discrimination in the United States*, ed. Thomas F. Pettigrew. New York: Harper & Row, 1975.

Gallen, David, ed., *Malcolm X As They Knew Him*. New York: Carroll & Graf Publishers, 1992.

Gallen, David, and Peter Skutches, eds., *Malcolm X As They Knew Him*. New York: Carroll & Graf Publishers, 1999.

Garrow David J. *Bearing the Cross: Martin Luther King Jr. and the Southern Christian Leadership Conference*. New York: William Morrow and Company, 1986.

——. "The Intellectual Development of Martin Luther King Jr: Influences and Commentaries." *Union Seminary Quarterly Review*, 40, no.1 (1986).

——, ed. *Martin Luther King Jr.: Civil Rights Leader, Theologian, Orator*. New York: Carlson Publishing Inc., 1989.

Gier, Nicholas. "Gandhi, Ahimsa and Self." *Gandhi Marg* 15, no. 1 (1993).

——. "Gandhi, Pre-Modern, Modern or Post-Modern?" *Gandhi Marg* 18, no. 3 (1996).

Godrej, Farah, *Cosmopolitan Political Thought: Method, Practice, Discipline*. New York: Oxford University Press, 2011.

Gopal S. *Jawaharlal Nehru*. 3 vols. London: Jonathan Cape, 1973–84.

Gordon, Leonard A. "Mahatma Gandhi's Dialogues with Americans." *Economic and Political Weekly*, January 26, 2002.

Gore, M. S. *The Social Context of an Ideology: Ambedkar's Political and Social Thought*. New Delhi: Sage,1993.

Gregg, Richard B., *The Power of Non-Violence*. London: J. B. Lippincott, 1934.

Griffiths, Percival, *To Guard My People: The History of the Indian Police*. London: Ernest Benn, 1971.

Guha, Ranajit. *Dominance without Hegemony: History and Power in Colonial India*. New Delhi: Oxford University Press, 1998.

Guru, Gopal, ed. *Humiliation: Claims and Content*. New Delhi: Oxford University Press, 2009.

Haksar, Vinit. *Rights, Communities and Disobedience: Liberalism and Gandhi*. New Delhi: Oxford University Press, 2001.

Hanigan, James. *Martin Luther King Jr. and the Foundations of Nonviolence*. Boston, MA: University of America Press, 1984.

Haque, Azizul. *A Plea for a Separate Electorate in Bengal*. Calcutta, 1931.

Hardiman, David. *Gandhi in His Times and Ours*. New Delhi: Permanent Black, 2003.

——. *Peasant Nationalists of Gujrat: Kheda district, 1917–34*. New Delhi: Oxford University Press, 1981.

Hardy P. *The Muslims of British India*. Cambridge: Cambridge University Press, 1972.

Harlan, Louis R., ed. *The Booker T. Washington Papers*. Vol. 1. Urbana: University of Illinois Press, 1972.

Hasan, Mushirul. *Legacy of a Divided Nation: India's Muslims since Independence*. New Delhi: Oxford University Press, 1997.

——, ed. *India Partitioned: The Other Face of Freedom*. Vol. 1. New Delhi: Roli Books, 1995.

——. *Inventing Boundaries: Gender, Politics and the Partition of India*. New Delhi: Oxford University Press, 2000.

Hashim, Abul. *In Retrospection*. Dhaka: Mowla Brothers, 1974.

Henningham, S. "The Social Setting of the Champaran Satyagraha: The Challenge of an Alien Rule." *Indian Economic and Social History Review*, 13, no. 1 (1976).

Herman, A. L. *Community, Violence and Peace*. Albany: State University of New York Press, 1999.

Himmelfarb, Gertrude. *The Roads to Modernity: The British, French and American Enlightenments*. New York: Alfred A. Knopf, 2004. Reprint.

Hodosn, H. V. *The Great Divide: Britain—India—Pakistan*. London: Hutchinson, 1969.

Horsburgh, H. J. N., *Non-Violence and Aggression: A Study of Gandhi's Moral Equivalent of War*. Oxford: Oxford University Press, 1968.

Iyer, Raghavan. *The Moral and Political Thought of Mahatma Gandhi*. New Delhi: Oxford University Press, 1973.

——, ed., *The Moral and Political Writings of Mahatma Gandhi*. Oxford: Clarendon Press, Vols. 1 & 2, 1986 and Vol. 3, 1987.

Jha, Sadan. "Charkha, 'Dear Forgotten Friend,' Of Widows: Reading the Erasures of Symbols," *Economic and Political Weekly*, July 10, 2004, 3113–20.

Jinnah, Muhammad Ali. *Speeches* Karachi: Pakistan Publications, 1963.

Juergensmeyer, Mark. *Fighting with Gandhi*. San Francisco: Harper and Row, 1984.

——. *Gandhi's Way: A Handbook of Conflict Resolution*. New Delhi: Oxford University Press, 2003.

Kamath, M. V., and V. B. Kher. *The Story of Militant but Non-Violent Trade Unionism: A Biographical and Historical Study*. Ahmedabad: Navjivan Trust, 1993. Reprint.

Kapur, Sudarshan. *Raising Up a Prophet: The African-American Encounter with Gandhi*. Boston, MA: Beacon Press, 1992.

Karenga, Maulana. "Du Bois and the Question of the Color Line: Race and Class in the Age of Globalization." *Journal of Socialism and Democracy* (online) 57, no. 25 (3) (2012).

Karunakaran, K. P. *New Perspectives on Gandhi*. Shimla: Indian Institute of Advanced Studies, 1969.

Kennedy, Randall. *Nigger: The Strange Career of a Troublesome Word*. New York: Vintage Books, 2003.

Khilnani, Sunil. "Gandhi and History." *Seminar*, no. 461 (annual) (January 1998).

King, Coretta Scott. *My Life with Martin Luther King Jr*. Chicago, IL: Holt, Rinehart and Winston, 1969.

King, Mary. *Mahatma Gandhi and Martin Luther King Jr.: The Power of Non-Violent Action*. Paris: UNESCO Publishing, 1999.

Koditschek, Theodore. *Liberalism, Imperialism and Historical Imagination*. Cambridge: Cambridge University Press, 2011.

Kosek, Joseph Kip. "Reichard Gregg, Mohandas Gandhi and the Strategy of Non-Violence." *The Journal of American History* 91, no. 1 (March 2005).

——. *Acts of Conscience: Christian Nonviolence and Modern American Democracy*. New York: Columbia University Press, 2009.

Kripalani, Krishna. *Gandhi: A Life*. New Delhi: National Book Trust, 1968.

Kripalani, Sucheta. *An Unfinished Biography*. Ahmedabad: Navjivan Publishing House, 1978.

Kumar, R., *Essays on Gandhian Politics: The Rowlatt Satyagraha of 1919*. Oxford: Clarendon Press, 1971.

Lal, Vinay. "Gandhi's West, the West's Gandhi." *New Literary History* 40, no.2 (2009).

Lewis, Catherine M., and J. Richard Lewis, eds. *Jim Crow America: A Documentary History.* Fayetteville: University of Arkansas Press, 2009.

Loomba, Ania. *Colonialism/Postcolonialism.* London: Routledge, 1998.

Mahajan, Sucheta. *Independence and Partition: The Erosion of Colonial Power.* New Delhi: Sage, 2000.

Manor, J. ed. *Nehrus to the Nineties: The Changing Office of Prime Minister in India.* London: Hurst, 1994.

Mansergh, Diana, ed. *Independence Years: The Selected Indian and Commonwealth Papers of Nicholas Mansergh.* New Delhi: Oxford University Press, 1999.

Mantena, Karuna. "Another Realism: The Politics of Gandhian Non-Violence." *American Political Science Review* 16, no. 2 (May 2012).

Marable, William Manning. *The Great Wells of Democracy: The Meaning of Race in American Life.* New York: Basic Ovitas Books, 2002.

———. *Malcolm X: A Life of Reinvention.* New York: Penguin Books, 2011.

Markovits, Claude. *The Un-Gandhian Gandhi: The Life and Afterlife of the Mahatma.* New Delhi: Permanent Black, 2003.

Mays, Benjamin E. *The Negro's God.* Boston, MA: Chapman and Grimes, 1938.

McAdam, Doug. "The US Civil Rights Movement: Power from Below and Above, 1945–70." In *Civil Resistance and Power Politics: The Experience of Non-Violent Action from Gandhi to the Present,* edited by Adam Roberts and Timothy Garton Ash. Oxford: Oxford University Press, 2009.

McNight, Gerald. *The Last Crusade: Martin Luther King Jr., the FBI, and the Poor People's Campaign.* Boulder, CO: Westview Press, 1998.

Mehta, V. R. *Foundations of Indian Political Thought.* New Delhi: Manohar Books, 1992.

Mehta, V. R., and Thomas Pantham *Political Ideas in Modern India.* Vol. 10, no. 7). New Delhi: Sage, 2006.

Menon, Dilip. "Religion and Colonial Modernity: Rethinking Belief and Identity." *Economic and Political Weekly,* April 27, 2002.

Menon, V. P. *The Transfer of Power in India.* Madras: Orient Longman, 1993. Reprint. Appendix 10.

Mitra, Ashok. *The New India, 1948–1955: Memoirs of an Indian Civil Servant.* Bombay: Popular Prakashan, 1991.

Mondal, Anshuman, "Gandhi, Utopianism and the Construction of Colonial Difference." *Interventions* 3, no. 3 (2001).

Moon, Penderel, ed. *Wavell: the Viceroy's Journal.* Oxford: Oxford University Press, 1973.

Moon, Penderel. *The British Conquest of Dominion of India.* London: Duckworth, 1989.

Moore, Barrington Jr. *Social Origins of Dictatorship and Democracy: Lord and Peasant in the Making of the Modern World.* Boston, MA: Beacon Press, 1966.

Morris-Jones, W. H. "Mahatma Gandhi: Political Philosopher." *Political Studies* 8, no.1 (February 1960).

Mukherjee, Hiren. *Gandhi: A Study.* New Delhi: People's Publishing House, 1991. Reprint.

Mukherjee, Rudrangshu, ed. *Leaves from a Diary: Shyama Prasad Mookherjee.* Calcutta: Oxford University Press, 1993.

———. *The Penguin Gandhi Reader.* New Delhi: Penguin, 1993.

Mukherjee, Subrata. *Gandhian Thought: A Marxist Interpretation*. New Delhi: Deep & Deep, 1997.

Mukherjee, Subrata, and Sushila Ramaswamy, eds. *Economic and Social Principles of Mahatma Gandhi*. New Delhi: Deep & Deep, 1998.

———. *Ethics, Religion and Culture*. New Delhi: Deep & Deep, 1998.

———. *Non Violence and Satyagraha*. New Delhi: Deep & Deep,1998.

———. *Political Ideas of Mahatma Gandhi*. New Delhi: Deep & Deep, 1998.

Mullane, Deirdre, ed. *Crossing the Danger Water: Three Hundred Years of African-American Writing*. New York: Anchor Books, 1993.

Muste, A. J. *Non-Violence in an Aggressive World*. New York: Harper, 1972. Reprint.

Myrdal, Gunnar. *An American Dilemma: The Negro Problem and Modern Democracy*. New York: Harper & Row Publishers,1962. Reprint.

Namboodiripad, E. M. S. *The Mahatma and the Ism*. New Delhi: People's Publishing House, 1959.

Nanda, B. R. *Gandhi and His Critics*. New Delhi: Oxford University Press, 1985.

———. *The Illegitimacy of Nationalism: Rabindranath Tagore and the Politics of Self*. New Delhi: Oxford University Press, 1994.

———. *In Search of Gandhi: Essays and Reflections*. New Delhi: Oxford University Press, 2002.

———. *Mahatma Gandhi*. New Delhi: Oxford University Press, 1996. Reprint.

———. *Mahatma Gandhi: 125 Years*. New Delhi: New Age International Publishers, 1995.

———. *The Nehrus: Motilal and Jawaharlal*. London: George & Allen, 1962.

Nandy, Ashis. *The Intimate Enemy: Loss and Recovery of Self under Colonialism*. New Delhi: Oxford University Press, 1983.

Narayan, R. K. *Waiting for the Mahatma*. Chennai: Indian Thought Publications, 2003. Reprint.

Nash, Andrew. "Gandhi in South Africa: An Interpretation." Paper presented at a seminar of the Department of History, University of Kwa-Zulu-Natal, August 11, 2004.

Nayar, Sushila. *Mahatma Gandhi's Last Imprisonment: The Inside Story*. New Delhi: Har-Anand, 1996.

Nehru, Jawaharlal. *The Discovery of India*. New Delhi: Oxford University Press, 1985. Centenary Edition.

———. *Jawaharlal Nehru: An Autobiography*. London: John Lane, The Bodley Head, 1941.

Niebuhr, Reinhold. *Moral Man and Immoral Society: A Study in Ethics and Politics*. New York: Charles Scribner's Sons, 1932.

———. "The Preservation of Moral Values in Politics." *Non-Violence in America: A Documentary History*, edited by Staughton Lynd. New York: The Bobbs-Merrill Company, 1966.

Nojeim, Michael J. *Gandhi and King: The Power of Non-Violent Resistance*. Westport, CT: Praeger, 2004.

Oates, Stephen B. *Let the Trumpet Sound: The Life of Martin Luther King, Jr*. New York: Harper & Row, 1982.

Orwell, George. "Reflections on Gandhi." *Partisan Review*, January 16, 1949.

Packard, Jerrold M. *American Nightmare: The History of Jim Crow*. New York: St. Martin's Press, 2002.

Pandey, Gyan. *A History of Prejudice: Caste and Difference in India and the USA*. Mimeograph, 2012.

Pandey, Gyanendra. *Hindus and Others: The Question of Identity in India Today*. New Delhi: Viking, 1997.

——. "The Prose of Otherness." In *Subaltern Studies*, edited by Ranajit Guha. Vol. 8. New Delhi: Oxford University Press, 1994.

——.*Remembering Partition: Violence, Nationalism and History in India*. Cambridge: Cambridge University Press, 2001.

Pantham, Thomas. "Habermas' Practical Discourse and Gandhi's Satyagraha." In *Political Discourse: Explorations in India and Western Political Thought*, edited by Bhikhu Parekh and Thomas Pantham. New Delhi: Sage, 1987.

——. "Gandhi: *Swaraj*, *Sarvadaya* and *Satyagraha*." In *Political Theories and Social Reconstruction: A Critical Survey of the Literature on India*. New Delhi: Sage, 1995.

——. "Thinking with Mahatma Gandhi: Beyond Liberal Democracy." *Political Theory* 11, no. 2 (1983).

Pantham, Thomas, and Kenneth L. Deutsch, *Political Thought in Modern India*. New Delhi: Sage, 1986.

Parekh, Bhikhu. *Colonialism, Tradition and Reform: An Analysis of Gandhi's Political Discourse*. New Delhi: Sage, 1999.

——. *Gandhi*. Oxford: Oxford University Press, 1997.

——. *Gandhi's Political Philosophy*. Notre Dame, IN: University of Notre Dame Press, 1989.

——. "Logic of Humiliation." In *Humiliation: Claims and Content*, edited by Gopal Guru. New Delhi: Oxford University Press, 2009.

——. "Nehru and the National Philosophy of India." *Economic and Political Weekly*, January 5, 1991, 35–48.

Parel, Anthony. J. *Gandhi's philosophy and the quest for harmony*. Cambridge: Cambridge University Press, 2006.

——, ed. *Gandhi, Freedom and Self Rule*. New Delhi: Vistaar, 2000.

——, ed. *Hind Swaraj and Other Writings*. Cambridge: Cambridge University Press, 1997.

Pettigrew, Thomas, ed. *Racial Discrimination in the United States*. New York: Harper & Row, 1975.

Pfeffer, Paula F. *A. Philip Randolph: Pioneer of the Civil Rights Movement*. Baton Rouge and London: Louisiana State University Press, 1990.

Pirzada, S. S., ed. *Foundations of Pakistan: All India Muslim League documents*. Vol. II. Karachi: National Publishing House, n.d.

Pouchepadas, Jacques, *Champaran and Gandhi: Planters, Peasants and Gandhian Politics*. New Delhi: Oxford University Press, 1999.

Prasad, Bimal. *Pathway to India's Partition: The Foundations of Muslim Nationalism*. Vol. I. New Delhi: Manohar Books, 1996.

——. *Pathway to India's Partition: A Nation within a Nation, 1877–1937*. Vol. II. New Delhi: Manohar Books, 2000.

Puri, Reshmi-Sudha. *Gandhi on War and Peace*. New York: Praeger, 1987.

Pyarelal. *Mahatma Gandhi, The Early Phase*. 2 vols. Ahmedabad: Navjivan Publishing House, 1956 and 1958.

Radhakrishnan, Sarvepalli, ed. *Mahatma Gandhi: Essays and Reflections*. Mumbai: Jaico Books, 2003. Reprint.

Raines, Howell, ed. *My Soul Is Rested: The Story of the Civil Rights Movement in the Deep South*. New York: Penguin, 1977.

Randolph, A. Philip. "Why Should We March?" *Survey Graphic*, no. 31 (November 1942).

Rauschenbush, Walter. *The Social Principles of Jesus*. New York: Association Press, 1920.

Ray, Rajat K., ed. *Mind, Body and Society: Life and Mentality in Colonial Bengal*. Calcutta: Oxford University Press, 1995.

——. *Exploring Emotional History: Gender, Mentality and Literature in the Indian Awakening*. New Delhi: Oxford University Press, 2001.

Ray, Sibnarayan, ed. *Selected Works of M. N. Roy*. Vol. II (1923–1927). New Delhi: Oxford University Press, 2000.

Richards, G., *The Philosophy of Gandhi: A Study of His Basic Ideas*. Surrey, UK: Curzon Press, 1982.

Ritterhouse, Jeniffer. *Growing up Jim Crow: How Black and White Southern Children Learned Race*. Chapel Hill: University of North Carolina Press, 2006.

Roberts, Adam, and Timothy Garton Ash. *Civil Resistance and Power Politics: The Experience of Non-Violent Action from Gandhi to the Present*. Oxford: Oxford University Press, 2009.

Roberts, Gene, and Hank Klibanoff. *The Race Beat: The Press, the Civil Rights Struggle and the Awakening of a Nation*. New York: Alfred A. Knopf, 2006.

Rodrigues, Valerian, ed. *The Essential Writings of B. R. Ambedkar*. New Delhi: Oxford University Press, 2004.

Rogers, Alex M. "On the Color Line: The Early Ideologies and Methodologies of Dr. W.E.B. Du Bois." *Colonial Academic Alliance Undergraduate Research Journal 2*, no. 1 (2011).

Rolland, Romain. *Mahatma Gandhi*. London: Allen and Unwin, 1924.

Roy, M. N. *India in Transition*. Bombay: Nachiketa Publications, 1971. Reprint.

Roy, Ramashray. *Self and Society: A Study of Gandhian Thought*. New Delhi: Sage, 1985.

Rudolph, Lloyd I. "Gandhi in the Mind of America." *Economic and Political Weekly*, November 20, 2010.

Rudolph, L. I., and S. H. Rudolph. *The Modernity of Tradition: Political Development in India*. Chicago and London: University of Chicago Press, 1967.

Rudolph, Susanne Hoeber, and Lloyd I. Rudolph. *Gandhi: The Traditional Roots of Charisma*. Delhi: Orient Longman, 1987.

Rustin, Bayard. "The Negro and Nonviolence." In *Down the Line: The Collected Writings of Bayard Rustin*. Chicago, IL: Quadrangle Books, 1971.

——. *Strategies for Freedom: The Changing Patterns of Black Protest*. New York: Columbia University Press, 1976.

Sarkar, Sumit. *Modern India, 1885-1947*. New Delhi: Macmillan India, 1983.

Scalmer, Sean. *Gandhi in the West: The Mahatma and the Rise of Radical Protest*. Cambridge: Cambridge University Press, 2011.

Seshachari, C. *Gandhi and the American Scene: An Intellectual History and Enquiry*. Bombay: Nachiketa Publications, 1969.

Sethi, J. D., *Gandhi Today*. Durham, NC: Carolina Academic Press, 1978.

Settar, S. and Indira B. Gupta, eds. *Pangs of Partition: The Human Dimension*. Vol. II. New Delhi: Manohar Books, 2002.

——. *Pangs of Partition: The Parting of Ways*. Vol. I. New Delhi: Manohar Books, 2002.

Shaikh, Farzana. "Muslims and Political Representation in Colonial India: The Making of Pakistan." *Modern Asian Studies* 20, no. 3 (1986).

Sharp, Gene. *The Politics of Non-Violent Action.* Boston, MA: Peter Sargent Publishers, 1972.

Sheppart, Mikleson Thomas Jarl, Th.D. "The Negro's God in the Theology of Martin Luther King Jr.: Social Community and Theological Discourses." PhD diss., Harvard University, 1988.

Singh, Anita Inder. *The Origins of the Partition of India, 1936–47.* New Delhi: Oxford University Press, 1987.

Sitaramayya, B. Pattabhi. *History of the Indian National Congress.* Vol. II (1935–47). Delhi: S. Chand & Co., 1969.

Sitkoff, Harvard. *King: Pilgrimage to the Mountaintop.* New York: Hill and Wang, 2008.

Southard, Barbara. "The Feminism of Mahatma Gandhi." In *Economic and Social Principles of Mahatma Gandhi,* edited by Subrata Mukherjee and Sushila Ramaswamy. Vol. 3. New Delhi: Deep & Deep Publications, 1998.

Southern, David W. *Gunnar Myrdal and Black-White Relations: The Use and Abuse of an American Dilemma, 1944–1969.* Baton Rouge and London: Louisiana State University Press, 1987.

Spear, Percival. *The Oxford History of Modern India, 1740–1947.* Oxford: Clarendon Press, 1965.

Sprigle, Ray. *In the Land of Jim Crow.* New York: Simon and Schuster, 1949.

Sridharani, Krishnalal J. *War without Violence: A Study of Gandhi's Method and Its Accomplishment.* New York: Harcourt Brace & Co., 1939.

Stegar, Manfred B. *Gandhi's Dilemma: Nonviolent Principles and Nationalist Power.* New York: St. Martin's Press, 2000.

Sundquist, Eric, ed. *The Oxford W.E.B. Du Bois Reader.* Oxford: Oxford University Press, 1996.

Tai, Yong Tan, and Gynesh Kudaisya. *The Aftermath of Partition in South Asia.* London: Routledge, 2000.

Taneja, Anup. *Gandhi, Women and the National Movement, 1920-47.* New Delhi: Har-Anand, 2005.

Tarchek, Ronald J. *Gandhi: Struggling for Autonomy.* New Delhi: Vistaar, 1998.

Taylor, Cynthia. *A. Philip Randolph: The Religious Journey of an African-American Labor Leader.* New York: New York University Press, 2006.

Tebble, Adam James. "What Is the Politics of Difference?" *Political Theory* 30, no. 2 (April 2002).

Tendulkar, D. G., *Mahatma: The Life of M. K. Gandhi.* New Delhi: Ministry of Information and Broadcasting, Government of India, 1961.

The Autobiography of Malcolm X, as told to Alex Haley. New York: Random House, 1973. Reprint.

Thoreau, Henry David. *Civil Disobedience and Other Essays.* New York: Dover Publications, 1993. Reprint.

Thornton, J. MillsIII. *Dividing Lines: Municipal Politics and the Struggle for Civil Rights in Montgomery, Birmingham and Selma.* Tuscaloosa: University of Alabama Press, 2002.

Thurman, Howard. *With Head and Heart: The Autobiography of Howard Thurman.* New York: Harcourt Brace & Co.,1979.

Tirmizi, S. A. I., ed. *The Paradoxes of Partition, 1937–47.* Vol. 1 (1937–39). New Delhi: Centre for Federal Studies, Jamia Hamdard, 1998.

Tour, Kwame, and Charles V. Hamilton. *Black Power: The Politics of Liberation.* New York: VintageBooks, 1992.

Turner, Arlin, ed. *The Negro Question: A Selection of Writings on Civil Rights in the South by George W. Cable.* New York: Doubleday Anchor Books, 1958.

Van der Veer, Peter, *Religious Nationalism: Hindus and Muslims in India.* New Delhi: Oxford University Press, 1996.

Walton, Hans, Jr. *The Political Philosophy of Martin Luther King, Jr.* Westport, CT: Greenwood Publishing Company, 1972.

Washington, Booker T. *Up from Slavery.* New York: Bantam Books, 1977. Reprint.

Washington, James M., ed. *A Testament of Hope: The Essential Writings and Speeches of Martin Luther King Jr.* New York: HarperOne, 1986.

——. *I Have a Dream: Writings and Speeches That Changed the World.* New York and San Francisco: Harper1992. Reprint.

Weber, Thomas. *Conflict Resolution and Gandhian Ethics.* New Delhi: The Gandhi Peace Foundation, 1991.

——. *Gandhi as Disciple and Mentor.* Cambridge: Cambridge University Press, 2004.

Weinberg, Meyer, ed. *W.E.B. Du Bois: A Reader.* New York: Harper & Row, 1970.

White, Walter. *A Man Called White: The Autobiography of Walter White.* New York: Viking Press, 1948.

Winant, Howard. "Dialectics of theVeil." In *The New Politics of Race: Globalism, Difference, Justice.* Minneapolis: University of Minnesota Press, 2004.

Wolpert, S., *Nehru: A Tryst with Destiny.* New York: Oxford University Press, 1996.

Woodward, C. Vann. *The Strange Career of Jim Crow.* New York: Oxford University Press, 2002.Commemorative Edition.

Wright, Kai, ed. *The African-American Experience: Black History and Culture through Speeches, Letters, Editorials, Poems, Songs and Stories.* New York: Black Dog & Leventhal Publishers, 2009. Reprint.Young, Andrew. *An Easy Burden: The Civil Rights Movement and the Transformation of America.* New York: HarperCollins, 1996.

Young, Iris Marion. *Justice and the Politics of Difference.* Princeton, NJ: Princeton University Press, 1990.

Zaidi, A. M., and S. G. Zaidi, eds. *The Encyclopedia of the Indian National Congress.* Vol. 12. New Delhi: S. Chand & Co., 1981.

Zhang, Junfu. "Black-White Relations: The American Dilemma." *Perspectives* (online) 1, no. 4 (February 2000).

Ziegler, P., *Mountbatten: The Official Biography.* Glasgow: Collins, 1985.

INDEX